Essentials of International Relations

EIGHTH EDITION

Karen A. Mingst
UNIVERSITY OF KENTUCKY

Heather Elko Mckibben
UNIVERSITY OF CALIFORNIA, DAVIS

Ivan M. Arreguín-Toft
BOSTON UNIVERSITY

W. W. NORTON & COMPANY
NEW YORK · LONDON

W. W. Norton & Company has been independent since its founding in 1923, when William Warder Norton and Mary D. Herter Norton first published lectures delivered at the People's Institute, the adult education division of New York City's Cooper Union. The firm soon expanded its program beyond the Institute, publishing books by celebrated academics from America and abroad. By midcentury, the two major pillars of Norton's publishing program—trade books and college texts—were firmly established. In the 1950s, the Norton family transferred control of the company to its employees, and today—with a staff of four hundred and a comparable number of trade, college, and professional titles published each year—W. W. Norton & Company stands as the largest and oldest publishing house owned wholly by its employees.

Editor: Peter Lesser
Editorial Assistant: Anna Olcott
Project Editor: Taylere Peterson
Managing Editor, College: Marian Johnson
Managing Editor, College Digital Media: Kim Yi
Associate Director of Production, College: Benjamin Reynolds
Media Editor: Spencer Richardson-Jones
Media Project Editor: Marcus Van Harpen
Media Associate Editor: Michael Jaoui
Media Assistant Editor: Ariel Eaton
Marketing Manager, Political Science: Erin Brown
Design Director: Rubina Yeh
Book design by: Lissi Sigillo
Photo Editor: Travis Carr
Permissions Associate: Elizabeth Trammell
Permissions Manager: Megan Schindel
Composition: Six**Red**Marbles–Brattleboro, VT
Manufacturing: Transcontinental

Permission to use copyrighted material is included in the credits section of this book, which begins on p. C-1.

Library of Congress Cataloging-in-Publication Data

Names: Mingst, Karen A., 1947- author. | McKibben, Heather Elko, author. | Arreguín-Toft, Ivan M., author.
Title: Essentials of international relations / Karen A. Mingst, University of Kentucky, Heather Elko McKibben, University of California, Davis, Ivan M. Arreguín-Toft, Boston University.
Description: Eighth Edition. | New York : W.W. Norton and Company, [2018] | Includes bibliographical references and index.
Identifiers: LCCN 2018034410 | ISBN 9780393643275 (paperback)
Subjects: LCSH: International relations.
Classification: LCC JZ1305 .M56 2018 | DDC 327—dc23 LC record available at https://lccn.loc.gov/2018034410

ISBN: 978-0-393-64327-5 (pbk.)

W. W. Norton & Company, Inc., 500 Fifth Avenue, New York, NY 10110
wwnorton.com
W. W. Norton & Company Ltd., 15 Carlisle Street, London W1D 3BS

3 4 5 6 7 8 9 0

BRIEF CONTENTS

CONTENTS

<u>6</u>   War and Security   187

FIGURES, TABLES, AND MAPS

FIGURES

TABLES

MAPS

ABOUT THE AUTHORS

Karen A. Mingst is Professor Emeritus at the Patterson School of Diplomacy and International Commerce at the University of Kentucky. She holds a PhD in political science from the University of Wisconsin. A specialist in international organization, international law, and international political economy, Professor Mingst has conducted research in Western Europe, West Africa, and Yugoslavia. She is the author or editor of seven books and numerous academic articles.

Heather Elko McKibben is an associate professor in the Department of Political Science at the University of California, Davis. She has been at Davis since 2009, after receiving her PhD from the University of Pittsburgh in 2008 and holding a postdoctorate position in the Niehaus Center for Globalization and Governance at Princeton University in the 2008–2009 academic year. In her research, Professor McKibben is interested in understanding when, why and how different countries negotiate with each other. When and why will countries come to the negotiating table to resolve problems instead of resorting to more coercive measures? What types of strategies do they use in those negotiations, and why do those strategies differ from country to country and negotiation to negotiation? When and why will countries be able to reach cooperative agreements, and what are the resulting agreements likely to look like? Examining international negotiations in a wide variety of settings, Professor McKibben seeks to answer these types of questions.

Ivan M. Arreguín-Toft is Assistant Professor of International Relations at Boston University, where he teaches introductory international relations, among other courses. He holds a PhD in political science from the University of Chicago. Professor Arreguín-Toft is a specialist in security studies, asymmetric conflict, and cyber warfare. He was recently the recipient of a U.S. Fulbright grant to Norway.

PREFACE

Brief textbooks are now commonplace in International Relations. This textbook was originally written to be not only smart and brief, but also—in the words of Roby Harrington of W. W. Norton—to include "a clear sense of what's essential and what's not." While this book's treatment of the essential concepts and information has stood the test of time through seven editions, this edition includes more substantial revisions.

The overall structure remains similar. Students need a brief history of international relations to understand why we study the subject and how current scholarship is informed by what has preceded it. Theories provide interpretative frameworks for understanding what is happening in the world. The levels of analysis—the international system, the state, and the individual—are introduced and then expanded in a chapter on the state and the tools of statecraft. Since conflict and cooperation are the foundation of international relations, a chapter is devoted to each. Then the other major issues of the day are examined from the international political economy, to international and nongovernmental organizations, human rights, and human security, namely migration, heath, and the environment.

This fully updated edition is enhanced by the addition of new material on the challenges to globalization posed by populism; the discussion of the perspectives using the 2014 and beyond Russia-Ukraine conflict; the introduction of cyberwarfare as a major type of war; the elaboration of international cooperation theory and new examples drawn from international law; the introduction of basic economic concept, including the role of the state and international monetary policy; the implications of Brexit for the future of the European Union; the expanded notion of human security with discussion on migration and refugees. As we add, so must we subtract to preserve the "brief" and "essential." Radicalism is dropped from the general theoretical discussions, but retained in the international political economy chapter. Discussion of the individual level of analysis is abbreviated, as was suggested by our valuable reviews.

The rich pedagogical program of previous editions has been revised based on suggestions from adopters and reviewers:

- Each chapter is introduced with a new story "ripped from the headlines," selected to help students apply the concepts discussed in the chapter to a contemporary problem.

- The popular Global Perspectives features have been updated with new perspectives, including: Brexit—view from Great Britain; development—view from Rwanda; going nuclear—view from North Korea; human rights—view from Canada. This feature encourages students to consider a specific issue from the vantage point of a particular state.

- End-of-chapter review materials include discussion questions and a list of key terms from the chapter to help students remember, apply, and synthesize what they have learned.

- Theory in Brief boxes, In Focus boxes, and numerous maps, figures, and tables appear throughout the text to summarize key ideas.

Many of these changes have been made at the suggestion of expert reviewers, primarily faculty who have taught the book in the classroom. While it is impossible to act on every suggestion (not all the critics themselves agree), we have carefully studied the various recommendations and thank the reviewers for taking time to offer critiques. We thank the following reviewers for their input on this new edition: Christopher J. Saladino, Virginia Commonwealth University; Alexei Shevchenko, California State University, Fullerton; Charles W. Mahoney, California State University, Long Beach; Mona Lyne, University of Missouri, Kansas City; Joseph M. Brown, University of Massachusetts, Boston; Phil Kelly, Emporia State University; Kelly M. Kadera, University of Iowa; John W. Dietrich, Bryant University; Fabian Borges, California State University, San Bernardino, and all those who provided feedback along the way.

Karen Mingst would like to offer a special thanks to Heather. It was a joy to work together even though they did so mostly over the Internet. Heather provided not only a "fresh eye" to the substance of the book, but also was quick to respond to inquiries, filling in key gaps, always with aplomb.

In this edition as in the others, Karen Mingst owes special thanks to her husband, Robert Stauffer. He has always provided both space and encouragement, while questioning another book, another edition! Together we are enjoying a new phase of life called retirement (or just old age). We continue to explore the political and natural world together, as we have for 45 years. Our son Brett and daughter-in-law Tara have given us Quintin, now five years old and Langley, one year old. Quintin just received a globe so he can see where grandma and papa are. Our daughter Ginger, an attorney, has found her own voice, while constantly trying to provide technical support to her "slow" parents. We are thrilled that they all continue to be a large part of our life even though we remain divided by the miles.

Heather Elko McKibben would like to thank Karen for inviting her to join the incredible journey of working on this book. Most of all, she is thankful for Karen's trust in her ideas (some of which were new and different), allowing Heather to help reshape the book that had been Karen's own "baby" for so long. It has been a true joy to work with her, and I look forward to continuing to do so. Thank you also to Peter Lesser, who took notice of the ideas I had, and introduced me to Karen to start this joint project together. Without Karen and Peter, my part in this story would not exist.

Heather would also like to give special thanks to her husband, Scott McKibben. Writing a book is always a team effort—not just among co-authors, but among those supporting us behind the scenes as well. Without Scott's patience and reinforcement, I would not have been able to pull this off. Thank you also to my parents, who have always been there to support me and continue to be there, pushing me to be the best I can in all things.

Special thanks to Ivan Arreguín-Toft for his important contributions to previous editions.

We have been fortunate to have several editors from W. W. Norton who have shepherded various editions: Peter Lesser has been the calm point person on this edition, taking a personal interest in making this new collaboration smooth and seamless. He has kept us on task and time and offered his own keen eye for substantive ambiguity and awkward wording. He has done this with grace and tact while at the same time welcoming a new member to his family and relearning the necessity of sleep. Ann Shin, the editor of the first four editions, continues to offer support, guidance, and enthusiasm. And Anna Olcott has expertly directed the editorial process in an expeditious fashion. In short, many talented, professional, and delightful people contributed to the making of this edition, which we feel is the best so far. And for that, we remain always grateful.

AFRICA

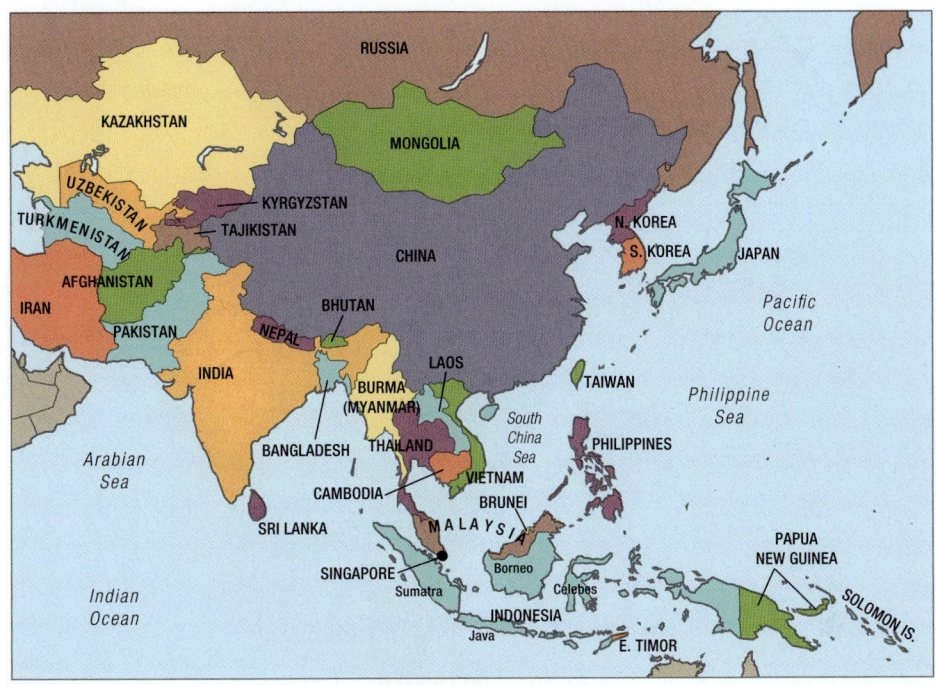

ASIA

THE MIDDLE EAST

EUROPE

NORTH AMERICA

CENTRAL AND SOUTH AMERICA

THE WORLD

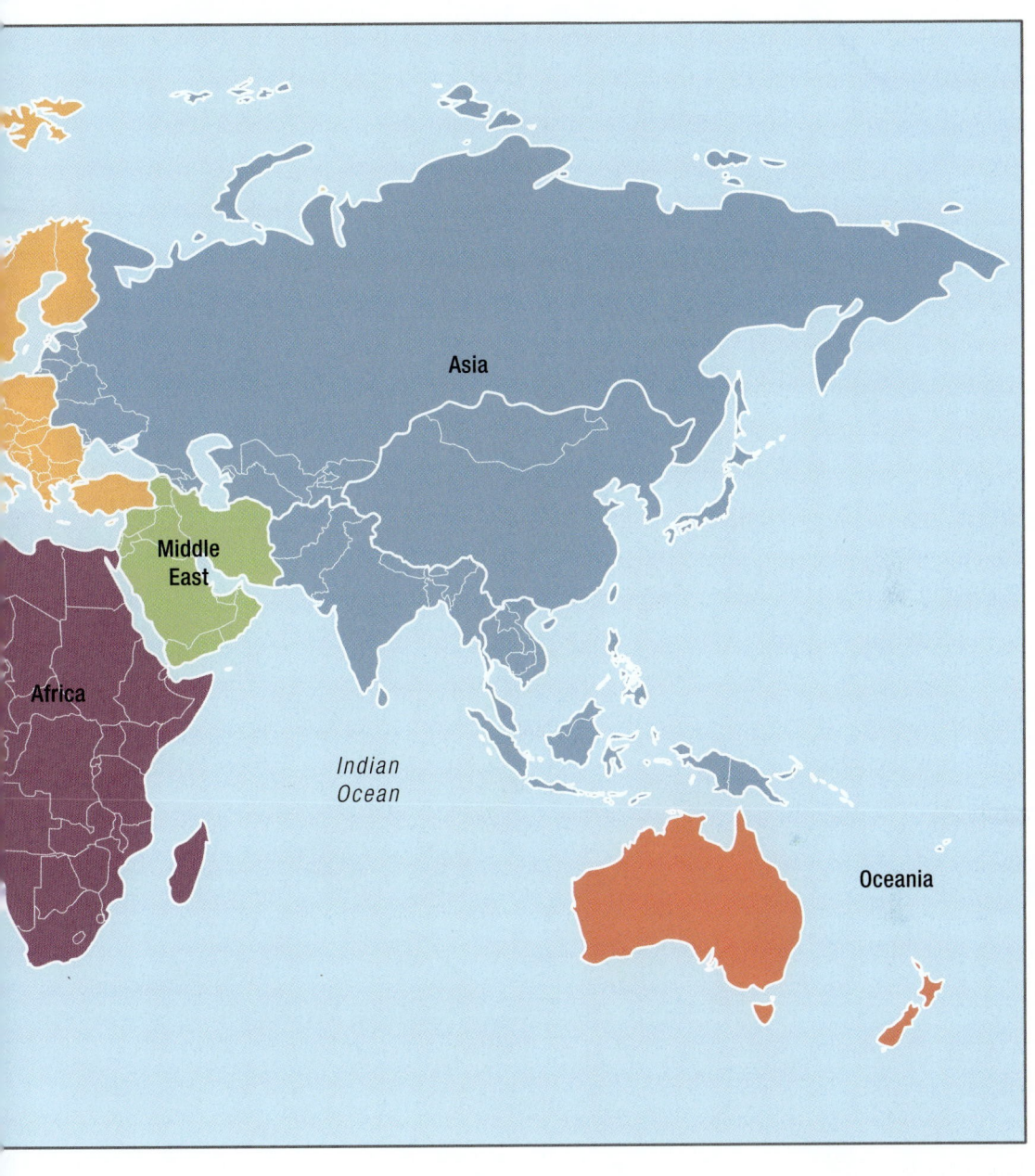

Essentials of International Relations

EIGHTH EDITION

Rohingya refugees flee Myanmar for neighboring Bangladesh after violence erupted in the Rhakine state in August 2017. The Rohingya are considered to be one of the most persecuted peoples in the world.

1

Approaches to International Relations

If we listen to the 24-hour news cycle and social media, we are flooded with reports of sympathizers of the Islamic State gunning down Europeans and threatening minorities in Syria and Iraq; drones hitting unintended Pakistani targets; the North Korean state setting off bombs and testing missiles over neighboring countries; men, women, and children clinging to rickety boats, fleeing conflict and economic hardship in Africa and Southeast Asia; and thousands in India, Nepal, and Bangladesh fleeing natural disasters. Vivid pictures make those events appear to be happening everywhere, perhaps just next door.

Amid these news stories is a debate over whether the world is being more peaceful. In 2011 psychologist Steven Pinker, author of *The Better Angels of Our Nature: Why Violence Has Declined*, concluded that "we may be living in the most peaceful era in our species' existence." A year later, Martin Dempsey, former chairman of the Joint Chiefs of Staff, remarked that the world is becoming "more dangerous than it has ever been."[1] Who is right? Why can one person be optimistic about our ability to live together more peacefully and another be more pessimistic? Are these observers coming at the question from different theoretical positions? Are they examining different data, using different time periods?

Your place in the world is complicated. You are a member of a family; your father or mother may work for a multinational corporation; you may be a member of a nongovernmental organization (NGO), supporting a particular cause that you hold dear; you may be a member of a church, synagogue, or mosque, or an ethnic group whose members span the globe; your state may be composed of different local units having responsibilities for issues with transnational significance; your state may have diplomatic relations and may trade with states across the globe, may participate in the activities of international NGOs, and may be a member of numerous intergovernmental organizations. The variety of actors in international relations includes not just the 193 states recognized in the world today, their leaders, and their government bureaucracies but also municipalities, for-profit and not-for-profit private organizations, international organizations, and you.

International relations, as a subfield of political science, is the study of the interactions among the various actors that participate in international politics. It is the study of the behaviors of these actors as they participate individually and together in international political processes. International relations is also an interdisciplinary field of inquiry, using concepts and substance from history, economics, and anthropology, as well as political science.

How can we begin to study this multifaceted phenomenon called international relations? How can we begin to think theoretically about what appear to be disconnected events? How can we begin to answer the foundational questions of international relations: What are the characteristics of human nature and the state? What is the relationship between the individual and society? How is the international system organized? In this book, we will help you answer these questions, and many more.

LEARNING OBJECTIVES

- ▶ Understand how international relations affects you in your daily life.
- ▶ Explain why we study international relations theory.
- ▶ Analyze how history and philosophy have been used to study international relations.
- ▶ Describe the contribution of behavioralism in international relations.
- ▶ Explain how and why alternative approaches have challenged traditional approaches in international relations.

Nongovernmental organizations and their members often respond to issues of international significance. Here, volunteers from NGOs operating in Lebanon distribute aid to Syrian refugees in Al-Masri refugee camp in October 2014.

THINKING THEORETICALLY

Political scientists develop theories or frameworks both to understand the causes of events that occur in international relations every day and to answer the foundational questions in the field. Although there are many contending theories in international relations, some take similar perspectives while others differ in significant ways. Three of the more prominent perspectives are developed in this book: realism and neorealism, liberalism and neoliberal institutionalism, and constructivism.

In brief, realism posits that states exist in an anarchic international system; that is, there is no overarching hierarchical authority. Each state bases its policies on an interpretation of its national interest defined in terms of power. The structure of the international system is determined by the distribution of power among states. In contrast, liberalism is historically rooted in several philosophical traditions that posit that human nature is basically good. Individuals form groups and, later, states. States generally cooperate and follow international norms and procedures that they have agreed to support. And international relations constructivists, in contrast to both realists and liberals, argue that the key structures in the state system are not material but instead social and dependent on ideas. The interests of states are not fixed but rather malleable and ever-changing. All three of these perspectives are subject to different interpretations by international relations scholars,

Foundational Questions of International Relations

- ▶ How can human nature be characterized?

- ▶ What is the relationship between the individual and society?

- ▶ What are the characteristics and role of the state?

- ▶ How is the international system organized?

and various theories therefore stem from each perspective. Those theories help us describe, explain, and predict. These different theories help us see international relations from different viewpoints. As political scientist Stephen Walt explains, "No single approach can capture all the complexity of contemporary world politics. Therefore, we are better off with a diverse array of competing ideas rather than a single theoretical orthodoxy. Competition between theories helps reveal their strengths and weaknesses and spurs subsequent refinements, while revealing flaws in conventional wisdom."[2] We will explore these competing ideas, and their strengths and weaknesses, in the remainder of this book.

DEVELOPING THE ANSWERS

How do political scientists find information to assess the accuracy, relevancy, and potency of their theories? The tools they use to answer the foundational questions of their field include history, philosophy, and the scientific method.

History

Inquiry in international relations often begins with history. Without any historical background, many of today's key issues are incomprehensible. History tells us that the continual violence in Jerusalem and in the West Bank is part of a dispute over territory between Arabs and Jews, a dispute having its origins in biblical times and its modern roots in the establishment of the state of Israel in 1948. Sudan's 20-year civil war between the Muslim north and Christian/animist south and the Darfur crisis beginning in 2003 are both products of the central government's long-standing neglect of marginalized areas, exacerbated by religious differences and magnified by natural disasters. Without that historical background, we cannot debate the appropriate solution in the Arab-Israeli dispute, nor can we understand the dynamics between Sudan and Darfur and within the new state of the Republic of South Sudan.

Thus, history provides a crucial background for the study of international relations. History has been so fundamental to the study of international relations that there was no separate international relations subfield until the early twentieth century. Before that time, especially in Europe and the United States, international relations was studied under the umbrella of diplomatic history in most academic institutions. Having knowledge of both diplomatic history and national histories remains critical for students of international relations.

History invites its students to acquire detailed knowledge of specific events, but it also can be used to test generalizations. Having deciphered patterns from the past, students of history can begin to explain the relationships among various events. For example, having historically documented the cases when wars occur and described the patterns leading up to war, the diplomatic historian can seek explanations for, or causes of, war. The ancient Greek historian Thucydides (c. 460–401 BCE), in *History of the Peloponnesian War*, used this approach. Distinguishing between the underlying and the immediate causes of wars, Thucydides found that what made that war inevitable was the growth of Athenian power. As Athens's power increased, Sparta, Athens's greatest rival, feared losing its own power. Thus, the changing distribution of power was the underlying cause of the Peloponnesian War.[3]

Many scholars following in Thucydides's footsteps use history in similar ways. But those using history must be wary because it is not always clear what history attempts to teach us. We often rely on analogies, comparing, for example, the 2003 Iraq War to the Vietnam War. In both cases, the United States fought a lengthy war against a little understood, often unidentifiable enemy. In both, the United States adopted the strategy of supporting state building so that the central government could continue the fight, a policy labeled *Vietnamization* and *Iraqization* in the respective conflicts. The policy led to a quagmire in both places when American domestic support waned and the United States withdrew. Yet differences are also evident; no analogies are perfect. Vietnam has a long history and a strong sense of national identity, forged by wars against both the Chinese and French. Iraq, in contrast, is a relatively new state with significant ethnic and religious divisions, whose various groups seek a variety of different objectives. In Vietnam, the goal was defense of the U.S. ally South Vietnam against the communist north, backed by the Soviet Union. In Iraq, the goal was first to oust Saddam Hussein, who was suspected of building weapons of mass destruction, and second to create a democratic Iraq that would eventually lead to greater stability in the region.[4] In both, although we cannot ignore history, neither can we draw simple "lessons" from historical analogies.

Analogies are incomplete. Lessons are often drawn that reflect one's theoretical orientation. Realists might draw the lesson from both Vietnam and Iraq that the United States did not use all of its military might—political actors constrained

Scholars often draw on history to help understand world politics. When the United States invaded Iraq first in the 1991 Gulf War and then in the 2003 Iraq War, some observers raised comparisons to the Vietnam War, when many Americans protested U.S. involvement. However, there were also significant differences between these events.

military actions—otherwise, the outcome may have been different. Liberals might conclude that the United States should never have been involved since the homeland was not directly affected and one country's ability to construct or reconstruct another state is limited. What lessons can we draw from the United States' acquiescence to the Russian takeover of Crimea in 2014? Was this another Munich, when the Allies appeased Germany at the early stages of World War II? Or was this an affirmation of national self-determination since the Crimeans, mostly ethnic Russians, voted to secede from Ukraine and rejoin Russia? Was the Joint Comprehensive Plan of Action, the 2015 agreement between the Western powers and Iran setting limits on Iran's nuclear program, another Munich or a Helsinki moment?[5] Helsinki refers to the 1975 accord officially ratifying post–World War II borders and advocating for respect of human rights. History offers no clear-cut lesson or guidance.

Philosophy

Philosophy can help us answer questions in international relations. Much classical philosophy focuses on the state and its leaders—the basic building blocks of international relations—as well as on methods of analysis. For example, the ancient Greek philosopher Plato (c. 427–347 BCE), in *The Republic*, concluded that in the "perfect state," the people who should govern are those who are superior in the ways of philosophy and war. Plato called these ideal rulers "philosopher-kings."[6] Though not directly discussing international relations, Plato introduced two ideas seminal to the discipline: class analysis and dialectical reasoning, both of which were bases for later Marxist analyses, in which economic class is the major divider in domestic and international politics. Chapter 8 explores this viewpoint in more detail. It helps us explain the tension between global and local policies, whereby, for example, local-level textile workers lose their jobs to foreign competition and are replaced by high-technology industries.

Just as Plato's contributions to contemporary thinking were both substantive and methodological, the contributions of his student, the philosopher Aristotle (384–322 BCE), lay both in substance (the search for an ideal domestic political system) and in method. Analyzing 168 constitutions, Aristotle looked at the similarities and differences among states, becoming the first writer to use the comparative method of analysis. He concluded that states rise and fall largely because of internal factors—a conclusion still debated in the twenty-first century.[7]

After the classical era, many of the philosophers of relevance to international relations focused on the foundational questions of the discipline. The English philosopher Thomas Hobbes (1588–1679), in *Leviathan*, imagined a state of nature, a world without governmental authority or civil order, where men rule by passions, living with the constant uncertainty of their own security. To Hobbes, the life of man is solitary, selfish, and even brutish. Society is in a "state of nature," or *anarchy*. Under anarchy there is no hierarchically superior, coercive authority that can create laws or enforce law and order. Extrapolating to the international system, which also lacks such an overarching authority, states in this anarchic condition act as man does in the state of nature. For Hobbes, the solution to the dilemma is a unitary state—a leviathan—where power is centrally and absolutely controlled.[8]

The French philosopher Jean-Jacques Rousseau (1712–78) addressed the same set of questions but, having been influenced by the Enlightenment, saw a different solution. In *Discourse on the Origin and Foundations of Inequality among Men*, Rousseau described the state of nature as an egocentric world, with man's primary concern being self-preservation—not unlike Hobbes's description of the state of nature. Rousseau posed the dilemma in terms of the story of the stag and the hare. In a hunting society, each individual must keep to his assigned task so the hunters can find and trap the stag for food for the whole group. However, if a hare happens to pass nearby, an individual might well follow the hare, hoping to get his next meal quickly and caring little for how his actions will affect the group. Rousseau drew an analogy between these hunters and states. Do states follow short-term self-interest, like the hunter who follows the hare? Or do they recognize the benefits of a common interest?[9] Rousseau's solution to the dilemma posed by the stag and the hare was different from Hobbes's leviathan. Rousseau's preference was for the creation of smaller communities in which the "general will" could be attained. Indeed, according to Rousseau, it is "only the general will," not a leviathan, that can "direct the forces of the state according to the purpose for which it was instituted, which is the common good."[10] In Rousseau's vision, "each of us places his person and all his power in common under the supreme direction of the general will; and as one we receive each member as an indivisible part of the whole."[11]

Still another philosophical view of the characteristics of international society was set forth by the German philosopher Immanuel Kant (1724–1804), in both *Idea for a Universal History* and *Perpetual Peace*. Kant envisioned a federation of states as a means to achieve peace, a world order in which man is able to live without fear of

TABLE 1.1

Contributions of Philosophers to International Relations Theory

Plato (c. 427–347 BCE) Greek	Argued that the life force in man is intelligent. Only a few people can have insight into what is good; society should submit to the authority of these philosopher-kings. Many of these ideas are developed in *The Republic*.
Aristotle (384–322 BCE) Greek	Addressed the problem of order in the individual Greek city-state. The first to use the comparative method of research, observing multiple points in time and suggesting explanations for the patterns found.
Thomas Hobbes (1588–1679) English	In *Leviathan*, described life in a state of nature as solitary, selfish, and brutish. Individuals and society can escape from the state of nature through a unitary state, a leviathan.
Jean-Jacques Rousseau (1712–78) French	In *Discourse on the Origin and Foundations of Inequality among Men*, described the state of nature in both national and international society. Argued that the solution to the state of nature is the social contract, whereby individuals gather in small communities where the "general will" is realized.
Immanuel Kant (1724–1804) German	Associated with the idealist or utopian school of thought. In *Idea for a Universal History* and *Perpetual Peace*, advocated a world federation of republics bound by the rule of law.

war. Sovereignties would remain intact, but the new federal order would be both preferable to a "super-leviathan" and more effective and realistic than Rousseau's small communities. Kant's analysis was based on a vision of human beings that was different from that of either Rousseau or Hobbes. In his view, though man is admittedly selfish, he can learn new ways of cosmopolitanism and universalism.[12]

The tradition laid down by these philosophers has contributed to the development of international relations by calling attention to fundamental relationships: those between the individual and society, between individuals *in* society, and between societies. These philosophers had varied, often competing, visions of what these relationships were and what they ought to be. (See Table 1.1.) The early philosophers have led contemporary international relations scholars to the examination of the characteristics of leaders, to the recognition of the importance of the internal dimensions of the state, to the analogy of the state and nature, and to descriptions of an international community. History and philosophy permit us to delve into foundational questions—the nature of people and the broad characteristics of the state and of international society. They allow us to speculate on the **normative** (or moral) elements in political life: What *should be* the role of the state? What *ought to be* the norms in international society? How *might* international society be structured to achieve order? When *is* war just? Should economic resources be redistributed? Should human rights be universalized?[13] Philosophical methods may not be useful for helping us answer specific questions; they may tell us what *should* be done, providing the normative guide, but philosophy generally does not help us make or implement policy. Nevertheless, both history and philosophy are key tools for international relations scholars.

The Scientific Method: Behavioralism

In the 1950s, some scholars began to draw upon one understanding of the nature of humans and on history to develop a more scientific approach to the study of international relations. They built upon the philosophical assumption that humans tend to act in predictable ways. If humans act in predictable ways, might not states do the same? Are there recurrent patterns to how states behave? Are there subtle patterns to diplomatic history? Are states as power hungry as some philosophers would have us believe? How can we explain empirical findings? Can we use those findings to predict the future?

Behavioralism proposes that individuals, both alone and in groups, act in patterned ways. The task of the behavioral scientist is to suggest plausible hypotheses regarding those patterned actions and to systematically and empirically test those hypotheses. Using the tools of the scientific method to describe and explain human behavior, these scholars hope to predict future behavior. Many will be satisfied, however, with being able to explain patterns, because prediction in the social sciences remains an uncertain enterprise.

The Correlates of War project permits us to see the application of behavioralism. Beginning in 1963 at the University of Michigan, the political scientist J. David Singer and his historian colleague Melvin Small investigated one of the fundamental questions in international relations: Why is there war?[14] Motivated by the normative philosophical concern with how peace can be achieved, the two scholars chose an empirical methodological approach. Rather than focusing on one "big" war that changed the tide of history, as Thucydides did, they sought to find patterns among a number of different wars. Believing that generalizable patterns may be found across all wars, Singer and Small turned to statistical data to discover the patterns.

The initial task of the Correlates of War project was to collect data on international wars between 1865 and 1965 in which 1,000 or more deaths had been reported in a 12-month period. For each of the 93 wars that fit these criteria, the researchers found data on its magnitude, severity, and intensity, as well as the frequency of war over time. This data-collection process proved a much larger task than Singer and Small had anticipated, employing a bevy of researchers and graduate students.

Once the wars were codified, the second task was to generate specific, testable hypotheses that might explain the outbreak of war. Is there a relationship between the number of alliance commitments in the international system and the number of wars that are fought? Is there a relationship between the number of great powers in the international system and the number of wars? Is there a relationship between the number of wars over time and the severity of the conflicts? Which factors are *most* correlated over time with the outbreak of war? And how are these factors related to each other? What is the correlation between international system–level factors—such as the existence of international organizations—and the outbreak of war? Although answering these questions will never *prove* that a particular factor is the cause of war, the answers could suggest some high-level correlations that merit theoretical explanation. That is the goal of this research project and many others following in the behavioralist scientific tradition.

Another example of research in the behavioral tradition can be found in human rights literature. The question many scholars probe is why countries violate human rights treaties. Is it because states never intended to follow the provisions? Is signing onto treaties just cheap talk? Is it because there is no threat of direct international enforcement? Or is it because states often lack the capacity to implement new standards? Sociologist Wade M. Cole began with a hypothesis, unlike in the Correlates of War project, which began with data collection, that "noncompliance with international treaty obligations is neither willful or premeditated."[15] Rather, it depends on a state's bureaucratic efficiency. Using data from each explanatory variable of state bureaucratic efficiency and dependent variables of state empowerment and physical-integrity rights data found in the Cingranelli-Richards (CIRI) Human Rights Dataset, Cole used sophisticated statistical models that confirmed his expectations. Improvements in a state's empowerment and physical-integrity rights after the signing of the International Covenant on Civil and Political Rights depend on state capacity.

Yet methodological problems occur in both projects. The Correlates of War database looks at all international wars, irrespective of the different political, military, social, and technological contexts. Can wars of the late 1800s be explained by the same factors as the wars of the new millennium? Answering that question has led subsequent researchers to expand the data set to include militarized interstate disputes, conflicts that do not involve a full-scale war. And those data include not only international and civil wars but also communal and nonstate wars.[16] The human rights study also involves major problems of measurement and definition of key variables. How can one measure concepts such as state's empowerment and state capacity? Many different indicators need to be combined. And data may not be available for all states across all the time periods studied. In each case, alternative explanations need to be investigated. Such studies are never an end in themselves, only a means to improve explanation and to provide other scholars with hypotheses that warrant further testing.

So, to return to the question posed at the beginning of the chapter, what explains the different conclusions reached by Pinker and Dempsey on whether contemporary international relations can be described as relatively peaceful? The data they are examining are different. Pinker, arguing that the world was much more violent over the past centuries, includes all types of violence—murder, tribal warfare, slavery, executions, rape. He cites statistics showing that tribal warfare was nine times as deadly as twentieth-century warfare and the murder rate in medieval Europe was 30 times more than it is today. While the numbers of deaths and violent acts today may be larger, they are much smaller compared to the size of the population: in the seventeenth century, the "wars of religion" killed about 2 percent of the population in the warring states, while in the twentieth century, the deadliest century in absolute numbers, just 0.7 percent of the people died in battle. World Wars I and II represent spikes from what is generally a downward trend. Post 1946, there has been a decline in deaths on a per capita basis in all different kinds of wars, including colonial wars, civil wars, internationalized civil wars, and genocide, as well as interstate conflicts. Dempsey, and certainly many others in the policy community, see a different reality. The total number of armed conflicts of all types tripled from the 1950s to the 1990s. And though most were relatively low-intensity conflicts with limited fatalities and wartime fatalities have declined dramatically—from 240 battle-related deaths per million of the world's population in 1950 to less than 10 per million in 2007—the numbers are still too high if you are responsible for the lives of others.

Given the data-selection problem as well as other issues, there is disillusionment with behavioral approaches. Different data may lead to substantially different conclusions, just as described above. Some critics suggest that attention to data and methods has overwhelmed the substance of behavioralists' research. Few would doubt the importance of Singer and Small's initial excursion into the causes of war, but even the researchers themselves admitted losing sight of the important questions in their quest to compile data and hone research methods. Some scholars, still within the behavioral orientation, suggest simplifying esoteric methods to refocus on the substantive questions. To still others, many of the foundational questions— the nature of humanity and society—are neglected by behavioralists because they are not easily testable by empirical methods. These critics suggest returning to the philosophical roots of international relations. But most scholars remain firmly committed to behavioralism and the scientific method, pointing to the slow incremental progress that has been made in explaining the interactions of states.

Does choosing one method over another make a difference in the research findings? Although there are few systematic comparisons, evidence suggests that in human rights research, the findings do tend to vary by method.[17] Qualitative researchers in the historical and philosophical tradition, often employing case studies of a specific human rights issue over a long period, generally find progress in human rights records. And they find that new human rights norms have emerged. In contrast, behavioral researchers, in general, find less evidence of changes in state behavior. Usually drawing on studies with large amounts of data, including data from many states over decades when available, researchers find only marginal improvements in a state's human rights record. What explains these divergent findings? Differences in ways of measuring human rights violations, differences in what human rights issues and periods of time are studied, and problems with the availability of data are all responsible for the differences among findings. This divergence has led researchers to plead for more mixed-method research. Multi-method projects can help us overcome the disturbing finding that different methods lead to different substantive conclusions.

Alternative Approaches

Some international relations scholars are dissatisfied with using history, philosophy, or behavioral tools. Some scholars approaching the study of international relations from the constructivist perspective have turned to discourse analysis to answer the foundational questions of international relations. To trace how ideas shape identities, constructivists analyze culture, norms, procedures, and social practices. They probe how identities are shaped and change over time. They use texts, interviews, and archival material, and they research local practices by riding public transportation and standing in lines. By using multiple sets of data, they create thick description. The case studies found in Peter Katzenstein's edited volume *The Culture of National Security* use this approach. Drawing on analyses of Soviet foreign policy at the end of the Cold War, German and Japanese security policy from militarism to antimilitarism, and Arab national identity, the authors search for security interests defined by actors who are responding to changing cultural factors. These studies show how social and cultural factors shape national security policy in ways that contradict realist or liberal expectations.[18]

The postmodernist scholars seek to deconstruct the basic concepts of the field, such as the state, the nation, rationality, and realism, by searching texts (or sources) for hidden meanings underneath the surface, in the subtext. Once those hidden meanings are revealed, the postmodernists seek to replace the once-orderly picture with disorder, to replace the dichotomies with multiple portraits. Cynthia Weber, for example, argues that sovereignty (the independence of a state) is neither well defined nor consistently grounded. Digging below the surface of sovereignty, going beyond evaluations of the traditional philosophers, she has discovered that conceptualizations of sovereignty are constantly shifting, depending on the needs of the moment and the values of different communities. The multiple meanings of sovereignty are conditioned by time, place, and historical circumstances.[19] More specifically, Karen T. Litfin shows how norms of sovereignty are shifting to address ecological destruction, although the process remains a contested one.[20] These analyses have profound implications for the theory and practice of international relations, which are rooted in state sovereignty and accepted practices that reinforce sovereignty. They challenge conventional understandings.

Postmodernist scholars also seek to find the voices of "the others," those individuals who have been disenfranchised and marginalized in international relations. Christine Sylvester illustrates her approach with a discussion of the Greenham Common Peace Camp, a group of mostly women who in the early 1980s walked more than 100 miles to a British air force base to protest plans to deploy missiles at the base. Although the marchers were ignored by the media—and thus were "voiceless"—they maintained a politics of resistance, recruiting other political action groups near the camp and engaging members of the military stationed at the base. In 1988, when the Intermediate Range Nuclear Force Treaty was signed, dismantling the missiles, the women moved to another protest site, drawing public attention to Britain's role in the nuclear era.[21] Scholars in this tradition also probe how the voiceless *dalit* (or untouchables) have fought for rights in South Asia, how the disabled have found a voice in international forums, and how some, like children born of rape, have not found a voice.[22]

No important question of international relations today can be answered with exclusive reliance on any one method. History, whether in the form of an extended case study (Peloponnesian War) or a study of multiple wars (Correlates of War or militarized interstate disputes), provides useful answers. Philosophical traditions offer both cogent reasoning and the framework for the major discussions of the day. But behavioral methods dominate because they are increasingly using mixed methods, combining the best of social-science methods and other approaches. And the newer methods of discourse analysis, thick description, and postmodernism provide an even richer base from which the international relations scholar can draw.

IN SUM: MAKING SENSE OF INTERNATIONAL RELATIONS

How can we, as students, begin to make sense of international political events in our daily lives? How have scholars of international relations helped us make sense of the world around us? This chapter has introduced the major perspectives of international relations, including the realist, liberal, and constructivist approaches.

These perspectives provide frameworks for developing theories designed to answer core foundational questions. To answer these questions, international relations scholars turn to many other disciplines, including history, philosophy, behavioral psychology, and critical studies (see Table 1.2). International relations is a pluralistic and eclectic discipline.

To understand the development of international relations theory, we need to examine general historical trends for developments in the state and the international

TABLE 1.2

Tools for Studying International Relations

TOOL	METHOD
History	Examines individual or multiple cases
Philosophy	Develops rationales from core texts and analytical thinking
Behavioralism	Finds patterns in human behavior and state behavior using empirical methods, grounded in scientific method
Alternatives	Deconstructs major concepts and uses discourse analysis to build thick description; finds voices of "others"

system, particularly events in Europe during the nineteenth and twentieth centuries. This "stuff" of diplomatic history is the subject of Chapter 2. Chapter 3 is designed to help us think about perspectives that have shaped the development of international relations theories—realism, liberalism, and constructivism. Chapter 4 builds on this discussion, introducing three "levels" from which we can analyze international relations: focusing on key characteristics of the international system, states, and individuals to understand international politics. Chapter 5 digs deeper into the study of the state and the tools of statecraft. The remaining chapters address important topics that international relations scholars seek to better understand. Chapter 6 examines issues of war and security, Chapter 7 analyzes international cooperation and international law, Chapter 8 looks at the international political economy, and Chapter 9 examines the roles that intergovernmental organizations (IGOs) and NGOs intergovernmental organizations play in international politics. Chapter 10 then turns to the study of human rights, and Chapter 11 examines issues that affect human security, including migration, health, and the environment. Throughout each topic, we use the perspectives of realism, liberalism, and constructivism as lenses for analysis.

Discussion Questions

1. A respected family member picks up this book and sees the word *theory* in the first chapter. She is skeptical about the value of theory. Explain to her the utility of developing a theoretical perspective.

2. Philosophy is your passion, but you find international relations moderately interesting. How can you integrate your passion with this pragmatic interest? What questions can you explore?

3. You are a history major skilled in researching historical archives. Suggest two research projects that you might undertake to further your understanding of international relations.

4. How can the study of international relations be made more scientific? What are the problems with doing so?

Key Terms

behavioralism (p. 11)

international relations (p. 4)

normative (p. 11)

Historical context is necessary to understand the complex politics between North Korea, South Korea, and the world. Although much of the world seeks to curb North Korean nuclear development as a first priority, many North and South Koreans wish for unification of their country. Every year, visitors place colorful ribbons on a fence in the Demilitarized Zone between the two countries to signify their desire for reunification.

2

The Historical Context of Contemporary International Relations

Students of international relations need to understand the events and trends of the past. Theorists recognize that historical circumstances have shaped core concepts in the field—concepts such as the state, the nation, sovereignty, power, and balance of power. It will prove difficult to understand the contemporary politics of the Koreas, China, and Japan, for example, without understanding how the peoples of each present-day state remember the events of World War II.

In large part, the roots of the contemporary international system are found in Europe-centered Western civilization. Of course, great civilizations thrived in other parts of the world, too. India and China, among others, had extensive, vibrant civilizations long before the historical events covered here. But the European emphasis is justified because in both theory and practice, contemporary international relations is rooted in the European experience. In this chapter, we begin by looking at Europe in the period immediately preceding and following the Thirty Years' War (1618–48). We then consider Europe's relationship with the rest of the world during the nineteenth century, and we conclude with an analysis of the major transitions during the twentieth and first two decades of the twenty-first centuries.

LEARNING OBJECTIVES

▶ Analyze which historical periods have most influenced the development of international relations.

▶ Describe the historical origins of the state.

▶ Understand why international relations scholars use the Treaties of Westphalia as a benchmark.

▶ Explain the historical origins of the European balance-of-power system.

▶ Explain how the Cold War became a series of confrontations between the United States and the Soviet Union.

▶ Analyze the key events that have shaped the post–Cold War world and the first two decades of the new millennium.

THE EMERGENCE OF THE WESTPHALIAN SYSTEM

Most international relations theorists locate the origins of the contemporary states system in Europe in 1648, the year the **Treaties of Westphalia** ended the Thirty Years' War. These treaties marked the end of rule by religious authority in Europe and the emergence of secular authorities. With secular authority came the principle that has provided the foundation for contemporary international relations: the notion of the territorial integrity of states—legally equal and sovereign participants in an international system.

The formulation of **sovereignty**—a core concept in contemporary international relations—was one of the most important intellectual developments leading to the

Westphalian revolution. Much of the development of the notion is found in the writings of the French philosopher Jean Bodin (1530–96). To Bodin, sovereignty is the "absolute and perpetual power vested in a commonwealth."[1] It resides not in an individual but in a state; thus, it is perpetual. It is "the distinguishing mark of the sovereign that he cannot in any way be subject to the commands of another, for it is he who makes law for the subject, abrogates law already made, and amends obsolete law."[2]

Although, ideally, sovereignty is absolute, in reality, according to Bodin, it is not without limits. Leaders are limited by divine law and natural law: "All the princes on earth are subject to the laws of God and of nature." They are also limited by the type of regime—"the constitutional laws of the realm"—be it a monarchy, an aristocracy, or a democracy. And lastly, leaders are limited by covenants, contracts with promises to the people within the commonwealth, and treaties with other states, though there is no supreme arbiter in relations among states.[3] Thus, Bodin provided the conceptual glue of sovereignty that would emerge with the Westphalian agreement.

The Thirty Years' War devastated Europe. The war, which had begun as a religious dispute between Catholics and Protestants, ended due to mutual exhaustion and bankruptcy. Princes and mercenary armies ravaged the central European countryside, fought frequent battles, and plundered the civilian population to secure needed supplies. The treaties that ended the conflict had three key impacts on the practice of international relations.

First, the Treaties of Westphalia embraced the notion of sovereignty. With one stroke, virtually all the small states in central Europe attained sovereignty. The Holy Roman Empire was dead. Monarchs—and not a supranational church—gained the authority to decide which version of Christianity was appropriate for their subjects. With the pope and the emperor stripped of this power, the notion of the territorial state came increasingly to be accepted as normal. Not only did the Treaties legitimize territoriality and the right of *states*—as the sovereign, territorially contiguous principalities came to be known—to choose their own religion, but the Treaties also established that states had the right to determine their own domestic policies, free from external pressure and with full jurisdiction in their own geographic space. The Treaties thus introduced the principle of noninterference in the affairs of other states.

Second, because the leaders of Europe's most powerful countries had seen the devastation wrought by mercenaries in war, after the Treaties of Westphalia, these countries sought to establish their own permanent national militaries. The growth of such forces led to increasingly centralized control, since the state had to collect taxes to pay for these militaries and leaders assumed absolute control over the troops. The state with a national army emerged as a powerful force—its sovereignty acknowledged and its secular base firmly established. And that state's power increased. Larger territorial units gained an advantage as armaments became more standardized and more lethal.

Third, the Treaties of Westphalia established a core group of states that dominated the world until the beginning of the nineteenth century: Austria, Russia, Prussia, England, France, and the United Provinces (the area that is now the Netherlands). Those in the west (England, France, and the United Provinces) underwent an economic revival under the aegis of liberal capitalism, whereas those in the east (Prussia and Russia) reverted to feudal practices. In the west, private enterprise was encouraged. States improved their infrastructure to facilitate commerce, and great trading companies and banks emerged. In contrast, in the east, serfs remained on the land, and economic development was stifled. Yet in both regions, states led by a monarch with absolute power dominated, with Louis XIV ruling in France (1643–1715), Peter the Great in Russia (1682–1725), and Frederick II in Prussia (1740–86).

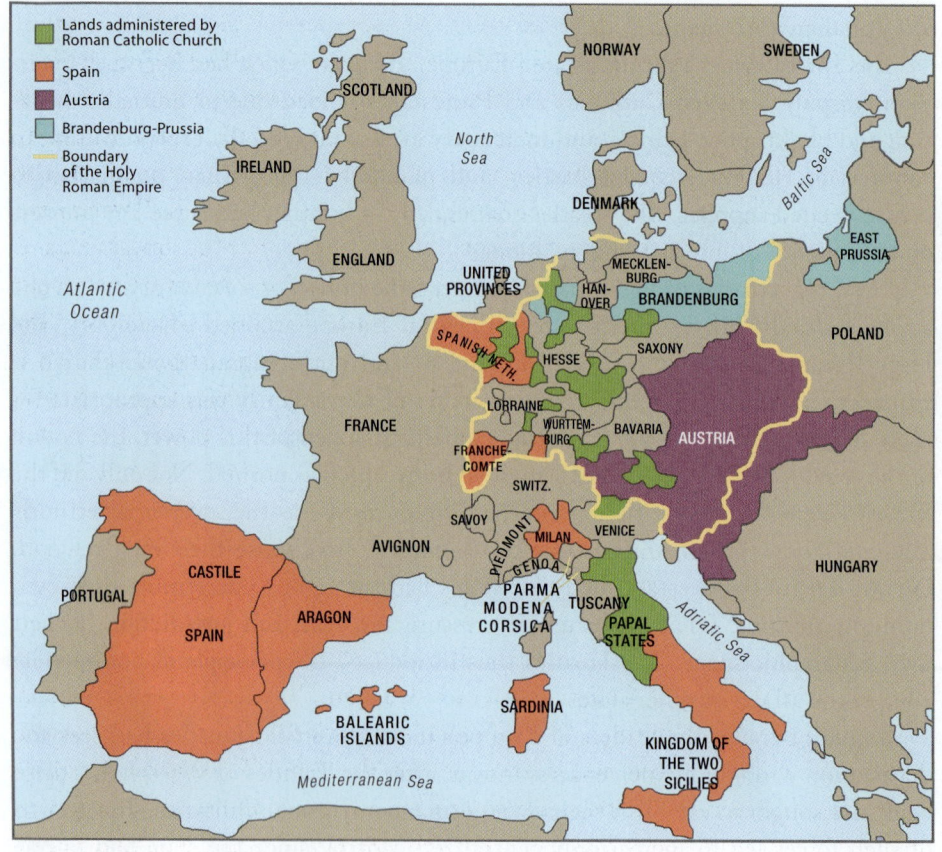

Europe, c. 1648

Key Developments after Westphalia

- ▶ Concept and practice of sovereignty develops.
- ▶ Centralized control of institutions to facilitate the creation and maintenance of military; military power grows.

- ▶ Capitalist economic system emerges (stable expectations facilitate long-term investment).

The most important social theorist of the time was the Scottish economist Adam Smith (1723–90). In *An Inquiry into the Nature and Causes of the Wealth of Nations,* Smith argued that the notion of a market should apply to all social orders. Individuals—laborers, owners, investors, consumers—should be permitted to pursue their own interests, unfettered by all but the most modest state regulations. According to Smith, each individual acts rationally to maximize her or his own interests. With groups of individuals pursuing their interests, economic efficiency is enhanced, and more goods and services are produced and consumed. At the aggregate level, the wealth of the state and that of the international system are similarly enhanced. What makes the system work is the so-called invisible hand of the market: when individuals pursue their rational self-interests, the system (the market) operates in a way that benefits everyone.[4] Smith's explication of how competing units enable market capitalism to ensure economic vitality has had a profound effect on states' economic policies and political choices, which we will explore in Chapter 8. But other ideas of the period would also dramatically alter governance in subsequent centuries.

EUROPE IN THE NINETEENTH CENTURY

The nineteenth century in Europe was a turbulent time. The American Revolution (1773–85) against British rule and the French Revolution (1789) against absolutist rule ushered in the new century, followed by the Napoleonic Wars and the expansion of imperialism and colonialism to other continents. The balance of power among the European states that had stabilized the region during that time began to break down by the end of the century as key alliances solidified.

The Aftermath of Revolution: Core Principles

Two core principles emerged in the aftermath of the American and French revolutions. The first was that absolutist rule is subject to limits imposed by man. In *Two Treatises of Government*, the English philosopher John Locke (1632–1704) attacked absolute power and the notion of the divine right of kings. Locke argued that the state is an institution created by rational men to protect both their natural rights (life, liberty, and property) and their self-interests. Men freely enter into this political arrangement, agreeing to establish government to ensure natural rights for all. The crux of Locke's argument is that political power ultimately rests with the people, rather than with a leader or monarch. The monarch derives **legitimacy** from the consent of the governed.[5]

The second core principle was **nationalism**, wherein a people comes to identify with a common past, language, customs, and territory. Individuals who share such characteristics are motivated to participate actively in the political process as a *nation*. For example, during the French Revolution, a patriotic appeal was made to the *French* masses to defend the French *nation* and its new ideals. This appeal forged an emotional link between the people and the state—France's territory with a government—as explained in Chapter 5. These two principles—legitimacy and nationalism—arose out of the American and French revolutions to provide the foundation for politics in the nineteenth and twentieth centuries.

The Napoleonic Wars

The political impact of nationalism in Europe was profound. The nineteenth century opened with war in Europe on an unprecedented scale. France's status as a revolutionary power made it an enticing target of other European states intent on stamping out the contagious idea of government by popular consent. Thus, France became embroiled in an escalating series of wars with Austria, Britain, and Prussia. Weakened and disorganized from the years of internal conflict, a Corsican artillery officer named Napoleon Bonaparte rose to leader of the French military and, eventually, to the rank of emperor of France.

Napoleon, with help from other talented officers, set about reorganizing and regularizing the French military. Making skillful use of French national zeal, Napoleon led large, well-armed, and passionately motivated armies. Modest changes in technology meant that war supplies could be stored in pre-positioned locations along likely campaign routes so troops could avoid having to stop and forage for food. In combination with nationalism, that system made it possible for the French to field larger, more mobile, and more reliable armies that could employ innovative tactics unavailable to the smaller professional armies of France's rivals like Prussia. Through a series of famous battles, Napoleon's armies shattered those of "invincible" Prussia, conquering nearly the whole of Europe in a few short years.

Yet the same nationalist fervor that brought about much of Napoleon's success also led to his downfall. In Spain and Russia, Napoleon's armies met nationalists who fought a different sort of war. Rather than facing French forces in direct confrontations, Spanish fighters used intimate local knowledge to mount hit-and-run attacks on French occupying forces. These fighters also enjoyed the support of Britain, whose unrivaled mastery of the seas meant the country could lend supplies and occasional expeditionary forces. When local French forces attempted to punish the Spanish into submission by looting, torture, rape, and execution of prisoners and suspected insurgents, resistance to French occupation escalated. The cost to France was high, draining away talented soldiers and cash and damaging French morale. When Napoleon invaded Russia in 1812 with an army of 422,000, the Russians retreated toward their areas of supply, destroying all available food and shelter behind them in what came to be known as a "scorched earth" policy. The French began to suffer from severe malnutrition, with the entire army slowly starving to death as it advanced to Moscow.

The dramatic successes and failures of France's Napolean Bonaparte illustrated both the power and the limits of nationalism, new military technology, and organization.

By the time the French reached the Russian capital, the government had already evacuated. The French army occupying Moscow had dwindled to a mere 110,000. Napoleon waited in vain for the tsar to surrender. After realizing the magnitude of his vulnerability, Napoleon attempted to return to France before Russia's harsh winter set in. But it was already too late. By the time French troops crossed the original line of departure at the Nieman River, Napoleon's *Grande Armeé* had been reduced to a mere 10,000. The proud emperor's final defeat in 1815 by English and Prussian forces at the Battle of Waterloo (in present-day Belgium) was assured.

Peace at the Core of the European System

Following the defeat of Napoleon in 1815 and the establishment of peace by the Congress of Vienna, the five powers of Europe—Austria, Britain, France, Prussia, and Russia—known as the Concert of Europe, ushered in a period of relative peace in the international political system. These great powers fought no major wars after the defeat of Napoleon until the Crimean War in 1854, and in that war, both Austria and Prussia remained neutral. Other local wars of brief duration were fought, and in these, too, some of the five major powers remained neutral. Meeting more than 30 times before World War I at a series of ad hoc conferences, the Concert became a club of like-minded leaders. Through these meetings, these countries legitimized both the independence of new European states and the division of Africa among the colonial powers.

The fact that peace among great powers prevailed during this time seems surprising since major economic, technological, and political changes were radically altering power relationships. Industrialization, a critical development during the nineteenth century, was a double-edged sword. During the second half of the nineteenth century, the powers focused all attention on the processes of industrialization. Great Britain was the leader, outstripping all rivals in its output of coal, iron, and steel and the export of manufactured goods. In addition, Britain became the source of finance capital, the banker for the continent and, in the twentieth century, for the world. Industrialization spread through virtually all areas of western Europe as the masses flocked to the cities and entrepreneurs and middlemen scrambled for economic advantage. In addition, more than any other factor, industrialization led the middle classes to capture political power at the expense of the aristocratic classes. Unlike the aristocratic classes, the middle classes did not depend on land for wealth and power; their ability to invent, use, and improve industrial machines and processes gave them political power.

The population of Europe soared and commerce surged as transportation corridors across Europe and the globe were strengthened. Political changes were

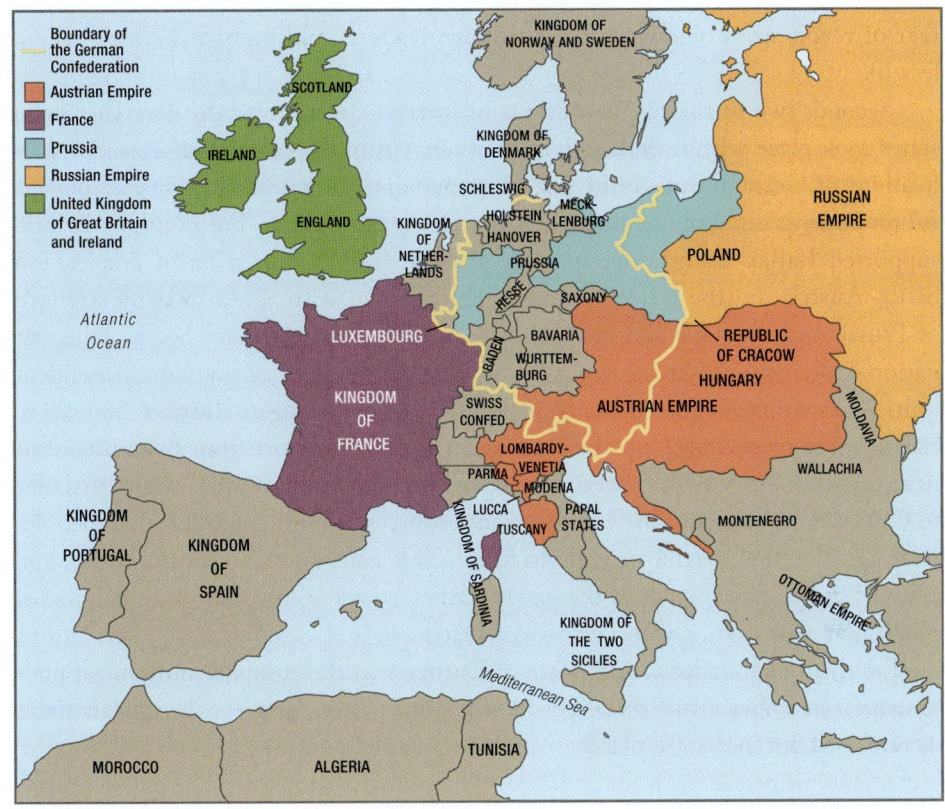

Europe, c. 1815

dramatic: Italy was unified in 1870; Germany was formed out of 39 different fragments in 1871; the United Kingdom of the Netherlands was divided into the Netherlands and Belgium in the 1830s; and the Ottoman Empire gradually disintegrated, leading to independence for Greece in 1829 and for Moldavia and Wallachia (Romania) in 1856. With such dramatic changes under way, what explains the absence of major war? At least three factors discouraged war.

First, Europe's political elites were united in their fear of revolution among the masses. In fact, at the Congress of Vienna, the Austrian diplomat Count Klemens von Metternich (1773–1859), architect of the Concert of Europe, believed that returning to the age of absolutism was the best way to manage Europe. Others envisioned grand alliances that would bring European leaders together to fight revolution by the lower classes. And in 1848, all five powers did face demands for reform from the masses. But soon, European leaders acted in concert, ensuring that mass revolutions did not spread from state to state. Thus, fear of revolt from below united European leaders, making war between them less likely.

Second, two of the major conflicts of interest confronting the core European states took place within, rather than between, culturally close territories: the unifications of Germany and Italy. Both German and Italian unification had powerful proponents and opponents among the European powers. For example, Britain supported Italian unification, making possible Italy's annexation of Naples and Sicily. Austria, on the other hand, was preoccupied with the increasing strength of Prussia and thus did not actively oppose what may well have been against its national interest—the creation of two sizable neighbors out of myriad independent units. German unification was acceptable to Russia, as long as Russian interests in Poland were respected. German unification also got support from Britain's dominant middle class, which viewed a stronger Germany as a potential counterbalance to France. Thus, because the energies and resources of German and Italian peoples were concentrated on the struggle to form single contiguous territorial states, and because the precise impact of the newly unified states on the European balance of power was unknown, a wider war was averted.

The third factor supporting peace in Europe was the complex and crucial phenomenon of imperialism-colonialism, wherein rivalries between European states were played out in distant places.

Imperialism and Colonialism in the European System

The discovery of the "New" World—as Europeans after 1492 called it—led to rapidly expanding communication between the Americas and Europe. The same advanced navigation technology also made contact with Asia less costly and more frequent. The first to arrive in the New World were explorers seeking discovery, riches, and personal glory; merchants seeking raw materials and trade relations; and clerics seeking to convert "savages" to Christianity. But the staggering wealth they discovered, and the relative ease with which it could be acquired, led to increasing competition among European powers for territories in far-distant lands. Most of the European powers became empires and, once established, claimed as sovereign territory the lands indigenous peoples occupied. These empires are the origin of the term **imperialism**, the annexation of distant territory (most often by force) and its inhabitants to an empire. **Colonialism**, which often followed or accompanied imperialism, refers to the settling of people from a home country like Spain among indigenous peoples of a distant territory like Mexico. The two terms are thus subtly different, but most scholars use them interchangeably.

This process of annexation by conquest or treaty continued for 400 years. As the technology of travel and communications improved, and as Europeans developed vaccines and cures for tropical diseases, the costs to European powers of imposing their will on indigenous people continued to drop. Europeans were welcomed in some places but were resisted in many. In most cases, Europeans overcame that resistance with very little cost or risk. They met spears with machine guns and horses with heavy artillery. In the dawning machine age, it became more common to target indigenous civilians deliberately, often with near genocidal results. By the close of the nineteenth century, almost the whole of the globe was "ruled" by European states. Great Britain was the largest and most successful of the imperial powers, but even small states, such as Portugal and the Netherlands, maintained important colonies abroad.

LA FRANCE VA POUVOIR PORTER LIBREMENT AU MAROC LA CIVILISATION LA RICHESSE ET LA PAIX

In the early twentieth century, French authorities took control of Morocco. Here, a magazine suggests the popular ideal of colonialism as "civilized" nations bringing peace and prosperity to "uncivilized" Morocco.

The Industrial Revolution provided the European states with the military and economic capacity to engage in territorial expansion. Some imperial states were motivated by economic gains, seeking new external markets for manufactured goods and obtaining, in turn, raw materials to fuel their industrial growth. For others, the motivation was cultural and religious—to spread the Christian faith and the ways of white "civilization" to the "dark" continent and beyond. For still others, the motivation was political. Since the European balance of power prevented direct confrontation in Europe, European state rivalries were played out in Africa and Asia.

Many leaders within the now-unified Italy and Germany felt that to have international respect and to guarantee cheap imports of raw materials, both states "needed" to annex or colonize countries in Asia or Africa. Italy attempted to conquer and colonize Ethiopia, a Christian empire in the Horn of Africa, but suffered a humiliating defeat in 1896. To mollify Germany's imperial ambitions, during the Congress of Berlin in 1885, the major powers divided up Africa, "giving" Germany a sphere of influence in east Africa (Tanganyika), west Africa (Cameroon and Togo), and southern Africa (Southwest Africa). European imperialism seemed to provide a convenient outlet for Germany's aspirations as a great power, without endangering the delicate balance of power within Europe itself. By the end of the nineteenth century, 85 percent of Africa was under the control of European states.

In Asia, only Japan and Siam (Thailand) were not under direct European or U.S. influence. China is an excellent example of the extent of external domination. Under the Qing dynasty, which began in the seventeenth century, China had slowly been losing political, economic, and military power for several hundred years. During the nineteenth century, British merchants began to trade with China for tea, silk, and porcelain, often paying for these products with smuggled opium. In 1842, the British defeated China in the Opium War, forcing China to cede various political and territorial rights to foreigners through a series of unequal treaties. European states and Japan were able to occupy large portions of Chinese territory, claiming to have exclusive trading rights in particular regions. Foreign powers exercised separate "spheres of influence" in China. By 1914, Europeans had colonized four-fifths of the world, and still controlled much of it. The United States eventually became an imperial power as well, having won the 1898 Spanish-American War, pushing the Spanish out of the Philippines, Puerto Rico, Cuba, and other small islands.

The struggle for economic power led to heedless exploitation of colonial areas, particularly in Africa and Asia. European weapons and communications technology

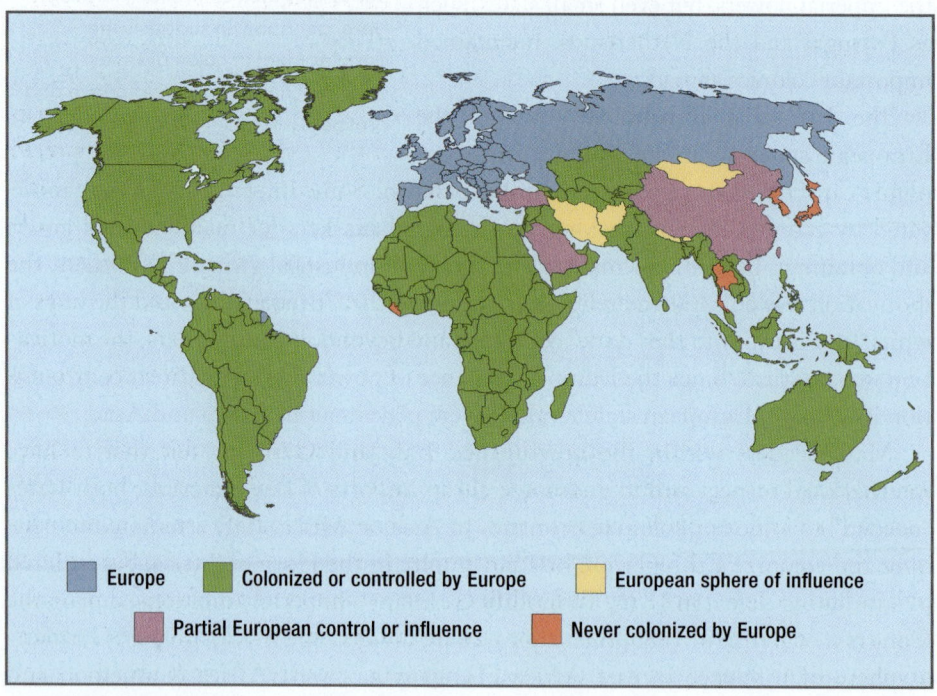

This map shows every country that had been under European control at any point from the 1500s to the 1960s. The United States, Mexico, and most of Latin America became independent of Europe in the eighteenth and nineteenth centuries, respectively, but much of the rest of the world remained under colonial control until after World War II.

proved very difficult for indigenous peoples to resist. Used to winning battles against vastly more numerous adversaries, one famous apologist for colonialism explained: "Thank God that we have got the Maxim gun, and they have not."[6]

The process of colonial expansion led to the establishment of a "European" identity. European states enjoyed a solidarity among themselves, based on their being European, Christian, "civilized," and white. These traits differentiated an "us"—white Christian Europeans—from an "other"—the rest of the world. With the rise of mass literacy and increasing contact with the colonial world due to industrialization, Europeans more than ever saw the uniqueness of being "European." This identity was, in part, a return to the same kind of unity felt under the Roman Empire and Roman law, a secular form of medieval Christendom, and a larger Europe as Kant and Rousseau had envisioned (see Chapter 1).

But, as the nineteenth century drew to a close, the assumption that imperialist countries could cheaply control vast stretches of distant territory containing large numbers of aggrieved or oppressed people with only a few colonial officers and administrators was being challenged with increasing frequency. For Great Britain, the world's most successful colonial power, the future of colonialism was clearly signaled by Britain's Pyrrhic victory in the Second Anglo-Boer War (1899–1902; also known as the South African War). British soldiers fought against Boer commandos, white descendants of Dutch immigrants to South Africa in the 1820s, in a lengthy and bitter counterinsurgency war that claimed the lives of more than 20,000 Boer women and children through the failure of the British to provide sanitary internment conditions, sufficient food, and fresh water. The war, which Britain expected to last no longer than three months and cost no more than 10 million pounds sterling, ended up costing 230 million pounds and lasting over two years. It proved the most expensive war, by far, in British colonial history. The war was largely unpopular in Europe and led to increased tensions between Britain and Germany. Still, the five European powers had not yet fought major wars directly against each other.

In sum, much of the competition, rivalry, and tension traditionally marking relations among Europe's states could be acted out far beyond Europe itself. Europeans raced to acquire colonies to achieve increased status, wealth, and power vis-à-vis their rivals. Europeans could imagine themselves as bringing the light of civilization to the "dark" regions, while at the same time acquiring the material resources they might need in a future war in Europe. Each colonial power understood it might take years to accumulate sufficient resources to gain an advantage in a major European war. Therefore, each state maintained an interest in managing crises so conflicts would not escalate to all-out war. Thus, the "safety valve" of colonialism both reinforced European unity and identity and slowed the buildup of tension in Europe.

Tensions, however, did gradually reemerge and become destabilizing. Germany's unification, rapid industrialization, and population growth led to an escalation of tension that could not be assuaged in time to prevent war. In 1870, France and Germany fought a major war, in which France suffered defeat. Through a humiliating peace treaty, France was forced to surrender the long-contested provinces of Alsace and Lorraine, which became part of the new Germany. The war and the simmering resentments to which it gave birth were mere harbingers of conflicts to come. In addition, the legacy of colonialism, which had served to defuse tension in Europe, laid the groundwork for enduring resentment of Europeans by many Asians and Africans. This resentment continues to complicate peace, humanitarian work, and development operations in these areas of the world today.

Balance of Power

During the nineteenth century, colonialism, the common interests of conservative European elites, and distraction over the troubled unifications of German and Italian principalities seemed to promote a long peace in Europe. But this condition of relative peace was underpinned by another factor as well: a **balance of power**. The independent European states, each with relatively equal power, feared the emergence of any predominant state (**hegemon**) among them. As a result, they formed alliances to counteract any potentially more powerful faction, thus creating a balance of power. The idea behind a balance of power is simple. States will hesitate to start a war with an adversary whose power to fight and win wars is relatively balanced or *symmetrical*, because the risk of defeat is high. When one state or coalition of states is much more powerful than its adversaries, *asymmetrical* war is relatively more likely. (These terms are discussed in more detail in Chapter 6.)

The treaties signed after 1815 were designed not only to quell revolution from below but also to prevent the emergence of a hegemon, such as France had become under Napoleon. Britain or Russia, at least later in the century, could have assumed a dominant leadership position—Britain because of its economic capability and naval prowess, and Russia because of its relative geographic isolation and extraordinary manpower. However, neither sought to exert hegemonic power; each one's respective capacity to effect a balance of power in Europe was declining and the status quo was acceptable to both states.

Britain and Russia did play different roles, however, in the balance of power. Britain most often played the role of offshore balancer; for example, it intervened on behalf of the Greeks in their struggle for independence from the Turks in the late 1820s, on behalf of the Belgians during their war of independence against Holland in 1830, on behalf of Turkey against Russia in the Crimean War in 1854–56, and again in the Russo-Turkish War in 1877–78. Thus, Britain ensured that power

Key Developments in Nineteenth-Century Europe

- ▶ From revolutions emerge two concepts: the idea that legitimate rule requires (some) consent of the governed, and nationalism.

- ▶ A system managed by the balance of power brings relative peace to Europe. Elites are united in fear of the masses, and domestic concerns are more important than foreign policy.

- ▶ European imperialism in Asia and Africa helps maintain the European balance of power.

- ▶ The balance of power breaks down due to imperial Germany's too-rapid growth and the increasing rigidity of alliances, resulting in World War I.

in Europe remained relatively balanced. Russia's role was as a builder of alliances. The Holy Alliance of 1815 kept Austria, Prussia, and Russia united against revolutionary France, and Russia used its claim on Poland to build a bond with Prussia. Russian interests in the Dardanelles, the strategic waterway linking the Mediterranean Sea and the Black Sea, and in Constantinople (today's Istanbul) overlapped with those of Britain. Thus, these two states, located at the margins of Europe, played key roles in making the balance-of-power system work.

During the last three decades of the nineteenth century, the Concert of Europe frayed, beginning with the Franco-Prussian War (1870) and the Russo-Turkish War (1877–78). Alliances began to solidify as the balance-of-power system began to weaken. The advent of the railroad gave continental powers such as Germany and Austria-Hungary an enhanced level of economic and strategic mobility equal to that of maritime powers such as Britain. This change reduced Britain's ability to balance power on the continent. Russia, for its part, began to fall markedly behind in the industrialization race, and its relatively few railroads meant that its massive manpower advantage would be less and less able to reach a battlefield in time to determine an outcome. So Russia's power began to diminish compared with that of France, Germany, and Austria-Hungary.

The Breakdown: Solidification of Alliances

Whereas in most of the nineteenth century, alliances had been flexible and fluid, by the later years, alliances became more rigid. Two camps emerged: the Triple Alliance (Germany, Austria-Hungary, and Italy) in 1882 and the Dual Alliance (France and Russia) in 1893. In 1902, Britain broke from the "balancer" role, joining in a naval alliance with Japan. For the first time, a European state (Great Britain) turned to an Asian one (Japan) to thwart a European power (Russia). And, in 1904, Britain joined with France in an alliance called the Entente Cordiale.

In that same year, Russia and Japan went to war in a contest Europeans widely expected to result in a Japanese defeat. After all, the Japanese had come late to industrialization, and although Japan's naval forces looked impressive on paper, their opponents would be white Europeans. But Russia's industrial backwardness would affect it severely. Russia's lack of sufficient railroads meant it could not reinforce its forces in the Far East, leaving it to send a naval flotilla from its Baltic home ports 18,000 miles away. In May 1905, the Russian and Japanese fleets clashed in Tsushima Bay, and the result was perhaps the greatest naval defeat in history: Russia lost eight battleships, some 5,000 sailors were killed, and another 5,000 were captured. The Japanese lost three torpedo boats and 116 sailors. The impact of Japan's victory would extend far beyond the defeat of Russia in the Far East. An Asian power's defeat of a white colonial power seriously compromised a core ideological foundation of colonialism—that whites were inherently superior to nonwhites. The Russian defeat spurred Japanese expansion and caused Germany to discount Russia's ability to interfere with German ambitions in Europe. Russia's defeat severely compromised the legitimacy of the tsar, setting in motion a revolution that, after 1917, was to topple the Russian empire and replace it with the Union of Soviet Socialist Republics (USSR, or the Soviet Union).

World War I

The final collapse of the balance-of-power system came with World War I. Germany's rapid rise in power intensified the destabilizing impact of the hardening of alliances at the turn of the twentieth century. By 1912, Germany had exceeded France and Britain in both heavy industrial output and population growth. Germany also feared Russian efforts to modernize its relatively sparse railroad network. Being "latecomers" to the core of European power, and having defeated France in the Franco-Prussian War (1870), many Germans felt that Germany had not received the diplomatic recognition and status it deserved. This lack of recognition in part explains why Germany encouraged Austria-Hungary to crush Serbia following the assassination of Archduke Franz Ferdinand (heir to the throne of the Austro-Hungarian Empire), who was shot in Sarajevo in June 1914. Like most of Europe's leaders at the time, Germany's leaders believed war made the state and its citizens stronger, and that backing down after a humiliation would only encourage further humiliations. Besides, the outcome of a local war between Austria-Hungary and Serbia was certain to be a quick victory for Germany's most important ally.

But under the tight system of alliances, the fateful shot set off a chain reaction. What Germany had hoped would remain a local war soon escalated to a continental war, once Russia's tsar ordered a premobilization of Russian forces. And once German troops crossed into Belgium, violating British-guaranteed Belgian neutrality, that continental war escalated to a world war when Britain sided with France and Russia. The Ottoman Empire (a Turkish-centered empire extending into the Middle East from the late thirteenth century), long a rival of Russia, entered the war on the side of Germany and Austria-Hungary. Both sides anticipated a short, decisive war, but this did not happen. Germany's Schlieffen Plan—its strategy for a decisive victory in a two-front war against Russia and France—failed almost immediately, leading to a ghastly stalemate. Between 1914 and 1918, soldiers from more than a dozen countries endured the persistent degradation of trench warfare and the horrors of poison gas.

The "Great War," as World War I came to be known, saw the introduction of aerial bombing and unrestricted submarine warfare as well. Britain's naval blockade of Germany caused widespread suffering and privation for German civilians.

Europe, c. 1914

More than 8.5 million soldiers and 1.5 million civilians lost their lives. Germany, Austria-Hungary, and the Ottoman Empire were defeated. Britain and France— two of the three "victors"—were seriously weakened. Only the United States, a late entrant into the war, emerged relatively unscathed. The defeat and subsequent dismemberment of the Ottoman Empire by France and Britain led to those countries' management of core territory in the Middle East, including British control over Palestine. Previously, in 1917, under the Balfour Doctrine, Britain had pledged to facilitate the establishment in Palestine of a homeland for the Jewish people, a pledge that would be honored 30 years later.

THE INTERWAR YEARS AND WORLD WAR II

The end of World War I saw critical changes in international relations. First, three European empires were strained and finally broke up during or near the end of World War I. With those empires went the conservative social order of Europe. In its place emerged a proliferation of nationalisms. Russia exited the war in 1917, as revolution raged within its territory. The tsar was overthrown and eventually replaced by not only a new leader, Vladimir Ilyich Lenin, but also a new ideology—communism. The Austro-Hungarian and Ottoman Empires disintegrated. Austria-Hungary was replaced by Austria, Hungary, Czechoslovakia, part of Yugoslavia, and part of Romania. The Ottoman Empire was also reconfigured. Having gradually weakened throughout the nineteenth century, its defeat resulted in the final overthrow of the Ottomans. Arabia rose against Ottoman rule, and British forces occupied Palestine (including Jerusalem) and Baghdad. Turkey became the largest of the successor states that emerged from the disintegration of the Ottoman Empire.

The end of the empires accelerated and intensified nationalisms. In fact, one of President Woodrow Wilson's Fourteen Points in the treaty ending World War I called for self-determination, the right of national groups to self-rule. Technological innovations in the printing industry and a mass literate audience stimulated the nationalism of these various groups. Now it was easy and cheap to publish material in the multitude of different European languages and so offer differing interpretations of history and national life.

A second critical change was that Germany emerged from World War I an even more dissatisfied power. Germany had been defeated on the battlefield, but German forces ended the war in occupation of enemy territory. Moreover, German leaders had not been honest with the German people. Many German newspapers had been predicting a major breakthrough and victory right up until the armistice of November 11, 1918, so the myth grew that the German military had been "stabbed in the back" by "liberals" (and later Jews) in Berlin. Even more devastating was the fact that the Treaty of Versailles, which formally ended the war, made the subsequent generation of Germans pay the entire economic cost of the war through reparations—$32 billion for wartime damages. As Germany printed more money to pay its reparations, Germans suffered from hyperinflation, causing widespread impoverishment of the middle and working classes. Finally, Germany was no longer allowed to have a standing military, and French and British troops occupied its most productive industrialized region, the Ruhr Valley. Bitterness over these harsh penalties provided the climate for the emergence of conservative groups such as the National Socialist Worker's Party, or Nazis, led by Adolf Hitler. Hitler publicly dedicated himself to righting the "wrongs" imposed on the German people after World War I.

Third, enforcement of the Treaty of Versailles was given to the **League of Nations**, the intergovernmental organization designed to prevent all future interstate wars. But the organization itself did not have the political weight, the legal instruments, or the legitimacy to carry out the task. The political weight of the League was weakened by the fact that the United States—whose president Woodrow Wilson had been the League's principal architect—itself refused to join, retreating instead to an isolationist foreign policy. Nor did Russia join, nor were any of the vanquished states of the war permitted to participate. The League's legal authority was weak, and the instruments it had for enforcing the peace, namely sanctions, proved ineffective.

Fourth, the blueprint for a peaceful international order enshrined in Wilson's Fourteen Points failed. Wilson had called for open diplomacy—"open covenants

IN FOCUS

Key Developments in the Interwar Years

▶ Three empires collapse: Russia by revolution, the Austro-Hungarian Empire by dismemberment, and the Ottoman Empire by external wars and internal turmoil. These collapses lead to a resurgence of nationalisms.

▶ German dissatisfaction with the World War I settlement (Versailles Treaty) leads to the rise of fascism in Germany. Germany finds allies in Italy and Japan.

▶ A weak League of Nations is unable to respond to Japanese, Italian, and German aggression. Nor can it prevent or reverse widespread economic depression.

of peace, openly arrived at, after which there shall be no private international understandings of any kind but diplomacy shall proceed always frankly and in public view."[7] Point three was a reaffirmation of economic liberalism, the removal of economic barriers among all the nations consenting to the peace. The League, a "general association of nations" that would ensure war never occurred again, would maintain order. But these principles were not adopted. In the words of historian E. H. Carr, "The characteristic feature of the twenty years between 1919 and 1939 was the abrupt descent from the visionary hopes of the first decade to the grim despair of the second, from a utopia which took little account of reality to a reality from which every element of utopia was rigorously excluded."[8] Liberalism and its utopian and idealist elements were replaced by realism as the dominant international relations theory—a fundamentally divergent theoretical perspective. (See Chapter 3.)

The world from which these realists emerged was a turbulent one. The German economy imploded; the U.S. stock market plummeted; and the world economy sputtered, and then collapsed. Japan marched into Manchuria in 1931 and into the rest of China in 1937; Italy overran Ethiopia in 1935; fascism, liberalism, and communism clashed.

World War II

In the view of most Europeans and many in the United States, Germany, and in particular Adolf Hitler, started World War II. But Italy and Japan also played major roles in the breakdown of interstate order in the 1930s.

In 1935, Italy invaded Ethiopia (Abyssinia) and occupied it the following year. The League of Nations responded to this act of aggression with sanctions, but member states refused to enforce them, dealing a blow to the League's very foundation.

In 1931, Japan staged the Mukden incident as a pretext for assaulting China and annexing Manchuria. The Japanese invasion of China was marked by horrifying barbarity against the Chinese people, including the rape, murder, and torture of Chinese civilians, and by the increasing inability of Japan's civilian government to restrain its generals in China. Japan's record in Korea was equally brutal. Japan's reputation for savagery against noncombatants in China reached its peak in the Rape of Nanking in 1937, when an estimated 300,000 were murdered. When news of the massacres and rapes reached the United States—itself already embroiled in a dispute with Japan over Japan's prior conduct in China—a diplomatic crisis ensued, the result of which was war, when Japanese forces attacked the U.S. Seventh Fleet at Pearl Harbor in December 1941.

But Nazi Germany, the **Third Reich**, proved to be the greatest challenge to the nascent interstate order that followed World War I. Adolf Hitler had come to power with a promise to restore Germany's economy and national pride. The core of his economic policies, however, was an overinvestment in armaments production. Germany could not actually pay for the foodstuffs and raw materials needed to maintain the pace of production, so it bullied its neighbors—mostly much weaker new states to the east, such as Bulgaria, Hungary, and Romania—into ruinous trade deals. As one economic historian of the period put it: "The process was circular. The economic crisis itself was largely caused by the extreme pace of German rearmament. One way out would have been to slacken that pace: when that was rejected, Germany was in a position where she was arming in order to expand, and then had to expand in order to continue to arm."[9] But once the other European powers realized how far behind they were, they used every diplomatic opportunity to delay confronting Germany until they themselves might have a chance to succeed. For these and other reasons, including the economic damage both Britain and France suffered in World War I, Britain and France did little to halt Germany's resurgence.

The Third Reich represented more than an economic juggernaut. Fascism as practiced by Hitler effectively mobilized the masses in support of the state, exalting the nation and race above the individual. It capitalized on the idea that war and conflict were noble activities from which ultimately superior civilizations would be formed. It drew strength from the belief that certain racial groups were superior and others inferior, and it mobilized the disenchanted and the economically weak on behalf of its cause. In autumn 1938, Britain agreed to let Germany occupy the westernmost region of Czechoslovakia, in the hope of averting a general war, or at least delaying war until Britain's defense preparations could be sufficiently strengthened. But this was a false hope. In spring 1939, the Third Reich annexed the remainder of Czechoslovakia, and in September 1939, after having signed a peace treaty with the Soviet Union that divided Poland between them, German forces stormed into Poland from the west while Soviet forces assaulted from the east. Hitler's real intent was to secure his eastern flank against a Soviet threat while he assaulted Norway, Denmark, the Netherlands, and, ultimately, France. His grand plan then called for Germany to turn east and conquer the Soviet Union. Poland was quickly overcome, but because Britain and France had guaranteed Polish security, the invasion prompted a declaration of war: World War II had begun.

In 1940, Hitler set his plans into motion and succeeded in a series of rapid conquests, culminating in the defeat of France in May. In the late summer and fall, after being repeatedly rebuffed in its efforts to coerce Britain into neutrality, the Third Reich prepared to invade and the Battle of Britain ensued. Fought almost

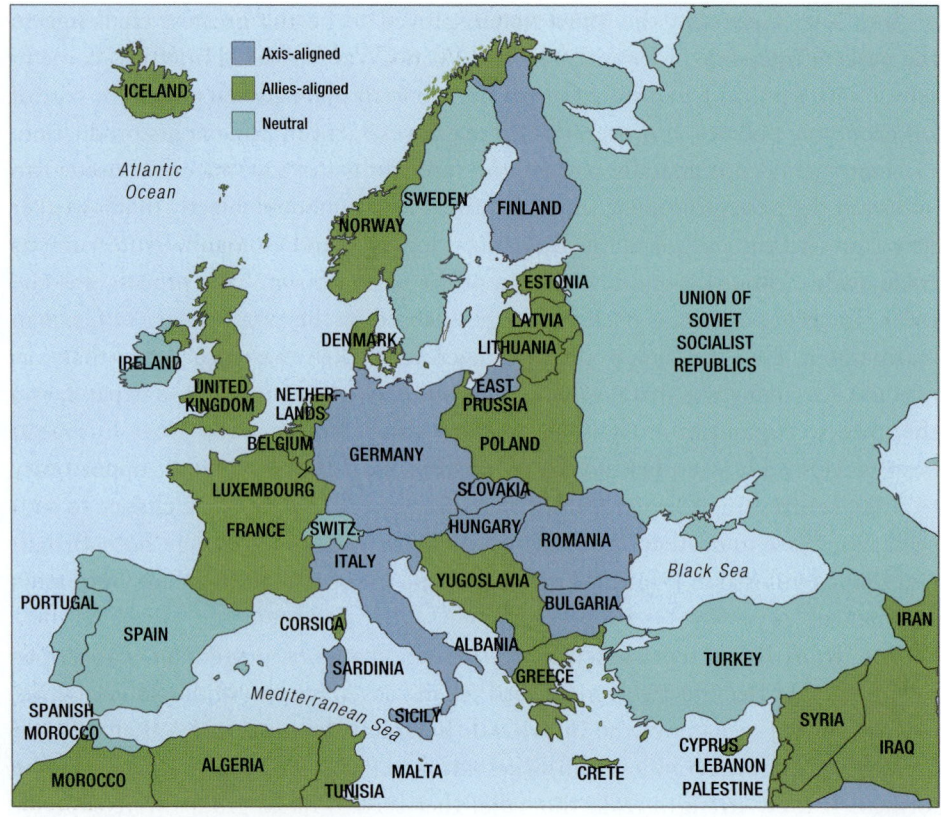

Europe, showing alliances as of 1939

entirely in the air, the battle was eventually won by Britain through a combination of extreme courage, resourcefulness, and luck; and Hitler was forced to turn east with a hostile Britain at his back. In June 1941, the Third Reich undertook the most ambitious land invasion in history: Operation Barbarossa—its long-planned yet ill-fated invasion of the Soviet Union. This surprise attack led the Soviet Union to join sides with Britain and France.

The power of fascism—in German, Italian, and Japanese versions—led to an uneasy alliance between the communist Soviet Union and the liberal United States, Great Britain, and France, among others (the Allies). That alliance sought to check the Axis powers (Germany, Italy, and Japan), by force if necessary. Thus, during World War II, those fighting against the Axis powers acted in unison, regardless of their ideological disagreements.

At the end of the war in 1945, the Allies prevailed. Italy had already surrendered in September 1943, and the Third Reich and imperial Japan lay in ruins. In Europe, the Soviet Union paid the highest price for the Third Reich's aggression, and, with some justification, considered itself the victor in Europe, with help from the United States and Britain. In the Pacific, the United States, China, and Korea paid the highest price for Japan's aggression. With some justification, the United States considered itself the victor in the Pacific.

Two other features of World War II demand attention as well. First, the Third Reich's military invasion of Poland, the Baltic states, and the Soviet Union was followed by organized killing teams whose sole aim was the mass murder of human beings, regardless of their support for, or resistance to, the German state. Jews in particular were singled out, but Nazi policy extended to gypsies (now called Roma), communists, homosexuals, and even ethnic Germans born with genetic defects. In Germany, Poland, the Baltic states, Yugoslavia, and the Soviet Union, persons on target lists were forced to abandon their homes. Nazi captors forced these people to work in labor camps under cruel conditions, and then either slowly or rapidly murdered them. In East Asia, Japanese forces acted with similar cruelty against Chinese, Vietnamese, and Korean noncombatants. The Japanese often tortured victims or forced them to become subjects in gruesome experiments before murdering them. In many places, women were forced into brothels, or "comfort stations," as Japanese rhetoric of the day described them. The nearly unprecedented brutality of the Axis powers against noncombatants in areas of occupation during the war led to war crimes tribunals and, ultimately, to a major new feature of international politics following the war: the Geneva Conventions of 1948 and 1949. These conventions—which today have the force of international law—formally criminalized many abuses, including torture, murder, and food deprivation, all perpetrated against noncombatants in areas of German and Japanese occupation during World War II. The conventions are collectively known as international humanitarian law (IHL), which is discussed in Chapter 10.

The Germans and Japanese were not the only forces for whom race was a factor in World War II. As documented by John Dower in his book *War without Mercy*, U.S., British, and Australian forces fighting in the Pacific tended to view the Japanese as "apes" or "monkey men." As a result, they rarely took prisoners and were more comfortable in undertaking massive strategic air assaults on Japanese cities. In the United States in 1942, citizens of Japanese descent were summarily deprived of their constitutional rights and interned for the duration of the war. In the Pacific theater, racism affected the conduct and strategies of armed forces on *both* sides.[10]

Second, although Germany surrendered unconditionally in May 1945, the war did not end until Japan surrendered in August of that year. By this point in the war, Japan had no hope of winning. Japan had made it clear as early as January that it might be willing to surrender, so long as Allied forces did not try or imprison Emperor Hirohito. But the Allies had already agreed they would accept no less than unconditional surrender, so Japan prepared for an invasion by U.S. and possibly

Soviet forces, hoping that the threat of massive Allied casualties might yet win it a chance to preserve the emperor from trial and punishment. Instead, on August 6, the United States dropped an atomic bomb on Hiroshima, and three days later, a second bomb on Nagasaki. The casualties were no greater than those experienced in fire-bombings of major Japanese cities earlier that year. But the new weapon, combined with a Soviet declaration of war on Japan the same day as the Nagasaki bombing, led to Japan's unconditional surrender on August 15, 1945.

The end of World War II resulted in a major redistribution of power. The victorious United States and Soviet Union emerged as the new world powers, though the USSR had been severely hurt by the war and remained economically crippled as compared to the United States. Yet what the USSR lacked in economic power, it gained from geopolitical proximity to the two places where the future of the international system would be decided: Western Europe and East Asia. The war also changed political boundaries. The Soviet Union virtually annexed the Baltic states (Latvia, Lithuania, and Estonia) and portions of Austria, Finland, Czechoslovakia, Poland, and Romania; Germany and Korea were divided; and Japan was ousted from much of Asia. Each of these changes contributed to the new international conflict: the **Cold War**.

THE COLD WAR

The leaders of the victors of World War II—Britain's prime minister, Winston Churchill; the United States' president, Franklin Roosevelt; and the Soviet Union's premier, Joseph Stalin—planned during the war for a postwar order. Indeed, the Atlantic Charter of August 14, 1941, called for collaboration on economic issues and prepared for a permanent system of security in a "united nations." These plans were consolidated between 1943 and 1945. The final conference in Potsdam, concluded weeks before the war officially ended, divided Germany into zones. This division, along with several other outcomes of World War II, help explain the emergence of what we now call the Cold War.

Origins of the Cold War

The first and most important outcome of World War II was the emergence of two **superpowers**—the United States and the Soviet Union—as the primary actors in the international system, which resulted in the decline of Western Europe as the epicenter of international politics. The second outcome of the war was the intensification of fundamental incompatibilities between these two superpowers in both national interests and ideology. Differences surfaced immediately over geopolitical national interests. Having been invaded from the west on several occasions, including during World War II, the USSR used its newfound power to solidify its sphere of influence in Eastern Europe, specifically in Poland, Czechoslovakia, Hungary, Bulgaria, and Romania. The Soviet leadership believed that ensuring friendly (or at least weak) neighbors on its western borders was vital to the country's national interests. In the United States, there raged a debate between those favoring an aggressive **rollback** strategy—pushing the USSR back to its own borders—and those favoring a less aggressive **containment** strategy. The diplomat and historian George Kennan published in *Foreign Affairs* the famous "X" telegram, in which he argued that because the Soviet Union would always feel military insecurity, it would conduct an aggressive foreign policy. Containing the Soviets, Kennan wrote, should therefore become the cornerstone of the United States' postwar foreign policy.[11] What Kennan meant was that the United States should devise policies that restrained the power of that hostile nation, keeping it under control, but not necessarily using military force.

The United States put the notion of containment into action in the Truman Doctrine of 1947. Justifying material support in Greece against the communists, President Harry Truman asserted, "I believe that it must be the policy of the United States to support free peoples who are resisting attempted subjugation by armed minorities or by outside pressures. I believe that we must assist free peoples to work out their own destinies in their own way."[12] Containment as policy—essentially, the use of espionage, economic pressure, and forward-deployed military resources—emerged from a comparative asymmetry of forces in Europe. After the Third Reich's surrender, U.S. and British forces rapidly demobilized and went home, whereas the Soviet army did not. In 1948, the Soviets blocked western transportation corridors to Berlin, the German capital—which had been divided into sectors by postwar agreement. The United States then realized that even as the sole state in possession of atomic weapons, it did not possess the power to coerce the Soviet Union into retreating to its pre–World War II borders. And, in August 1949, the Soviets successfully tested their first atomic bomb. Thus, containment, based on U.S. geostrategic interests and a growing recognition that attempting rollback would likely lead to another world war, became the fundamental doctrine of U.S. foreign policy during the Cold War.

The United States and the Soviet Union also had major ideological differences. The United States' democratic liberalism was based on a social system that accepted the worth and value of the individual; a political system that depended on the participation of individuals in the electoral process; and an economic system, **capitalism**, that provided opportunities to individuals to pursue what was economically rational with minimal government interference. At the international level, this translated into support for other democratic regimes and support of liberal capitalist institutions and processes, including, most critically, free trade.

Soviet communist ideology also influenced that country's conception of the international system and state practices. The failure of the Revolutions of 1848 cast Marxist theory into crisis; Marxism insisted that peasants and workers would spontaneously rise up and overthrow their capitalist masters, but this had not happened. The crisis in Marxist theory was partly resolved by Vladimir Lenin's "vanguard of the proletariat" amendment, in which Lenin argued that the masses must be led or "sparked" by intellectuals who fully understand **socialism**. But the end result was a system in which any hope of achieving communism—a utopian vision in which the state withered away along with poverty, war, sexism, and the like—had to be led from the top down. This result meant that to the United States and its liberal allies, the Soviet system looked like a dictatorship, bent on aggressively exporting that system under the guise of worldwide socialist revolution. Popular sovereignty vanished in every state allied to the Soviet Union (e.g., Czechoslovakia, Hungary, Romania, Lithuania, Latvia, Estonia, and Poland). For their part, Soviet leaders felt themselves surrounded by a hostile capitalist camp and argued that the Soviet Union "must not weaken but must in every way strengthen its state, the state organs, the organs of the intelligence service, the army, if that country does not want to be smashed by the capitalist environment."[13]

These "bottom up" versus "top down" differences between the United States and Russia were exacerbated by mutual misperceptions. Once each side became distrustful, it tended to view the other side's policies as necessarily threatening. For example, the formation of the **North Atlantic Treaty Organization (NATO)** in 1949 became a contentious worldwide issue. NATO's twelve founding members sought to defend Western Europe from the fully mobilized Soviet Army; while from the Soviet perspective, NATO seemed clearly an aggressive military alliance aimed at depriving the USSR of the fruits of its victory over the Third Reich. In 1955, Russia formed its own postwar alliance—the **Warsaw Pact**—together with six East European states. When the USSR reacted in ways it took to be defensive, Britain and the United States interpreted these actions as dangerous escalations.

The third outcome of the end of World War II was the collapse of the colonial system, a development few foresaw. The defeat of Japan and Germany meant the immediate end of their respective empires. The other colonial powers, faced with the reality of their economically and politically weakened position, and confronted with newly powerful indigenous movements for independence, were spurred by the United Nations Charter's endorsement of the principle of national self-determination. These movements were equipped with leftover small arms from World War II, led by talented commanders employing indirect defense strategies such as "revolutionary" guerrilla warfare, and inspired to great self-sacrifice by the

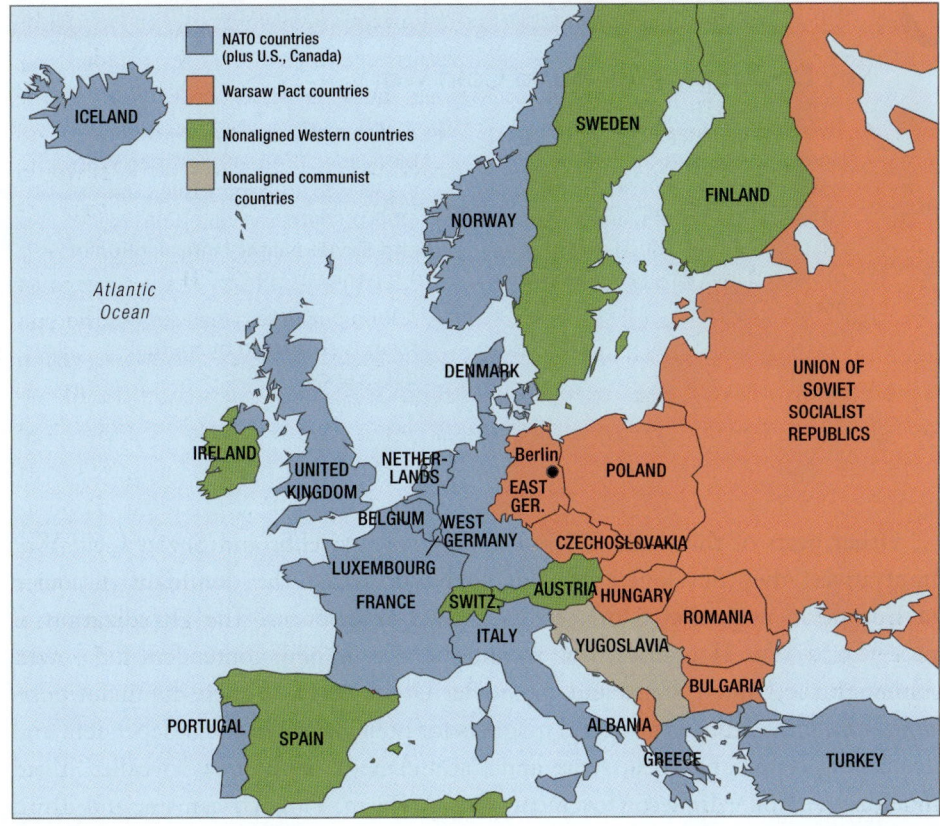

Europe during the Cold War

ideals of nationalism. Victorious powers were forced—by local resistance, their own decline, or pressure from the United States—to grant independence to their former colonies. This started with Britain, which granted India independence in 1947. It took the military defeat of France in Indochina in the early 1950s to bring decolonization to that part of the world. African states, too, became independent between 1957 and 1963.

The fourth outcome was the realization that the differences between the two emergent superpowers would be played out indirectly, on third-party stages, rather than through direct confrontation. Both rivals came to believe that the risks of a direct military confrontation were too great and that the "loss" of any potential ally, no matter how poor or distant, might begin a cumulative process leading to a significant shift in the balance of power. Thus, the Cold War resulted in the globalization of conflict to all continents. International relations became truly global.

Key Developments in the Cold War

▶ Two superpowers emerge—the United States and the Soviet Union. They are divided by national interests, ideologies, and mutual misperceptions. These divisions are projected into different geographic areas.

▶ A series of crises occur—Berlin blockade (1948–49), Korean War (1950–53), Cuban missile crisis (1962), Vietnam War (1965–73), and Soviet military intervention in Afghanistan (1979–89).

▶ A long peace between superpower rivals is sustained by mutual deterrence.

Other parts of the world did not merely react to U.S. and Soviet Cold War imperatives: they developed new ideologies or recast the dominant discourse of Europe in ways that addressed their own experiences. The globalization of post–World War II politics thus meant the rise of new contenders for power. Although the United States and the Soviet Union retained their dominant positions, new ideas acted as powerful magnets for populations in the independent and developing states of Africa, Asia, and Latin America—the new so-called Third World. The Non-Aligned Movement, Pan-Arabism, Pan-Africanism, and Third World socialism developed as reactions to the dominant U.S.-Soviet Union confrontation.

The Cold War as a Series of Confrontations

We can characterize the Cold War (1945–89) as 45 years of overall high-level tension and competition between the superpowers but with no direct military conflict. The advent of nuclear weapons created a stalemate in which each side acted, at times reluctantly, with increasing caution. As nuclear technology advanced, both sides realized that a nuclear war would likely result in the destruction of each power beyond hope of recovery. This state of affairs was called "mutual assured destruction"—aptly underlined by its acronym: MAD. Though each superpower tended to back down from particular confrontations—either because its national interest was not sufficiently strong to risk a nuclear confrontation, or because its ideological resolve wavered in light of military realities—several confrontations very nearly escalated to war.

The Cold War, then, can be understood as a series of confrontations. Most were conflicts between proxies (North Korea versus South Korea, North Vietnam versus South Vietnam, Ethiopia versus Somalia) that, in all likelihood, neither the United

States nor the Soviet Union had intended to escalate as they did. Thus, the Cold War involved not only superpower confrontations but also confrontations between two blocs of states. The non-communist bloc consisted of the NATO allies (the United States, Canada, Australia, and most of Western Europe), South Korea, Japan, and the Philippines; and the communist bloc consisted of the Warsaw Pact states (the Soviet Union with its allies in Eastern Europe), North Korea, Vietnam, and the People's Republic of China, along with Cuba. Over the life of the Cold War, these blocs loosened, and states sometimes took positions different from that of the dominant power. But for much of this time, bloc politics operated. Table 2.1 shows a timeline of major events related to the Cold War.

One of the high-level, direct confrontations between the superpowers took place in Germany. Germany had been divided immediately after World War II into zones of occupation. The United States, France, and Great Britain administered the western portion; the Soviet Union, the eastern. Berlin, Germany's capital, was similarly divided but lay within Soviet-controlled East Germany. In 1948, the Soviet Union blocked land access to Berlin, prompting the United States and Britain to airlift supplies for 13 months. In 1949, the separate states of West and East Germany were declared. In 1961, East Germany erected the Berlin Wall around the West German portion of the city to stem the tide of East Germans trying to leave the troubled state. U.S. president John F. Kennedy responded by visiting the city and declaring, "*Ich bin ein Berliner*" (improper German for the sentiment "I am a Berliner"), committing the United States to the security of the Federal Republic of Germany at any cost. Not surprisingly, the dismantling of that same wall in November 1989 became the most iconic symbol of the end of the Cold War.

TABLE 2.1

Important Events of the Cold War

1945–48	Soviet Union establishes communist regimes in Eastern Europe.
1947	Announcement of Truman Doctrine; United States proposes Marshall Plan for the rebuilding of Europe.
1948–49	Soviets blockade Berlin; United States and Allies carry out airlift.
1949	Soviets test atomic bomb, ending U.S. nuclear monopoly. Chinese communists under Mao win civil war, establish People's Republic of China. United States and Allies establish NATO.
1950–53	Korean War.

1957	Soviets launch the satellite *Sputnik*, causing anxiety in the West and catalyzing superpower scientific competition.
1960–63	Congo crisis and UN action to fill power vacuum.
1962	Cuban missile crisis; nuclear war narrowly averted.
1965	United States begins large-scale intervention in Vietnam.
1967	Israel defeats Egypt, Syria, and Jordan in the Six-Day War. Glassboro summit signals détente, loosening of tensions between the superpowers.
1968	Czech government liberalization halted by Soviet invasion. Nuclear Nonproliferation Treaty (NPT) signed.
1972	U.S. president Nixon visits China and Soviet Union. United States and Soviet Union sign Strategic Arms Limitations Treaty (SALT I).
1973	Yom Kippur War between Israel and Arab states leads to global energy crisis.
1975	Proxy and anticolonial wars fought in Angola, Mozambique, Ethiopia, and Somalia. South Vietnam falls to communist North Vietnam.
1979	United States and Soviet Union sign SALT II (but U.S. Senate fails to ratify it). Soviet Union invades Afghanistan. Shah of Iran (a major U.S. ally) overthrown in Islamic revolution. Israel and Egypt sign a peace treaty.
1981–89	Reagan Doctrine provides basis for U.S. support of "anticommunist" forces in Nicaragua and Afghanistan.
1985	Gorbachev starts economic and political reforms in Soviet Union.
1989	Peaceful revolutions in Eastern Europe replace communist governments. Berlin Wall is dismantled. Soviet Union withdraws from Afghanistan.
1990	Germany reunified.
1991	Resignation of Gorbachev. Soviet Union collapses.
1992–93	Russia and other former Soviet republics become independent states.

The Cold War in Asia and Latin America

China, Indochina, and especially Korea became the symbols of the Cold War in Asia. In 1946, after years of bitter and heroic fighting against the Japanese occupation, communists throughout Asia attempted to take control of their respective states following Japan's surrender. In China, the wartime alliance between the Kuomintang (non-communist Chinese nationalists) and Mao Zedong's "People's Liberation Army" dissolved into renewed civil war, in which the United States attempted to support the Kuomintang with large shipments of arms and military equipment. By 1949, however, the Kuomintang had been defeated, and its leaders fled to the island of Formosa (now Taiwan). With the addition of one-fourth of the world's population to the communist bloc, U.S. interests in Japan and the Philippines now seemed directly threatened.

In 1946, in what was then French Indochina (an amalgamation of the contemporary states of Cambodia, Laos, and Vietnam), Ho Chi Minh raised the communist flag over Hanoi, declaring Vietnam to be an independent state. The French quickly returned to take Indochina back, but though French forces fought bravely and with great skill, they proved unable to defeat the communists, the Viet Minh. In 1954, after having laid a trap for the Viet Minh in a fortified town called Dien Bien Phu, the French were themselves trapped and decisively defeated. France abandoned Indochina; a peace treaty signed in Geneva that same year divided Indochina into the political entities of Laos, Cambodia, and Vietnam, with Vietnam being divided into two zones: North Vietnam and South Vietnam.

After having spent years seeking support from the USSR to unify the Korean peninsula under communist rule, North Korean leader Kim Il-Sung finally persuaded Joseph Stalin to lend him the military equipment needed to conquer non-communist South Korea. On June 25, 1950, communist North Korean forces crossed the frontier into South Korea and rapidly overwhelmed the South's defenders. The North Korean offensive quickly captured Seoul, South Korea's capital, and then forced the retreat of the few surviving South Korean and American armed forces all the way to the outskirts of the southern port city of Pusan. In one of the most dramatic military reversals in history, U.S. forces—fighting for the first time under the auspices of the United Nations because of North Korea's "unprovoked aggression" and violations of international law—landed a surprise force at Inchon. Within days, the U.S. forces cut off and then routed the North Korean forces. By mid-October, UN forces had captured North Korea's capital, Pyongyang, and by the end of the month, the destruction of North Korea's military was nearly complete.

Yet the war did not end. Against the wishes of U.S. president Harry Truman, U.S. general Douglas MacArthur ordered his victorious troops—now overconfident of victory and spread thin—to finish off the defeated North Koreans, who by this time were encamped very close to the border with communist China. The Chinese had warned they would intervene if their territory was approached too closely, and in November, they did. The relatively poorly equipped but more numerous and highly motivated Chinese soldiers attacked the UN forces, causing the longest retreat of U.S. armed forces in American history. The two sides then became mired in a stalemate. With numerous diplomatic skirmishes over the years—provoked by the basing of U.S. troops in South Korea, the use of the demilitarized zone between the north and the south, and North Korean attempts to become a nuclear power—the peninsula remains a source of conflict today.

The 1962 Cuban missile crisis was a high-profile direct confrontation between the superpowers in another area of the world. The United States viewed the Soviet Union's installation of nuclear missiles in Cuba as a direct threat to its territory: no weapons of a powerful enemy had ever been located so close to U.S. shores. The way in which the crisis was resolved suggests unequivocally that neither party sought a direct confrontation, but once the crisis became public, neither side could back down and global thermonuclear war became a very real possibility. The United States chose to blockade Cuba—another example of containment strategy in action—to prevent the arrival of additional Soviet missiles. The U.S. president, John F. Kennedy, rejected the more aggressive actions the U.S. military favored, such as a land invasion of Cuba or air strikes on missile sites. Through behind-the-scenes, unofficial contacts in Washington and direct communication between Kennedy and Soviet premier Nikita Khrushchev, the Soviets agreed to remove the missiles from Cuba and the United States agreed to remove similarly capable missiles from Turkey. The crisis was defused, and war was averted.

Vietnam provided a test of a different kind. The Cold War was also played out there, not in one dramatic crisis but in an extended civil war. Communist North Vietnam and its Chinese and Soviet allies were pitted against the "free world"—South Vietnam, allied with the United States and assorted supporters, including South Korea, the Philippines, and Thailand. To most U.S. policy makers in the late 1950s and early 1960s, Vietnam was yet another test of the containment doctrine: communist influence must be stopped, they argued, before it spread like a chain of falling dominos through the rest of Southeast Asia and beyond (hence the term **domino effect**). Thus, the United States supported the South Vietnamese dictators Ngo Dinh Diem and later Nguyen Van Thieu against the rival communist regime of Ho Chi Minh in the north, which was underwritten by both the People's Republic of China and the Soviet Union. But, as the South Vietnamese

For the United States, Vietnam became a symbol of the Cold War rivalries in Asia. The United States supported the South Vietnamese forces against the communist regime in the north. Here, Vietnamese soldiers stand atop a downed U.S. B-52 bomber.

government and military faltered on their own, the United States stepped up its military support, increasing the number of its troops on the ground and escalating the air war over the north.

In the early stages, the United States was confident of victory; after all, a superpower with all its military hardware and technically skilled labor force could surely beat a poorly trained Vietcong guerrilla force. American policy makers were quickly disillusioned, however, as communist forces proved adept at avoiding the massive technical firepower of U.S. forces, and a corrupt South Vietnamese leadership siphoned away many of the crucial resources needed to win its more vital struggle for popular legitimacy. As U.S. casualties mounted, with no prospects for victory in sight, the U.S. public grew disenchanted. Should the United States use all of its conventional military capability to prevent the "fall" of South Vietnam and stave off the domino effect? Should the United States fight until victory was guaranteed for liberalism and capitalism, or should it extricate itself from this unpopular quagmire? Should the United States capitulate to the forces of ideological communism? These questions, posed in both geostrategic and ideological terms, defined the middle years of the Cold War, from the Vietnam War's slow beginning in the late 1950s until the dramatic departure of U.S. officials from the South Vietnamese capital, Saigon, in 1975— symbolized by U.S. helicopters leaving the U.S. embassy roof while dozens of desperate Vietnamese tried to grab on to the boarding ladders and escape with them.

The U.S. effort to avert a communist takeover in South Vietnam failed, yet contrary to expectations, the domino effect did not occur. Cold War alliances were shaken on both sides: the friendship between the Soviet Union and China had long before degenerated into a geostrategic fight and a struggle over the proper form of communism, especially in Third World countries. But the Soviet bloc was left relatively unscathed by the Vietnam War. The U.S.-led Western alliance was seriously jeopardized, as several allies (including Canada) strongly opposed U.S. policy toward Vietnam. The bipolar structure of the Cold War–era international system was coming apart. Confidence in military alternatives was shaken in the United States, undermining for more than a decade the United States' ability to commit itself militarily. The power of the United States was supposed to be righteous power, but in Vietnam, it was neither victorious in its outcome nor righteous in its effects.

Was the Cold War Really Cold?

It was not always the case that when the United States or the Soviet Union acted, the other side responded. In some cases, the other side chose not to act, or at least not to respond in kind. Usually this was out of concern for escalating a conflict to a major war. For example, the Soviet Union invaded Hungary in 1956 and Czechoslovakia in 1968, both sovereign states and allies in the Warsaw Pact. Under other circumstances, the United States might have responded with counterforce, but while it verbally condemned these aggressive Soviet actions, the actions themselves went unchecked. In 1956, the United States, preoccupied with the Suez Canal crisis, kept quiet, aware that it was ill prepared to respond militarily. In 1968, the United States was mired in Vietnam and beset by domestic turmoil and a presidential election. The United States was also relatively complacent, although angry, when the Soviets invaded Afghanistan in 1979. The Soviets likewise kept quiet when the United States took aggressive action within the U.S. sphere of influence, invading Grenada in 1983 and Panama in 1989. Thus, during the Cold War, even blatantly aggressive actions by one of the superpowers did not always lead to a response by the other.

Many of the events of the Cold War involved the United States and the Soviet Union only indirectly; proxies often fought in their place. Nowhere was this so true as in the Middle East. For both the United States and the Soviet Union, the Middle East was a region of vital importance because of its possession of an estimated one-third of the world's oil, its strategic position as a transportation hub between Asia and Europe, and its cultural significance as the cradle of three of the world's major religions. The establishment of Israel itself in 1948 was a controversial act. At the end of World War II, Britain had concluded that it could no longer manage Palestine, referring the issue to the United Nations. The UN recommended the partition of Palestine into two states, one Jewish and one Arab; the Jews accepted the proposal, and the Arabs did not. Thus, when British control terminated in 1948, Israel announced the formation of a new state, to which the United States immediately gave diplomatic recognition.

The region thus became the scene of a superpower confrontation by proxy between the U.S.-supported Israel and the Soviet-backed Arab states Syria, Iraq, and Egypt. During the Six-Day War in 1967, Israel crushed the Soviet-equipped Arabs in six short days, seizing the strategic territories of the Golan Heights, Gaza, and the West Bank. During the Yom Kippur War of 1973, which the Egyptians had planned as a limited war, the Israeli victory was not so overwhelming, because the United States and the Soviets negotiated a cease-fire before more damage could be done. But throughout the Cold War, these "hot" wars were followed by guerrilla actions supported by all parties. As long as the basic balance of power was maintained between Israel and the United States on one side and the Arabs and the Soviets on the other, the region was left alone; when that balance was threatened, the superpowers acted through proxies to maintain the balance. Other controversies also plagued the region, as evidenced by events after the end of the Cold War.

In parts of the world that were of less strategic importance to the two superpowers, confrontation through proxies was even more regular during the Cold War. Africa and Latin America present many examples of such events. When the colonialist Belgians abruptly left the Congo in 1960, civil war broke out as various contending factions sought to take power and bring order out of the chaos. One of the contenders, the Congolese premier Patrice Lumumba (1925–61), appealed to the Soviets for help in fighting the Western-backed insurgents and received both diplomatic support and military supplies. However, Lumumba was dismissed by the Congolese president, Joseph Kasavubu, an ally of the United States. Still others, such as Moïse Tshombe, leader of the copper-rich Katanga province, who was also closely identified with Western interests, fought for control. The three-year civil war could have become another protracted proxy war between the United States and the Soviet Union. However, the United Nations averted such a confrontation by sending in peacekeepers, whose primary purpose was to stabilize a transition government and prevent the superpowers from making the Congo yet another violent arena of the Cold War.

In Latin America, too, participants in civil wars were able to transform their struggles into Cold War confrontations by proxy, thereby gaining military equipment and technical expertise from one of the superpowers. In most cases, Latin American states were led by governments beholden to wealthy elites who maintained a virtual monopoly on the country's wealth. When popular protest against corruption and injustice escalated to violence, communist Cuba was often asked to support these armed movements, and in response, the United States tended to support the incumbent governments—even those whose record of human rights abuses against their own citizens had been well established. In Nicaragua, for example, after communists called Sandinistas captured the government from its dictator in 1979, the Ronald Reagan administration supported an insurgency known as the "Contras" in an attempt to reverse what it feared would be a "communist foothold" in Latin America. Such proxy warfare enabled the superpowers to project power and support geostrategic interests (e.g., oil in Angola, transportation routes around the Horn of Africa, the Monroe Doctrine in Latin America) and ideologies without directly confronting one another and risking major or thermonuclear war.

In sum, the Cold War was really only relatively cold in Europe, and very warm, or even hot, in other places. In Asia, the Middle East, Africa, and Latin America, over 40 million people lost their lives in superpower proxy wars from 1946 to 1990.

But the Cold War was also "fought" and moderated in words, at **summits** (meetings between leaders), and in treaties. Some Cold War summits were relatively successful: the 1967 Glassboro summit between U.S. and Soviet leaders began the loosening of tensions known as **détente**. Others, however, did not produce results. Treaties between the two parties placed self-imposed limitations on nuclear arms. For example, the first Strategic Arms Limitations Treaty (SALT I), in 1972, placed an absolute ceiling on the numbers of intercontinental ballistic missiles (ICBMs), deployed nuclear warheads, and multiple independently targetable reentry vehicles (MIRVs); and limited the number of antiballistic missile sites each superpower maintained. So the superpowers did enjoy periods of accommodation, when they could agree on principles and policies.

THE IMMEDIATE POST–COLD WAR ERA

The fall of the Berlin Wall in 1989 symbolized the end of the Cold War, but its actual end was gradual. The Soviet premier at the time, Mikhail Gorbachev, and other Soviet reformers had set in motion two domestic processes—*glasnost* (political openness) and *perestroika* (economic restructuring)—as early as the mid-1980s. *Glasnost*, combined with a new technology—the videocassette player—made it possible for the first time since the October Revolution for average Soviet citizens to compare their living standards with those of their Western counterparts. The comparison proved dramatically unfavorable. It also opened the door to criticism of the political system, culminating in the emergence of a multiparty system and the massive reorientation of the once-monopolistic Communist Party. *Perestroika* undermined the foundation of the planned economy, an essential part of the communist system. At the outset, Gorbachev and his reformers sought to save the system, but once initiated, these reforms led to the dissolution of the Warsaw Pact, Gorbachev's resignation in December 1991, and the disintegration of the Soviet Union itself in 1992–93.

Gorbachev's domestic reforms also led to changes in the orientation of Soviet foreign policy. Needing to extricate the country from the political quagmire and economic drain of the Soviet war in Afghanistan while seeking to save face, Gorbachev suggested that the permanent members of the UN Security Council "could become guarantors of regional security."[14] Afghanistan was a test case, in which a small group of UN observers monitored and verified the withdrawal of more than 100,000 Soviet troops in 1988 and 1989—an action that would have been impossible during the height of the Cold War. Similarly, the Soviets agreed to and supported the 1988 withdrawal of Cuban troops from Angola. The Soviet Union had retreated from international commitments near its borders, as well as others farther abroad. Most important, the Soviets agreed to cooperate in multilateral activities to preserve regional security.

The first post–Cold War test of the so-called new world order came in response to Iraq's invasion and annexation of Kuwait in August 1990. Despite its longstanding support for Iraq, the Soviet Union (and later Russia), along with the four other permanent members of the UN Security Council, agreed first to implement

IN FOCUS

Key Developments in the Immediate Post–Cold War Era

- ▶ Changes are made in Soviet/Russian foreign policy, with the withdrawals from Afghanistan and Angola in the late 1980s, monitored by the United Nations.

- ▶ Iraqi invasion of Kuwait in 1990 and the multilateral response unite the former Cold War adversaries.

- ▶ *Glasnost* and *perestroika* continue in Russia, as reorganized in 1992–93.

- ▶ The former Yugoslavia disintegrates into independent states; civil war ensues in Bosnia and Kosovo, leading to UN and NATO intervention.

- ▶ Widespread ethnic conflict arises in central and western Africa, Central Asia, and the Indian subcontinent.

Explaining the End of the Cold War: A View from the Former Soviet Union

Many scholars of American diplomatic history attribute the end of the Cold War to policies the United States initiated: the buildup of a formidable military capable of winning either a nuclear or conventional war against the Soviet Union and the development of the strongest, most diversified economy the world has ever known. However, those within the Soviet Union perceived the events leading to the end of the Cold War differently.

The predominant viewpoint in the former Soviet Union is that the explanation for the end of the Cold War can be found in a very long and complex chain of domestic developments in the Soviet Union itself. Political, economic, and demographic factors led to what seemed to be an abrupt disintegration of the Soviet Union and hence the end of the Cold War. International relations theorists did not predict it; perhaps they were not looking at domestic factors within the Soviet state itself and did not have a sufficiently long historical perspective.

The political dominance and authority of the Communist Party, the main ideological pillar of the Soviet Union, had significantly eroded by the late 1980s. The revelation of Joseph Stalin's horrific crimes against the Soviet people, especially ethnic minorities, intensified animosity in the far-flung parts of the Soviet empire. Many of the smaller republics and subnational regions bore a grudge against the central government for forced Russification, the resettlement of certain minorities, and other atrocities such as induced famines in Russia and Ukraine in the early 1930s. Increasingly open discussion of such events undermined the ideological fervor of the common population and shook their trust in the "people's government."

During the 1960s, some Soviet leaders saw stagnation in the economic, technological, and agricultural spheres. Internal critics of the regime blamed the top-level political leadership, which had become ossified. The policy of lifelong appointments to leading posts, a policy that remained in effect until the mid-1980s, meant that political appointees stayed in their posts for 20 or more years, regardless of their performance. There were few efforts to reform and modernize the system, and younger people had little opportunity to exercise political leadership. These failures in leadership, exemplified by the poor economy, led to widespread discontent and resentment in all layers of the society.

Moreover, the Soviet Union was a very ethnically diverse state, consisting of 15 major republics, some of which also contained "autonomous" republics and regions, inhabited by hundreds of ethnicities. Although the Soviet Union had benefited economically from extracting resources found in the far reaches of its territories, the costs of keeping the empire together were high. Subsidies flowed to the outer regions at the expense of the Soviet state. With growing economic discontent and the erosion of the ideology promoted by the Communist Party, local nationalist movements started to fill the ideological vacuum by the late 1980s.

Before the mid-1980s, the inherent distortions and inefficiencies of the Soviet planned economy were partially offset by the profits from the energy sector based on oil and

Mikhail Gorbachev addresses the Russian parliament in 1991.

gas exports. However, the Soviet industrial and agricultural sectors lagged behind, inefficient and uncompetitive. Technological development stagnated, too. The sharp decline in world oil prices in the 1980s compounded the problems. The resulting rationing of basic food products and the poor quality of domestically manufactured products totally discredited the socialist economic model and added to the general discontent. The declining state budget could no longer bear the burden of the arms race with the United States, finance an expensive war in Afghanistan, and keep the increasingly fractured empire within its orbit.

The interplay of all these factors came to a climax when Mikhail Gorbachev took power in 1985. Acknowledging the urgent need for change, he launched ambitious domestic reforms collectively referred to as *perestroika*, literally, "restructuring" of economic relations, including stepping back from central planning and curbing government subsidies. *Glasnost* was the political component, an "opening" that relaxed censorship and encouraged democratization. In foreign policy, "New Thinking" meant improving relations with the United States and the possibility of the coexistence of the capitalist and socialist systems through shared human values. The underlying reasons for most of these domestic changes were economic. Reducing military expenditures and gaining access to Western loans became critical for the survival of the troubled state.

The rapid dissolution of the Eastern bloc led to a dramatic shift in the balance of power in the international system. Rising nationalist movements and local liberal forces gained momentum and won significant representation in the local parliaments after the first competitive elections in the former Socialist republics. Eventually, Russia became one of the first to declare independence and affirm sovereignty, with the rest of the republics following suit in the "sovereignty parade" in 1991. The de facto dissolution of the Soviet Union marked an important chapter in the history of the Cold War, but given events in Russia and Ukraine—especially Russia's 2014 annexation by force of Crimea—we cannot yet say that the collapse of the Soviet Union is the Cold War's final chapter.

FOR CRITICAL ANALYSIS

1. How can we balance the traditional view that Western economic and military dominance caused a Soviet "defeat" with the Soviet view that internal weaknesses and contradictions were primarily to blame?

2. *Glasnost* was supposed to make it possible for Soviet citizens to share information, but it also made it possible for them to compare their own lives with those beyond the USSR. How might this development have affected the legitimacy of the Communist Party?

3. If states "learn" from their own mistakes and achievements as well as those of other states, what might a state like China have learned from the collapse of the USSR?

economic sanctions against Iraq. Then they agreed in a Security Council resolution to support the means to restore the status quo—to oust Iraq from Kuwait with a multinational military force. Finally, they supported sending the UN Iraq-Kuwait Observer Mission to monitor the zone and permitted the UN to undertake humanitarian intervention and create safe havens for the Kurdish and Shiite populations of Iraq. Although forging a consensus on each of these actions (or in the case of China, convincing it to abstain) was difficult, the coalition held—a unity unthinkable during the Cold War.

The 1990s were marked by the struggle of former allies and enemies to find new identities and interests in a more complex world. As the threat of World War III vanished, what was the purpose of an organization such as NATO? What was the purpose or focus of state foreign policy to be if not the deterrence of aggression by other states? The United States and Israel, for example, were unparalleled in their capacity to fight and win interstate wars. But who might these other states be? What role might armed forces specialized to win interstate wars play in sub-state violence? Yugoslavia's violent disintegration played itself out over the entire decade, despite Western attempts to resolve the conflict peacefully. At the same time, the world witnessed ethnic tension and violence in central Africa. Genocide in Rwanda and Burundi was effectively ignored by the international community. And, despite U.S. military primacy, Russia maintained enough military power and political influence to prevent U.S. intervention in ethnic hostilities in the Transcaucasus region.

These dual realities converged and diverged throughout the 1990s and continue to do so today. The disintegration of Yugoslavia culminated in an American-led war against Serbia to halt attacks on the ethnic Albanian population in Kosovo. The 78-day air war by NATO against Serbia ended with the capitulation of the Serbs and international administration of the province of Kosovo. The war also severely challenged core principles of international law: technically, the action of NATO in Kosovo was a violation of Serbian sovereignty. Yet NATO's leaders held that Serb rapes, lootings, and murders constituted a greater harm: violating the principle of sovereignty was less harmful than allowing Serbians to murder and torture Kosovar Albanians. The repercussions affect international politics to this day.

Clearly, the end of the Cold War in the 1990s denotes a major change in international relations, the end of one historical era and the beginning of another. The overwhelming military power of the United States, combined with its economic power, appeared to many to usher in an era of U.S. primacy in international affairs to a degree not matched even by the Romans or Alexander the Great. The United States seemed able to impose its will on other states, even against the strong objections of its allies. Yet this moment of primacy now appears doubtful; it proved insufficient to deter or prevent ethnic conflict, civil wars, and human rights abuses from occurring, whether in Somalia, Rwanda, or the former Yugoslavia. And many threats, like terrorism, cyberattacks, and the global financial crisis of 2008, have shown themselves, by their very nature, to demand *multilateral* engagement: no single state, however, powerful, can remain secure against these threats on its own.

THE NEW MILLENNIUM: THE FIRST TWO DECADES

The most significant change in interstate politics following the end of the Cold War has been the emergence of terrorism—once a relatively minor threat—from a law-enforcement problem to a vital national security interest for many states. On September 11, 2001, the world witnessed lethal, psychologically disorienting, and economically devastating terrorist attacks organized and funded by Al Qaeda against New York City and Washington, DC. These attacks, directed by Osama bin Laden, set into motion a U.S.-led global "war on terror." Buoyed by an outpouring of support from around the world and by the first-ever invocation of Article V of the North Atlantic Treaty Organization's Charter, which declares an attack on one NATO member to be an attack on all, the United States undertook to lead an ad hoc coalition to combat terrorist organizations with global reach. That new **war on terrorism**, which continues today, involved multiple campaigns in different countries and began in October 2001 when the United States launched a war in Afghanistan to oust the Taliban regime, which was providing safe haven to Osama bin Laden's Al Qaeda organization.

Following an initially successful campaign in Afghanistan in 2001 and 2002, which specifically targeted terrorists and their supporters and paved the way for popular elections, the United States broke from its allies. Convinced that Iraq maintained clandestine **weapons of mass destruction (WMD)** and posed a continued threat by backing terrorist organizations, the United States attempted to build support in the United Nations for authorization to remove Saddam Hussein forcibly from power and find the hidden WMD. When United Nations Security Council members refused to back this request, the United States built its own coalition, including its key ally Great Britain. This coalition destroyed the Iraqi military and overthrew Iraq's government in 2003, and Hussein himself was executed in 2006. But when no weapons of mass destruction were found, additional justifications for the invasion were offered, including promoting democracy for Iraq's three main peoples—Kurds, Sunni Arabs, and Shia Arabs—within a single state. Fighting in Iraq continues today. Iraq remains torn by sectarian conflict, and its U.S.-built and

IN FOCUS

Key Developments in the First Two Decades of the New Millennium

▶ Al Qaeda terrorist network commits terrorist acts against the homeland of the United States and U.S. interests abroad; U.S. and coalition forces respond militarily in Afghanistan and Iraq; terrorist attacks occur in Saudi Arabia, Spain, Great Britain, Nigeria, France, and Belgium, among other countries.

▶ A financial crisis in the United States in 2008 devastates its economy and rapidly spreads to other countries. The euro debt crisis in Europe and the subsequent vote by Great Britain to leave the European Union threaten the viability of that arrangement.

▶ In the Arab Spring beginning in 2011, Tunisia becomes the first in a series of Arab countries in which a popular uprising topples a long-established dictator. But the uprisings are not all successful and lead to civil war in Syria.

▶ Amid instability in Syria and Iraq, the Islamic State rises, declaring itself a worldwide caliphate in 2014

and laying claim to territory with 10 million inhabitants.

▶ In 2014, presumed Russian soldiers begin occupying eastern Ukraine and Crimea. Crimea votes overwhelmingly to rejoin Russia, a move that is unsettling to Europeans and states bordering Russia. The war in eastern Ukraine continues.

▶ China's military budget expands, making it the second largest after the United States. China begins asserting its ambitious territorial claims in the South China Sea, thereby escalating tensions between China, its neighbors, and the United States.

▶ In reaction to globalization, perceived economic stagnation, and the onslaught of refugees fleeing war and economic hardship, there is a resurgence of nationalism and populism in both the United States and many European countries including France, the Netherlands, Hungary, and Poland.

trained armed forces have suffered repeated defeats and setbacks since the United States withdrew most of its troops. Likewise, even though most American troops left Afghanistan in 2014, that country remains mired in civil conflict, with a resurgent Taliban and an emboldened Islamic State fighting a weak Afghan state. In a bold move in the spring of 2017, the United States dropped the largest conventional weapon in its arsenal, a 22,000-pound "mother of all bombs," on tunnels in eastern Afghanistan where Islamic State fighters were hiding.

With many Western powers fighting militarily in both Afghanistan and Iraq, an international financial crisis developed in the United States in 2008, devastating the U.S. economy and spreading to Europe, and eventually to the developing world. Global stock markets plummeted; one of the world's largest banks collapsed; both industrial output and world trade levels dropped far more than they had in 1929; global foreign direct investment and flows of remittances from migrant workers plunged. Amid this turmoil, the economic health and long-term sustainability of the European Union states that had adopted the common monetary unit, the euro, has come into question. EU members Greece, Portugal, Ireland, Spain, and Cyprus struggled to repay or refinance their government debt. This inability led to serious political tensions between Germany and the "northern tier" of Eurozone states. The wealthier nations have come under pressure to forgive the debt. And the debtor states claim that whatever the causes of their economic problems, allowing them to go bankrupt would destroy the European Union. The fate of the EU itself was jeopardized by the referendum in Great Britain in 2016 approving the exit of Great Britain from the EU. These issues—along with closely linked issues of migration and refugees—are covered in greater detail in Chapters 8, 9, and 11.

In December 2010, a local protest by a single man in Tunisia sparked a massive social protest against the cruelty and corruption of Tunisia's long-standing dictator, Zine al-Abidine Ben Ali. In January 2011, Ben Ali was overthrown and fled to exile in Saudi Arabia. But protests against corrupt and brutal Arab leaders did not stop there. Soon popular protests broke out in Egypt, Libya, Yemen, Bahrain, and later Syria—events that have been labeled the Arab Spring. Egypt's leader, Hosni Mubarak, was taken by surprise and faced massive protests. With Egypt's military refusing to kill protesters, Mubarak was forced to step down. The fate of Libya's dictator, Muammar Qaddafi, was more severe: after having been forced from power by a rebellion actively supported by France and the United States, Qaddafi was captured and later murdered by his captors. And in other parts of the Middle East, Arab rulers made what some saw as concessions. In 2011, when Syrians began to protest against their government, the Bashar al-Assad regime released jihadists from prison. Thus, the Arab Spring gave lie to the claims of radical and militant Islamists such as Al Qaeda that only through Islamic revolution, terror attacks on "the West," and the reestablishment of strict Islamic law could Arab dictators be overthrown. The Arab Spring gave the world hope that young people armed with mobile phones, courage, and conviction could change entrenched regimes.

But the outcomes of these mass uprisings were neither uniform nor anticipated. In Bahrain, protest was brutally suppressed. And in Egypt, the fall of Mubarak was followed by the election of Mohamed Morsi, then his ouster by the Egyptian military, with a quasi-democratic government following. In Syria, the release of the violent jihadists served as a pretense for the Assad regime to lash out against protesters, unleashing a violent civil war.

That weakening of powerful dictators in the Arab Spring, as well as the civil strife in Iraq and Syria, gave rise to the Islamic State (IS), sometimes called ISIS (Islamic State in Iraq and Syria) or ISIL (Islamic State in Iraq and the Levant). In 2014, the IS declared itself to be a worldwide **caliphate** with Abu Bakr al-Baghdadi as its caliph. At its pinnacle of power in 2016, the IS laid claim to territory containing more than 10 million people in Iraq and Syria, relying on brutality and religious conservatism to subdue its Sunni subjects and systematically destroying cultural heritage sites. Since 2016, a coalition of Western states led by the United States, along with Turkey, has systematically fought back, liberating territory held by the IS in Iraq. In 2017, the coalition, together with the Syrian Democratic Forces, also succeeded in liberating territory in Syria, including the city of Raqqa, the IS's proclaimed "capital." But terrorist acts inspired by IS supporters continue to wreak havoc across Europe from Paris nightclubs to the streets of Nice, Brussels, Stockholm, Manchester, and London, and even in Iran. Thus, as the territory held by the IS continues to shrink, the violence perpetrated by its supporters and those inspired by the IS has escalated.

Syria is now the center of a complex situation involving both states and non-state actors in various overlapping coalitions. The Assad regime is supported by both Russia and Iran; Russia and Iran opposes the Islamic State and moderate rebels fighting the Syrian government. The United States supports Syrian Kurds, the moderate rebels, Saudi Arabia, and the Gulf states, but opposes the IS, the Assad regime, and Iran. Turkey supports the moderate rebels, Saudi Arabia, and its Gulf allies, but opposes Assad, the IS, Iran, and the Syrian Kurds. The United States and Russia are each flying combat air missions over Syria supporting their various allies, leading to the possibility of a direct military engagement. When Assad used chemical weapons for the second time against his own people in 2017, the United States responded militarily by firing 60 Tomahawk cruise missiles at a Syrian air base, escalating the tension between the United States and the Russian Federation.

That hostility between the United States and the Russian Federation had already escalated in 2014 when the Russian Federation invaded Ukraine—an independent sovereign state—and then annexed the Ukrainian province of Crimea along with its strategic port of Sevastopol. The action was undertaken not by Russian Federation soldiers in national uniforms, but by soldiers (often special forces) wearing uniforms without insignia. This tactic enabled both the Russian government and NATO and EU representatives to support the argument that no violation of international law had actually taken place, although outside Russia, no credible authorities believe this assertion. What is perhaps most dangerous about Russia's foreign policy in Ukraine is not its annexation of Crimea as such, but the precedent the action has set. In a move reminiscent of Germany's claims about Sudeten Germans in 1938, Russia argued that its citizens in Crimea and Ukraine were being physically threatened after the legitimate government of Ukraine had fallen in a coup. NATO members Poland, Slovakia, the Czech Republic, Estonia, Latvia, and Lithuania are concerned that Russia might use similar tactics to bring down their governments and annex large portions of their respective territories. That concern has led to a strengthening of NATO's commitment to the region.

Great power confrontations have also begun to occur in East Asia. China's framing of its growing use of economic, military, and diplomatic power as "China's peaceful rise" in 2003 was designed to assure its neighbors of China's benign intentions. Yet since 2014, China has been expanding its military at a very high rate, making it the world's second-largest military spender, behind only the United States. And in the same year, China began the practice of dredging large quantities of sand onto fragile coral reefs in the disputed waters of the Spratly Islands in the South China Sea. These islands are a critical strategic resource for Vietnam, the Philippines, Malaysia, and Taiwan, which have each responded with their own smaller dredging programs. If China's "peaceful rise" was intended to allay regional or international concerns about rising Chinese power, China's military spending and dredging have had the opposite effect. And North Korea's provocative actions—testing nuclear weapons and intercontinental ballistic missiles—coupled with U.S. president Donald Trump's threatening rhetoric, have escalated tensions in the peninsula. The possibility that North Korea could in the near future put nuclear weapons on ICBMs that are capable of reaching U.S. territory has made the issue an urgent priority to U.S. foreign policy decision makers.

Finally, economic and political globalization, such prominent features of international relations since the end of the Cold War, has spawned **populism** and nationalist reactions.[15] Condoleezza Rice describes the trends as "the Four Horsemen of the Apocalypse": populism, nativism, protectionism, and isolationism.[16] Europeans and Americans have realized that the economic gains from globalization have not been evenly distributed, that wages have stagnated, and that living standards have fallen. They blame the "other"—elites within their own country, other states' unfair policies, migrants, and refugees; the response is protectionism and isolationism. The vote in Great Britain in 2016 in favor of leaving the European Union was one of the first concrete indicators of this populist rebellion, and the election of President Donald Trump later that year was another. While populism and its nationalist expression remain strong, electoral victories in both the Netherlands and France by mainstream political parties suggest that the trend is not universal. Yet clearly, globalization is under attack in its economic and political manifestations, and nationalism is on the rise. We will explore these trends in subsequent chapters.

IN SUM: LEARNING FROM HISTORY

Will the coming years be ones of conflict among states and a resurgence of old ideas? Do recent conflicts of interest in North Africa, the South China Sea, and Russia's geographic periphery signal a return to yet another Cold War? How will changing state identities and the interaction of nonstate actors and organizations affect the interests and capabilities of states moving forward?

We have taken the first step toward answering these questions by looking to the past. Our examination of the development of contemporary international relations has focused on how core concepts of international relations have emerged and evolved over time, most notably the state, sovereignty, the nation, and the balance of power. Each concept developed within a specific historical context, providing the building blocks for contemporary international relations. The state is well established, but its sovereignty may be eroding from without and from within. The principal characteristics of the contemporary international system are in the process of changing as the Cold War divisions end.

Moreover, we have seen that the way peoples and their leaders remember events dramatically affects their sense of the legitimacy of any given cause or action. China's remembrance of the Rape of Nanking in 1937 and its feeling that Japan has never satisfactorily acknowledged its racist brutality in China during World War II still complicate China-Japan relations today. And Iran's memories of U.S. and British support for the former shah of Iran (whom Iran considers an evil dictator), and their recent invasions of two predominantly Muslim states—Iraq and Afghanistan—strongly affect Iran's views on acquiring an independent nuclear deterrent. And Russia's actions in Ukraine are strangely reminiscent of the Soviet Union's actions in the past. Thus, understanding historical events is a good way to understand the motives of *contemporary* leaders and the peoples they lead.

To help us further understand the trends of the past and how they influence contemporary thinking, we turn to theory. Theory gives order to analysis; it provides generalized explanations for specific events. In Chapter 3, we will look at competing theories of international relations. These theories view the past from quite different perspectives.

Discussion Questions

1. The Treaties of Westphalia are often viewed as the beginning of modern international relations. Why are they a useful benchmark? What factors does this benchmark ignore?

2. Colonization by the great powers of Europe has officially ended. However, the effects of the colonial era linger. Explain with specific examples.

3. The Cold War has ended. Discuss two current events in which Cold War politics persist.

4. The developments of international relations as a discipline have been closely identified with the history of Western Europe and the United States. With this civilizational bias, what might we be missing?

Key Terms

balance of power (p. 32)

caliphate (p. 62)

capitalism (p. 43)

Cold War (p. 42)

colonialism (p. 28)

containment (p. 43)

détente (p. 54)

domino effect (p. 50)

hegemon (p. 32)

imperialism (p. 28)

League of Nations (p. 37)

legitimacy (p. 24)

nationalism (p. 24)

North Atlantic Treaty Organization (NATO) (p. 44)

populism (p. 63)

rollback (p. 43)

socialism (p. 44)

sovereignty (p. 20)

summits (p. 54)

superpowers (p. 42)

Third Reich (p. 39)

Treaties of Westphalia (p. 20)

war on terrorism (p. 59)

Warsaw Pact (p. 44)

weapons of mass destruction (WMD) (p. 59)

Protesters rally outside the Russian embassy in Washington, DC to denounce Russian involvement in the Syrian Civil War in October 2015. A month after agreeing to pursue a political solution to the growing crisis in Syria, Russia launched a military strategy targeting the Islamic State and Syrian rebels.

3

International Relations Theories

In August 2015, the United States, Russia, and Saudi Arabia agreed on a renewed effort to reach a political solution to the Syrian crisis. Just a month later, however, the Russian parliament gave formal consent to President Putin to use the nation's military in Syria. Russian air strikes followed against targets in Syria—both the Islamic State and rebel groups opposing the Syrian regime of Bashar al-Assad (the rebels were being supported by the United States). "Volunteer" ground troops were also sent. Why did Russia pursue this military strategy rather than the political one agreed to earlier?

Some international relations scholars argue that Russia intervened to expand and defend its interests in the Middle East and to weaken the power of the United States and its allies in the region. Other scholars point to the domestic situation in Russia, which was characterized by economic decline. According to these scholars, Russia engaged militarily in Syria to turn attention away from its poor record of governance at home. Still others point to the importance of Russian identity. Russia was in decline in material terms relative to other states. But by acting according to the "great power script" by showing a willingness to use armed forces abroad in pursuit of state interests, Russia was able to increase its prestige in the international system, boosting its own identity in the process.

What explains Russia's involvement in Syria? Were interstate relations at work? Or were domestic politics driving the decision? Or was an identity crisis the cause? The facts are the same, but the explanations differ widely. Which one is right? Can several be right? In this chapter, we seek to answer these types of questions by better understanding the different perspectives that various scholars use to approach the explanation of international politics.

LEARNING OBJECTIVES

▶ Explain the value of studying international relations from a theoretical perspective.

▶ Explain the central tenets of realism, liberalism, constructivism, and radicalism, as well as the feminist critiques of them.

▶ Analyze contemporary international events using different theoretical perspectives.

THINKING THEORETICALLY

A **theory** is a collection of propositions that combine to explain phenomena by specifying the relationships among a set of concepts. It is a story of "why" a relationship exists between those concepts. The concept whose variation is being explained is referred to as the "dependent variable," and the concepts that are thought to do the explaining are referred to as "explanatory variables." For example, consider the concepts of war and power. An example of a theory about the relationship between power and war would be an argument that wars like World War I break out when other states rise in power. Germany's power increased with its unification prior to World War I. Other states feared a potential future attack from that rising power and therefore attacked before the power of the rising state surpassed their own. In this theory, variation in whether or not we see war break out (the dependent variable) can be "explained," in part, by variation in the power of opponent states (the explanatory variable).

To evaluate the strength of a theory's ability to explain a particular phenomenon, we generate testable **hypotheses**: specific *falsifiable* statements that question the proposed relationship among two or more concepts. For example, a falsifiable statement derived from the theory proposed above is, "If we see a significant rise in power of one state, we should then see war break out between that state and nearby states." If we see a pattern that war tends to break out after one state begins to quickly rise in power, this would support our theory. If we do not see such a pattern, this would call our theory into question. Even if our theory is supported, it is important to remember that theories are never absolute. There are many potential explanations for the outbreak of war, and theories cannot necessarily explain all cases of a particular phenomenon. What we see when we test hypotheses is that our theory can help explain a pattern of variation in war. It is not the only explanation for war, and it is not an absolute explanation for war.

Good theories are generalizable. They can explain events across space (e.g., this explanation for war works just as well in Europe as it does in Africa) and time (e.g., it works just as well today as it did in the tenth century). Theories that can explain patterns across space and time are powerful theories.

A famous example of a powerful theory from the natural sciences is Charles Darwin's theory of evolution. Darwin's theory of natural selection and his concept of survival of the fittest explain what had previously been puzzling variation in the coloration and beak shapes of identical species of birds in different environments. We say that Darwin's theory is powerful because it has survived testing and modifications over the years. Its logic is consistent, even with evidence unavailable to Darwin at the time he formulated his theory. The theory is therefore very general in the sense that it can explain seemingly unique variations across space and time. Yet in neither natural nor social sciences do we ever consider theories to be "proven" or "settled" or "fact." Theories, whether Darwin's or Albert Einstein's natural science theories or Kenneth Waltz's neorealist theory of international relations, can always be overturned or refuted by new evidence or a better theory. Theories are therefore not explanations that scientists "believe in." Rather, we say they are stronger or weaker, or more or less supported.

Moving from description to explanation to theory, and from theory to testable hypotheses, is not an entirely linear process. Although theory depends on a logical deduction of hypotheses from assumptions and a testing of the hypotheses as more and more data are collected in the empirical world, we often must revise or adjust theories. This process is, in part, a creative exercise, in which we must be tolerant of ambiguity, concerned about probabilities, and distrustful of absolutes.

International relations (IR) theories come in various forms. In this chapter, we introduce four theoretical perspectives in the study of international relations. The first three are the main tenets of studies of international relations today: realism, liberalism, and constructivism. A fourth perspective, radicalism, is not as prevalent

In addition to military action, Russian troops have provided aid to war-torn areas of Syria. Here, a Russian soldier distributes food to a child in the Quneitra province of Syria.

in the study of international relations today, but its arguments are important to consider. These **theoretical perspectives** are sets of theories united by some common themes. There are common actors, concepts, and issues on which they focus their explanations for various international events. The theories within these perspectives seek to explain many different phenomena such as war, peace, cooperation, oppression, economic development, the creation of international law, efforts to protect human rights and the environment, and many others. The chapters that follow demonstrate how these theories seek to explain some of these phenomena in more detail. This chapter focuses on highlighting the common themes that connect the various theories within each perspective.

COMPONENTS OF INTERNATIONAL RELATIONS THEORIES

Within each perspective, different theories focus on different factors in international politics. Some of these factors are material entities (entities with a physical presence) such as states, international institutions, multinational corporations, and individuals. Some are more conceptual factors and include an idea of an international system, as well as ideas about norms and identities.

The state is a key actor in international politics in many international relations theories. As discussed in Chapter 2, states are considered to be sovereign entities in the international system, meaning that that they are not subject to the commands of others; they have independent control over themselves and their decisions. As discussed in more detail in Chapter 5, to be considered a state, an entity must have a defined territory, a stable population, and an effective government, and must be recognized by other states as having the capacity to enter into relations with them. Many international relations theories treat the state as a unitary actor in international politics. In other words, they personify the state, treating it as an actor that has its own defined interests and chooses its own actions in the international system. It speaks and acts with one voice. However, not all theories use this unitary actor approach. Some theories look at characteristics of the state and its domestic politics in order to explain various phenomena in international politics.

International institutions are also central actors in international politics for many international relations theories. By **international institutions**, international relations scholars mean more than just formal organizations. Institutions are defined in a broader way as sets of rules meant to govern international behavior. Rules, in this context, are conceived of as statements that forbid, require, or permit particular kinds of actions.[1] An institution can be a formal organization such as the United Nations or the European Union that embodies particular sets of rules, but it can also be a treaty such as the Law of the Sea Treaty or the Vienna Convention for the Protection of the Ozone Layer. Both organizations and international treaties (and international laws, more generally) lay out rules, and those rules are meant to govern state behavior. They all therefore fall under the heading of international institutions.

Some international relations theories focus attention on the role that multinational corporations play in international politics. These corporations span state borders, connecting states together in important ways. IBM, a U.S.-based company, operates in more than 170 countries, spanning all continents except Antarctica. Hyundai is a Korean car manufacturer, but it has manufacturing, engineering, and research and design facilities across the United States. These corporations not only invest in other countries by building up operations within them but also acquire interest in foreign companies, or engage in mergers or joint ventures with them. Multinational corporations also trade with one another both within and across state borders, creating important economic connections between states, as discussed in Chapter 8.

Some international relations theories focus on individuals and their actions in order to explain various events in international politics. Individual state leaders and their personal characteristics influence their state's foreign policy choices and hence international relations. Russia governed by Vladimir Putin today is very different from Russia governed by Mikhail Gorbachev in the 1980s. The foreign policy of President Donald Trump is very different from the foreign policy of his predecessor, President Barack Obama. The leaders in charge influence foreign policy, and thus international politics, in important ways. Non-elite individuals acting alone or in groups can also influence international politics.

Factors that influence outcomes in international politics can also be more conceptual in nature. For example, some theories focus on the role that the international system plays in affecting outcomes. The idea that the international system can influence international politics means that characteristics of a set of states taken together and their relationships contribute in important ways to international relations. Attributes of the international system as a whole, such as how many major powers exist in the system at any given time, are therefore important to consider when studying international politics.

Two other conceptual factors that some international relations theories focus on are identities and norms. An identity is a sense of self based on certain qualities and beliefs that serve to define a person or group. For some theories in international relations, group identities, in particular, are central for understanding interactions in the international system. These group identities can be associated with the state (such as living in the state of France) and particular state characteristics (such as living in a democracy). They can also be associated with ethnicity, language, and religion. These identities allow groups to identify similarities and differences between themselves and others, thus shaping their behavior toward each other. Groups also act based on particular norms associated with their identities.

Norms are collective expectations for the proper behavior of actors with a given identity. A norm can be as simple as shaking hands when you meet someone in the United States or bowing to show appreciation and respect in many Asian societies. In the international system, norms can provide expectations about the proper behavior of states, such as respecting human rights and being transparent on international security issues. Most states, most of the time, respect these norms. These norms can even become codified into international treaties. Many treaties deal with human rights issues, and there are multiple treaties governing transparency issues in which states agree to report information about their military capabilities and activities to other states. Even without codification in treaties, however, some theories of international relations argue that the norms associated with various types of identities can influence state behavior, and thus international politics, in important ways.

Different theories focus attention on different factors that they argue influence international politics. Theories within each perspective, however, tend to focus on similar factors. It is therefore important to understand these perspectives, in order to understand how the various theories that fall within each perspective approach the study of international relations.

REALISM

Realism is the first key perspective from which some theories approach the study of international politics. The factors on which realists focus most attention are the state and the international system. For most realists, states are unitary actors that rationally pursue their own national interests when they act within an anarchic international system. This idea of **anarchy** refers to the fact that in the international system there exists no hierarchically superior, coercive authority that can create laws, resolve disputes, or enforce law and order. International politics is therefore very different from domestic politics. In domestic politics, the government sits above its citizens. It can create laws that the citizens must follow and can enforce those laws by punishing those who do not. In the anarchic international system, no such authority exists. Given this condition of anarchy, realists argue that states can rely only on themselves to protect against attacks or other forms of coercion from other states in the system. Their most important interest is therefore to increase their power—the material resources necessary to physically harm or coerce other states. Realists see states as increasing their power in two possible ways: (1) through war (and conquest) or (2) by **balancing** against powerful states by taking actions to offset their power and thus fend off a potential attack. According to realists, states' main focus is their security.

The Roots of Realism

Even though its direct application to international affairs is more recent, realism is the product of a long historical and philosophical tradition. At least four of the central assumptions of realism are found as far back in history as Thucydides's *History of the Peloponnesian War*, which was written in the 400s BCE.[2] First, for Thucydides, the state (in this case, Athens or Sparta) is the principal actor in war and in politics in general, just as today's realists posit. Although other actors, such as international institutions, may participate, their impact on the system is marginal.

Second, the state is assumed to be a unitary actor. Although Thucydides includes fascinating debates among different officials from the same state, he argues that once a state decides to go to war or capitulate, no subnational actors are trying to overturn the government's decision or subvert the state's interests. The state acts as a single entity.

Third, states are assumed to be **rational actors**. In other words, they make decisions by weighing the costs and benefits of various options against the goal to be achieved. Like most educated Greeks, Thucydides believed that individuals are essentially rational beings. Thucydides admitted that potential impediments to rational decision making exist, including wishful thinking by leaders, confusing intentions and national interests, and misperceiving the characteristics of the counterpart decision maker. However, the core notion that leaders use rational decision-making processes to pursue the national interest remains. Realists argue that states, as unitary actors, act the same way that Thucydides assumed leaders do: rational decisions are used to advance the interests of the state.

Fourth, Thucydides, like contemporary realists, was concerned with security issues—the state's need to protect itself from enemies both foreign and domestic. A state augments its security by increasing its domestic capacities, strengthening its economic prowess, and forming alliances with other states based on similar interests. In fact, Thucydides found that before and during the Peloponnesian War, fear of rivals motivated states to join alliances, a rational decision by their leaders.

Thucydides did not identify all the tenets of what we think of as realism today. Indeed, the tenets and rationale of realism have unfolded over centuries, and not all realists agree on what they are. For example, eight centuries after Thucydides lived, the Christian bishop and philosopher Saint Augustine (354–430) added a fundamental assumption of realism, arguing that humanity is flawed, egoistic, and selfish, although not predetermined to be so. Augustine blames war on these basic characteristics of humanity.[3] Although subsequent realists dispute Augustine's biblical explanation for humanity's flawed, selfish nature, few realists dispute the fact that humans are basically power seeking and self-absorbed.

The central tenet virtually all realist theorists accept is that the chief constraint on states' behavior is that states exist in an anarchic international system. This tenet was articulated by Thomas Hobbes, who lived and wrote during one of history's greatest periods of turmoil (the Thirty Years' War, 1618–48, and the English Civil Wars, 1641–51). Hobbes maintained that individuals in a hypothetical "state of nature" have the responsibility and the right to preserve themselves. This includes the right to use violence against others. States in the anarchic international system, which is like the state of nature for individuals, have the same rights. In his most famous treatise, *Leviathan*, Hobbes argued that the only cure for perpetual war within a state was the emergence of a single powerful prince who could overawe all others: a leviathan. Applying his arguments to relations among sovereign states, Hobbes depicted a condition of anarchy where the norm for states is "having their weapons pointing, and their eyes fixed on one another."[4] In the absence of an international sovereign to enforce rules, few rules or norms can restrain states. War—defined by Hobbes as a climate in which peace cannot be guaranteed—would be perpetual.

In sum, by the twentieth century, most of the central tenets of realism were well established. Given a system in which no authority exists to enforce law and order (an anarchic system), states have to rely on self-help. It is thus essential for states to seek power to protect themselves. According to prominent post–World War II realist Hans Morgenthau (1904–80), this idea explains why peace in the international system would always prove elusive.[5]

Realism in the Twentieth and Twenty-First Centuries

In the aftermath of World War II, Morgenthau wrote the seminal synthesis of realism in international politics. For Morgenthau, just as for Thucydides, Augustine, and Hobbes, international politics is best characterized as a struggle for power. In this context, both military and economic power matter. Economic power can be used for coercion, in and of itself, and can also be translated into military power, if needed. Both types of power are therefore sought by states in order to protect themselves.

Because of this constant struggle for power, realists argue that states are concerned with **relative gains**. In contrast to absolute gains, which refers to how much one state gains for itself, relative gains refers to how much more one state gains over another. When one state gains relative to another state, it can feel more secure because it can better fend off an attack from the other, or can more successfully launch its own attack against the other. At the same time, a relative loss makes a state more susceptible to attack, and thus more insecure. States are therefore concerned with relative, rather than absolute, gains. In a realist world, a state's survival depends on having more power than other states do. As realist scholar John Mearsheimer argued, power (and gains in power) are therefore viewed in relative rather than absolute terms.[6]

Thus, even if both states can gain in absolute terms from cooperative interactions—be they cooperative security efforts or cooperative economic exchanges—the state that gains more relative to the other has a security advantage, and the one that gains less becomes more insecure and susceptible to attack. Despite being able to gain something in absolute terms, the state that would lose in relative terms has an incentive not to cooperate with the other. It needs to protect itself from the insecurity that would result from the relative gain for the other (and thus loss for itself) that would result. Cooperation is therefore difficult to achieve, and tensions between states are likely to result.

This concern for relative gains can lead to what realists call a **security dilemma**. As the political scientist John Herz described, a state working to ensure security from attack is driven to acquire more and more power. This, however, renders other states more insecure, which drives them to acquire more power. This makes the first state less secure, and it thus works to gain more power. And the spiral continues.[7] The security dilemma, then, results in a permanent condition of tension and power conflicts among states, even if none actually seek conquest and war. In other words, security is a zero-sum game. A gain in security for one state is a loss for the other.

Relative gains concerns and the security dilemma are important explanations for why we see costly arms races. For example, India and Pakistan have been engaged in a nuclear arms race since the 1970s. By 2017, both sides had over 100 nuclear warheads. Escalating the race, India said in 2016 that it had begun testing its first homemade nuclear-powered submarine, as well as a nuclear missile capable of striking all of Pakistani territory from far offshore. In 2017, Pakistan said it had tested its own undersea nuclear missile that was capable of carrying out a retaliatory strike. In early 2017, India tested interceptor missiles as part of its plan to develop a ballistic missile defense shield. Pakistan responded, testing a missile with multiple warheads capable of evading the shield. In other words, the concern that India was achieving greater gains by increasing its arms made Pakistan more insecure. So it increased its own arms. In turn, the concern about Pakistan's gain in power made India feel less secure, thus leading it to further increase its arms in order to ensure its own security. The focus on relative gains has led to a security dilemma and arms race between India and Pakistan. According to realists, the struggle for power is ever present in the international system.

In this struggle for power, one focus of many realists is the idea of managing power through "balancing." Balancing can take two forms: internal or external. **Internal balancing** refers to a state's building up its own military resources and capabilities in order to be able to stand against more powerful states. **External balancing** refers to allying with other states to offset the power of more powerful states. In both cases, the objective is to ensure the ability to fend off an attack from more powerful states, with the goal of deterring such attacks in the first place. A relative balance can deter both sides from engaging in an attack, thus helping to prevent war.

Both George Kennan (1904–2005), a writer and chair of the State Department's policy-planning staff in the late 1940s and later the U.S. ambassador to the Soviet Union, and Henry Kissinger (b. 1923), a scholar, foreign policy adviser, and secretary of state to presidents Richard Nixon and Gerald Ford, are known to have based their policy recommendations on this balance-of-power realist theory. As we saw in Chapter 2, Kennan was one of the architects of the U.S. Cold War policy of containment, an interpretation of the balance of power. The goal of containment was to prevent Soviet power from extending into regions beyond its immediate, existing sphere of influence (Eastern Europe), thus balancing U.S. power against Soviet power. Containment was an important alternative to the competing strategy of "rollback," in which a combination of nuclear and conventional military threats would be used to force the Soviet Union out of Eastern Europe and, in particular, Germany. Rollback would increase U.S. power relative to that of the Soviet Union, upsetting the balance. Kennan's fear of uncontrolled escalation to a third world war ultimately led to the adoption of containment as U.S. foreign policy. During the 1970s, Kissinger encouraged the classic realist balance of power by supporting weaker powers such as China to exert leverage over the Soviet Union, and Pakistan to offset India's growing power, as India was an ally of the Soviet Union at the time.

While realism appears to offer clear policy prescriptions, not all realists agree on what an ideal foreign policy might look like. In particular, a divide exists between defensive and offensive realists. Defensive realists observe that few, if any, major wars in the last century ended up benefiting the state or states that started them. Threatened states, they argue, tend to balance against aggressors, invariably overwhelming and reversing whatever initial gains were made for the state that started the war. Offensive realists, on the other hand, argue that conquest can yield significant benefits to a state by creating a reputation for a willingness to use force. That reputation can help a state get others to do what it wants for fear of war being waged against them as well. Two different sets of foreign policy actions help illustrate the defensive and offensive realists' argument.

Defensive realists would point to Iraqi leader Saddam Hussein's attempt to conquer and annex neighboring Kuwait in 1990 as an illustration of their argument that war is more costly than it is beneficial. In August 1990, Iraq's armed forces quickly overwhelmed the defenses of Kuwait. Before the invasion, Kuwait had been a little-known, oil-rich Arab state in which a repressive hereditary elite ruled over a population composed mainly of servants hired from surrounding Arab countries (in particular, Palestinian Arabs). However, although critics pointed out that Kuwait was itself a less-than-ideal candidate for rescue, Saddam's aggression provoked a powerful international reaction. In 1991, an international coalition of armed forces, led by the United States, invaded Kuwait and rapidly forced the retreat and later surrender of the Iraqi army. Iraq was forced to repay all the damages from its aggressive actions. Conquest, in other words, did not pay for Iraq.

For defensive realists, the outcome of Iraq's 1990 war forms part of a long historical pattern of effective (and inevitable) balancing. In this case, Saudi Arabia, the United States, and others supported Kuwait to balance against Iraq's regional power. Because this balancing against an aggressor is inevitable, defensive realists argue that states should pursue policies of restraint, whether through military, diplomatic, or economic channels. Such moderate defensive postures can be pursued without leading to dangerous levels of mistrust among states and, more importantly, without fear of unintended or uncontrolled escalation to counterproductive wars.

Offensive realists, by contrast, note that periodically demonstrating a willingness to engage in war, though perhaps costly in the short run, may pay huge dividends in reputation enhancement later. The credible threat of conquest can often act as a motivation to alter other states' interests by making them believe that they could be the targets of conquest as well. To avoid a war waged against them, states that might have opposed the threatening state thus choose to ally with it instead—a process international relations theorists call **bandwagoning**. The logic is that the more power you have, the more power you get. Conquest, in other words, pays. States may thus pursue expansionist politics, building up their relative power positions and intimidating potential rivals into cooperation.

Consider the case of Libya's decision in December 2003 to publicly acknowledge and then abandon its years-long efforts to acquire nuclear, chemical, and biological weapons, along with the vehicles to launch them. To an offensive realist, Libya's decision to abandon its efforts could well have been the result of the U.S. decision to invade Iraq in March 2003—an invasion that the United States justified as an effort to halt Iraq's production or dissemination of weapons of mass destruction. In the face of this demonstration of U.S. power, Libya chose to bandwagon with the United States, after years of having stood opposed to it, and gave up its policy to acquire weapons of mass destruction. By offensive realist logic, the costs of the war against Iraq were at least partly redeemed by Libya's change of policy; conquest, or the credible threat of conquest, paid for the United States.

Neorealism

Realism, as a general perspective, encompasses a family of related arguments that share common assumptions and premises. It is not itself a single, unified theory. Among the various reinterpretations of what is referred to as "classical realism," the most important is neorealism (or structural realism), as delineated in Kenneth Waltz's *Theory of International Politics*.[8] Reasoning that lack of progress in the social scientific theory of international politics was due to lack of theoretical rigor (especially in comparison to steady theoretical progress in the natural sciences), Waltz undertook this reinterpretation of classical realism to make political realism a more rigorous theory of international politics. Neorealists therefore propose general laws to explain events: they simplify explanations of behavior in anticipation of being better able to explain and predict trends.

While traditional realists attach importance to the characteristics of states and human nature, neorealists give precedence in their analyses to the structure of the international system as an explanatory factor. Attempting to understand the international system by reference to states is analogous, in Waltz's view, to attempting to understand a market by reference to individual firms: unproductive at best. Neorealism thus advances two normative arguments and one theoretical argument. The first normative argument is that we need theory to understand international politics (and that prior to the publication of Waltz's book, we had none), and the second is that his theory, neorealism, explains international politics since 1648, the date scholars cite for the advent of the Westphalian state system. Waltz's theoretical argument is that the amount of peace and war in an anarchic international system depends critically on the distribution of power, described in terms of system structure.

Critics of classical realism asked, "If the human desire for power attributed to states is driving the recurrence of interstate war, how can we explain long periods of peace?" Waltz argued that the distribution of power in the international system

THEORY IN BRIEF
Realism/Neorealism

Key Actors	States (most powerful matter most)
Characteristics of Individuals	Insecure, selfish, power seeking
Characteristics of States	Unitary actors, rational, power seeking
Characteristics of the International System	Anarchic (implies perpetual threat of war)
Beliefs about Change	Possibility of perpetual peace logically precluded; emphasis shifted to managing the frequency and intensity of war
Major Theorists	Thucydides, Saint Augustine, Hobbes, Morgenthau, Waltz, Gilpin, Mearsheimer

can be described as having one of three possible forms: (1) unipolar, where one state in the system has sufficient power to defeat all the others combined against it; (2) bipolar, where most of the system's power is divided between two states or coalitions of states; and (3) multipolar, in which power is divided among three or more states or coalitions of states. According to neorealists, the structure of the system and the distribution of power within it, rather than the characteristics of individual states, determine outcomes. Some realists argue that the closer the overall distribution of power approaches to unipolarity, the greater the likelihood (but never the certainty) of peace.[9] Balance-of-power theorists, in contrast, would highlight the importance of a bipolar system for increasing the likelihood of peace, as the bipolar system represents a basic balance of power between the two most powerful states.

Other interpretations of realism have also been developed. Although neorealism simplifies the classical realist theory and focuses on a few core concepts (such as system structure), other reinterpretations add increased complexity to realism. In *War and Change in World Politics*, Robert Gilpin offers one such reinterpretation. Accepting the realist assumptions that states are the principal actors, decision makers are basically rational, and the international system structure plays a key role in determining power, Gilpin examines 2,400 years of history, finding that the distribution of power among states is central in understanding every international system. What Gilpin adds is the notion of dynamism, of history as a series of cycles—cycles of the birth, expansion, and demise of dominant powers. Whereas classical realism offers no satisfactory rationale for the decline of powers, Gilpin finds the answer in economic power. Hegemons decline because of three processes: (1) the tendency for the returns from controlling an empire to decrease over time; (2) the tendency for economic hegemons to consume more and invest less over time; and (3) the diffusion of technology through which new powers challenge the hegemon. As Gilpin explains, "Disequilibrium replaces equilibrium, and the world moves toward a new round of hegemonic conflict."[10]

In short, there is no single tradition of political realism; there are multiple realist theories, each of which focuses on different explanatory variables to help explain various characteristics of international politics. Although each theory is predicated on a key group of assumptions, each attaches different importance to the various core propositions. What unites the various realist theories is their emphasis on the unitary state in an anarchic international system, the importance of power and the ability to use force as an effective tool of foreign policy, and the existence of the threat of war that can be managed but never done away with. These emphases distinguish them from other schools of thought.

LIBERALISM

Like realism, liberalism has a diverse set of theories, rooted in centuries-old thinking that continues to be updated today. Realists, however, focus mostly on the unitary state actor and the international system to explain international politics. Liberal theories also highlight various internal state characteristics as important explanatory factors. Different liberal theories focus on different factors.

The Roots of Liberalism

The origins of liberal theory are found in eighteenth-century Enlightenment optimism, nineteenth-century political and economic liberalism, and twentieth-century Wilsonian idealism. The contribution of the Enlightenment to liberalism rests on the Greek idea that individuals are rational human beings, able to understand the universally applicable laws governing both nature and human society. Understanding such laws means that people have the capacity to improve their condition by creating a just society. Thus, liberals believe that injustice, war, and aggression are not inevitable but can be moderated or even eliminated through institutional reform or collective action.

The writings of the French philosopher Charles-Louis de Secondat, Baron de La Brède et de Montesquieu (1689–1755), reflect Enlightenment thinking. Montesquieu argued that human nature is not defective, but rather, problems arise as humanity enters civil society and forms separate nations. War is a product of society, not an attribute inherent in individuals. To overcome defects in society, education is imperative; it prepares one for civil life. Groups of states are united according to the law of nations, which regulates conduct even during war. Montesquieu optimistically stated that "different nations ought in time of peace to do one another all the good they can, and in time of war as little harm as possible, without prejudicing their real interests."[11]

Likewise, the writings of Immanuel Kant (1724–1804) form the core of Enlightenment beliefs. According to Kant, international anarchy can be overcome through a particular kind of collective action—a federation of republics in which sovereignties would be left intact. Like other liberal philosophers, Kant held out the possibility that nations could transcend the limitations of anarchy in the international system and war could wither away. Unlike others, however, Kant did not assume or require moral actors in his philosophy. On the contrary, Kant assumed that states would act in self-interested ways and that the repeated interaction of self-interested states would eventually lead to an expanding zone of peace, *in spite of that self-interest.* As he famously put it, what is required for the emergence of perpetual peace is not moral angels, but "rational devils."[12]

Nineteenth-century liberalism took this rational approach from the Enlightenment and reformulated it by adding a preference for democracy over aristocracy and for free trade over national economic self-sufficiency. Sharing the Enlightenment's optimistic view of human nature, nineteenth-century liberalism saw humanity as capable of satisfying its natural needs and wants in rational ways. These needs and wants could be met most efficiently when each individual pursued his or her own freedom and autonomy in a democratic state, unfettered by excessive governmental restrictions. Likewise, political freedoms are most easily achieved in capitalist states, where rational and acquisitive human beings can improve their own conditions, maximizing both individual and collective economic growth and economic welfare. Free markets must be allowed to flourish, and governments must permit the free flow of trade and commerce. Liberal theorists believe that free trade and commerce create interdependencies among states, thus raising the cost of war and reducing its likelihood.

Early-twentieth-century "idealist" theory also contributed to liberalism, finding its greatest adherent in U.S. president Woodrow Wilson, who authored the covenant of the League of Nations. The basic proposition of Wilson's idealism is that war is preventable through the collective action of states. More than half of the League covenant's 26 provisions focused on preventing war. The covenant even included a provision legitimizing the notion of **collective security**, whereby aggression by one state would be countered by automatic and collective reaction, embodied in a "league of nations."

Thus, the League of Nations illustrated the importance that liberals place on the potential of international institutions to deal with war and the opportunity for collective problem solving in a multilateral forum. Liberals also place faith in international law and legal instruments such as mediation, arbitration, and international courts. Still other liberals think that all war can be eliminated through disarmament. Whatever the specific prescriptive solution, the basis of liberalism remains firmly embedded in the belief in the rationality of human beings, the notion that humans are inherently social, living and working in groups, and that through learning and education, humans can develop institutions capable of ensuring and advancing human welfare.

During the interwar period, when the League of Nations proved incapable of maintaining collective security, and during World War II, when atrocities like the Holocaust made many question the basic goodness of humanity, liberalism came under intense criticism. *Was* humankind inherently good? How could an institution

Liberalism/Neoliberal Institutionalism

Key Actors	States, nongovernmental groups, international organizations
Characteristics of Individuals	Basically good; social; capable of cooperating
Characteristics of States	States are rational; states have relationships (enduring friends and rivals); state characteristics (democratic-liberal, authoritarian-autarkic) matter; actors within states can influence state actions
Characteristics of the International System	Anarchy abridged by interdependence among actors; an international order
Beliefs about Change	Self-interest managed by structure (institutions) leads to possibility of cooperation and peace
Major Theorists	Montesquieu, Kant, Wilson, Keohane, Moravcsik

fashioned under the best assumptions have failed so miserably? Liberalism as a theoretical perspective fell out of favor and was replaced by realism and its preferred solution to the scourge of war: a balance of power.

Neoliberal Institutionalism

In the 1970s, a new branch of liberalism arose based on the observation that states in the international system actually cooperate most of the time. This is contrary to the realist predictions that cooperation is very difficult for states to achieve because of their concern for relative gains and the existence of the security dilemma. Liberals like Robert O. Keohane and Joseph S. Nye asked *why we see so much cooperation*, even under the anarchic conditions of the international system. Their answer lies in their idea of **complex interdependence**, which has three components.[13] First, states are connected through multiple channels, not just through direct formal interactions. Informal interactions between governments often take place, and actors like multinational corporations span state borders, connecting states in important ways. Second, there is not a hierarchy of issues. States are concerned not only about security but also about other issues on which they share common interests. Third, the result is a decline in the use of military force.

Building on Keohane and Nye's argument and focus on cooperation, neoliberal institutionalist theory has developed since the 1970s. The assumptions of neoliberal

Although formal meetings between global leaders often foster cooperation, informal talks between heads of state can facilitate discussion on difficult issues more effectively. It is an important type of connection between states, as highlighted by the theory of complex interdependence. Here, German chancellor Angela Merkel and French president Emmanuel Macron are meeting informally during travel from the formal West Balkans Conference.

institutionalism are the same as those of realism—states are key unitary actors in international politics that rationally pursue their own self-interest in an anarchic international system. Yet even though neoliberal institutionalists accept these realist assumptions, they argue that states can cooperate. As discussed in Chapter 7 in more detail, neoliberal institutionalists posit that cooperation arises because states are engaged in continuous interactions and are not solely focused on relative gains. They care about absolute gains as well. Moreover, states focus not only on security but also on other issues on which they might share common interests. Trade and the environment are key examples. When states care about absolute gains, the gains from cooperative interactions become a key part of states' interests. When states interact over time, the gains from cooperation can accumulate and thus overcome a state's incentives to exploit the others' cooperative actions for its own short-term gain. This is particularly true with regard to nonsecurity issues such as economics, in which gains from cooperation in trade and investment can be had by all. Reciprocity over time can help sustain this incentive, especially when complex interdependence characterizes states' relationships and there are multiple channels and multiple issues in which reciprocity can be implemented.[14] Power, therefore, does not rest solely on military might. Economic and social power also matter.

According to neoliberal institutionalists, international institutions—both organizations and treaties—play a key role in international politics by fostering these cooperative interactions. International organizations provide a guaranteed framework for interactions, thus creating a situation in which continuous interaction is expected and reciprocity is fostered. For example, states in the European Union expect to engage in multiple interactions with each other across issues and over time. International treaties also create expectations of repeated interactions over time. For example, the North American Free Trade Agreement that was negotiated between the United States, Canada, and Mexico created an environment in which those states could expect to engage in trade relationships long into the future.

Neoliberal institutionalists arrive at the same prediction that other liberals do—cooperation—but their explanation for why cooperation occurs is different. For classical liberals, cooperation emerges from humanity's establishing and reforming institutions that permit cooperative interactions and prohibit coercive actions. For neoliberal institutionalists, cooperation emerges because when actors have continuous interactions with each other, it is in their *self-interest* to cooperate.

Other Liberal Theories

In contrast to neoliberal institutionalism, other branches of liberal theory do not treat the state as a unitary actor. They argue that state behavior at the international level is influenced in important ways by the domestic level. They have a "bottom up" view of international politics. As Andrew Moravcsik described, these liberal theories share several key assumptions.[15] First, they argue that the key actors in international politics are individuals and private groups such as unions, nongovernmental organizations (NGOs), and corporations. Second, states' actions represent some subset of those individuals and private groups. It is the interests of this subset of domestic society that define states' preferences and shape their actions. Third, state behavior is defined by the configuration of state preferences, rather than the configuration of state power. When states' underlying preferences are compatible, cooperation is likely to result. When they are at odds with one another, there is a high probability of tension and conflict. The substance and depth of cooperation or conflict depends on the constellation of states' preferences.

For example, free trade is more likely when its net benefits are conferred to the most powerful domestic actors. This can happen, for example, when the actors that are most able to shape their governments' preferences are exporting industries that want to be able to compete in other states' markets. In contrast, protectionist policies are more likely when domestic groups (such as unions) and nonexporting industries that would incur costs from having to contend with foreign competitors have the greatest ability to shape their governments' preferences. In other words, it matters who the domestic group is that state leaders are responding to and whose preferences they choose to represent.

Other important liberal theories build on the work of Immanuel Kant and nineteenth-century liberalism. They highlight three key factors that can contribute to peace: democracy, economic interdependence, and international institutions. "Democratic peace" theorists argue (and have shown) that democracies rarely, if ever, go to war with one another. As discussed in Chapter 6, a variety of explanations are proposed by different theories in this branch of liberalism for why this is the case. "Commercial peace" theorists argue that war reduces the benefits of economic relations between states. States that are more economically interdependent are therefore less likely to go to war. Finally, a wide variety of theories focus on the role international institutions play in world politics. Classical liberal and neoliberal institutionalism's arguments about the role of institutions are prime examples. In addition, some liberal theories argue that when states share membership in a greater number of international institutions, they are likely to be more cooperative with one another, and thus less likely to engage in conflict.

Overall, as in realism, there are a wide variety of theories in the liberal perspective. Each focuses on different factors that, theorists argue, influence international politics, and each provides different insights into why states act the way they do. Liberal theories are united by their assumption that actors in international politics are largely rational, that cooperation is possible and more likely than realists posit, and that states focus on issues beyond just security and survival.

CONSTRUCTIVISM

A late-twentieth-century addition to international relations, constructivism explains events in international politics through a focus on norms and identities—both of individuals and of states. It has returned international relations scholars to foundational questions, including the nature of the state itself, how state interests are formed, and the nature of key concepts such as sovereignty. Yet, like liberalism and realism, constructivism is not a uniform theory. It is an overarching perspective with a set of core ideas that most constructivists share.

For constructivists, the objects of study in international relations should be the identities of actors, and the norms and practices of individuals and groups that stem from those identities. Ted Hopf offers a simple analogy that highlights the importance of understanding identities and norms:

The scenario is a fire in a theater where all run for the exits. Absent knowledge of social norms, even this seemingly overdetermined circumstance, the outcome is indeterminate. In a theater with just one door, while all run for that exit, who goes first? Are they the strongest or the disabled, the women or the children, the aged or the infirm, or is it just a mad dash? Determining the outcome will require knowing more about the situation than just the distribution of material power or the structure of authority. One will need to know about the culture, norms, institutions, procedures, rules, and social practices that constitute the actors and the structure alike.[16]

Note that had realist logic been employed to predict the outcome of Hopf's fire-in-a-theater example, or, say, the demographic composition of the *Titanic*'s lifeboats in 1912, the focus on one's own survival and self-interests, and on relative power, would have caused an incorrect prediction. In real life, the strong sometimes yield to the weak, rather than forcing the weak to "suffer what they must." That is why the *Titanic*'s lifeboats were filled not with strong men, but with the ship's physically weaker passengers: women and children. The identities of the individuals, and the norms and practices that stem from those identities, are what influence their behavior.

The relationship between different identities is also an important facet of understanding international politics from the constructivist perspective. States' identities can be convergent, meaning that those states share similar characteristics and ideals, or they can be divergent, meaning that they do not share similar characteristics and ideals. This difference does not mean that states necessarily have interests and ideals that are opposed to one another, but they could. Understanding the relationship between different identities is of central importance in international politics today. For example, one of the main divides between states like Saudi Arabia and Iran stems from their divergent Sunni (Saudi Arabia) and Shia (Iran) Islamic identities. This identity divergence can create a political divergence between the states themselves. This is arguably part of the reason that Saudi Arabia and Iran support opposing sides of the Syrian conflict that began in 2011. Iran backs the Bashar al-Assad government in Syria, while Saudi Arabia supports rebel groups. In addition to Syria's inclusion in Iran's sphere of influence, Bashar al-Assad also practices a Shia branch of Islam, sharing that identity with Iran. The rebels supported by Saudi Arabia share their Sunni identity. Iran and Saudi Arabia politically and militarily support the actors in the conflict with which they share an identity. Because their identities diverge, the sides they have chosen to support stand opposed to one another.

In addition to focusing attention on the role of norms and identities, constructivism offers the major theoretical proposition that neither objects nor concepts have any necessary, fixed, or objective meaning. Instead, their meanings are *constructed* through social interaction. For example, constructivists see sovereignty not as an absolute but rather as a contested concept. They point out that states have never had exclusive control over territory. State sovereignty has always been challenged, and is continuously being challenged by globalization, new institutional forms, and the development of new transitional problems that states must face. Constructivists argue that the idea of sovereignty still exists as a concept that governs state behavior only because when states interact, they do so in a way that treats themselves and other states as sovereign entities. State sovereignty is therefore a socially constructed facet of reality.

Identities are similarly socially constructed. State behavior thus depends not on the objective reality of a situation but on our subjective interpretation of that reality. An important part of that social construction of identities (and the resulting behavior) is our **discourse**. How we choose to talk about ourselves and others influences our interpretation of our respective identities, as well as others' interpretations of those identities. Therefore, in addition to how we act toward others, how we choose to talk about and frame our identities is important for understanding how those identities (and the resulting behavior) come to be formed. For example, a state that is viewed and treated as aggressive by other states might begin to act more aggressively, making that interpretation of reality real. After the attacks in the United States on September 11, 2001, Iran engaged in cooperative relations with the United States to fight the Taliban and Al Qaeda in Afghanistan. In 2002, however, President George W. Bush gave a speech labeling Iran part of the "axis of evil." Iran concluded that the United States was hostile toward it, and ceased cooperative activities in the war. Relations between them deteriorated to the point where, instead of assisting the United States, Iran even began to work against U.S. goals. According to constructivist logic, labeling and treating Iran as an enemy led it to pursue policies that coincided with that reality.

Constructivists argue that it is not only states' behaviors that are shaped by beliefs about themselves and others, but also states' very interests. For constructivists, states' interests are the result of their socially constructed identities. Moreover, those identities and interests are not fixed. They can change as experience, discourse, and practices change. This stands in contrast to realist and liberal approaches to the study of international relations, which view state interests as based on purely material factors.

For example, Germany and Japan had highly militaristic cultures and behavior leading into, and during, World War II. However, as Thomas Berger argues, the way their historical experiences during World War II have been interpreted and internalized by individuals at the domestic level has reshaped their national identities and interests.[17] In particular, their identities have been reconstructed in such a way that they are averse to resorting to the use of force in their relations with other states. Understanding Germany's national identity can help explain why, despite its fears that it could no longer rely on the United States to deter Russian aggression, there was little to no public support in Germany for its acquisition of nuclear weapons when the issue of obtaining them was floated in 2017. Similarly, this identity change can help explain why there was strong opposition in the mid-2010s to a proposal to revise the Japanese constitution by removing Article 9, which legally prohibits Japan from waging war or obtaining "war potential." Indeed, the argument that Japan's pacifist ideals are a foundation of their democracy has been widely cited by opponents of the change.

Overall, constructivists dispute the idea that material structures have a necessary, fixed, or inherent meaning. Alexander Wendt, one of the best-known constructivists, argues that, on its own, the political structure of the international system (that is, whether the distribution of power is unipolar, bipolar, or multipolar) cannot tell us much of interest. It does not predict whether two states will be friends or enemies, whether they will recognize each other's sovereignty, whether they will have revisionist or status quo ideals, and so on.[18] It is the identities of states and the relationship between their identities, along with the norms that stem from those identities, that matter most.

Constructivists do align with realists and liberals in that they view power as important. However, whereas realists and liberals primarily see power in material terms (military, economic, or political), constructivists also see power in discursive terms—they focus on the power of ideas, culture, and language. In some constructivist theories, power rests in the ability to persuade when deliberating or arguing with others. Other theories invoke the idea of legitimacy as an important source of power. States may alter their actions so other members of the international community will view them as legitimate. These arguments about persuasion and legitimacy lead to the idea of *soft power*—the power of a state to attract states to change their behavior based on the legitimacy of its values or policies, rather than having to coerce them into doing so.[19] In other words, the legitimacy of one state's actions can help that state persuade others to adopt similar behavior. For example, the European Union has chosen to take the lead in addressing environmental issues like climate change, with the hope that their example will lead states outside the EU to follow suit.

Constructivist theories also offer explanations of change that differ from those of realism and liberalism. Change can occur through diffusion of ideas or the internationalization of norms, as well as through **socialization** (the process through which one adopts the identities of peer groups). These explanations help us understand that ideas are spread both within a national setting and cross-nationally. This is how democracy is diffused, how ideas about human rights protection have been internationalized, and how states such as the new members of the European Union become socialized into the community's norms and practices. Put another way, realism and liberalism both have a more difficult time explaining the advent, spread, and real-world impact

A Policy Perspective: A View from India

Focusing on different IR theories may lead to the pursuit of different kinds of foreign policies. Recent policy choices that have been made by India's Narendra Modi illustrate the influence of different aspects of the different theoretical perspectives. From which of these orientations does Narendra Modi seem to approach his policy choices? Given the characteristics of his policies, this question is an interesting one, and one that deserves careful thinking.

Since coming into power in 2014, the government of Narendra Modi has adopted clear policy positions in the areas of security and economics—policies that seem to reflect the influence of different IR perspectives. First, the Modi government has endorsed a policy of nuclear deterrence. The policy is based not on first-strike use but rather on the credibility of assured retaliation if a nuclear weapon is used against India. The government has therefore focused on building up the survivability and reliability of its nuclear arsenal, and demonstrating these capabilities to its adversaries through regular testing of its delivery systems. Such a strategy, the government believes, can strengthen its overall strategy of deterrence. This policy position seems to indicate a defensive realist orientation.

However, with regard to Kashmir—a region that presents one of India's most prominent security issues—the Modi government seems more oriented toward offensive realism. Its policy is seen as a continuation of the "Doval doctrine" begun in 2010. The doctrine is based on the idea that India must change the "mind-set" of Pakistan and Kashmir through the exercise of power. It must not back down in the face of civilian protests and is justified in using force against them. The goal is to establish full territorial control in Kashmir, forcing Pakistan to come to terms with India's resolve and Kashmiri separatists to cut their links with Pakistan.

But not all policies of the Modi government are realist in nature. In fact, it is pursuing a more liberal policy of cooperation and multilateralism in the area of maritime security. The scale and complexity of maritime security challenges India faces have increased in recent years. They stem from piracy and terrorism emanating from the seas, the changing balance of power in the Indo-Pacific region, the militarization in the South China Sea, and the increasing number of naval platforms in the Indian Ocean. In response to these challenges, the Modi government has taken actions to further cooperation with its neighbors and island states in the Indian Ocean, with the belief that stability on the seas cannot be achieved by a single nation alone. It has supported multilateral initiatives such as the Indian Ocean Rim Association and the Indian Ocean Naval Symposium, as well as working at the bilateral level with coastal states such as Kenya and Tanzania and island countries such as the Seychelles, the Maldives, and Sri Lanka—states that lack maritime military prowess and thus are vulnerable to the threats arising from the seas. Proactively engaging with these states, India has become a "formidable and reliable" maritime partner, according to a report by the Institute of Peace and Conflict Studies.[a]

In the economic realm, the Modi government's trade policies have been interesting and mixed. The government has actively dis-

Prime Minister Narendra Modi with Sri Lankan president Maithripala Sirisena.

cussed improving bilateral trade cooperation with a number of states but has shied away from, and has even taken steps backward from, multilateral cooperation. It has discussed pursuing a bilateral agreement with the United Kingdom post-Brexit, while negotiations with the European Union have broken down. It expressed no intention of ever joining the Trans-Pacific Partnership and held up the World Trade Organization's (WTO) trade facilitation agreement. The policies have been argued to reflect a concern with domestic political interests (a more liberal approach), as well as Modi's own personal characteristics (a more constructivist reasoning). The preference for bilateral agreements highlights Modi's inclination for personal, one-on-one diplomacy, and the overall pursuit of open trade policies reflects the government's desire to lessen constraints on India's ability to develop its economy and create jobs. At the multilateral level, however, the government faces political pressures beyond a simple concern with the general state of the economy. Negotiations with the EU broke down, in part, because of the government's desire to protect the automotive and dairy sectors, as well as demands for concessions from India's information technology companies. India held up the WTO agreement in order to secure the right to stockpile grain as part of a public distribution system, which helped increase the government's popularity in rural areas. Moreover, by adopting actions that affect many nations at once, India has raised its profile in the international system, instilling a domestic sense of national pride that motivates its people to support the government.

These different policies reflect different perspectives of IR theory. Some of them focus on the use of force, while others focus on cooperation. Others focus on "mind-sets," national pride, or Modi's own personality. So is Modi a realist? Or do you think his policies reflect a more liberal approach? Or does he use more constructivist-oriented tactics?

a. Institute of Peace and Conflict Studies, Special Report 191, "3 Years of the Modi Government," 2017, p. 18, www.ipcs.org/pdf_file/issue/Modi_Compendium_Final.pdf (accessed 1/9/18).

FOR CRITICAL ANALYSIS

1. Why do the Modi government's security policies differ so widely—with some focused on the active use of force, others focused on deterrence, and others focused on cooperation? Can these policies be reconciled?

2. If you were in Modi's position, which policies would you approach differently? Why?

3. Which of the three security policies—those involving nuclear weapons, Kashmir, or maritime issues—do you think will be most effective in achieving India's interests? Why?

Constructivism

Key Actors	People, elites, cultures
Characteristics of Individuals	Key actors in creation of meaning; bound by education, socialization, and culture; their identities matter
Characteristics of States	Artifacts whose significance is socially constructed through discourse; their identities matter
Characteristics of the International System	An artifact whose significance is socially constructed through discourse; distribution of identities matters
Beliefs about Change	Possible through socialization, diffusion of ideas, or internationalization of norms
Major Theorists	Kratochwil, Hopf, Wendt

of ideas and norms such as taboos against land mines or the "responsibility to protect" (discussed in Chapter 10). Constructivist theories offer an answer.

Like realism and liberalism, however, constructivism has its shortcomings. Until recently, constructivism remained mainly a powerful tool of criticism rather than an approach capable of explaining outcomes in the real world. This situation is changing, however. Throughout this textbook, examples of constructivist scholarship will allow you to see this approach in use so that you can make your own judgments concerning this crucial and still relatively new theoretical perspective.

THE RADICAL PERSPECTIVE

While radicalism is not as prominent as other views are today, it offers another perspective on the study of international relations. Theories from this perspective place primacy on the role of economics in explaining international phenomena. This focus differs from that of the three main perspectives in international relations, which place the most importance on political interactions. Economics has a place in these perspectives, but it is not the main factor contributing to explanations of international politics. For realists, economic factors are one of the ingredients of power, one component of the international structure. For liberals, economic interdependence (and the role multinational corporations play in fostering that interdependence) is one possible explanation for international cooperation, but only one among many factors. In neither theory, though, is economics the determining factor. Both realists and liberals accept that the *state* is the primary unit of analysis. Constructivists do not focus solely on the state as the main actor in world politics, but their focus on identities and norms leads them more to political than economic explanations. For radicals, the factors that affect international politics are economic rather than political. They focus on the role of the economic system and actors such as economic classes and multinational corporations. Following this line of logic, two main schools of thought are the most pervasive in the radical perspective: Marxism and dependency theory.

Marxism

The writings of Karl Marx (1818–83) are fundamental to all radical thought, even though his theories did not directly address many contemporary issues. Marx based his theory of the evolution of capitalism on economic class conflict: he believed that the capitalism of nineteenth-century Europe emerged out of the earlier feudal system. According to Marx, in the capitalist system, private interests control labor and market exchanges, creating bondages from which certain classes try to free themselves. For Marx, there are two main economic classes: a bourgeoisie—which owns the means of production—and a proletariat—exploited labor.[20] Not only do radical theories seek to understand the relationship between those classes, but some have also applied Marxist ideas to help explain the relationship between states in the international system.

One important group of radical beliefs centers on the structure of the global system. That structure, according to Marxist thinking, is hierarchical and is largely the by-product of "imperialism," or the expansion of certain economic forms into other areas of the world. The British economist John A. Hobson (1858–1940) theorized that expansion occurs because of three conditions in the more developed states: overproduction of goods and services, underconsumption by workers and the lower class because of low wages, and oversaving by the upper class. Corporations are making goods that they need people to buy in order to sustain the corporations' economic well-being and the state's economy. However, workers cannot afford to buy these goods because of low wages, and the upper class is saving its money rather than buying goods. Corporations need to sell these good somewhere. To solve this problem, developed states have expanded abroad, and radicals argue that developed countries still see expansion as a solution. Goods find new markets in underdeveloped regions, workers' wages are kept low because of foreign competition, and savings are profitably invested in new markets rather than in improving the lot of the workers at home.[21] Critically, for radicals, states intervene, but they do so on behalf of the bourgeoisie class rather than on behalf of the exploited workers. States are therefore part of the problem in keeping the lower class suppressed.

For radicals, imperialism produces a hierarchical international system, which offers opportunities to some states, organizations, and individuals, but imposes

	Marxism	Dependency Theory
Key Actors	Social classes (upper-class bourgeoisie and lower-class proletariat); multinational corporations; emphasis on economics	Dominant and dominated states; multinational corporations; emphasis on economics
Characteristics of States	States act on behalf of the bourgeoisie class	Advanced industrialized countries dominate developing countries
Characteristics of the International System	Hierarchical; by-product of the expansion of certain economic forms into other areas of the world	Hierarchical; controlled by dominant states
Result of Current Situation	Imperialism	Underdevelopment in the dominated states
Major Theorists	Marx, Hobson	Prebisch, Pinto

significant constraints on behavior for others. Techniques of domination and suppression arise from the uneven economic distribution inherent in the capitalist system. This empowers and enables the dominant class and dominant states to exploit the others. The dynamics of capitalism and economic expansion make such exploitation necessary if the dominant actors are to maintain their position and the capitalist structure is to survive. Marxists and radicals view the economic techniques of domination and suppression as the means of power in the world.

Dependency Theory

Not all radical theorists, however, are Marxist. **Dependency theory**, whose development is closely associated with the work of economists such as Raúl Prebisch (1901–86) and Aníbal Pinto (1919–96), is a key strand of the radical school of thought. It differs from Marxism in that Marxist theories of imperialism explain the expansion of dominant states while dependency theory focuses on explaining the underdevelopment of the dominated states. Marxist theories explain the reasons for dominant state expansion (imperialism), while dependency theory focuses on the consequences of that expansion within the states where it has occurred.

There are a variety of theories within the dependency theory school of thought, but they are united by several core arguments.[22] First, just as Marx saw society as

Mining for minerals in Latin American countries is a common example of dependency theory at work. Here, miners sponsored by both North American and Peruvian companies extract gold from South America's largest gold mine, Yanacocha, located in Peru.

comprising two separate economic classes, dependency theorists see the international system as comprising two sets of states: those that are dominant and those that are dependent. The advanced industrial countries are the dominant states, while the dependent states are the developing countries that are dependent on the exports of primary products (commodities) to the developed states for their income.

Second, dependency theorists assume that external forces such as multinational corporations are central to the economic activities within dependent states. However, multinational corporations are controlled by the dominant states, which use them to represent their own economic interests in the dependent countries. Multinational corporations are thus key players in establishing and maintaining dependency relationships. For dependency theorists, they are not benign actors, as liberals would characterize them, or marginal actors, as realists would. Multinational corporations are agents through which dominant states can exploit dependent states and their workers.

Third, dependency theorists argue that the relationship between dominant and dependent states is dynamic. Their interactions reinforce each other. Dependent states supply the dominant states with cheap primary products. The dominant countries and their multinational corporations use those primary products to manufacture goods (either in their own country or by exploiting the cheap labor in dependent countries) and then sell those goods to the dependent states. These goods are always more expensive than the primary products used to create them.

Dependent countries can therefore never earn enough from their exports to rise out of their impoverished state. This spiral continues and, over time, intensifies states' unequal positions in the international system. Dependency theorists argue that this is a central reason for underdevelopment in many areas of the world.

Overall, because they focus mostly on economic factors, radical theories are less helpful for explaining more political phenomena in international politics. In the realm of economics, however, they do have some conceptual ideas to offer. The chapters that follow therefore do not focus on radical theories, but they are discussed in Chapter 8 on international political economy. Because of its contributions in economics, the radical perspective is important to at least consider, even if it is not in the mainstream of current studies of international relations.

FEMINIST CRITIQUES OF IR THEORY

To some IR scholars, feminism represents yet another IR theory. But to most theorists, feminism offers a variety of illuminating critiques of the mainstream perspectives. Many of the critiques share core propositions. Chief among them is the proposition that the world would be a better place—more just, more peaceful, more prosperous—if women were given more space to define, describe, and lead in domestic and international affairs. Thus, both realist and liberal feminists argue for greater participation of women in national and international decision making, and in economic life. Liberal feminists, for example, call for developing organizational policies that affect women, especially the role of women in economic development, women as victims of crime and discrimination, and women in situations of armed conflict. For too long, states have neglected these issues.

Radical feminists critique international relations theories as well. Unlike other radicals, who point to the structure of the international economic system as determinant of international relations, radical feminists define the problem as overarching patriarchy. The patriarchal system permeates national and international systems. For example, engaging in war seems desirable or rational. Until this system is changed, war will always be more likely, and women will always be in a subservient position—the victims of a neoliberal capitalist model of economic governance, in which poor women are exposed to the ravages of global competition.

Feminist critics are also found among social constructivists, postmodernists, and critical theorists. To these feminists, studying gender involves more than just counting women in elite positions or cataloging programs targeting women.

Just as constructivists assert more broadly, the meaning of things is established, supported, and changed through a process of social interaction, namely discourse.

According to J. Ann Tickner, for example, classical realism is based on a very limited—indeed, *masculine*—notion of both human nature and power. She argues that human nature is not fixed and unalterable; it is multidimensional and contextual. Power cannot be equated exclusively with physical control and domination. Tickner thinks that all international relations theory must be reoriented toward a more inclusive notion of power, in which power is the ability to act in concert (not just in conflict) or to engage in a symbiotic relationship (instead of outright competition). In other words, power can also be a concept of connection rather than one of only autonomy. [23]

For Tickner, as well as many other feminist scholars, such as Cynthia Enloe and Christine Sylvester, discourse has been dominated by a narrowly male perspective. This domination affects not only the issues IR theorists and policy makers consider important, but also the very standards by which a given policy is thought to be effective or ineffective. For example, if we want to understand violent conflict in terms of intensity, we may think that the number of combatants killed constitutes a sound measure of how important a given conflict is. Yet feminist IR scholars have pointed to rape as a serious cost of conflict that does not often result in a physical death. By privileging deaths in conflict over rape, we discount the true costs and consequences of a violent conflict such as a civil or interstate war. Paying little attention to the voices of women affects the kinds of questions we ask and the way we evaluate the answers.

Tickner has also pointed to the masculinization of many aims of foreign policy. For example, to the extent males tend to frame problems as dichotomous, gender suggests a hierarchy of associations that often lead states to give unwarranted or counterproductive priority to armed conflict as the core meaning of "security." Some countries are "feminine" or "childlike," and therefore in need of guidance or discipline from "masculine" or "grown-up" states (e.g., Britain or Germany). This situation creates incentives to intervene (rescue fantasies) and, at the same time, channels the forms of "effective" intervention to military force at the high (masculine) end, and diplomatic or economic intervention at the low (feminine) end.

Other feminists, such as Cynthia Enloe, have argued that contrary to Tickner's assertion that women have been absent from international politics, they have in fact been key participants.[24] The problem, according to Enloe, is that their participation goes almost entirely unnoticed (and, she might add, unrewarded). Enloe calls attention to the ways that the domestic roles for women condition our understanding of their potential as leaders and agenda-setters in international politics.

Even today, we see a strong gap between women's potential and women's *visible* participation and leadership in international politics as compared to men's. Perhaps, then, the strongest argument is that the core values of justice, peace, and prosperity, which both sexes share, cannot help but be advanced by the active participation and leadership of more women. And international relations theories can benefit from the various critiques that feminists of all theoretical persuasions offer.

THEORY IN ACTION: ANALYZING THE 2014 (AND BEYOND) RUSSIA–UKRAINE CONFLICT

The contending theoretical perspectives discussed in the preceding sections see the world and even specific events quite differently. What theorists and policy makers choose to see, what they each seek to explain, and what implications they draw vary widely, even though the facts of an event remain the same. Applying arguments from the three main perspectives (realism, liberalism, and constructivism) to the military conflict between Russia and Ukraine that began in early 2014 allows us to compare and contrast these perspectives in action.

Background on the Russia–Ukraine Conflict

In order to analyze the 2014 Russia-Ukraine conflict, we must understand the background of the case. In 1999 and in 2004, the North Atlantic Treaty Organization (NATO) expanded east, moving ever closer to Russia's border and bringing in states that had previously been part of the Soviet Union's sphere of influence. Russia opposed these NATO expansions from the start but was in a weak position to stop them. In 2008, NATO issued a statement in support of Georgia's and Ukraine's aspirations to join. Russian president Putin believed that the possibility of admitting Georgia and Ukraine, which share fairly expansive borders with Russia, was a "direct threat" to Russia. [25]

In addition to this potential NATO expansion, the European Union proposed a plan in May 2008 for an Eastern Partnership initiative to begin to integrate countries such as Ukraine into the EU economy. Russian leaders also viewed this move as hostile to their interests. The Russian foreign minister accused the EU of trying to create a "sphere of influence" in eastern Europe. The initiative, however, was strongly supported by Ukraine and its leaders at the time.

The domestic situation in Russia contributed in important ways in the lead-up to the Russia-Ukraine conflict. In late 2011 and early 2012, tens of thousands protested in Moscow over what was considered fraud in the 2011 Russian legislative elections, as well as Putin's decision to run for a third presidential term. Violence broke out and some opposition leaders were arrested. By the end of 2013, the opposition movement had collapsed, and Putin began a campaign of geopolitical actions and propaganda that some dubbed "make Russia great again."[26] The goal was to strengthen the people's Russian patriotism, and thus build up popular support.

Domestic politics in Ukraine, characterized by tensions between pro-Western and pro-Russian groups, also became very important. In November 2013, the new pro-Russian president of Ukraine, Viktor Yanukovych, chose to terminate the plans to sign the political association and trade agreement with the EU. The result was immediate pro-Western protests in Ukraine's capital, which quickly grew into a large movement. The protesters urged Yanukovych to sign the deal with the EU, but he began to expand ties with Russia instead.

In February 2014, the Ukrainian protesters succeeded in overthrowing Yanukovych. The new government they put in place was strongly pro-Western. This new government was viewed by Putin (and those of Russian descent living in Ukraine) as another example of the West's encroachment into Russia's sphere of influence.

The fears of pro-Russian Ukrainians were realized when one of the first actions the new government took was to ban Russian as the second official language of Ukraine. In response, pro-Russian protests broke out in Crimea. Crimea is an important area in Russian-Ukrainian relations. Crimea was a republic of Ukraine when the conflict began, but it had been part of Russia (and subsequently the Soviet Union) from 1783 until 1954, when it was handed over to Ukraine, which was then one of the Soviet republics. Many people in Crimea are therefore Russian speaking and of Russian descent. Crimea was thus a central area where people resented the anti-Russian sentiments of the new government.

The pro-Russian protesters in Crimea seized government buildings and other strategic sites. Pushed in part by Russian propaganda, they demanded that Crimea secede from Ukraine and become part of Russia. Soon after, Russia's parliament voted to approve Putin's request to use force against Ukraine to protect Russian interests. Thousands of Russian soldiers then moved onto the Crimean Peninsula. On March 16, Crimea held a referendum in which the people voted to secede from Ukraine (many in the West argued that the vote was fraudulent), and Crimea was annexed by Russia two days later. In response to the Russian actions, the United States, the European Union, and several European countries outside the EU imposed sanctions on Russia.

Continuing the "make Russia great again" campaign, state-controlled media in Russia immediately began to vilify the West and to hail the "return" of Crimea to Russia as one of the greatest moments in Russian history since the defeat of the Nazis in World War II. The citizens of Russia responded with patriotic pride, and polls showed a significant "rally around the flag" effect.

Pro-Western and pro-Russian divides in the Crimean Peninsula have led to sharp conflicts on the peninsula. Although some cities in Crimea have aligned with Russia (such as Sevastopol, pictured here), others remain in opposition to Putin's increasing nationalistic pressure.

The conflict has yet to subside. By mid-2017, Russia still had a significant military presence in Crimea and was actively practicing military exercises close to Ukraine's border. Skirmishes between Ukrainian and Russian troops were regularly breaking out, and Russia was beginning to support Russian rebel groups in other areas of Ukraine in their fight against the Ukrainian government.

So why did all this happen? The three major perspectives in international relations can help us understand, though as you will see, they interpret these events in very different ways.

Realist Perspectives

Realist interpretations of the Russia-Ukraine conflict would focus on the security interests of the states involved, as well as the distribution of power between them. First, leading up to the outbreak of the conflict, Russia clearly felt the intrusion of the West into its sphere of influence. The growing Western influence in Ukraine is exemplified by its aspiration of joining NATO, its possible trade agreement with the EU, and the pro-West government that took over in Ukraine just weeks before Russian troops moved into Crimea and annexed it.

As realists argue, security is a zero-sum game. A relative gain for one side is a loss for the other. The intrusion of the West into eastern Europe, and the movement of Ukraine farther toward the West, was thus a direct security threat to Russia, shifting the distribution of power in the region toward the United States and the EU. The security threat to Russia is further illustrated by the fact that NATO, one of the institutions actively building connections with Ukraine, is a military alliance specifically designed to counter outside states such as Russia.

Following realist logic, Russia's actions were designed to prevent the encroachment of the United States and the EU into its own sphere of influence, which would shift the distribution of power toward the West, and thus threaten Russia's security. Russia directly subverted Ukraine's move toward the West by proposing a counteroffer that led the Ukrainian president to reject the agreement between Ukraine and the EU. Russia also worked to weaken and destabilize Ukraine, preventing it from becoming a power that the West could use against Russia. After the annexation of Crimea, Russia supported pro-Russian groups that were fighting the Ukrainian government within the country, and it established a military presence and began to conduct military exercises at the border with Ukraine. Russia took actions that it saw as necessary steps to protect its security.

An offensive realist would also highlight the fact that Russia's military actions relating to Ukraine helped further its reputation regarding its willingness to engage in conflict. The creation of such a reputation is demonstrated by fears in Finland, Poland, and the Baltic states that the same type of action taken by Russia in Crimea might occur in their own states. All were once either part of Russia (or the Soviet Union) or in its sphere of influence. In addition, like Crimea, several of these countries have fairly significant Russian-speaking populations. Not only has Russia clearly created a reputation for a willingness to engage in conquest, but a bandwagoning effect by some states resulting from this reputation might even be evident. For example, shortly after the annexation of Crimea, Russia also began to increase its military power in the Black Sea. Rather than work to balance against Russia, however, Turkey increased both military and economic cooperation with it. Turkey and Russia signed a gas pipeline deal, pledged to increase bilateral trade more than fivefold, brokered a ceasefire in Aleppo, and agreed on a plan to stop the fighting in the rest of Syria. Demonstrating a willingness to engage in conquest can, according to offensive realists, pay off.

Liberal Perspectives

Liberal interpretations of the Russia-Ukraine situation would focus on characteristics of the states and the domestic politics at work within them, as well as the role that international institutions have played in influencing the conflict.

A theorist arguing from the liberal perspective would counter the realist argument by emphasizing that states are not unitary actors. Domestic actors and the preferences of those domestic actors are important factors in international politics, and examining them can help us understand the outbreak of the conflict between Russia and Ukraine. Under the power of Viktor Yanukovych, the pro-Russian president of Ukraine who came to power in 2010, Ukraine was not seen by Russia as much of a threat. In fact, Russia actively pursued cooperative relations with Ukraine, offering to buy up Ukrainian debt and lower the price of gas exports to Ukraine. The pro-Russian preferences that were represented by the Yanukovych government, as evidenced by the fact that it cut off the EU agreement and accepted Russia's cooperative offer, meant that Ukraine was not much of a threat at the time.

It was when a government supporting pro-Western domestic actors came to power in February 2014 that Russia came to view Ukraine as a threat. The government of Ukraine now represented pro-Western rather than pro-Russian preferences. The new Ukrainian government was thus likely to actively pursue connections with the West, bringing Ukraine closer to the Western (rather than the Russian) sphere of influence. The pro-Western protesters' demand that the Yanukovych government sign the EU association agreement is evidence that these actors desired to engage in these types of relations. According to this liberal argument, it was fear of the actions that the pro-Western government would take that led Russia to work to destabilize the country by mobilizing pro-Russian domestic actors in Crimea, and the same fear led Russia to continue to support pro-Russian rebel groups in eastern Ukraine after Crimea's annexation.

Other liberal arguments would highlight the important role that international institutions played—both international organizations like NATO and the EU and treaties like the association agreement Ukraine sought to forge with the EU. In particular, Russia associated the threat that stemmed from the pro-Western groups within Ukraine with their attempts to align their interests and actions with the EU and NATO. If these institutions had not been key actors in international relations, Ukraine's alignment with them would probably not have been seen as a threat by Russia and pro-Russian groups within Ukraine. But, according to liberal theorists, international institutions play a key role in fostering interdependence and influencing state behavior. Joining NATO and forging an association agreement (which included important trade provisions) with the EU would link Ukraine with the West in ways that could not be achieved without these institutions. Joining NATO would align the West's security interests with those of Ukraine—creating a threat to the security interests of Russia. The association agreement designed to facilitate trade between Ukraine and the EU would increase the interdependence between these countries, and in doing so, lessen Ukraine's trade dependence on Russia—creating a threat to the economic interests of Russia. In other words, because of the important role international institutions play in creating connections between states, Ukraine's attempts to join these institutions were an important factor influencing the threat felt by Russia.

Constructivist Perspectives

Constructivist interpretations of the Russia-Ukraine conflict would focus on the importance of the identities of the states involved, as well as the social constructions that came to define them. Identities come into play in several important ways.

First, the encroachment of the West into the Russian sphere of influence is not, in and of itself, a threat to Russian interests. The threat is made real because the states involved have divergent identities—the pro-democracy identity of the West and the more autocratic identity of Russia under Putin's leadership. The importance of these divergent identities can be seen in the fact that prior to 2013, Western states had begun to work to spread democratic values to post-Soviet eastern European states such as Ukraine. It is estimated that the United States has spent over $5 billion supporting organizations aimed at promoting democratic civil society, as well as supporting opposition groups against pro-Russian president Yanukovych after his election in 2010. This "social engineering" was seen as a threat to the leaders of Russia. This argument is backed up by this statement by the president of the nonprofit organization National Endowment for Democracy: "Ukraine's choice to join Europe will accelerate the demise of the ideology of Russian imperialism that Putin represents. . . . Russians too, face a choice, and Putin may find himself on the losing end not just in the near abroad but within Russia itself."[27]

Second, identities come into play in the way Putin used discourse to stimulate a patriotic Russian identity among the people who had previously been opposing him. The "make Russia great again" campaign was an effort to secure popular support at home. It shaped the identity of Russians in a way that led them to view Crimea as an important part of their history and identity. The annexation of Crimea mobilized this identity and led to a significant increase in popular support for Putin. Polls show that in response to the annexation of Crimea, popular support for Putin rose significantly and remained high through at least the end of 2017. Putin's need to secure support, and his efforts to construct Russian identity in specific ways, played a key role in his choice to annex Crimea and the effects that it had.

Overall, the realist, liberal, and constructivist perspectives provide very different explanations for the conflict that broke out between Russia and Ukraine in 2014. While the facts of the case are the same, the factors that each perspective highlights are different. None of the theorists associated with these perspectives are necessarily right or wrong; their explanations are simply more or less convincing. Which perspective's theories do you think best help us understand the outbreak of the conflict?

IN SUM: SEEING THE WORLD THROUGH THEORETICAL LENSES

Without theory, we are reduced to educated guesses on how to resolve crises or how to constructively advance human values such as justice and peace. How each of us sees international relations depends on our own theoretical lens. Do you see events through a realist framework? Are you inclined toward a liberal interpretation? Do you adhere to a constructivist view of the world? These theoretical perspectives differ not only in who they identify as key actors, but also in what counts as a threat or a benefit. They also differ in their views about the relative explanatory power that stems from considering individual actors, states, and the international system in the study of international politics. Better understanding these three "levels of analysis" is the focus of the next chapter.

Discussion Questions

1. Choose a current event in world politics. Describe and explain that event using the three main theoretical perspectives.

2. A realist and a liberal are discussing the role of domestic politics in influencing international outcomes. Re-create that conversation, highlighting the differing perspectives.

3. Constructivists assert that the power of norms and ideas is continuously shaping and reshaping state behavior. Select a political idea—equality, democracy, or human rights. How has that idea changed over time? How has state behavior changed, if at all?

4. What feminist critique of international relations theory do you find the most convincing? Why?

Key Terms

anarchy (p. 73)

balancing (p. 73)

bandwagoning (p. 78)

collective security (p. 82)

complex interdependence (p. 83)

dependency theory (p. 94)

discourse (p. 88)

external balancing (p. 76)

hypotheses (p. 68)

internal balancing (p. 76)

international institutions (p. 71)

norms (p. 72)

rational actors (p. 74)

relative gains (p. 75)

security dilemma (p. 76)

socialization (p. 89)

theoretical perspectives (p. 70)

theory (p. 68)

The Saudi-Iraqi border is now open for trade between the two Muslim-majority countries. Is this a sign of reconciliation between the two countries, or a method to stabilize a volatile region?

4

Levels of Analysis

In the 2010s, relations between Saudi Arabia and Iraq, while historically rocky, appeared to be improving. After Iraq's invasion of Kuwait in 1990, Saudi Arabia shut down its Baghdad embassy, cut diplomatic ties, and closed the border. But things have changed in recent years. The embassy reopened in 2015. In mid-2017, an agreement was reached for Saudi Arabia to donate $10 million in aid to the Iraqi government and study the possibility for investments in the Shia regions in the south of Iraq. In September 2017, the Saudi government announced that it had established a joint trade commission with Iraq, and the two countries announced a plan to reopen the border crossing to allow trade in goods between them. Why the drastic change in the previously rocky relationship between these countries? And why now?

Observers put forth several arguments about why this change came about. Some cite the growing influence of Iran in the region and its destabilizing effect. The Saudi government, fearing an Iran-friendly Iraq that would further destabilize the region, is seeking to woo it to its own side. It is the regional distribution of power that matters. Others highlight the fact that Iran is backing the anti-Saudi rebels in Yemen and recently threatened military action against Saudi Arabia itself. The desire of Saudi Arabia to protect its own power and interests is driving the move toward Iraq. Still others highlight the importance of the individuals involved. In July 2017, Iraqi cleric Muqtada al-Sadr traveled to Saudi Arabia to meet with Saudi crown prince Mohammed bin Salman. Sadr had long had a large following in Iraq's poorer regions and had been an anti-American ally of Iran for most of the era after Saddam Hussein had been ousted from power in 2003. The change in Sadr's own approach was central for the positive breakthrough in their relations. Indeed, it was this meeting that resulted in the $10 million aid donation.

The three explanations for why relations between Iraq and Saudi Arabia improved point to different factors that matter. Is it the distribution of power between the states in the system? Is it the relationship between the states themselves? Or is it the individuals that matter most? All three highlight a different "level" at which we can analyze international politics. Like the theoretical perspectives, none are necessarily right or wrong. They simply highlight different ways to approach the analysis. In this chapter, we look at these different "levels of analysis" to understand how each can help us better understand various events in international politics.

LEARNING OBJECTIVES

▶ **Understand how the various theoretical perspectives view the international system, the state, and the individual as levels of explanation for international events.**

▶ **Describe how each of the contending theoretical perspectives explains change in the international system.**

▶ **Describe how political scientists measure state power.**

▶ **Analyze what psychological factors have an impact on elite foreign policy decision making.**

▶ **Describe the roles private individuals and the mass public play in international relations.**

In Chapter 3, we introduced different perspectives through which international relations theorists study various events in world politics. These theoretical perspectives do not only differ in whom they identify as key actors and what counts as a threat or a benefit. They also differ in their views about the relative explanatory power of three levels of analysis: the international system, the state, and the individual. Dividing the analysis of international politics into levels helps orient our questions and suggests the appropriate type of evidence to explore. Paying attention to levels of analysis helps us make logical deductions and enables us to explore all categories of explanation.

A categorization first used by Kenneth Waltz and later amplified by J. David Singer offers three different sources of explanations for why there is war. If the *international system level* is the focus, then the explanation rests with the characteristics of that system (such as the distribution of "power") or with international and regional organizations and their relative strengths and weaknesses. If the *state level*, or domestic factors, is the focus, then the explanation is derived from characteristics of the state: the type of government (e.g., democratic or authoritarian), the type of economic system (e.g., capitalist or socialist), interest groups within the country, and/or the national interest. If the focus is on the *individual level*, then the personality, perceptions, choices, and activities of individual decision makers and individual participants provide the explanation.[1]

In this chapter, we examine in more detail how the international relations perspectives see the international system, the state, and the individual and how using these different levels of analysis can help us better understand international politics (see Figure 4.1). We can approach the study of international relations not only by

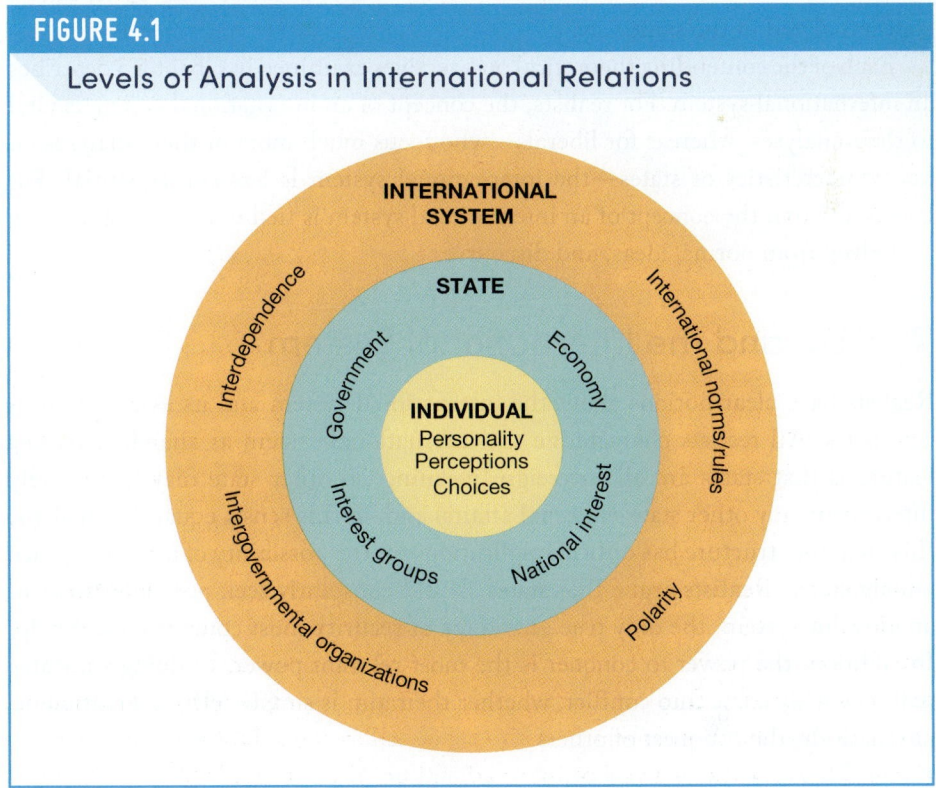

FIGURE 4.1

Levels of Analysis in International Relations

looking through the lenses of the various perspectives, as discussed in Chapter 3, but also by highlighting explanatory factors that occur at the different levels of analysis. We can therefore further evaluate international events such as the conflict between Russia and Ukraine that broke out in 2014 using these levels of analysis.

THE INTERNATIONAL SYSTEM

To understand the *international* system, we must first clarify the notion of a system itself. Broadly defined, a **system** is an assemblage of units, objects, or parts united by some form of regular interaction. The concept of systems is essential to the physical and biological sciences; systems are composed of different interacting units, whether at the micro (cell, plant, animal) or the macro (natural ecosystem or global climate) level. Because these units interact, a change in one unit causes changes in the others. With their interacting parts, systems tend to respond in regularized ways; their actions have patterns. Boundaries separate one system from another, but exchanges can occur across these boundaries. A system can break down when changes within it become so significant that, in effect, a new system emerges. The international system, composed of states as interacting units, can be conceptualized in the same way.

Each of the contending theoretical perspectives examined in Chapter 3 describes an international system. For realists, the concept of an international system is vital to their analyses, whereas for liberals—who focus much more of their analyses on key characteristics of states—the international system is less consequential. For constructivists, the concept of an international system is tied to notions of identity as derived from norms, ideas, and discourse.

Realism and the International System

Realists have clear notions about the international system and its essential characteristics. All realists characterize the international system as anarchic. Its key feature is that states are all sovereign (meaning no other state may legitimately intervene in any other state's internal affairs) and, in this sense, equal. For realists, this anarchic structure has critical implications for the possibility of enduring peace among states. Realists argue that states should constantly seek power because, in an anarchic system, the only true guarantee of security must come from self-help. In addition, the power to conquer is the most relevant power. In doing so, states will inevitably come into conflict, whether their aim is simply self-preservation or, alternatively, the conquest of others.

To characterize the possibilities of war and peace in the international system, realists rely on the concept of polarity. As discussed in Chapter 3, system polarity describes the distribution of capabilities among states in the international system by counting the number of "poles" (states or groups of states) where material power is concentrated. There are three types of system polarity: multipolarity, bipolarity, and unipolarity (see Figure 4.2).

A **multipolar** system is any system in which the distribution of the power to conquer is concentrated in more than two states. In the system preceding World War I, five states—Great Britain, Russia, Prussia, France, and Austria-Hungary—composed a multipolar system that had evolved from the balance of power after the Napoleonic Wars.

In a stable multipolar system—a balance-of-power system—the essential norms of interaction are clear to each of the state actors: norms of competition, cooperation, and shifting alliances. In systems in which these norms are shared and observed, alliances are formed for a specific purpose, have a short duration, and shift according to advantage rather than ideology. Any wars that do erupt are expected to be limited in nature, designed to preserve a balance of power. As we saw in Chapter 2, however, when an essential actor ignores the understood norms, the system may become unstable.

Bipolar systems are those in which the distribution of the power to conquer is concentrated in two states or coalitions of states. In the bipolar system of the Cold War, each of the blocs (the Warsaw Pact and the North Atlantic Treaty Organization, or NATO) sought to negotiate rather than fight, and to fight proxy wars outside of Europe rather than major wars among themselves. In a bipolar system, alliances tend to be longer term, based on relatively permanent interests, not shifting ones. Unlike in a multipolar system, each bloc in a bipolar system is certain about the direction and magnitude of its biggest threat. In a tight bipolar system, international organizations either do not develop or are relatively ineffective, as the United Nations was during the height of the Cold War. In a looser bipolar system, international organizations may develop primarily to mediate between the two blocs, and individual states within the looser coalitions may try to use the international organizations for their own advantage. During much of the Cold War era, particularly in the 1950s and 1960s, the international system was bipolar—the United States and its European and Asian allies (NATO, and Japan, South Korea, South Vietnam [until 1975], the Philippines, and Australia, respectively) faced the Soviet Union and its European and Asian allies (the Warsaw Pact, and the People's Republic of China, North Korea, and North Vietnam, respectively; and after 1962, Cuba). But over the course of the Cold War, the relative tightness or looseness of the bipolar system shifted, as powerful states such as the People's Republic of China, India, and France pursued independent paths.

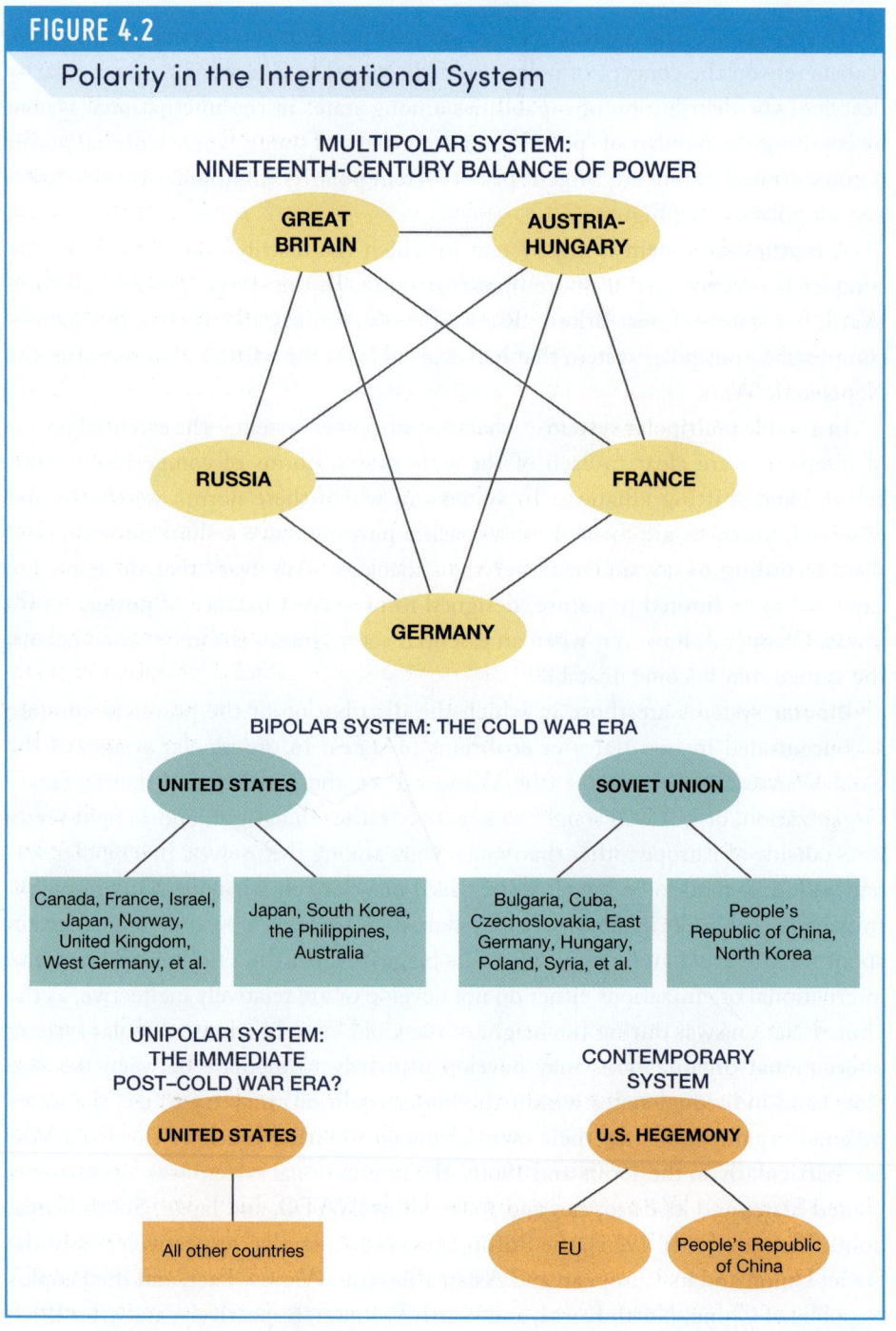

FIGURE 4.2

Polarity in the International System

MULTIPOLAR SYSTEM:
NINETEENTH-CENTURY BALANCE OF POWER

- GREAT BRITAIN
- AUSTRIA-HUNGARY
- RUSSIA
- FRANCE
- GERMANY

BIPOLAR SYSTEM: THE COLD WAR ERA

UNITED STATES

- Canada, France, Israel, Japan, Norway, United Kingdom, West Germany, et al.
- Japan, South Korea, the Philippines, Australia

SOVIET UNION

- Bulgaria, Cuba, Czechoslovakia, East Germany, Hungary, Poland, Syria, et al.
- People's Republic of China, North Korea

UNIPOLAR SYSTEM:
THE IMMEDIATE
POST–COLD WAR ERA?

UNITED STATES

- All other countries

CONTEMPORARY
SYSTEM

U.S. HEGEMONY

- EU
- People's Republic of China

A **unipolar** system is one in which the power to conquer all other states in the system combined resides within a single state. Realists of all sorts still disagree about whether the world has actually seen a true unipolar system (which, if it were to happen, would do away with anarchy and its interstate conflict implications). But immediately after the Gulf War in 1991, many states, including the United States' closest allies and virtually all developing states, grew concerned that the international system *had* become unipolar. After all, its chief rival bloc—the USSR and Warsaw Pact—had collapsed, U.S. defense expenditures were greater than those of the next 15 states combined, and its economy was three times stronger than the next three economies combined. With that superiority, other states were worried there might be no effective counterweight to the power of the United States. In the twenty-first century, this concern remains.

There is little debate about whether the United States still commands overwhelming material capabilities, but there is much more discussion over whether the United States can translate those capabilities into effective dominance. Even though U.S. dominance in military expenditures has gone largely unchallenged, save perhaps modestly by China and Russia, U.S. power in relative terms is on the decline. China and the European Union are rising economically, as are Brazil and India. The trend clearly suggests that not only is the global distribution of material power widening, but material power itself may be less important than many assume, especially as compared to other sorts of power such as the power of ideas (as constructivists would argue).

The type of international system in place at any given time has implications for system management and stability. Are certain polarities more manageable and hence more stable than others are? Are wars more likely to occur in bipolar systems, multipolar systems, or unipolar systems? These questions have dominated much of the discussion among realists, but so far, studies of these relationships have been inconclusive.

Bipolar systems are very difficult to regulate formally, because neither uncommitted states nor international organizations can reliably direct the behavior of either of the two poles. Informal regulation may be easier. If either of the blocs is engaged in disruptive behavior, the consequences are immediately evident, especially if one of the blocs gains in strength or position as a result. The neorealist theorist Kenneth Waltz, for one, argues that because of this visibility, the bipolar international system is the most stable structure in the long run: the two sides are "able both to moderate the other's use of violence and to absorb possibly destabilizing changes that emanate from uses of violence that they do not or cannot control."[2] In such a system, a clear difference exists in how much power each pole holds compared with what other state actors hold. Because of the power disparity, each of the two poles can focus its activity almost exclusively on the other. Each can anticipate

The International System: A View from China

Realists posit that the international system changes as great powers gain or lose power relative to other states. As China's economic and political power has grown, many scholars have speculated about whether China will catch up to the United States, leading to a new bipolarity, or surpass the United States, becoming the new hegemon in a unipolar system. Chinese government officials have stated their intentions.

Following almost a century of seeing itself as a victim of the great powers and after decades of internal revolution when it was closed to the world, China is becoming a confident great power. The country wields increasing economic and political influence, using both bilateral and multilateral diplomacy. It now operates within the rules of the contemporary international system and it has become socialized into prevailing international norms.

The economic revolution in China, its embrace of free markets, and its opening to foreign investment and enterprise have led to almost four decades of unprecedented economic growth of more than 9 percent per year. As the world's second-largest economy, China has maintained that it is in China's interest to continue this "peaceful rise," or *zhongguo heping jueqi*, serving as a viable economic model for many states.

China's participation in world trade regimes has increased its global presence to the benefit of all parties. China's accession to the World Trade Organization (WTO) has allowed it to maximize economic output while demonstrating to the world that it can adhere to WTO regulations, such as nondiscrimination policies and elimination of price controls. China is also now actively engaged in regional trade and economic agreements, particularly with Association of Southeast Asian Nations (ASEAN) states and within the Asia-Pacific Economic Cooperation forum. In 2015, China launched the Asian Infrastructure Investment Bank, a rival to the World Bank, International Monetary Fund, and Asian Development Bank. Over the objections of both the United States and Japan, 56 states had joined the bank as of 2017, and 24 had memberships pending.

In its rise, China has acted responsibly toward both the advanced capitalist states and the developing world. China finances a large portion of American debt because of its large balance-of-trade surplus with the United States. During the 2008 international financial crisis, China refrained from putting pressure on the U.S. dollar and interest rates. To help rebalance the international economy after the 2008 financial crisis, China is encouraging domestic consumption, increasing workers' pay, and allowing its currency to appreciate gradually. China is also supporting massive infrastructure projects as part of the "One Belt, One Road" initiative. These projects are designed to provide a conduit for its imports and exports, connecting China with Central and south Asia, all the way to Istanbul, Moscow, and Venice.

China has also forged relationships with many African countries by investing in infrastructure, technology, and raw materials. With trade of more than $210 billion, China is Africa's top business partner. Chinese private companies, businesses, and tourists are finding Africa fertile territory. Whereas the West colonized these lands and often stripped them of their resource wealth, China seeks a peaceful, mutually beneficial relationship without interfering with domestic affairs.

Like all great powers, China has increased its military expenditures, although the United

China has built the Subi Reef, pictured here, into a man-made island in the Spratly Island group.

States spends six times more on defense than China spends. China will continue to modernize its nuclear forces and strengthen its second-strike abilities. It will develop cyber-warfare capabilities. But the threat posed by these advances may have been exaggerated by Western observers.

China so far has chosen not to use its military capabilities. Nor has China fought militarily to expand its territory. It has, however, worked to defend its national interest in ways consistent with the One-China policy: the view that Tibet, Taiwan, and the islands in the South China Sea are part of China. Since 2014, China has undertaken a policy of dredging thousands of metric tons of sand onto coral reefs to create artificial islands in the Spratly Island group to strengthen its territorial claims. As expected of the actions of a great power, China refused to recognize the 2016 ruling of the Permanent Court of Arbitration, which found that these actions violated international law, and China will continue to oppose the designs of neighboring states, which consistently refute its claims on the islands.

China is building the capacity—mainly naval capacity—to deploy armed forces farther and farther abroad. China argues that as a global power with global interests, its armed forces will need to be able to reach Chinese citizens when they are stranded or threatened abroad. China has benefited from the international order of the last decades and is committed to a stable continuation of that order.

FOR CRITICAL ANALYSIS

1. How are China's actions affecting the configuration of the international system in terms of the distribution of power, interdependence, and identities?

2. If China continues with its current trajectory and actions, what do you think the international system will look like in 20 years?

3. How do China's actions differ from those of other great powers? How are they similar?

4. If we looked at China's policies from the state or individual level of analysis, what might we conclude that would be different if we were looking only at the level of the international system?

the other's actions and accurately predict its responses because of their history of repeated interactions. Each pole tries to preserve this balance of power to preserve itself and the nature of the system. In 2012, Waltz reprised a similar argument in "Why Iran Should Get the Bomb." He argues that Israel's nuclear capability is destabilizing the region: "If Iran goes nuclear, Israel and Iran will deter each other, as nuclear powers always have." That would bring stability.[3]

Multipolar systems can also be "balance of power" systems. According to some realists, multipolar systems can be very stable so long as the system's key actors internalize norms of competition and cooperation. For neorealists, however, balance of power is more difficult in multipolar systems because they involve more inherent uncertainty about where and when a threat might emerge (including the threat of a given state's ignoring important balance-of-power norms). For this reason, neorealists argue that bipolar systems are likely to be more peaceful. Again, the empirical evidence is mixed.

In contrast, hegemonic stability theorists claim that an approximation of unipolarity—hegemony—may be sufficient to create and maintain a stable international system. So long as the hegemon—a term coming from the Greek word for "to lead"—is able and willing to act, and act in ways that benefit those it leads as well as itself, enduring and prosperous peace can result. In *The Rise and Fall of the Great Powers*, historian Paul Kennedy argues that the hegemony of Britain in the nineteenth century and the United States in the immediate post–World War II era led to the greatest stability.[4] Other theorists, such as Robert O. Keohane, contend that hegemonic states are willing to pay the price of enforcing norms, unilaterally if necessary, to ensure the continuation of the system that benefits them. When the hegemon loses material capability or is no longer willing to exercise its advantage in relative power, then system stability is jeopardized.[5]

It is clear, then, that realists do not entirely agree among themselves about the relationship between polarity and stability. Individual and group efforts to test this relationship have been inconclusive.

Liberalism and the International System

For liberals, the international system is less consequential as an explanatory level of analysis. Therefore, it is not surprising to find at least three different conceptions of the international system in liberal thinking.

The first conception sees the international system not as an unchanging structure, but rather as an interdependent system in which multiple and fluid interactions occur among different parties and where various actors learn from their interactions. Actors in this process include not only states but also international governmental organizations (such as the United Nations), nongovernmental

	Realism/ Neorealism	Liberalism/ Neoliberal Institutionalism	Constructivism
Characterization	Anarchic	Three liberal interpretations: interdependence, international order, and neoliberal institutionalism	International system exists as social construct
Actors	State is primary actor	States, international governmental institutions, nongovernmental organizations, substate actors	Individuals matter; no differentiation between international and domestic
Constraints	Polarity; distribution of power	Interdependence; institutions	Ongoing interactions
Possibility of Change	Slow change when the balance of power shifts	Low possibility of radical change; constant incremental change as actors are involved in new relationships	Emphasis on change in social norms and identities

organizations (such as Human Rights Watch), multinational corporations, and substate actors (such as parliaments and bureaucracies). With so many different kinds of actors interacting with all of the others, a plethora of national interests defines the liberal international system. Although security interests, so dominant for realists, are also important to liberals, other interests, such as economic and social issues, are also considered important. In their book *Power and Interdependence*, the political scientists Robert Keohane and Joseph Nye describe the international system as an interdependent system in which the different actors are both sensitive to (affected by) and vulnerable to (suffering costly effects from) the actions of others. Interdependent systems have multiple channels connecting states; these channels exist among governmental elites, nongovernmental elites, and transnational organizations. Multiple issues and agendas arise in the interdependent system. Military force may be useful in some situations, but it is not useful for all issues.[6]

Negotiating and coordinating in the liberal international system often occur through **multilateralism**. Multilateralism is the conduct of international activity by three or more states in accord with shared general principles, often, but not always, through international institutions. One of those core principles of cooperation is belief in the collective security system. Briefly, collective security rests on the idea that peace is indivisible: a war against one is a war against all, meaning that the international community is obligated to respond. That idea will be examined in greater detail in Chapter 6; it is a key liberal approach to war and security. Thus, the possibility of coordinating behavior through multilateralism is a critical component of the liberal view of the international system.

A second liberal conception sees the international system in terms of a specific international order. Building on the tradition of Immanuel Kant and U.S. president Woodrow Wilson, as Chapter 3 discussed, this view holds that a liberal international order governs arrangements among states by means of shared rules and principles, similar to the principles that realists see under varying conditions of polarity. But unlike the realists' principles, this order is an acknowledged order; it is not just patterned behavior or some interconnections. In this order, institutions play a key role. As John Ikenberrry in *After Victory* argues, the acknowledged goal of a dominant power in this international order is to establish rules that are "both durable and legitimate, but rules and arrangements that also serve the long-term interests of the leading state."[7] To do that, the dominant power limits its own autonomy and agrees to make credible commitments.

A third liberal view of the international system is held by neoliberal institutionalists. Like realists, neoliberal institutionalists see the international system as anarchic and acknowledge that each individual state acts in its own self-interest. But neoliberal institutionalists draw different conclusions about state behavior in the international system. It may be a cooperative system, wherein states choose to cooperate because they realize that they will have future interactions with the same actors, as Chapter 7 explains in more detail. Those repeated interactions provide the motivation for states to create international institutions, which in turn moderate state behavior, providing a guaranteed framework for interactions and a context for bargaining. International institutions provide focal points for coordination and serve to make state commitments more credible by specifying what is expected, thereby encouraging states to establish reputations for compliance. Thus, for neoliberals, institutions have important and independent effects on interstate interactions, both by providing information and by framing actions, but they do not necessarily affect states' underlying motivations. The international system may be anarchic, but cooperation may emerge through institutions.

Constructivism and the International System

Constructivists argue that the whole concept of an international system is a European idea that, over time, became accepted as a natural fact (at least among

Europeans and North Americans). They hold that we can explain nothing by international material structures alone. Martha Finnemore in *The Purpose of Intervention* suggests that there have been different international orders with changing purposes, different views of threat, and different ways to maintain order. She traces at least four European international orders: an eighteenth-century balance order; a nineteenth-century concert order; a sphere-of-influence system for much of the twentieth century; and, since the end of the Cold War, an evolving new order whose purpose is the promotion of liberal democracy, capitalism, and human rights. Constructivists agree with other theorists that power matters in the international system, but they propose that the meaning of "power" can change over time. As Finnemore writes, "What made 1815 a concert and 1950 a cold war was not the material distribution of capabilities but the shared meanings and interpretations participants imposed on those capabilities."[8]

Constructivists see not a material structure in the international system but rather a socially constructed process. While the prominent constructivist Alexander Wendt, in *Social Theory of International Politics*, agrees with the fundamental premise of realists that the system is anarchic, he contends that the whole notion of anarchy is socially constructed: anarchy is what states make of it.[9] The meaning of anarchy is not constant across geographic space or through time. Anarchy leads to no particular outcome unless we agree it does. States debate anarchy's meaning and in turn give it meaning. Neither sovereignty nor balance of power objectively exist. Thus, constructivists reject the notion that the international system exists objectively or gives rise to objective rules or principles.

Change in the International System

Theories from all three perspectives recognize that the international system not only can affect international politics but also can change over time. For realists, the nature of the change in the system can be reduced to the distribution of peace and war between great powers (small and medium powers matter less). If that structure affects the likelihood of war and peace in the system, then logically, any understanding of what causes structural change (e.g., in polarity) will result in an understanding of what makes war or peace more likely. Changes in either the number of major actors or the relative power of those actors may cause a fundamental change in the structure of the international system. According to realists, wars are most often responsible for such fundamental changes in power relationships. For example, World War II caused a relative decline of Great Britain and France, even though they were the victors. The war also signaled the end not only of Germany's and Japan's imperial aspirations but of their considerable military and economic capabilities as well. Their militaries were soundly defeated; their civil societies were destroyed and their infrastructures demolished. Two other powers emerged in dominant positions—the United States, now willing to assume the international role it had shunned after World War I, and the Soviet Union, buoyed by its victory, although economically weakened. The international system had fundamentally changed; the multipolar world had been replaced by a bipolar one.

Robert Gilpin, in *War and Change in World Politics*, sees another mechanism of system change: states grow at uneven rates because states respond differently to political, economic, and technological developments. Those uneven rates eventually lead to a redistribution of power and thus change the international system. For example, the rapidly industrializing East Asian states—South Korea, Taiwan, and Hong Kong (now part of China)—have responded to technological change the fastest. By responding rapidly and with single-mindedness, these states have improved their relative positions. Thus, the actions of a few can change the characteristics of the international system.[10]

Exogenous shifts in technology may also lead to a shift in the international political system. Technological advances—such as the instruments for oceanic navigation, the airplane for transatlantic crossings, satellites and rockets for the exploration of space, and cyber and Internet technology—have not only expanded the boundaries of accessible geographic space but also brought about changes in the boundaries of the international political system. The same is true of global warming and the receding Arctic ice cap: previously unexplored territory and unnavigable waterways have created new strategic interests in the area, and states bordering the Arctic are not alone in seeking to establish territorial and economic interests there. These exogenous shifts changed the relative power of state actors, all reflecting different political interests and different cultural traditions.

Perhaps no technological change has had a stronger impact on the international system than the development of nuclear weapons and their use in warfare. Their destructiveness, their inability to discriminate between combatants and civilians, and their evident harm to future generations have led policy makers to reconsider the political utility of the power to destroy. During the Cold War, this led the superpowers to spar through non-nuclear proxies using conventional military technology, rather than fight directly, as Chapter 2 discussed. Since nuclear weapons have not been used in war since 1945, they are no longer seen as credible in some circles. Nevertheless, their use remains greatly feared. Efforts or threats by non-nuclear states to develop such weapons have provoked sharp resistance, such as the uproar that occurred when North Korea claimed to have tested a hydrogen bomb in January 2016 and when it tested missiles in 2017 that some experts say are capable of reaching New York. The nuclear states do not want a change in the status quo; in their view, nuclear proliferation, particularly in the hands of "rogue" states such as North Korea and Iran, leads to international system instability. That is why the Joint Comprehensive Plan of Action for Iran denuclearization—a compromise plan between Iran, P5+1 (the five permanent members of the UN Security Council plus Germany), and the EU in which Iran agreed to halt production of nuclear weapons in exchange for the lifting of costly economic sanctions—was pursued with such unity and vigor.

Thus, in the view of realists, international systems can change, yet the inherent bias among realist interpretations is for continuity. The reason is that all states have an interest in preventing the one structural change that might do away with the possibility of war in the system: unipolarity. The closer the system gets to a single actor exercising all the power in its own interests, the greater the incentives of actors in the system to countervail that actor. Put differently, we might say that most states prefer independence (sovereignty) and some risk of war, over a guarantee of peace under the absolute rule of a single state. This argument explains why, for realists, peace in the international system must prove elusive.

Liberals, too, see the role of states, and peace, as critical features of the international system. Liberals see change as coming from several sources. First, like some realists, liberals recognize that changes in the international system may occur as the result of exogenous technological developments. They see these developments as progress that occurs independently, outside the control of states in the system.

U.S. Secretary of State John Kerry shakes hands with Iranian Foreign Minister Javad Zarif as talks to curb Iran's nuclear proliferation and relieve hurtful sanctions progressed. This global agreement was seen as a successful effort to bring stabilization to a "rogue" nation.

For example, changes in communication and transportation are responsible for the increasing level of interdependence among states within the international system.

Second, change may occur because of changes in the relative importance of different issue areas. Although realists give primacy to issues of national security, liberals identify the relative importance of other issue areas. Specifically, in the last decades of the twentieth century, economic issues replaced national security issues as the leading topic of the international agenda. In the twenty-first century, transnational concerns such as human rights, the environment, and health have assumed a much more prominent role. These are fundamental changes in the international system, according to most liberal thinking.

Third, change may occur when new actors, including multinational corporations, nongovernmental organizations, or other participants in global civil society, augment or replace state actors. The various new actors may enter into new kinds of relationships and may alter both the international system and individual state behaviors. These types of changes are compatible with liberal thinking and are discussed by liberal writers. And, like their realist counterparts, liberal thinkers also acknowledge that change *may* occur in the overall power structure among the states. On the critical question of whether war is something we must live with, liberals are distinct from realists in arguing that a different feature of human nature—besides fear and greed—helps explain how we might transcend and eradicate war. In the liberal view, the economic or material self-interest of states can lead to cooperation, including cooperation across what were once considered zero-sum issues. For example, in the liberal view, cooperation to reduce tariff barriers to trade, after a while, may lead to cooperation on professional standards, immigration controls, and even, eventually, security cooperation. Change in the system, and in the likelihood of war in the system, then comes after decades, even centuries, of painstaking, at times reversed, but ultimately more comprehensive, cooperation. In sum, whereas realist theory remains pessimistic about the possibilities of transcending perpetual war, liberal theory holds out an optimistic possibility of an evolution toward perpetual peace.

Constructivists believe that changes in the system stem from changes in norms, although not all norm changes will be transforming. Social norms can be changed through both the actions of the collective and the efforts of charismatic individuals. Individuals matter in both realist and liberal theory, but they matter differently. For constructivists, they matter in how they affect discourse (how we frame and understand our world in talking, writing, and performing). Collectively, norms may change through coercion, but most likely, they will change through international institutions, law, and social movements. So although material capabilities do matter in explaining change, just as realists and many liberals argue, "why one order emerges rather than another" can only be seen, Martha Finnemore argues, "by examining the ideas, culture, and social purpose of the actors involved."[11]

Constructivists, then, are interested in understanding the major changes in the normative structure of the system: how the use of force has evolved over time, how the view of who is human has changed, how ideas about democracy and human rights have internationalized, and how states have been socialized—or resisted socialization—in turn.

The International System as a Level of Analysis: The Russia-Ukraine Conflict

How can the international system level of analysis explain real-world international relations? Consider arguments from the three theoretical perspectives that would use the international system level to explain the outbreak of the Russia-Ukraine conflict in 2014 (discussed in detail in Chapter 3).

Analyzing the international system as a source of possible explanations for the conflict, a realist would likely highlight the distribution of power in the system, and how that distribution could change. In particular, the move of Ukraine toward the West would shift the distribution of power in its own region toward the United States and states of Europe. Russia took military actions to prevent this change in the balance of power between itself and the West.

A liberal theorist might highlight the interdependence between the states involved as an important international system–level explanation for the conflict. The trade agreement that Ukraine was seeking to sign with the EU would increase the interdependence between them. This would not only decrease Ukraine's level of dependence on Russia, but also connect Ukraine's own interests to those of the West. Seeking to prevent Ukraine from forming stronger ties with the EU, Russia took action.

A constructivist would likely highlight the important role of the distribution of identities among the states. Following constructivist logic, Russia saw the prospect of Western encroachment into the Russian sphere of influence as a threat because the identities of the states involved diverged and in many ways were incompatible.

As these examples show, looking at the international system level can help us understand various aspects of international politics. However, using the international system level of analysis has both advantages and disadvantages. It allows us to see the big picture and the relationship among the various parts. Specifics, however, are lacking. Looking at the state level and the individual level can help add more detail to our understanding of international politics.

THE STATE

The state is a second level of analysis from which we can derive explanations of international phenomena. As discussed in detail in Chapter 5, to be legally considered a state, an entity must have a defined territory, a stable population, and an effective government and must be recognized by other states as having the capacity to enter into relations with them. Some conceptualizations of the state, however, emphasize ideas absent from this legalistic definition. Other concepts of the state include the following: the state is a normative order, a symbol for a particular society and the beliefs that bind the people living within its borders; the state is an entity that has a monopoly on the legitimate use of violence within a society; the state is a functional unit that assumes a number of important responsibilities, centralizing and unifying them. These different views of the state reflect the general international relations perspectives discussed in Chapter 3.

International Relations Perspectives and the State

Realists generally hold a statist, or state-centric, view. They believe that the state is an autonomous actor constrained only by the structural anarchy of the international system. The state enjoys sovereignty—the authority to govern matters that are within its own borders and that affect its people, economy, security, and form of government. As a sovereign entity, the state has a consistent set of goals—that is, a national interest—defined in terms of power. When the state acts to pursue its national interests, according to the realists, it does so as an autonomous, unitary actor.

In the liberal view, the state enjoys sovereignty but is not an autonomous actor. Just as liberals believe the international system is a process occurring among many actors, they see the state as a pluralist arena whose function is to maintain the basic rules of the game. These rules ensure that various interests (both governmental and societal) compete fairly and effectively in the game of politics. There is no single explicit or consistent national interest; there are many. These interests often compete against each other within a pluralistic framework. A state's national interests change over time, reflecting the interests and relative power positions of competing groups inside and sometimes also outside the state.

Because constructivists see both national interests and national identities as social constructs, they conceptualize the state very differently than theorists who have other perspectives. To constructivists, national interests are neither material nor given. They are ideational and ever-changing and evolving, in response to both domestic factors and international norms and ideas. States share a variety of goals and values, which they are socialized into by international and nongovernmental organizations. Those norms can change state preferences, which in turn can influence state behavior. So, too, do states have multiple identities, including a shared understanding of national identity, which also changes, altering state preferences and hence state behavior. In short, the state "makes" the system and the system "makes" the state.[12]

State Power

All three perspectives see states as important actors in international relations. One of the most important reasons for this is that they have **power**. Power refers to the ability not only to influence others but also to control outcomes, producing results that would not have occurred naturally. States have power with respect to each other and with respect to actors within the state. Whether a state can actually be effective at influencing outcomes and others depends on the **power potential** of each party. A state's power potential depends on the resources it has at its disposal to try to wield possible influence. Those resources can be natural, tangible, and/or intangible.

All theoretical perspectives acknowledge the importance of power, but each pays attention to different types of power. Realists and liberals conceptualize power in materialist terms; realists focus primarily on natural and tangible power sources, while liberals pay attention to natural, tangible, and intangible sources. Constructivists emphasize the nonmaterialist sources found in the power of ideas, one of the intangible sources. Although many of these sources of power are domestic in origin, power is situational, multidimensional, and dynamic.

Natural Sources of Power Potential

The first source of power potential is natural—it flows from innate characteristics of the state. The three most important natural sources of power potential are geographic size and position, natural resources, and population.

Geographic size and position were the natural sources of power that international relations theorists recognized first. A large geographic expanse gives a state automatic power potential (when we think of power, we think of large states— Russia, China, the United States, Australia, India, Canada, or Brazil, for instance). Long borders, however, may be a weakness: they must be defended, an expensive and often problematic task.

Two different views about the importance of geography in international relations emerged at the turn of the last century within the realist tradition. In the late 1890s, the naval officer and historian Alfred Mahan (1840–1914) wrote of the importance of controlling the sea. He argued that the state controlling the ocean routes controls the world. To Mahan, sovereignty over land was not as critical as having access to, and control over, sea routes.[13] In 1904, the British geographer Sir Halford Mackinder (1861–1947) countered this view. To Mackinder, the state that controlled the Eurasian geographic "heartland" had the most power: "He who rules Eastern Europe commands the Heartland of Eurasia; who rules the Heartland commands the World Island of Europe, Asia, and Africa, and who rules the World Island commands the world."[14]

Both views have empirical validity. British power in the eighteenth and nineteenth centuries was determined largely by its dominance on the seas, a power that allowed Britain to colonialize distant places, including India, much of Africa, and North and Central America. Russia's lack of easy access to the sea and its resultant inability to wield naval power has been viewed as a persistent weakness in that country's power potential. Control of key oceanic choke points—the Straits of Malacca, Gibraltar, and Hormuz; the Dardanelles; the Persian Gulf; and the Suez and Panama Canals—is viewed as a positive indicator of power potential.

Yet geographic position in Mackinder's heartland of Eurasia has also proven to be a significant source of power potential. More than any other country, Germany has acted to secure its power through its control of the heartland of Eurasia, acting very clearly according to Mackinder's dictum, as interpreted by the German geographer Karl Haushofer (1869–1946). Haushofer, who had served in both the Bavarian and the German armies, was disappointed by Germany's loss in World War I. Arguing that Germany could become a powerful state if it could capture the Eurasian heartland, he set out to make geopolitics a legitimate area for academic inquiry. He founded an institute and a journal, thrusting himself into a position as the leading supporter and proponent of Nazi expansion.

But geographic power potential is magnified or constrained by natural resources, a second source of natural power potential. Controlling a large geographic expanse is not a positive ingredient of power unless that expanse contains natural resources. Petroleum-exporting states such as Kuwait, Qatar, and the United Arab Emirates, which are geographically small but have a crucial natural resource, have greater power potential than their sizes would suggest. States need oil and are ready to pay dearly for it, and will even go to war when access to it is denied. States that have such valuable natural resources, regardless of their geographic size, wield power over states that do not. The United States, Russia, and South Africa have vast power potential because of their diverse natural resources—oil, copper, bauxite, vanadium, gold, and silver. Russia has leveraged its power from its control of natural resources to influence political outcomes in other states. For instance, Russia cut off natural gas supplies to Ukraine, thereby slowing supplies to Europe, which gets one-quarter of its gas through Ukraine. Mainland China, which supplies over 95 percent of the demand for rare earth minerals that are essential in high-tech manufacturing, has been able to use its monopoly to deny access for political purposes and drive up prices. Yet China's monopoly is not assured as new mines in Australia, the United States, India, and Vietnam open. Even natural resource–based power may have its limits.

Of course, having a sought-after resource may prove a liability, making states targets for aggressive actions, as Kuwait soberly learned in 1990. Nor does the absence of natural resources mean that a state has no power potential; Japan is not rich in natural resources, but it has parlayed other elements of power potential to make itself an economic powerhouse.

Population is a third natural source of power potential. Sizable populations, such as those of China (1.4 billion people), India (1.3 billion), the United States (323 million), Indonesia (261 million), Brazil (208 million), and Russia (144 million), automatically give power potential, and often great power status, to a state. Although a large population produces a variety of goods and services, characteristics of that population (health status, age distribution, level of social services) may magnify or constrain state power. States with small, highly educated, skilled populations, such as Switzerland, Norway, Austria, and Singapore, can fill disproportionately large economic and political niches. States with large but relatively poor populations,

Though small in population and geographic size, Japan's power potential can be understood through its vast economic influence. Here, Japanese-made cars are on sale in Germany, another country that is a top producer of automobiles.

FIGURE 4.3

Ingredients of State Power Potential

NATURAL SOURCES OF POWER:	TANGIBLE SOURCES OF POWER:	INTANGIBLE SOURCES OF POWER:
Geography	Industrial development	National image
Natural resources	Level of infrastructure	Public support
Population	Characteristics of military	Leadership

such as Ethiopia, with 102 million people but a gross domestic product of only $706 per capita, can exercise less power. States with a declining population, like Russia, or a rapidly aging one, like South Korea and Japan, may in the future suffer from a decline in this natural source of power.

Both tangible and intangible sources can affect the degree to which these natural sources of power potential are translated into actual power. These sources are used to enhance, modify, or constrain power potential (see Figure 4.3).

Tangible Sources of Power Potential

Industrial development, economic diversification, level of infrastructure, and characteristics of the military are critical tangible sources of power potential. With an advanced industrial capacity, the advantages and disadvantages of geography diminish. Air travel, for example, makes geographic expanse less of a barrier to commerce, yet at the same time, makes even large states militarily vulnerable. Industrialization modifies the importance of population, too. Large but poorly equipped armies are no match for small armies with advanced equipment. Industrialized states generally have higher educational levels and more advanced technology, and use capital more efficiently, all of which add to their power potential.

Intangible Sources of Power Potential

Intangible sources of power potential—national image, quality of government, public support, leadership, and morale—may be as important as the tangible ones. People within states have images of their own state's power potential—images that translate into an intangible power ingredient. Canadians have typically viewed themselves as internationally responsible and eager to participate in multilateral peacekeeping missions, to provide generous foreign-aid packages, and to respond unselfishly to international emergencies. The state has acted on and, indeed, helped to shape that image, making Canada a more powerful actor than its small population (36.2 million) would otherwise dictate. But images can slowly change as policy positions change. In recent years, Canada's view of itself as "helpful fixer" has waned as its defense spending and development spending—the two funding areas used to measure a state's global engagement—have lagged compared to those of other developed states.

The perception by other states of public support and cohesion is another intangible source of power. China's power was magnified during the leadership of Mao Zedong (1893–1976), when there appeared to be unprecedented public support for the communist leadership and a high degree of societal cohesion. A state government's actual support among its own population can also be a powerful mediator of state power. Israel's successful campaigns in the Middle East in the 1967 and 1973 wars can be attributed in large part to strong public support, including the willingness of Israeli citizens to pay the cost and die for their country when necessary.

When that public support is absent, particularly in democracies, the power potential of the state diminishes. Witness the U.S. loss in the Vietnam War, when challenges to, and disagreement with, the war effort undermined military effectiveness. Loss of public support may also inhibit authoritarian systems. In both the 1991 Gulf War and the 2003 Iraq War, Saddam Hussein's support from his own troops was woefully inadequate: many were not ready to die for the Iraqi regime and fled. In 2015, Iraqi soldiers once again dropped their weapons and discarded their uniforms when faced with the Islamic State onslaught. They were not ready to fight for the regime. Neither were the mercenaries Muammar Qaddafi hired ready to fight for Libya in 2011 as they left with their arms, making their way to West African states like Mali, ready to fight another day.

Leadership is another source of intangible power. Visionaries and charismatic leaders, such as India's Mohandas Gandhi, Germany's Otto von Bismarck, and Britain's Winston Churchill, were able to augment the power potential of their states by taking bold initiatives. Poor leaders, those who squander public resources and abuse the public's trust, such as Zimbabwe's Robert Mugabe, Iraq's Nouri al-Maliki, and Syria's Bashar al-Assad, diminish the state's power capability and its capacity to exert power over the long term. Liberals, in particular, pay attention to leadership: good leaders can avoid resorting to war; bad leaders may not be able to prevent it.

States can exercise intangible power characteristics in various ways. Joseph S. Nye labeled one such mechanism **soft power**, the ability to attract others because of the legitimacy of the state's values or its policies.[15] Rather than exerting its power potential to coerce states, a state can influence others through the power of its example. For the United States, its soft power resources may include its model of functioning democracy and commitment to political and civil rights. Recognizing its importance, China has tried to increase its soft power resources, spending an estimated $10 billion per year in its overseas publicity work since 2007.

Critics disagree, however, about the effectiveness of soft power. Realists might argue that it is ineffective compared to hard power. Yet when coupled with tangible sources, intangible sources of power potential might influence a state's capacity in important ways. Liberals, who have a more expansive notion of power, would more than likely place greater importance on these intangible ingredients because several reflect domestic political processes. Yet different combinations of the sources of power may produce different outcomes. The NATO alliance's victory over Slobodan Milošević's Yugoslavian forces in 1999 and Libya in 2011 can be explained by the alliance's overwhelming natural sources of power coupled with its strong tangible sources of power. But how can we explain Afghanistan's victory over the Soviet Union in the early 1980s, or the North Vietnamese victory over the United States in the 1970s, or the Algerian victory over France in the early 1960s? In each case, a country with limited natural and tangible sources of power prevailed over those with strong natural and tangible power resources. In these cases, the intangible sources of power, including the willingness of the populations to continue fighting against

Although China wields enormous economic and geographic power, it has recently made attempts to increase its influence via soft power. Funded by China, Confucian Institutes that educate students on Chinese culture have been installed in universities across the world. Here, an instructor teaches a student at the University of Zambia about Chinese culture and tradition through painting.

overwhelming odds, explain victory by the objectively weaker side.[16] Success often involves using a combination of the hard power of coercion with the soft power of persuasion and attraction. Nye calls the use of this combination "**smart power**."[17]

Constructivists recognize that power comes from tangible and intangible sources. But, they argue, it comes from more than that. It includes the power of ideas and language. State identities and nationalism are forged and changed through socialization to certain ideas and the discourse used to talk about them. All these factors matter.

The State as a Level of Analysis: The Russia-Ukraine Conflict

How can these state-level factors (their characteristics, interests, and power) help us explain the case of the Russia-Ukraine conflict? Realists would highlight the states involved as the key actors, and their security interests as central in influencing the outbreak of the conflict. It was Russia's desire to protect its national security, which leaders perceived would be threatened by the growth of the power of the United States and Europe in the region, that led Russia to act militarily against its weaker next-door neighbor, Ukraine. Preventing Ukraine from allying with these Western states would help ensure that Russian security was not jeopardized.

Liberals would also highlight the importance of the state level of analysis in understanding the conflict. However, they would more likely look to Russia's domestic characteristics, rather than just its power and security interests. For example, many liberals argue that democracies, based on their domestic characteristics, are unlikely to engage in conflict with one another. Both Russia and Ukraine lacked many of the important characteristics that help prevent democracies from going to war with each other. It is therefore not surprising that a conflict broke out when their interests clashed.

Constructivists could also make an argument about the conflict focusing on the state level of analysis. For example, constructivists would highlight the identities of the states involved. They would argue that conflict in the ideas and identities of Russia and the West led Russia to see an increase in the power of the Western states in the region as a threat.

As is the case with the international system level, using the state level of analysis has both advantages and disadvantages. The centrality of the state in international politics cannot be disputed, and looking to the state level helps highlight the interactions that define international politics today. However, states are not actually unitary actors. Individuals within states make the decisions that are then reflected in what we observe as state actions. Looking at the individual level will therefore help us better understand why some policy decisions are adopted and others are not, as well as how those decisions are made.

THE INDIVIDUAL

The third level of analysis focuses on the role of individuals in international politics. Sometimes, individual motives and preferences seem to make a difference in international politics. The example of Soviet leader Mikhail Gorbachev illustrates the ability of individual leaders to effect real change. After coming to power in 1985, he began to frame the challenges confronting the Soviet Union differently, identifying the Soviet security problem as part of the larger problem of weakness in the Soviet economy. Through a process of trial and error, and by living through and then studying failures, Gorbachev realized that the economic system had to be reformed to improve the country's security. He then took action to implement major reforms. Although he eventually lost power, he was responsible for initiating broad economic foreign policy change, including extricating the Soviet Union from its war in Afghanistan. Similarly, the Chinese leader Deng Xiaoping established himself as the architect of the new China after 1978. Under his socialist market economy, the state permitted limited private competition and gradually opened itself economically to the outside world.

Were these individuals in fact responsible for these major changes, or did individual leaders just happen to be the right people at the time? Given the same situation, would different individuals have made different decisions, thus charting different courses through international relations? The main perspectives differ in how they view the extent to which individuals matter in explaining international relations.

International Relations Perspectives and the Individual

For realists, individuals are of little importance. This position comes from the realist assumption that states are unitary actors. States are differentiated not by their government type or the personalities or styles of the leaders in office but by the relative power they hold in the international system. To the extent that mass publics can influence international relations, their actions may be reflected in the national interest. Hans J. Morgenthau explained as follows:

> The concept of national interest defined as power imposes intellectual discipline upon the observer, infuses rational order into the subject matter of politics, and thus makes the theoretical understanding of politics possible. On the side of the actor, it provides for rational discipline in action and creates the astounding continuity in foreign policy which makes American, British, or Russian foreign policy appear as an intelligible, rational continuum, by and large consistent with itself, regardless of the different motives, preferences, and intellectual and moral qualities of successive statesmen.[18]

Realists see state leaders as constrained by the state they inhabit, and neorealists see them as constrained by the international system. Those are the most relevant levels of analysis.

Most liberals recognize that leaders do make a difference and individuals may be an appropriate level of analysis. Whenever a leadership change happens in a major power such as the United States, China, or Russia, speculation always arises about possible changes in the country's foreign policy. This speculation reflects the general belief that individual leaders, and their personal characteristics and decision-making processes, do make a difference in foreign policy, and hence in international relations. According to most liberals, mass publics can also influence international relations through mass actions that pressure state leaders to pursue particular foreign policies.

Constructivists also recognize the importance of individuals. Individual state leaders can shape popular understanding of certain events through the discourse that they use to explain those events. In doing so, they shape the interests that they are expected to represent in their foreign policy decisions. For example, Iran's pursuit of nuclear technology is perceived as a threat in the United States, while the United Kingdom's possession of this technology is not. This is due, in part, to the fact that political elites talk about Iran's pursuit of this technology in a way that frames it as a threat, while this is not the case for the United Kingdom. Mass publics are also agents of potential change through discourse. For example, constructivists credit the changes made in the Soviet Union in the 1980s not only to Gorbachev as a leader but also to a network of Western-oriented policy entrepreneurs who promoted new ideas, which were then implemented.[19]

The main international relations perspectives differ not only in how they view the role of the individual, but also in how they describe the types of individuals who are likely to matter in international politics. These individuals are often political elites (political leaders and decision makers), but mass publics and even private individuals not holding official positions can play a central role.

The Role of Elites

Political elites play an important role in shaping states' foreign policies. However, some individuals seem to have a greater impact on foreign policy than others. This variation in influence is caused by the personal characteristics of individuals, their thought processes, and situational factors.

The Influence of Personality and Personal Interests

Political psychologist Margaret Hermann has found a number of personality characteristics that affect elite foreign policy behaviors, which orient individuals' views of foreign affairs. Two orientations emerge from individuals' personality traits. One type—leaders with high levels of nationalism, a strong belief in their own ability to control events, a strong need for power, low levels of conceptual complexity, and high levels of distrust of others—tends to develop an "independent" orientation to foreign affairs. The other type—leaders with low levels of nationalism, little belief in their ability to control events, a high need for affiliation, high levels of conceptual complexity, and low levels of distrust of others—tends to develop a "participatory" orientation to foreign affairs. [20] Figure 4.4 summarizes these different sets of personality characteristics.

Both Hermann and subsequent researchers using the same schema have found that these characteristics and orientations matter. For example, one study analyzed the personality characteristics of the former British prime minister Tony Blair using Hermann's categories to organize Blair's foreign policy answers to questions posed in the House of Commons.[21] The researcher found that Blair had a strong belief in his own ability to control events and a high need for power, accompanied by low conceptual complexity. These personality findings go a long way toward explaining British foreign policy toward the 2003 Iraq War, a policy that many in the government and the British public opposed. Thus, even in democracies, where institutional constraints are high, individual personality characteristics influence foreign policy orientation and behavior.

Personality characteristics affect the leadership of dictators perhaps more than that of democratic leaders because of the absence of effective institutional checks. Betty Glad analyzed the personalities of tyrants—those who rule without attention to law, capitalize on grandiose self-presentations and projects, look for every advantage, and utilize cruel, often extreme tactics. Comparing Hitler, Stalin, and Saddam Hussein, she labels them as having malignant narcissism syndrome. Glad explains how "project over-reach and creation of new enemies leads to increasing vulnerability, a deepening of the paranoiac defense, and volatility in behavior."[22]

Vladimir Putin's personal characteristics have also played an important role in shaping Russian policies. Putin has carefully crafted a strong personal image—a 5-foot-7-inch, bare-chested, horseback-riding, tiger-wrestling, race car–driving, hockey-playing macho man. He sees weakness in former leaders like Tsar Nicholas II and Mikhail Gorbachev, and has thus vowed never to bend to others. He has established excellent relations with the various religious groups in Russia and shown strong support for the Orthodox Church, a purveyor of traditional Russian values.

These personal characteristics are reflected in many Russian policies. Russia's strong stance against the expansion of NATO—to the point of taking military action against Ukraine—reflects Putin's strong desire to stand up to others (the West, in particular). His response to the "travesty" of Soviet leader Nikita

FIGURE 4.4

Personality Characteristics of Leaders

PERSONALITY CHARACTERISTICS OF LEADERS

Nationalism:	strong emotional ties to nation; emphasis on national honor and dignity
Perception of control:	belief in ability to control events; high degree of control over situations; governments able to influence state and nation
Need for power:	need to establish, maintain, and project power or influence over others
Need for affiliation:	concern for establishing and maintaining friendly relationships with others
Conceptual complexity:	ability to discuss with other people places, policies, and ideas in a discerning way
Distrust of others:	feelings of doubt, uneasiness about others; doubt about motives and actions of others

FOREIGN POLICY ORIENTATIONS

Independent leader:	high in nationalism
	high in perception of control
	high in need for power
	low in conceptual complexity
	high in distrust of others
Participatory leader:	low in nationalism
	low in perception of control
	high in need for affiliation
	high in conceptual complexity
	low in distrust of others

Source: Margaret G. Hermann, "Explaining Foreign Policy Behavior Using the Personal Characteristics of Political Leaders," *International Studies Quarterly* 24:1 (March 1980): 7–46.

Khrushchev's cession of Crimea to Ukraine in 1954 was the retaking of the peninsula in 2014, to great popular acclaim. The passage of a controversial law banning homosexual propaganda in 2013 and the failure of the government to prevent homophobic violence help illustrate Putin's support of traditional values.

Personal characteristics can even be important in explaining war. In *Why Leaders Fight*, three IR scholars show that leaders' beliefs, worldviews, and tolerance for risk and military conflict are shaped by their life experiences. Using data on these characteristics of leaders from 1875 to 2004, they show that within the constraints of domestic political institutions and the international system, the individual leader plays an important role in determining when and why states go to war.[23]

Personality characteristics, then, partly determine what decisions individual leaders make, and thus the policies adopted by the state. But to make those decisions, they have to process information about the issue at hand.

The Influence of Information Processing

Individual elites, like all people, use a variety of psychological techniques to process and evaluate information. In perceiving and interpreting new and often contradictory information, individuals rely on existing perceptions, usually based on prior experiences. Such perceptions are the "screens" that enable individuals to process information selectively; these perceptions have an integrating function, permitting the individual to synthesize and interpret the information. Perceptions also serve an orienting function, providing guidance about future expectations and expediting planning for future contingencies. If those perceptions form a relatively integrated set of images, then they are called a **belief system**.

International relations scholars have devised methods to test the existence of elite perceptions, although research has not been conducted on many individuals because sufficient data are usually unavailable. Ole Holsti systematically analyzed 434 of the publicly available statements of Secretary of State John Foster Dulles concerning the Soviet Union during the years 1953–54. His research showed convincingly that Dulles held an unwavering image of the Soviet Union, focusing on atheism, totalitarianism, and communism. To Dulles, the Soviet people were good, but their leaders were bad; the state was good, the Communist Party bad. This image was unvarying; the character of the Soviet Union did not change. Whether this perception, gleaned from Dulles's statements, affected U.S. decisions during the period cannot be stated with certainty. He was, after all, only one among a group of top leaders. Yet a plethora of decisions made during that time all consistent with his perception.[24]

Such elite mind-set studies are possible when individuals leave behind extensive written records from before, during, and after the period when they held key policy-making positions. Since few leaders leave such a record, however, our ability to empirically reconstruct elite beliefs, perceptions, or operational codes is limited, as is our ability to state with certainty their influence on a specific decision. Often, both political scientists and historians publish interpretative biographies, based on reexamination of the historical record, as previously classified documents become available. For many leaders, such as Vladimir Putin, authoritative biographies do not exist, and some leaders may try to shape their personal image for political purposes. So, based on our knowledge at this time, is Putin a realist? An idealist? Or just a pragmatist?

Our images and perceptions of the world are continually bombarded by new, sometimes overwhelming, and often discordant information. Images and belief systems, however, are not generally changed, and almost never are they radically altered. Thus, individual elites use, usually unconsciously, several psychological mechanisms to process the information they encounter in the world. Table 4.1 summarizes these different processes.

First, individuals strive for **cognitive consistency**, ensuring that their beliefs fit together into a coherent whole. For example, individuals like to believe that the enemy of an enemy is a friend, and the enemy of a friend is an enemy. Because of the tendency to be cognitively consistent, individuals select or amplify information that supports existing beliefs and ignore or downplay contradictory information. For example, because both Great Britain and Argentina were friends of the United States prior to their war over the Falkland/Malvinas Islands in 1982, U.S. decision makers denied the seriousness of the conflict. They did not think that their ally would go to war with Argentina over barren islands thousands of miles from Britain's shores. However, the United States underestimated the strength of British public support for military action and misjudged the precarious domestic position of the Argentinian generals, who were trying to bolster their power by diverting attention to a popular external conflict.

Individuals also perceive and evaluate the world according to what they have learned from past events. They look for details of a present episode that look like those of a past one, perhaps ignoring the important differences. Such similar details are often referred to as an **evoked set**. During the 1956 Suez crisis, for instance, British prime minister Anthony Eden saw Egyptian president Gamal Abdel Nasser as another Hitler. Eden recalled Prime Minister Neville Chamberlain's failed effort to appease Hitler with the Munich agreement in 1938 and thus believed that Nasser, likewise, could not be appeased. Similar thinking led some American elites to describe Iraq as another Vietnam or to see the Soviet defeat in Afghanistan as that country's Vietnam, despite critical differences.

Individual perceptions are often shaped in terms of **mirror images**: whereas one considers one's own actions good, moral, and just, one automatically finds the

TABLE 4.1

Psychological Mechanisms Used to Process Information

TECHNIQUE	EXPLANATION	EXAMPLE
Cognitive consistency	The tendency to accept information that is compatible with what has previously been accepted, often ignoring inconsistent information.	Just prior to the Japanese attack on Pearl Harbor, military spotters saw unmarked planes approaching Hawaii. Not believing the evidence, they discounted the sightings.
Evoked set	Details from a present situation that are similar to information gleaned from past situations.	During the Vietnam War, U.S. decision makers saw the Korean War as a precedent, although there were critical differences.
Mirror image	Seeing in one's opponent the opposite of characteristics seen in oneself. One views the opponent as hostile and uncompromising, whereas one views oneself as friendly and compromising.	During the Cold War, the U.S. elites and public viewed the Soviet Union in terms of their own mirror image: the United States was friendly, the Soviet Union hostile.
Groupthink	The tendency of individuals to strive for cohesion and sometimes unanimity to achieve cohesion, at the risk of not examining alternative policies	During the U.S. planning for the Bay of Pigs operation against Cuba in 1961, opponents were ostracized from the planning group.

enemy's actions evil, immoral, and unjust. Mirror imaging often exacerbates conflicts, making it even more difficult to resolve a contentious issue.

The psychological mechanisms that we have discussed so far affect the functioning of both individuals and small groups. But small groups themselves also have psychologically based dynamics that can influence decision making, such as the pressure for group conformity and solidarity. Psychologist Irving Janis identified another small group dynamic: **groupthink**.[25] Groupthink is the tendency of individuals to strive for cohesion and sometimes unanimity to achieve cohesion, at the risk of not examining alternative policies. The dynamics of the group, which include the illusion of invulnerability and unanimity, excessive optimism, the belief in the group's own morality and the enemy's evil, and the pressure placed on dissenters to change their views, lead to groupthink.

During the Vietnam War, for example, a top group of U.S. decision makers, unified by bonds of friendship and loyalty, met in what they called the Tuesday lunch group. In the aftermath of President Lyndon Johnson's overwhelming electoral win in 1964, the group basked in self-confidence and optimism, rejecting pessimistic information about North Vietnam's military buildup. When information mounted about increasing South Vietnamese and American casualties and external stresses intensified, the group further closed ranks, its members taking solace in the security of the group. Individuals who did not share the group's thinking were both informally and formally removed from the group because their prognosis that the war effort was going badly was ignored.

Political scientist Robert Jervis offers suggestions on how decision makers can safeguard their thinking and minimize mistakes due to the misperceptions that can stem from these psychological processes.[26] They need to make their assumptions and beliefs as explicit as possible, be cognizant of the pitfall of interpreting data only as consistent with one's own theory, and be willing to consider information from different angles. Yet even this awareness does not necessarily lead to rational decision making.

The Influence of Situational Factors

Individual elites and their personal characteristics and decision-making processes do not always matter to the same degree in all situations. They can most clearly affect the course of events when at least one of several factors is present. Figure 4.5 summarizes these situational factors.

First, when political institutions are unstable, young, or collapsed, leaders are able to wield significant influence. In these situations, institutions and practices are in the process of being established. An opportunity therefore exists for individual elites to shape the course of their states' trajectory by shaping these institutions and practices in particular ways. Founding fathers such as the United States' George Washington, India's Mohandas Gandhi, Russia's Vladimir Lenin, or South Africa's Nelson Mandela were able to have a great impact because they led in the early years of their nations' lives. Second, when a state's economy is in crisis, individuals can also affect their state's policies in important ways. For example, Adolf Hitler, Franklin Roosevelt, and Mikhail Gorbachev had significant influence on the policies of their states because their economies were in crisis when they came to power.

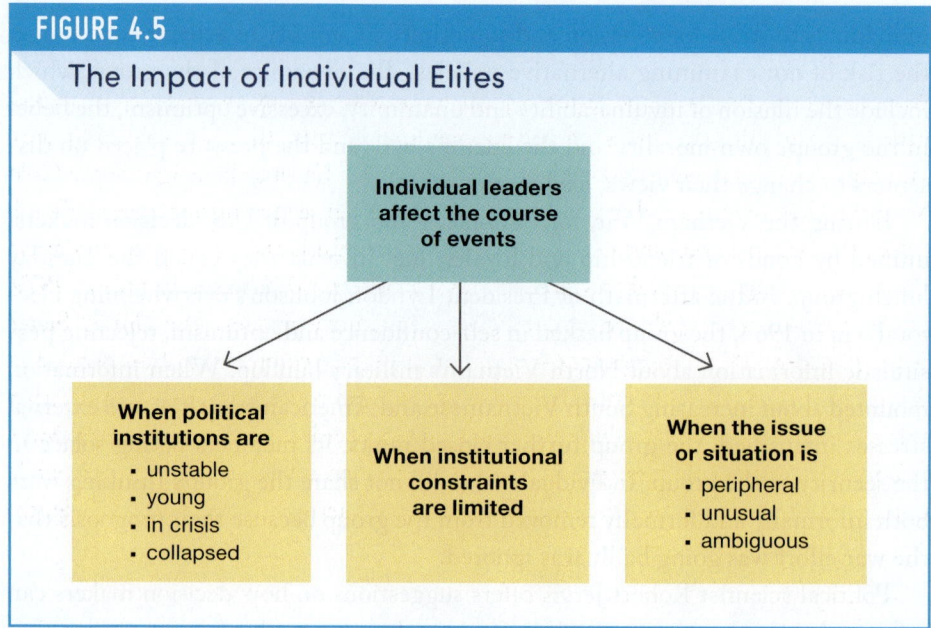

FIGURE 4.5

The Impact of Individual Elites

Individual leaders affect the course of events

When political institutions are
- unstable
- young
- in crisis
- collapsed

When institutional constraints are limited

When the issue or situation is
- peripheral
- unusual
- ambiguous

The particular solutions they chose to implement shaped their states' policies in significant ways.

Individuals also affect the course of events when they have few institutional constraints. In dictatorial or highly centralized regimes, top leaders are relatively free from domestic constraints, such as political opposition or societal inputs, and thus are able to chart courses and implement foreign policy relatively unfettered. In younger and struggling democracies, the institutions may not be well established. Indeed, Hamid Karzai of Afghanistan admitted that he relied "the very least" on his own governmental institutions, but rather, he depended on informal networks and ad hoc governance.[27]

However, political elites in democracies are also occasionally able to change policy in a dramatic fashion. For example, U.S. president Richard Nixon in 1972 was able to engineer a complete foreign policy reversal in relations with the People's Republic of China, secretly sending his top foreign policy adviser, Henry Kissinger, for several meetings with the Chinese premier Zhou Enlai and his advisers. These moves were an unexpected change, given Nixon's Republican Party affiliation and prior anticommunist record. President Barack Obama in 2015 also announced an unexpected policy reversal, opening up dialogue with Cuba after almost five decades, and the administration negotiated a framework nuclear agreement with Iran after almost four decades of little contact. But such changes may be the exception, since many democratic leaders are constrained by bureaucracies and societal groups.

The Role of Mass Publics and Private Individuals

Mass publics have the same psychological tendencies as elite individuals and small groups. They think in terms of perceptions and images, they see mirror images, and they use similar information-processing strategies. During the height of the Cold War, the United States and the Soviet Union were often seen as mirror images of each other: the one generous and peace loving, the other selfish and aggressive. Following the seizure of the U.S. embassy and the taking of over 50 hostages in Iran in 1979, public-opinion surveys showed the prevalence of mirror images. The United States (strong and brave) and its leader (safe and humane) were compared to Iran (weak and cowardly) and its leader Ayatollah Khomeini (dangerous and ruthless). Yet whether this public perception of Iran had an impact on top decision makers is unclear.[28] Mass publics' influence on foreign policy could be explained in two ways: by mass public opinion influencing decision makers, or by the masses acting (relatively) independently.

Public Opinion

The mass public might influence foreign policy via the effects of public opinion on state leaders. Masses might have opinions and attitudes about foreign policy and international relations that are different from those of the elites. If so, mass publics could affect international relations when elites listen to these opinions and adopt policies accordingly.

Sometimes a public's general foreign policy orientation reflects a perceived general mood of the population that leaders can detect. President George W. Bush was able to capitalize on the public mood in the aftermath of the attacks on September 11, 2001 (distress after being attacked on home soil) to build support for the war in Afghanistan. Even leaders of authoritarian regimes pay attention to dominant moods, with Chinese leaders curbing corruption at the local and provincial level in response to public anger.

More often than not, however, publics do not express a single, dominant mood; top leaders are usually confronted with an array of public attitudes. These opinions are registered in elections, but elections are an imperfect measure of public opinion because they merely select individuals for office—individuals who may share voters' attitudes on some issues but not on others.

In most democratic regimes, public-opinion polling provides information about public attitudes. The European Union, for example, conducts the Eurobarometer, a scientific survey of public attitudes on a wide range of issues in EU countries. Because the same questions are asked during different polls over time, state officials and the EU leadership can avail themselves of reliable data on public opinion. Likewise, the Latin American Public Opinion Project has conducted systematic surveys of Latin American citizens since the 1970s. And Afrobarometer polls conducted since 2000 chart citizen attitudes on governance and economics in almost 35 countries. But do leaders fashion policy with these attitudes in mind? Do elites change policy to reflect the preferences of the public?

Evidence from the United States suggests that elites do care about the preferences of the public, although they do not always directly incorporate those attitudes into policy decisions. Presidents care about their popularity because it affects their ability to work; a president's popularity is enhanced if he or she follows the general mood of the masses or fights for generally popular policies. Such popularity gives the president more leeway to set a national agenda, but mass attitudes may not always be directly translated into policy.

Occasionally, and quite extraordinarily, the masses may vote directly on an issue with foreign policy significance. For example, many issues related to the European Union have been put to public referendum, including the Maastricht Treaty, the EU Constitution, and the Treaty of Lisbon, as we will discuss in Chapter 9. In 2002, the Swiss people voted in a referendum to join the United Nations. In 2016, the British voted to leave the European Union. These are rather rare instances of direct public input on a foreign policy decision.

Mass Actions

The masses might also sometimes have a profound impact on international relations, regardless of anything that the elites do. At times, the masses, essentially appearing leaderless, take collective actions that have significant effects on the course of world politics. Individual acts of thousands fleeing East Germany led to the construction of the Berlin Wall in 1961. Twenty-eight years later, the spontaneous exodus of thousands of East Germans through Hungary and Austria led to the tearing down of the wall in 1989. The spontaneous movement of "boat people" fleeing Vietnam and the ragged ships leaving Cuba and Haiti for the U.S. coast resulted in changes in U.S. immigration policy. Several months of public demonstrations in Guatemala by people seeking an end to widespread corruption ultimately brought down that government in 2015. Currently, the spontaneous movement of Syrians and Iraqis fleeing their war-torn countries in masses has led to the refugee crisis in Europe.

At other times, a small elite may have acted behind the scenes or even organized mass protests, as illustrated by the "people's putsch" during October 2000 against the Yugoslavian leader Slobodan Milošević. After 13 years of his rule, people from all walks of Serbian life joined 7,000 striking miners, crippled the economic system, blocked transportation routes, and descended on Belgrade, the capital. Aided by the new technology of the time—the cell phone—they were able to mobilize citizens from all over the country, driving tractors into the city, attacking the

Parliament, and disrupting Milošević's radio and TV stations. But the opposition elite was behind the scenes, aiding in the mobilization of the masses for policy change, and as *Time* reported, "the Serbs took back their country and belatedly joined the democratic tide that swept away the rest of Eastern Europe's communist tyrants a decade ago."[29]

The people's revolution in Serbia against Milošević (the Bulldozer Revolution) proved to be a blueprint for action in other states of the postcommunist world. In Georgia, in 2003, the Rose Revolution brought a new president to power and a political dynasty was broken. In Ukraine in 2004, the Orange Revolution brought into power an opposition leader, Viktor Yushchenko, who fled to Russia a decade later following the Euromaidan Revolution, named for the central square in Kiev where the demonstrators amassed. Although these events illustrate the power of the masses and of mass communications, opposition elites played a key role.

Although the events of the Arab Spring were galvanized by the public action of a Tunisian vendor, it was a group of young private citizens, led by Google executive Wael Ghonim in late 2010, who organized a Facebook and YouTube campaign, calling on over 130,000 followers for the ouster of the government of President Hosni Mubarak of Egypt. They connected with human rights groups, raising the public awareness of the average Egyptian about governmental abuses. Collaborating

Protests in Italy evoking an "Italy First" message erupt after refugees from Syria and Iraq flood Europe in 2016. Tensions between Europeans and refugees increased after ISIS claimed responsibility for terrorist attacks in Paris.

with Mohamed ElBaradei (former director-general of the International Atomic Energy Agency and leader of an opposition political party), they became the voice behind the January 25, 2011, demonstration. Ghonim wrote, "This is Revolution 2.0. No one was a hero because everyone was a hero."[30]

The long-term impact of these revolutions, in which the masses played a role with elite support, remains in doubt. In several color-revolution states, newly instituted reforms have been overturned, or the reforms weakened, and the NGOs that they spawned have been severely restricted. In Iran, a mass opposition challenging Iranian religious and political elites in the 2009 Green Movement lost the election, and its momentum. And the future for democracy is unclear in Egypt and other Arab states. While new regimes have been voted into power, they face high expectations, steep challenges, and lingering societal opposition.

Private Individuals

Although leaders holding formal positions have more opportunity not only to participate in but also to shape international relations, private individuals can and do play key roles. Private individuals, independent of any official role, may by virtue of circumstances, skills, or resources carry out independent actions in international relations. They are less bound by the rules of the game and institutional norms. Many of these individual voices can magnify their impact through social media, including Facebook, Twitter, and blogs. From Tunisia to Colombia, Iran, and China, individuals have used these new tools to expose grievances and corruption and organize protests and demonstrations in support of their individual position.

A few individuals become crusaders for a cause because of what they have achieved or stood for. No better example exists than Malala Yousafzai, the youngest ever recipient, in 2014, of the Nobel Peace Prize. In 2009, blogging for the BBC, she gained a worldwide audience by describing the harsh life under the Taliban in Pakistan and condemning the discriminatory treatment of girls, who were banned from public schools. In 2012, a gunman shot her for speaking out, elevating her status as a fighter for women's and children's rights. Using that celebrity status, she is able to lobby heads of state and delegates to the United Nations, as well as use the public media and her own foundation to promote the cause of education for girls. Her book *I Am Malala* and a recent documentary, *He Named Me Malala*, have won high accolades.[31]

There are other individual crusaders, as well. Mohamed Bouazizi, a Tunisian vendor, set himself on fire outside a government building after state authorities confiscated his goods in 2010. The video posted on the Internet of his self-immolation was seen around the Arab world, not only leading to the overthrow of the Tunisian president, Zine al-Abidine Ben Ali, in the Jasmine Revolution but also providing the spark for the broader democratic opening in the Arab world, the Arab Spring.

The Individual

	Realism/ Neorealism	Liberalism/ Neoliberal Institutionalism	Constructivism
Overall Role of Individuals	Of little importance; states are key actors	Can make a difference in international relations	Can make a difference through their ideas and discourse
Foreign Policy Elites	Constrained by their state and the international system	Affect international relations through choices made and personality factors	Shape popular understanding of certain events through their discourse
Private Individuals	Have effect only in aggregate, as reflected in the national interest	Secondary role to elites and mass publics, but can have some influence	Actions of individuals less important than beliefs
Mass Publics	Actions may be reflected in the national interest	May affect international relations through mass actions that pressure state decision makers	Agents of potential change through discourse

The Individual as a Level of Analysis: The Russia–Ukraine Conflict

How does the individual level of analysis help us better understand the Russia–Ukraine conflict that broke out in 2014? While realists do not focus much attention on the individual, the centrality of power in their explanations of international relations could apply to this level of analysis. For example, an argument could be made that it was Putin's drive for power that led to the instigation of the conflict with Ukraine and the annexation of Crimea. His personal image, which involved standing up to the West and saying no to NATO expansion, boosted his approval ratings, thus helping to secure his power domestically.

An explanation at the individual level of analysis from the liberal perspective would likely highlight the important role that the mass public played in influencing Putin's decision to enter the conflict. Russia was in an economic crisis in 2014—an external factor that opened up the possibility for individual leaders to exert important effects on policy. In order to shift public opinion in his direction,

Putin used the diversionary tactic of war to rally the mass public around him. Pressure to secure domestic public support influenced Putin's decision.

A constructivist would go farther in focusing on Putin as an individual and the effects he had on Russia's instigation of the conflict with Ukraine. In particular, it was not simply the act of engaging in the conflict that mattered, and that rallied public opinion. It was the discourse that Putin used prior to the conflict—molding Russian identities around the importance of Crimea as an important part of Russian history and identity—that was key. With their identities shaped by Putin's discourse, Russians increasingly supported Putin after the annexation of Crimea.

As with the other levels of analysis, looking at the individual level has both advantages and disadvantages when we seek to understand international politics. It helps us understand the microfoundations of policy decisions, and thus provides important insights into how state relations play out. At the same time, however, when we look at this level of detail, we can often miss the bigger picture. Individuals do not act in a vacuum. They act within states, which exist within the overall international system. Looking at these macrolevels can help us identify patterns in state interactions that might be lost if we look solely at individual decision making.

IN SUM: SEEING THE WORLD THROUGH DIFFERENT LEVELS OF ANALYSIS

Together, the three levels of analysis provide a place to look for explanations for various international phenomena. Different perspectives place varying degrees of importance on these various levels, but each provides important insights into our understanding of international relations.

Central in all perspectives' analyses of international relations is the role played by the state. Clearly, the state is worthy of additional study. We therefore turn to a discussion of states and their tools of statecraft in the next chapter.

Discussion Questions

1. Neorealists and neoliberals agree on an essential characteristic of the international system. How do they disagree? Why is that disagreement important?

2. Leaders such as Iran's former president Mahmoud Ahmadinejad, Equatorial Guinea's Teodoro Obiang Nguema Mbasogo, and North Korea's Kim Jong-Un are often dismissed as "crazy" or "nuts." What do we mean by these characterizations? What other explanations can be offered for their behavior?

3. Mass publics are often stimulated by the media and connected by new technologies. How? Show how the Internet, cell phones, and Twitter have made a difference to international relations.

4. Find two newspaper articles that suggest the use of soft power. How can you tell whether soft power "works"?

Key Terms

belief system (p. 136)

bipolar (p. 111)

cognitive consistency (p. 137)

evoked set (p. 137)

groupthink (p. 138)

mirror image (p. 137)

multilateralism (p. 117)

multipolar (p. 111)

power (p. 125)

power potential (p. 125)

smart power (p. 131)

soft power (p. 129)

system (p. 110)

unipolar (p. 113)

CLOSED

OFFICE HOURS
VISA DESK CLOSED

PASSPORT LEGAL DESK
2 PM - 5PM
MONDAY — FRIDAY

TABBEE

As a result of the removal of American diplomatic staff in Russia, the Russian embassy in San Francisco was closed in September 2017. What does this mean for Russian–American citizens living in the United States and Russia?

5

The State and the Tools of Statecraft

Though they were bitter adversaries during the Cold War, in the 1990s the United States and Russia began to fuse a friendlier, though uneasy, relationship. Recently, however, relations between the United States and Russia have become bitter once again. In 2014, Russia took coercive military actions against Ukraine. The United States responded by placing economic sanctions on Russia. In response to possible Russian interference in the 2016 U.S. presidential election, the United States ejected 35 Russian diplomats from the country. In July 2017, the U.S. Congress increased its sanctions on Russia, in part, for its continued military actions in eastern Ukraine, and Russia responded by ordering the United States to remove 755 of its diplomatic staff from the country. The United States closed a Russian consulate in San Francisco in September 2017. A Russian spokeswoman said Russia "reserved the right to take retaliatory measures."[1] What form will that response take?

States adopt a variety of different types of policies when they interact, and these policies are often tit-for-tat actions taken in response to the behavior of the other side. But states do not always take the same actions as the states they are interacting with. How can we explain the different actions and strategies states use? When will they use force? When will they instead use economic sanctions? And when will they choose diplomatic actions as the strategy of choice? To answer these questions, first, we must understand the nature of the state and its place in the international system. Second, we must understand the types of policies available to states. Third, we must understand how decisions regarding which policies to adopt are made. We turn to these questions in this chapter.

LEARNING OBJECTIVES

▶ **Define the state, the major actor in international relations.**

▶ **Explain how the various theoretical perspectives view the state.**

▶ **Explain the various tools of statecraft.**

▶ **Analyze how democracies behave differently from nondemocracies.**

▶ **Understand the models that help us explain how states make foreign policy decisions.**

▶ **Analyze the major contemporary challenges to the state.**

THE STATE AND THE NATION

In the practice of international politics and in thinking about international relations, the state is central. What the state does and the tools of **statecraft** it exercises (its strategies for action vis-à-vis other states) are critical. Much of the history traced in Chapter 2 was the history of how the state emerged from the post-Westphalian framework and developed in tandem with sovereignty and the nation. Two of the theoretical perspectives—realism and liberalism—acknowledge the primacy of the state. Yet despite this emphasis on the state, it is inadequately conceptualized. As the scholar James Rosenau laments, "All too many studies posit the state as a symbol without content, as an actor whose nature, motives, and conduct are so self-evident as to obviate any need for precise conceptualizing. Often, in fact, the concept seems to be used as a residual category to explain that which is otherwise inexplicable in macro politics."[2] We need to do better. How do states behave in international relations, and why do they matter?

For an entity to qualify as a **state**, it must meet four fundamental legal conditions, as outlined in the 1933 Montevideo Convention. First, a state must have a territorial base, with geographically defined boundaries. Second, a stable population must reside within its borders. Third, this population should owe allegiance to an effective government. Finally, other states must recognize this state diplomatically.

These legal criteria are not absolute; they are often subject to various interpretations. Most states do have a territorial base, though the precise borders are often disputed. Until the Palestinian National Authority was given a measure of control over the West Bank, for instance, Palestine was not territorially based. Also, it is not officially recognized as a state, despite its attempt to further its status in international bodies. Possessing territory is so important that states try to extend their territory. China, for example, asserts its claims in the South China Sea by dredging sand and building landmasses on reefs in the contested Spratly Islands, in an attempt to solidify access to oil and gas reserves.

Most states have a stable population, but migrant communities and nomadic peoples cross borders, as the Maasai peoples of Kenya and Tanzania do, undetected by state authorities. Most states have some type of institutional structure for governance, but whether the people are obedient to it can be unknown due to lack of information. Such a structure might also be problematic if the government's institutional legitimacy is constantly questioned. A state need not have a particular form of government, but most of its people must acknowledge the legitimacy of that government. In 2010, the people of Egypt told the international community that they no longer recognized the legitimacy of the government led by Hosni Mubarak, leading to demonstrations and ultimately the downfall of his administration.

Finally, other states must recognize the state diplomatically. But, how many states' recognition does it take to fulfill this criterion? The Republic of Transkei—a tiny piece of real estate carved out of South Africa—was recognized by just one state, South Africa. That proved insufficient to give Transkei status as a state, and the territory was soon reincorporated into South Africa.

Some states are currently contested. In early 2008, Kosovo, once a semiautonomous part of Yugoslavia and later a province of Serbia, declared independence from Serbia. It adopted a constitution and established a ministry of foreign affairs. In 2013, Facebook gave users the option to identify themselves as citizens of Kosovo, rather than Serbia, an act that Kosovar leaders hailed as raising the country's profile and reinforcing its independence. By the end of 2016, more than 100 states had recognized Kosovo's independence, but these states did not include Serbia, Russia, and five EU members, each battling their own insurgency, which they feared might seek independence.

Other states that fulfill the four criteria but are unrecognized in the international system include Abkhazia, Nagorno-Karabakh, and South Ossetia, among others. They are variously described as "quasi-countries teetering on the brink of

Becoming a State: A View from Palestine

Palestine has been a contested territory for more than 2,000 years. Since the establishment of Israel in 1948, there have been numerous proposals for creating two states in the region—Israel for the Jewish people and Palestine for the Arab Muslim people. But after six wars and numerous rounds of negotiations, no solution to the territorial contestation has been found. Palestine has not yet become a state. But what makes a state?

The criteria for statehood are well established: a defined territory, a people living on that territory, a government to which those people are obedient, and recognition by other states. Does Palestine not meet these criteria? The territory of Palestine is known (though contested), and a people live on that territory. It has a government to which its people answer: the Palestinian National Authority. Moreover, most states in Asia, Latin America, and Africa recognize Palestine as a state. It also became a "nonmember observer state" in the United Nations in 2012 and was admitted to the International Criminal Court in 2015. Why, then, is Palestine not a state? It seems to meet all of the criteria.

The issue is a political one. To join the UN, membership must be approved by both the UN Security Council and the General Assembly. The United States, a strong ally of Israel, has veto power over Security Council decisions. Israel strongly opposes Palestinian membership and the granting of statehood through a UN process. The United States therefore opposes it as well. Both argue that rather than being granted statehood by the United Nations, a negotiated agreement must be reached between Israel and Palestine for Palestine to become a state.

That potential agreement is known as the "two-state solution." This solution would establish an independent state of Palestine alongside the state of Israel—two states for two peoples. This would allow Israel to keep its Jewish majority and democratic government while also granting the Palestinians a state.

Four main problems have been barriers to reaching this two-state solution, and thus to Palestine's ability to become a state. The first problem is that there is no consensus on where to draw the borders. Most believe that Palestine should be defined by the border that existed before the Arab-Israeli War of 1967. But Israel has constructed barriers along and within the West Bank that many worry are creating a new border that differs from that one. Israel has also built settlements in the West Bank that would make it very difficult to establish that land as part of a Palestinian state.

The second problem is that both sides claim Jerusalem as their capital. It is considered a center of worship, holy sites, and cultural heritage by both sides. The two-state solution calls for dividing Jerusalem into an Israeli west and a Palestinian east. Israel, however, has already declared Jerusalem as its "undivided capital" and is building constructions in the eastern half to entrench its control of the city. The United States further complicated the matter when President Trump formally recognized Jerusalem as the capital of Israel on December 6, 2017. These issues have made a two-state solution difficult, and Palestine does

Women Wage Peace, an Israeli and Arab women's group aimed towards establishing peace between the warring nations, gather in Jerusalem to call on their respective leaders to form a peace agreement.

not want to give up its claims on Jerusalem. Recognizing the problems the U.S. pronouncement has made for the two-state solution, the United Nations General Assembly passed a resolution on December 21, 2017, with an overwhelming vote (128 to 9, with 35 abstentions) demanding that the United States rescind its declaration on Jerusalem. As the minister of foreign affairs of Palestine has argued, "There is no two-state solution possible without East Jerusalem as the capital of Palestine."[a]

The third problem is that during the 1948 Arab-Israeli War, a large number of Palestinians fled or were forced from their homes on territory that is now part of Israel. They believe they have the right to return. This is not an option that Israel is even willing to consider.

Finally, the fourth problem is security. Palestine seeks an end to foreign military occupation. Israel, however, wants to protect its ability to defend against other states, which would require keeping a military presence in parts of the West Bank. Israel also fears that a new Palestinian state would either be sensitive to the preferences of Hamas—a group that controls the Gaza Strip and that does not want peace with Israel—or be too weak to prevent Hamas from taking over the West Bank.

Together, these seemingly irreconcilable differences, combined with frequent outbreaks of violence between the two sides, have made achieving a two-state solution extremely difficult. Palestine has thus chosen to adopt a unilateral diplomatic approach, which has led to its recognition by many other states in the system, "observer state" status in the United Nations, and membership in the International Criminal Court. Whether these diplomatic efforts will eventually result in international legal statehood and full membership in the United Nations, however, has yet to be seen. In all likelihood, whether or not it does will depend on how its political relationship with Israel and the United States continues in the future.

a. United Nations, "Jerusalem Critical in Negotiated Two-State Solution to Palestine Question, Says Secretary-General's Special Representative as International Conference Opens" (press release), GA/PAL/1362, May 3, 2016, www.un.org/press/en/2016/gapal1362.doc .htm (accessed 12/4/17).

FOR CRITICAL ANALYSIS

1. Beyond simply being a full member of the UN, what would formal statehood give Palestine that it does not have with its current status? What is so important about being formally recognized as a state?

2. Do you think Palestine's unilateral diplomatic approach to achieving statehood will eventually work? Or will it have to reach an agreement with Israel to be granted formal state status? What would it take for Palestine's unilateral approach to work?

to the small island of Taiwan. Both governments claimed to represent the Chinese nation, and the PRC has always maintained that Taiwan is an inseparable part of China—a policy it calls "the One-China policy." The relationship between China and Taiwan became more complicated after democracy was established in Taiwan in 1990, since one major political party supports independence for Taiwan while the other supports a continuation of the status quo.

The so-called China question—the conflict over the state and nation of China—continues today. A top-level contact, the first in 66 years, occurred in late 2015 between President Xi Jinping of the mainland and President Ma Ying-jeou of Taiwan. However, in response to President Ma's "warming" toward China, an electoral backlash followed. Tsai Ing-wen, a member of the opposing party with nationalist Taiwanese sentiments, won the presidential election in early 2016. China responded by suspending official contact with Taiwan. At the 19th national congress in China in 2017, President Xi announced in a speech that China has the ability to thwart any independence attempts by Taiwan, but tempered that statement with calls for unobstructed exchanges between the two sides. Whether any change in Chinese-Taiwanese relations will occur, however, remains unknown.

Disputes over state territories and the desires of nations to form their own states have been major sources of instability and even conflict since the end of colonialism in Africa and the Middle East, and most recently, after the break-ups of the Soviet Union and Yugoslavia. Another of these intractable conflicts is that between Israeli Jews and Palestinian Arabs, who each claim the same territory. This conflict has been complicated by several factors: Jews, Christians, Muslims, and Bahá'ís each claim certain land and monuments as sacred; Arab states intensely oppose the existence of the state of Israel; and Israel has gradually expanded its territory through war and settlements. Since the founding of Israel in 1948, the Arab and Jewish peoples of Palestine have been involved in six interstate wars and three popular uprisings. Civilians on both sides have been harmed and killed, and many continue to live as refugees. Policy makers have debated several alternatives. Should Israel and the Palestinian territories be divided into two separate independent states? The complicated boundaries exacerbated by the increasing number of Jewish settlers on the West Bank make that solution increasingly unlikely. Should the two nations be part of one multinational state? That would likely mean the end of the Jewish democratic state. Or should the Palestinians focus on attaining rights other than self-determination—basic political and civil rights—within the current structure?

States are central actors in international relations. Being recognized as a state therefore has great significance, as it influences a people's ability to act in the international system. But *how* do states act in the international system? What are the methods they use to influence one another and pursue their interests?

TOOLS OF STATECRAFT

States use a variety of techniques to exert influence in international relations. These techniques include diplomacy, economic statecraft, and the use of force. All three techniques require **credibility** on the part of the state that seeks to use them to exert influence. In other words, a state must have both the *ability* and the *incentive* to act using a certain policy in order for other states to believe that it will see it through. If it lacks either the ability or the incentive to carry out a stated policy, the policy is not a credible one. Other states are not likely to believe the state will actually act on the policy, and will thus not change their behavior. The effects of the stated policy will be lost. However, if its policy choices are seen as credible by others, a state can potentially exert influence over other states using policies of diplomacy, economic statecraft, and/or force.

In a particular situation, a state may begin with one approach and then try several others to influence the intended target. In other cases, a state may use several different techniques simultaneously. The techniques that political scientists think states emphasize vary across the theoretical perspectives. In addition, different types of states may make different choices.

The Art of Diplomacy

In traditional **diplomacy**, states try to influence the behavior of other actors by bargaining, negotiating, taking a specific action or refraining from such an action, or appealing to the foreign public for support of a position.

According to Harold Nicolson, a British diplomat and writer, diplomacy usually begins with negotiation, through direct or indirect communication, in an attempt to reach agreement. Parties may conduct this negotiation tacitly, with each party recognizing that a move in one direction leads the other to respond in a way that is strategic. The parties may also conduct open, formal negotiations, in which one side offers a formal proposal and the other responds. This process is generally repeated many times until the parties reach a compromise. In either case, reciprocity usually occurs, whereby each side responds to the other's moves in kind.

States seldom enter diplomatic bargaining or negotiations as power equals. Each state knows its own goals and power potential, of course, and has some idea of its opponent's goals and power potential, although information about the opponent may be imperfect, incomplete, or just wrong. Thus, although the outcome of the negotiating is almost always mutually beneficial (if not, why bother?), that outcome is not likely to please the parties equally. And the satisfaction of each party may change as new information is revealed or as conditions change over time.

Bargaining and negotiations are complex processes, complicated by at least two critical factors. First, most states carry out two levels of bargaining simultaneously. The first level is international bargaining between and among states. The second level is bargaining between the state's negotiators and its various domestic constituencies, both to reach a negotiating position and to ratify the agreement. The political scientist Robert Putnam refers to this as a "two-level game."[6]

The negotiations between Iran and the P5+1 over Iran's nuclear weapons programs illustrate the two-level game. Each country conducted two sets of negotiations: one with the foreign states and the other within its own domestic political arena. Iran's negotiators had to satisfy the demands of Supreme Leader Ali Khamenei, whose strident words to the country's conservative constituency extolled Iran's sovereignty to make its own security choices, while at the same time keeping the United States and its partners hopeful that a compromise could be negotiated. The U.S. negotiators had to mollify the demands of their domestic opposition, including members of the Republican Party, supporters of Israel, and the pro-Israel American Israel Public Affairs Committee (AIPAC), which opposed any negotiations with terrorist state Iran. What makes the game unusually complex, according to Putnam, is that "moves that are rational for one player at one board . . . may be impolitic for that same player at the other board."[7] The negotiator is the formal link between the two levels of negotiation. Realists see the two-level game as constrained primarily by the structure of the international system, whereas liberals more readily acknowledge domestic pressures and incentives.

Second, bargaining and negotiating are, in part, a culture-bound activity. Approaches to bargaining vary across cultures—a view accepted among liberals, who place importance on state differences. At least two styles of negotiations have been identified.[8] These two different styles may lead to contrasting outcomes. The more advanced industrialized states, like the United States, Great Britain, and Germany, favor discussion of concrete detail, eschewing grand philosophical debate. Other states, many in the developing world, argue in a deductive style—from general principles to particular applications. This approach may mask conflict over details until a later stage in the process. These differences in negotiating approaches can lead to stalemate or even, occasionally, negotiation failure.

The use of **public diplomacy** is an increasingly popular diplomatic technique in a communication-linked world. Public diplomacy involves targeting both foreign publics and elites, attempting to create an overall image that enhances a country's ability to achieve its diplomatic objectives. For instance, as secretary of state, Hillary Rodham Clinton traveled to more than 100 countries, highlighting the role of women and promoting values, democracy, and human rights. China's public diplomacy has used Confucius Institutes to promote Chinese language and culture worldwide.

Before and during the 2003 Iraq War, public diplomacy became a particularly useful diplomatic instrument. American administration officials not only made the case for war to the American people in news interviews and newspaper op-ed pieces but also lobbied friendly and opposing states, both directly in negotiations and indirectly through various media outlets, including independent Arab media such as the Qatar-funded Al Jazeera television network. The U.S. Department of State established the Middle East Radio Network, comprising both Radio Sawa and Alhurra. Radio Sawa broadcasts both Western and Middle Eastern popular music with periodic news briefs. The more controversial Alhurra, begun in 2004, has attracted much of the Iraqi market, and during the Arab Spring in Egypt, an estimated 25 percent of people living in Cairo and Alexandria listened to this news source. Al Jazeera remains the number-one news source for an estimated 55 percent of the Arab world. States in the communication age clearly have public diplomacy as a diplomatic policy instrument at their disposal. However, whether public diplomacy changes "hearts and minds" is debatable.

Track-two diplomacy is another type of diplomacy, but one that is not directly linked to the government of the state. Track-two diplomacy uses individuals outside the government to carry out negotiations. In some cases, this type of diplomacy has resulted in success. In the spring of 1992, for example, Eritrea signed a declaration of independence, seceding from Ethiopia after years of both low- and high-intensity conflict. The foundation for the agreement was negotiated in numerous informal meetings in Atlanta, Georgia, and elsewhere, between the affected parties and former president Jimmy Carter, acting through the Carter Center's International Negotiation Network at Emory University.

Other types of track-two diplomacy involve the lengthier process of sustained dialogue. In some cases, unofficial individuals from different international groups are brought together in small problem-solving workshops so they can develop personal relationships and an understanding of the problems from the perspective of others. It is hoped that these individuals will then seek to influence public opinion in their respective states, trying to reshape, and often rehumanize, the image of the opponent. This approach has been used to address the Protestant-Catholic conflict in Northern Ireland and the Arab-Israeli dispute. Problem-solving workshops have been conducted over decades, and cooperative activities encouraged. Systematic studies about their effectiveness have yet to be written.

While it can be effective, diplomacy may need to encompass more than conducting negotiations and persuading the public. Negotiators may find they need to use other measures of statecraft, including positive incentives (such as diplomatic recognition or foreign aid in return for desired actions) and the threat of negative consequences (such as reduction or elimination of foreign aid, severance of diplomatic ties, or use of coercive force) if the target state continues to move in a specific direction. The tools of statecraft are not only diplomatic but also economic and military.

The liberal view is that talking, via all forms of diplomacy, is better than not talking to one's adversaries. Whatever the differences, liberals assert, discussion clarifies the issues, narrows differences, and encourages bargaining. Use of more forceful actions, like economic statecraft and military force, may make diplomacy less effective and should be a last resort.

Realists are more skeptical about the value of diplomacy. While they acknowledge that diplomacy has some benefits, realists tend to see state goals as inherently conflictual. Thus, to them, negotiations and diplomacy are apt to be effective only when backed by force, either economic or military.

Economic Statecraft

States use more than words to exercise power. They may use economic statecraft—both **engagement** (sometimes called positive sanctions) and **sanctions** (or negative sanctions)—to try to influence other states.[9] Engaging another state involves offering a "carrot," enticing the target state to act in the desired way by rewarding moves it makes in the desired direction. The assumption is that positive incentives will lead the target state to change its behavior. Sanctions, however, may be imposed more often: a state may threaten to act, or actually take actions, to punish the target state for moves it makes in the direction not desired. The goal of using the "stick" (sanctions) may be to punish the target state for actions it has already taken or may be to try to change the future behavior of the target state. Table 5.1 provides examples of both positive engagement and negative sanctions.

Since the mid-1990s, states have increasingly imposed **smart sanctions**, including freezing assets of governments and/or individuals and imposing commodities sanctions (e.g., on oil, timber, or diamonds). Targeting has involved not just "what" but also "who"; the international community has tried to affect specific individuals and rebel groups, reduce ambiguity and loopholes, and avoid the high humanitarian costs of general sanctions. Despite these modifications, liberals are still wary of sanctions, believing instead that diplomacy is a more effective way for states to achieve international goals. Realist theorists, on the other hand, believe it is necessary in exercising power to resort to, or threaten to use, sanctions or force more regularly.

A state's ability to use these instruments of economic statecraft depends on its power potential. States with a variety of power sources have more instruments at their disposal. Clearly, only economically well-endowed countries can offer investment guarantees, grant preferences to specific countries, house foreign assets, grant licenses, or boycott effectively.

TABLE 5.1

Instruments of Economic Statecraft

POSITIVE ENGAGEMENT

THE ACTIVITY	EXAMPLE
Give the target state the same trading privileges given to your best trading partner (most-favored-nation [MFN] status) as incentive for policy change.	The United States granted MFN status to China, in spite of that country's poor human rights record.
Allow sensitive trade with target state, including militarily useful equipment.	France exports military equipment to Saudi Arabia, Qatar, and Egypt to build positive alliances in the region, despite their repressive political tactics.
Give corporations investment guarantees or tax breaks as incentives to invest in target state.	The United States offered insurance to U.S. companies willing to invest in post-apartheid South Africa.
Allow importation of target state's products into your country at best tariff rates.	Industrialized states allow imports from developing countries at lower tariff rates.

NEGATIVE SANCTIONS

THE SANCTION	EXAMPLE
Freeze target state's assets.	The United States froze Iranian assets during 1979 hostage crisis; Islamic State and al-Nusra Front assets, 2014 to present.
Arms embargo.	South Africa, 1977–94, in reaction to apartheid regime; North Korea, 2006 to present, in reaction to its military developments.
Export or import limits of selected technology and products.	Côte d'Ivoire (ban on diamonds, a significant source of income for violent groups), 2004–14; Somalia (ban on charcoal industry, the main source of income for al-Shabaab), 2012 to present.
Comprehensive sanctions.	U.S. sanctions against Myanmar, 1997–2016, to isolate military junta ruling the country; U.S. sanctions against Iraq, 1990–2003, to pressure regime to dismantle weapons of mass destruction.

Some liberals, however, argue that developing states do have some leverage in economic statecraft under special circumstances. If a state or group of states controls a key resource whose production is limited, their power is strengthened. Among the primary commodities, petroleum has this potential, and it gave the Arab members of the Organization of the Petroleum Exporting Countries (OPEC) the ability to impose oil sanctions on the United States and the Netherlands when those two countries strongly supported Israel in the 1973 Arab-Israeli War.

The ability of sanctions to alter a target state's behavior appears mixed. South Africa illustrates a case of relative success in the use of economic sanctions. When the Reagan administration's "constructive engagement" policy failed to work, the U.S. Congress approved harsh sanctions against South Africa's apartheid regime in 1986, over a presidential veto. Under the Comprehensive Anti-Apartheid Act, the United States joined with other countries and the United Nations, which had already imposed economic sanctions. In 1992, the white-controlled South African regime announced a political opening that led to the end of apartheid and white-minority rule. Most commentators conclude that sanctions probably had an important effect on the regime's decision to change policy, but that was not the sole explanation.

Economic statecraft does not always lead to the intended outcome. In 1960, the United States imposed an economic, commercial, and financial embargo against Cuba, designed to punish the communist regime under Fidel Castro. Those restrictions were strengthened and codified in 1992, making it the longest trade embargo in history. Despite these sanctions, however, a transition of power away from the communist government of Cuba has never taken place. Concluding that the sanctions had not worked, the Obama administration began a new era of positive engagement in late 2014. Talking with Cuba's leaders and bureaucrats, reopening the U.S. embassy in Havana, and using executive power to loosen a host of travel and commercial restrictions, including removing Cuba from the list of states sponsoring terrorism, would begin the engagement process. While only Congress can lift the economic embargo, the Obama administration embarked on a totally different strategy, to the consternation of some Florida-based older Cubans and many Republicans. In 2017, the Trump administration announced that it would reverse this positive engagement process. While most of the changes implemented by the Obama administration remained in place, restrictions on travel would be more stringently enforced, travelers would face new restrictions on how they could spend money in Cuba, and a confrontational rhetoric came to define U.S. policy. Whether or not moving away from positive engagement will influence the government of Cuba's policies, however, is unknown.

Iraq and Russia represent cases of ambiguous results for sanctioning, albeit for different reasons, and illustrate the difficulty in evaluating the policy's effectiveness. Between 1991 and 2003, Iraq was subject to comprehensive sanctions designed to pressure the Saddam Hussein regime to dismantle its weapons of mass destruction, and ultimately to bring down the government. The sanctions may have achieved the first goal of driving the disarmament process. The more general goal of removing Saddam from power was not achieved; accomplishing that goal would require military action. We can also see ambiguous results in the sanctions the European Union and the United States imposed against Russia in 2014. These sanctions were in response to Russia's annexation of the Crimean Peninsula and its support of separatists in Ukraine. The Russian economy was clearly hurt. It shrank in early 2015 by 2 percent, losing $26.8 billion in value. Russian officials acknowledged "meaningful" economic harm but maintained that the price was worth it. They would continue to support Ukrainian separatists, even if sanctions adversely affected their economy. In 2017, the U.S. Congress imposed a new wave of sanctions on Russia for a variety of reasons, including its continued military activity in eastern Ukraine. Whether this round of sanctions will be more effective in eliciting policy change, however, has yet to be seen.

Sanctions the United States and the European Union took against Iran and its petrochemical and oil industries in 2011–13, designed to cut off that country from the international financial system, produced different results. Iran experienced an estimated $9 billion loss every quarter, leading to a dramatic decline in the value of its currency and weakening the Iranian economy; this decline directly affected the population, which experienced shortages in all sectors. That outcome may have led Iran to the negotiating table in 2014–15, although we cannot prove that was the cause or the reason for the final agreement.

So how successful are sanctions as a tool of statecraft? One empirical study of UN-imposed sanctions (62 cases) differentiates between various kinds of sanctions: sanctions that intend to change behavior; sanctions that constrain access to critical goods or funds; and sanctions that signal or stigmatize targets in support of international norms. The study found that sanctions were effective 22 percent of the time in achieving at least one of the three purposes. They were more effective in signaling or constraining a target than in coercing a change in behavior. In only 10 percent of the cases were sanctions effective in actually changing behavior.[10]

These findings suggest that while sanctions are typically viewed as a cheaper and easier tool for coercion and punishment than the use of armed force, they may be effective only in limited cases. These outcomes have led realist theorists to conclude that states must use the threat of force to achieve their objective of changing the behavior of another state.

The Use of Force

Force (and the threat of force) is another critical instrument of statecraft and is central to realist thinking. As with economic statecraft, a state may use force or the threat of force either to get a target state to do something or to undo something that state has already done—compellence—or to keep an adversary from doing something in the future—deterrence.[11]

With the strategy of **compellence**, a state threatens to use force to try to get another state to do something or to undo an act it has undertaken. An excellent example is the prelude to the 2003 Iraq War, when the United States and others threatened Saddam Hussein that if certain actions were not taken, then war would follow. Threats began when George W. Bush labeled Iraq a member of the "axis of evil," and escalated when the United Nations found Iraq to be in material breach of a UN resolution. Then in March 2003, Great Britain, one of the coalition partners, gave Iraq ten days to comply with the UN resolution. And on March 17, the last compellent threat was issued: President George W. Bush gave Saddam's Baathist regime 48 hours to leave Iraq as its last chance to avert war. In all of these cases, it was necessary to resort to an invasion because compellence via an escalation of threats failed.

With the strategy of **deterrence**, states commit themselves to punishing a target state if that state takes an undesired action. Threats of actual war are used as an instrument of policy to dissuade a state from pursuing certain courses of action. If the target state does not take the undesired action, deterrence is successful and conflict is avoided. If it does choose to act, despite the deterrent threat, then the first state will presumably deliver a devastating blow.

Since the advent of nuclear weapons in 1945, deterrence has taken on a special meaning. Today, if a state chooses to resort to violence against a nuclear state, nuclear weapons might be launched against it in retaliation. If this happens, the cost of the aggression will be unacceptable, especially if both states have nuclear weapons—the viability of both societies would be at stake. Theoretically, states that recognize the destructive capability of nuclear weapons will therefore be hesitant to take aggressive action. It is difficult for a state to know with absolute certainty that it could annihilate its adversary's nuclear capability in one go (the ability to do so is called first-strike capability). Even the possibility that the adversary could respond with its second-strike capability would result in restraint. Deterrence is then successful.

For either compellence or deterrence to be effective, states must lay the groundwork. They must clearly and openly communicate their objectives and capabilities, be willing to make good on threats or fulfill promises, and have the capacity to follow through with their commitments. In short, a state's credibility is essential for compellence and deterrence. Yet this is not a one-sided, unilateral process. It is a strategic interaction in which the behavior of each state is determined not only by each state's own behavior but also by the actions and responses of the other.

Compellence and deterrence can fail, however. If they do, states may go to war. But even during war, states have choices. They choose the type of weaponry (nuclear or nonnuclear, strategic or tactical, conventional or cyber), the kind of targets (military or civilian, urban or rural), and the geographic location to be targeted (city, state, region). They may choose to respond in kind, to escalate, or to de-escalate.

Which of these policies to adopt—as well as the broader question of whether to use diplomatic, economic, or military strategies when engaging with other states—is a strategic choice states must make. It is therefore important to understand how these foreign policy decisions are made.

MODELS OF FOREIGN POLICY DECISION MAKING

How do states actually make specific foreign policy decisions? How do they decide which instruments of statecraft to use? Do democracies make foreign policy choices differently from the way nondemocracies do? How do the different theories view the decision-making process? Differences depend in large part on how we view subnational actors—state leaders, the mass public, interest groups, nongovernmental organizations (NGOs), and businesses.

The Rational Model: The Realist Approach

Most policy makers—particularly during crises—and most realists begin with the rational model, which conceives of foreign policy as actions the national government chooses to maximize its strategic objectives. The state is assumed to be a unitary

In addition to consulting with various experts when confronting a foreign policy decision, leaders will often consult with their own staff to devise a strategy for reaching their intended goals. Here, Spain's prime minister Mariano Rajoy speaks with advisers during a summit for European leaders.

actor with established goals, a set of options, and an algorithm for deciding which option best meets its goals. The process is relatively straightforward. Taking as our case the 1996 incident in which the People's Republic of China (PRC) tested missiles by launching them over the Republic of China (ROC; Taiwan), a rational approach would view Taiwan's decision-making process about how to respond in the following manner (the numbers correspond to the numbered steps in Figure 5.1):

1. The PRC was testing missiles over the ROC in direct threat to the latter's national security.

2. The goal of both the ROC and its major supporter, the United States, was to stop the firings immediately.

3. The ROC decision makers had several options: do nothing; wait until after the upcoming elections; issue diplomatic protests; bring the issue to the UN Security Council; threaten or conduct military operations against the PRC; or threaten or use economic statecraft (cut trade, impose sanctions or embargoes).

4. The ROC leaders analyzed the benefits and costs of these options: doing nothing would suggest that the missile testing was acceptable; the PRC would exercise its veto in the UN Security Council; any economic or military actions the ROC undertook were unlikely to be successful against the stronger adversary, potentially leading to the destruction of Taiwan.

5. The ROC weighed these costs against the possible benefits of each policy, and chose the one with the most benefits relative to costs. With U.S. support, it chose diplomatic protest as a first step.

Crises such as this have a unique set of characteristics: decision makers are confronted by a surprising, threatening event; they have only a short time to make a decision about how to respond; often a limited number of decision makers are involved in top-secret proceedings; and there is little time for substate actors to have much influence. In these circumstances, using the rational model as a way to assess the other side's behavior is an appropriate choice.

In a noncrisis situation, when a state knows very little about the internal domestic processes of another state—as the United States knew little about mainland China during the era of Mao Zedong—decision makers have little alternative but to assume that the other state will follow the rational model. Indeed, in the absence of better information, most U.S. assessments of decisions the Soviet Union took during the Cold War were based on a rational model. Only after the opening of the Soviet governmental archives following the end of the Cold War did historians find that, in fact, the Soviets had no concrete plans for turning Poland, Hungary, Romania, or other East European

FIGURE 5.1

The Rational Model of Decision Making

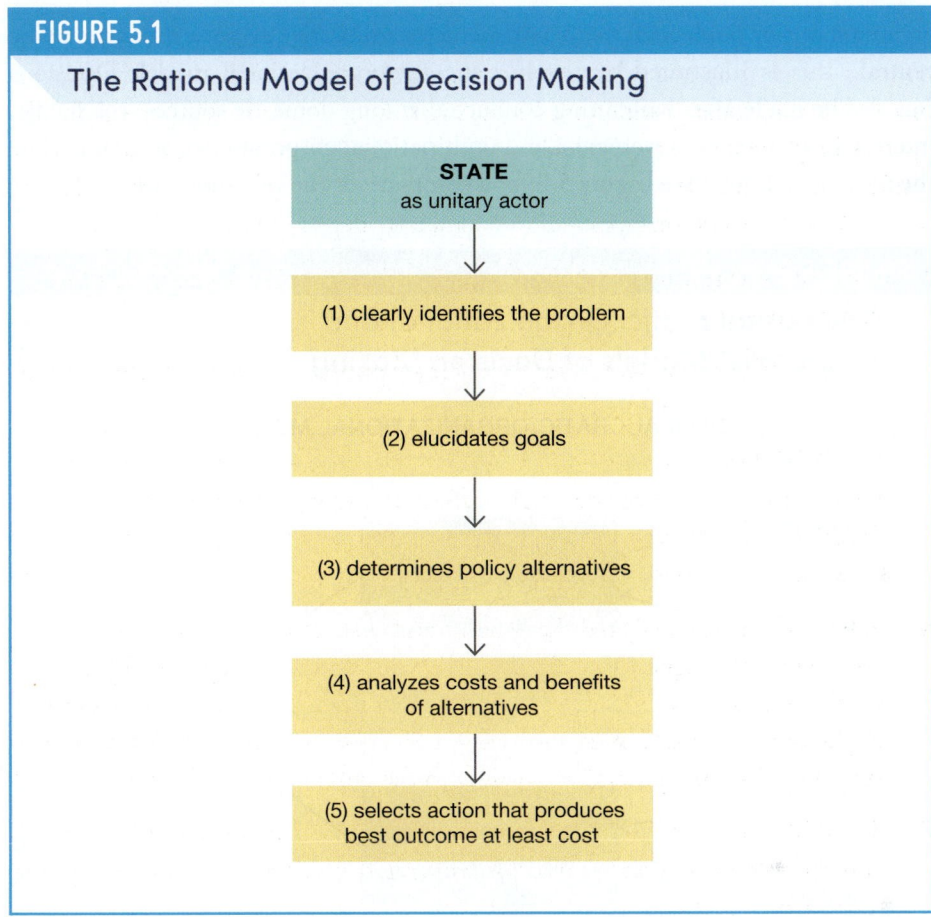

STATE
as unitary actor

(1) clearly identifies the problem

(2) elucidates goals

(3) determines policy alternatives

(4) analyzes costs and benefits
of alternatives

(5) selects action that produces
best outcome at least cost

states into communist dictatorships or socialist economies, as the United States had believed. The Soviets appear to have been guided by events happening in the region, not by specific ideological goals and rational plans.[12] The United States was incorrect in imputing the rational model to Soviet decision making, but in the absence of complete information, this was the least risky approach: the anarchy of the international system means a state assumes that its opponent engages in rational decision making.

The Bureaucratic/Organizational Model and the Pluralist Model: The Liberal Approaches

Not all decisions occur during crises, and not all decisions are made with so little knowledge of domestic politics in other countries. In these instances, foreign policy decisions may be products of other types of processes. Subnational governmental organizations or bureaucracies (departments or ministries of government) may be central. This is illustrated by the bureaucratic/organizational model. Decisions can also be made after bargaining conducted among domestic sources (the public, interest groups, mass movements, and multinational corporations), as captured by the pluralist model. (See Figure 5.2 for a summary of the two models.)

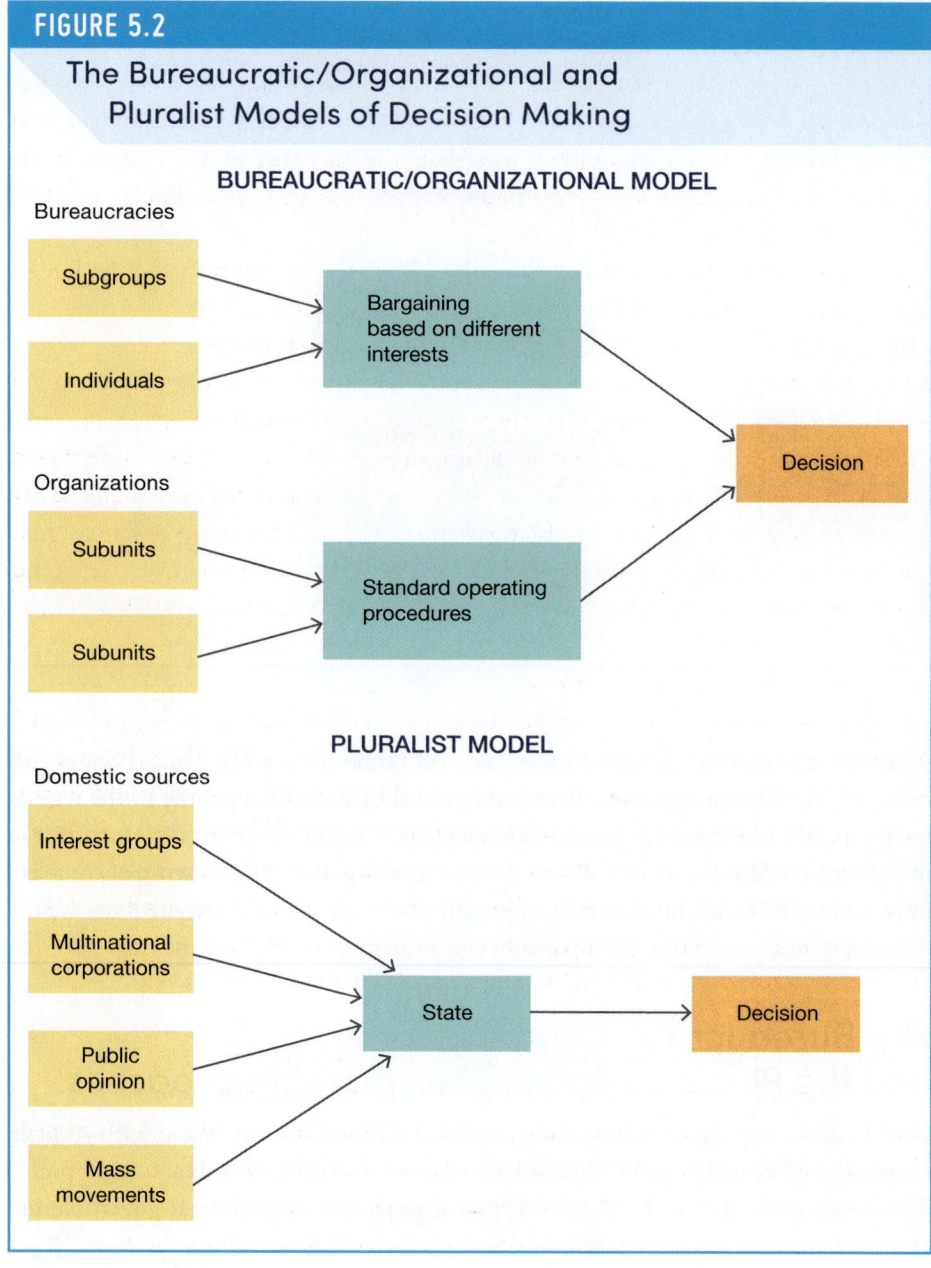

FIGURE 5.2

The Bureaucratic/Organizational and Pluralist Models of Decision Making

The first case—the bureaucratic/organizational model—highlights the role that subnational governmental organizations and bureaucracies can play in influencing foreign policy decisions. **Organizational politics** emphasizes an organization's standard operating procedures and processes. Decisions arising from organizational processes depend heavily on precedents; major changes in policy are unlikely. Conflicts can occur when different subgroups within the organization have different goals and procedures. Often particular interest groups or NGOs have strongly influenced those different goals. In models of **bureaucratic politics**, members of the bureaucracy representing different interests negotiate decisions. Decisions determined by bureaucratic politics flow from the push and pull, or tug-of-war, among these departments, groups, or individuals. In either political scenario, the ultimate decision depends on the relative strength of the individual bureaucratic players or the organizations they represent.

Both trade and environmental policy are prominent examples of the bureaucratic/organizational model of decision making at work in noncrisis situations. Bureaucracies in the ministries of agriculture, industry, and labor in the case of trade, and environment, economics, and labor in the case of the environment, fight particularly hard within their own governments for policies favorable to their constituencies. Substate groups develop strong relationships with these ministries to ensure favorable outcomes. When time is no real constraint, informal bureaucratic groups and departments are free to mobilize. They hold meetings, hammering out positions that satisfy all the contending interests. The decisions reached are not always the most rational ones; rather, the groups are content with **satisficing**—that is, settling for a decision that is a minimally acceptable solution, even if that decision is not the best possible outcome.

Liberals especially turn to this model of decision-making behavior in their analyses because, for them, the state is only the playing field; the actors are the competing interests in bureaucracies and organizations. The model is most relevant in large democratic countries, which usually have highly differentiated institutional structures for foreign policy decision making and where responsibility and jurisdiction are divided among several different units. But to use this model in policy-making circles to analyze or predict other states' behavior, or to use it to analyze decisions for scholarly purposes, one must have detailed knowledge of a country's foreign policy structures and bureaucracies.

The second case—the **pluralist model**—focuses on the fact that societal groups may play very important roles in the foreign policies adopted by states. This is especially the case in noncrisis situations and on particular types of issues, often economic ones. The pluralist model captures decision-making processes involving these types of actors. Societal groups have a variety of ways of forcing favorable decisions or constraining adverse decisions. They can mobilize the process. They help us understand where foreign policies come from. However, they do not tell us what the content of the resulting policies will be. What are states' foreign policies actually going to look like? We now turn to this question, focusing on the content of the foreign policies of different states—democracies and autocracies, in particular.

DEMOCRACIES, AUTOCRACIES, AND FOREIGN POLICY

Do democratic states conduct foreign policy and make policy choices that are any different from the choices and policies authoritarian states and leaders make? We might expect that in democratic states, the intangible sources of power discussed in Chapter 4—national image, public support, and leadership—would matter more, because the leaders are responsible to the public through elections. If that expectation is true, then do the foreign policies adopted by democratic states differ from the policies of nondemocratic or authoritarian states?

This question has occupied philosophers, diplomatic historians, and political scientists for centuries. In *Perpetual Peace* (1795), Immanuel Kant argued that the spread of democracy would change international politics by eliminating war. He reasoned that the public would be very cautious in supporting war because they, the public, would likely suffer the most devastating effects. Thus, leaders would act in a restrained fashion and tend to abstain from war because of domestic constraints.[14] Since Kant's time, other explanations have been added to the democratic-peace hypothesis. Liberals point to the notion of shared domestic norms and joint membership in international institutions to explain peace among democracies. And because democratic states trade more with each other than with nondemocratic states, they prefer to benefit from those economic gains made during peacetime. Many of these ideas found resonance with Woodrow Wilson, a major advocate of the democratic peace. Realists, too, point to the fact that democracies are more likely to adopt more peaceful policies toward each other. By belonging to the same alliances, democratic states are more effective at practicing balance-of-power politics, decreasing the probability of war.

Political scientists have developed an extensive research agenda related to this idea of a democratic peace. Are democracies more peaceful than nondemocracies are? Do democracies fight each other less than nondemocracies do? Do democracies fight nondemocracies more than they fight each other? Or is there a "capitalist peace"? Does capitalism explain the pacifying effects of democracy on interstate conflict? Gathering data on different kinds of warfare over several centuries, researchers have addressed these questions. One study has confirmed the hypothesis that democracies do not go to war against each other: since 1789, no wars have been fought strictly between independent states with democratically elected governments. Another study has found that wars involving democracies have tended to be less bloody but more protracted, although between 1816 and 1965 democratic governments were not noticeably more peaceable or passive. Other studies have shown that socioeconomic factors and globalization have a more important pacifying effect than democracy or economic interdependence has.[15] But the evidence is not that clear-cut, and explanations are partial.

Why have some of the findings on the democratic peace been so divergent? Scholars who use the behavioral approach themselves point to some of the difficulties. Some researchers analyzing the democratic peace use different definitions of the key variables, democracy and war. Some researchers distinguish between liberal democracies (for example, the United States and Germany) and illiberal democracies (Yugoslavia in the late 1990s). Also, the data for war would be different if wars with fewer than 1,000 deaths were included, as they are in some studies. And other studies of the democratic peace examine different time periods. Such differences in research protocols might well lead to different research findings. Yet even with these qualifications, the basic finding from the research is that democracies do not engage in militarized disputes against each other. That finding is statistically significant—that is, it does not occur by random chance. Overall, democracies are not more peaceful than nondemocracies are; democracies simply do not fight each other. In fact, autocracies are just as peaceful with each other as democracies are. State structure—whether a state is democratic or authoritarian— matters for foreign policy outcomes only some of the time. Much depends on the state the policy is directed toward.

CHALLENGES TO THE STATE

The state, despite its centrality in international affairs, is facing challenges from the processes of globalization, religiously and ideologically based transnational movements, ethnonational movements, transnational crime, and fragile states (see Table 5.2). In each of these processes, new and intrusive technologies—e-mail, Facebook, Twitter, cell phones with cameras, direct satellite broadcasting, and worldwide television networks such as CNN and Al

How do attacks such as the one in Nice, France, impact state security? Are there realistic measures states can take to prevent further attacks? Here, French citizens leave tokens to remember those lost in the terror attack.

6

War and Security

In June 2016, France witnessed a new kind of mass murder when a truck plowed into a crowd in Nice that had gathered to watch fireworks in celebration of Bastille Day. Eighty-six people were killed, including ten children. In August 2017, Spain witnessed a similar attack when a van driver plowed into a crowd of people on a pedestrian walkway in Barcelona. At least 14 people were killed and dozens of others injured. The attacks have instigated new questions about national security. Such vehicle attacks do not require extensive planning or a wide network to carry out. Little opportunity therefore exists for authorities to detect and stop them. How can states protect their citizens from attacks such as these?

Another type of attack has begun to plague state leaders concerned with national security: cyberattacks. In June 2017, a cyberattack hit Ukraine and spread across the globe within hours. Countries' infrastructures and companies around the world were affected, including those in the United States, France, Britain, Russia, and Australia. Because such attacks stem from cyberspace, identifying the attackers is nearly impossible and the effects can spread across state borders easily and quickly. How can states protect their vital infrastructures, companies, and citizens from cyberattacks if they cannot even find the attackers after the fact and cannot secure borders to prevent them?

The question of national security has been a central one for centuries. The nature of what is needed to protect national security, however, has changed significantly over time. A more conventional concern about physical violence stemming from other states has expanded to include concerns about individual terrorists and cyberspace. Are these attacks acts of war? Or are they something different? What types of responses are warranted when the perpetrators are not necessarily another state but individuals who reside in another state? Can a state simply go into another state to attack those individuals?

The challenge of dealing with these new issues of national security is a central problem for state leaders today. To understand the choices they face, we must answer several questions. How has the nature of national security changed over time? What constitutes war and what does not? What are the appropriate types of responses to different types of threats to national security? How might war and other threats to national security be prevented? This chapter seeks to provide answers to these fundamental questions.

LEARNING OBJECTIVES

▶ **Define war and identify the different categories of war.**

▶ **Explain how the theoretical perspectives help us explain the causes of wars.**

▶ **Describe the key characteristics of conventional and unconventional warfare.**

▶ **Highlight the circumstances under which a war can be considered "just."**

▶ **Explain how realists, liberals, and constructivists differ in their approaches to managing state security.**

One of the central concerns of all foreign policy makers as well as scholars studying international relations is that of state (or "national") security. We can think of **national security** as the ability of a state to protect its interests, secrets, and citizens from threats—both external and internal—that endanger it. This definition has three components. The first is a focus on threat: the fact that there is some actor, object, or potential action that can endanger a nation's interests, secrets, or citizens. This threat could stem from outside or inside the state. The second is a focus on protection: the need of the nation to ensure the safety of the state's interests, secrets, and citizens from harm by those threats. The third is a focus on capability: the actual ability of the state to provide that protection.

In the past, national security focused on military threats to the state and a state's ability to stave off those threats. Today, the definition of national security covers a variety of factors, including economic and environmental threats as well as nonphysical threats arising in cyberspace. National security has even expanded to include the idea that threats to individuals themselves endanger the security of the state—that human security is an important component of national security. This chapter focuses on two central types of security: military security and cybersecurity. Chapter 11 discusses several issues of human security.

MILITARY SECURITY AND WAR

Wars—in particular, major wars between states—have been the focus of historians of international relations for centuries. Major works on war include Thucydides's *History of the Peloponnesian War* (431 BCE) and Carl von Clausewitz's *On War* (1832). World War I and its aftermath (the founding of the League of Nations) led American diplomatic historians and legal scholars to create a new discipline called international relations. Since that time, prominent scholars in this field have addressed many of the critical and vexing issues surrounding war: its causes, its conduct, its consequences, its prevention, and even the possibility of its elimination. This attention to war and security is clearly warranted. Of all human values, physical security—security from violence, starvation, and the elements—comes first. All other human values that are crucially important to the quality of our lives— good government, economic development, a healthy environment—presuppose a minimal level of physical security.

History suggests that a minimum level of physical security has not always been attainable. In the past 3,400 years, the world has been entirely at peace for only 268 of them. Estimates of deaths from war throughout human history range from 150 million to 1 billion people (depending on how war is defined). Over 108 million were killed in the twentieth century alone.[1]

Following the world wars and the Korean War (1950–53), both the frequency and intensity of interstate war began a slow decline. This trend, however, is not the same for internal conflicts. In recent years, there has been a significant rise in the number of deaths from internal conflict, in particular, about a 440 percent increase from 2007 to 2016, not counting the Syrian conflict. If the Syrian conflict were included, it would be a 732 percent increase. The number of countries experiencing deaths from internal conflict has also risen over the past decade, from 26 countries in 2007 to 30 countries in 2016. Overall, the global peace index—which ranks countries according to their level of peacefulness using a variety of indicators—shows that by 2017 the global level of peace had deteriorated by 2.14 percent since 2008. War therefore remains perhaps the most compelling issue in world politics, and international relations theorists continue to analyze why it occurs.[2]

WHAT IS WAR?

International relations scholars debate how to define war. Over time, however, three features have emerged. First, a war involves organized, deliberate violence by an identifiable political authority. Riots are often lethal, but they are not considered "war" because, by definition, a riot is neither deliberate nor organized. Second, wars are relatively more lethal than other forms of organized violence. Pogroms, bombings, and massacres are deliberate and organized but generally not sufficiently lethal to count as war. Currently, most international relations scholars accept that at least 1,000 deaths in a calendar year are needed in order for an event to count as a war. Third, and finally, for an event to count as a war, both sides must have some

Many Rwandans fled their homes to escape persecution and violence during the 1994 genocide. What factors kept the international community from intervening?

real capacity to harm each other, although that capacity need not be equal on both sides. We do not count genocides, massacres, terrorist attacks, and pogroms as wars because in a genocide, for example, only one side has any real capacity to kill, while the other side is effectively defenseless.

In sum, **war** is an organized and deliberate political act by an established political authority that causes 1,000 or more deaths in a 12-month period and involves at least two actors capable of harming each other.

Defining war is not simply academic. These definitions have real-world consequences. An important case in point was the 1994 Rwandan genocide, in which over 750,000 men, women, and children were murdered in just four months. Had the international community named this violence properly as a genocide, the pressure to intervene militarily to halt it might have been greater, since in a genocide the side being murdered would have no chance of winning. However, the violence was instead characterized as a renewal of civil war, raising the question of whether international intervention should occur in Rwanda's internal affairs.

TYPES OF WAR

International relations scholars have developed many ways to categorize wars that pose physical threats to national security. At the broadest level, we distinguish between wars that take place between sovereign states (interstate war) and wars that take place within states (intrastate war). Scholars also distinguish between conventional and unconventional warfare, terrorism, and cyberwarfare.

Interstate War

Since the advent of the state system in the years following the conclusion of the Thirty Years' War (1618–48), the state as a form of political association has proven ideal at organizing and directing the resources necessary for waging war. As Charles Tilly famously put it, "War made the state and the state made war."[3] As a result, wars between states, also known as **interstate wars**, have captured the bulk of attention from international relations theorists and scholars.

Theorists are interested in wars between states, in particular, for two reasons. First, by definition, states have recognizable leaders and locations. When we say "France," we understand we are speaking about a government that controls a specific territory that others recognize as France. Therefore, states make good subjects for analysis and comparison. Second, states have formal militaries—some tiny and not much more than police forces, others vast and capable of projecting force across the surface of the globe and even into outer space. These militaries, and the state's capacity to marshal resources in support of them, make states formidable adversaries. Thus, interstate wars are often characterized by relatively rapid loss of life and destruction of property. At the end of World War II, the world's states faced the prospect that a future interstate war might not only destroy them as such, but also, in a nuclear exchange, destroy all human life.

World War I and World War II are two of the most prominent examples of interstate war and illustrate how devastating it can be. The same great powers fought in both wars: Britain, France, Austria-Hungary (in World War II, Germany), Japan, Russia/the Soviet Union, and the United States. Industrialization, which had occurred leading up to the beginning of World War I, revolutionized the killing power of states. The Industrial Revolution had led workers to move from rural areas to cities, making cities distinct targets to attack and allowing a state to inflict significant damage on the enemy all at once. The scope of the battlefield, once restricted to physical areas over which soldiers fought, expanded soon after World War I to include armaments and munitions workers, and eventually, even agricultural workers. The scope of the wars was astonishing. Weapons of mass destruction such as chemical weapons and nuclear weapons were employed, and the overall casualties were horrific: most belligerents lost 4 to 5 percent of their population in World War I, and double that in World War II.

More recently, however, wars have tended to be more limited in scope. One important set of examples of more limited interstate war is the Arab-Israeli disputes, described in Chapter 2. Israel has fought six interstate wars against its neighbors—Egypt, Syria, Jordan, and Lebanon—and struggled against repeated Palestinian uprisings in the West Bank and Gaza. Since the conclusion of the

 IN FOCUS

Characteristics of War

- ▶ Is an organized and deliberate political act
- ▶ Causes 1,000 or more deaths in a 12-month period
- ▶ Can be interstate or intrastate
- ▶ Can be asymmetric (between parties of unequal power) like terrorism
- ▶ Can be an act taken by established political authority
- ▶ Involves at least two actors capable of harming each other
- ▶ Can be conventional or unconventional
- ▶ Can take place in cyberspace when an act is endorsed or carried out by a state government

1973 Yom Kippur War, however, none of the opposing states have sought the complete destruction of their foes, and the conflict has blown hot and cold. With the increased destructiveness of modern warfare, adopting more limited actions has become states' most common option when contemplating violence against other states.

Intrastate War

Intrastate wars (civil wars) are wars that take place within a state. Examples of intrastate wars include a faction and a government fighting over control of territory (Boko Haram in Nigeria); rival groups fighting to establish a government to control a failed or fragile state (Somalia or Liberia); ethnonationalist movements fighting for greater autonomy or secession (Chechens in Russia, Kachins in Myanmar); and ethnic, clan, or religious groups fighting for control of the state (Rwanda, South Sudan, Burundi, Yemen).

Civil wars tend to share several characteristics. They often last a long time, even decades, with periods of fighting punctuated by periods of relative calm. Whereas the goals may seem relatively limited in comparison to those of interstate wars, in the context of the rivalry between incumbent governments and rebels, the stakes are often very high—including secession, group autonomy, and control of the state. The human costs are therefore often substantial. Both combatants and civilians are killed and maimed, food supplies are interrupted, diseases spread as health systems suffer, money is diverted from constructive economic development to purchasing armaments, and generations of people grow up knowing only war.

The African continent provides examples of these major intrastate wars. Ethiopia's war with two of its regions (Ogaden and Eritrea) lasted decades, as did the civil wars between the north and south in both Sudan and Chad. Liberia and Sierra Leone have also been sites of civil conflict in which various factions, guerrilla groups, paramilitary groups, and mercenaries have fought for control.

The Democratic Republic of the Congo (DRC) provides another example of a major civil war, but one that became so internationalized and so destructive that it is often called the "Great African War" or "African World War." In 1996, an internal rebellion broke out in the DRC against the longtime dictator Mobutu Sese Seko. Very quickly, both Uganda and Rwanda supported the rebellion, with the latter interested in eliminating Hutu militias that had fled Rwanda during the 1994 genocide. After Mobutu was ousted and replaced with a new leader, Laurent Kabila, a wider war erupted two years later. Powerful Congolese leaders and ethnic groups, supported by Rwanda and Uganda, opposed the new government. Angola and Zimbabwe supported Kabila's government, as did Chad and Sudan. A major conflict broke out, and rebel groups and the armies of the various countries involved fought intensely—not only for control of the government but also for control of the DRC's vast natural resources. The war formally ended in 2003, but the repercussions lasted long after. The war destroyed the DRC's infrastructure and millions were forced to flee their homes. It is estimated that more than 5 million people died during the war and its aftermath. Despite the efforts of a large UN peacekeeping force, examined in Chapter 9, more people were killed in this war than in any other conflict since World War II.

The most prominent intrastate wars that have broken out in the twenty-first century are those following the Arab Spring of 2011, especially those in Libya (February–October 2011) and Syria (2011–present). Both qualify as wars because well over 1,000 battle deaths resulted from conflict between an incumbent government and rebels, and because each side had military capacity to harm the other (though government forces had the greater capacity). Both followed a similar course: government forces harshly repressed peaceful protests by mostly young people, which then led to an escalation of protests and international condemnation. That escalation led to a harsher government response, with protests becoming both more widespread and more violent. After evidence of government murders, rapes, torture, and massacres, there were calls for international intervention. In Libya's case, both the incumbent government and its international supporters were caught by surprise, and limited military intervention by NATO on behalf of Libyan rebels accelerated the collapse of the incumbent government. In Syria, the incumbent government was better prepared, and more importantly, it received political and military support from allies such as Russia. As if a civil war between rebel groups and Syria's government were not complicated enough, in 2013 the Islamic State (IS) began making territorial gains in eastern Syria. In 2014, the United States, along with multiple states in the Middle East, began to attack the IS inside Syria. In 2015, Russia became officially involved in the conflict militarily, conducting air strikes throughout Syria. These air strikes focused not only on the IS but also on rebel groups involved in the civil war, bringing Russia into the conflict on the side of the Syrian government. The United States also eventually became involved in the civil war (beyond just fighting the IS). It supported rebel groups standing against the Syrian government, and in direct response to a chemical weapons attack that the Syrian government carried out against its citizens in 2017, the United States fired missiles at a Syrian government airbase, thus officially entering militarily into the civil conflict. Iran, Saudi Arabia, and Turkey are also involved, with Iran supporting the Syrian government, Saudi Arabia supporting the rebel groups, and Turkey providing weapons and safe havens to some rebel groups. Currently, the civil war in Syria, which has provoked a flood of refugees seeking safe haven in Europe and neighboring countries (see Chapter 11), ranks among the world's most complicated and deadly civil wars.

As the cases of the DRC and Syria demonstrate, civil wars can become internationalized, with outside actors getting involved in the conflict on one side or the other. States, groups, and individuals from outside the warring country become involved by funding particular groups, selling weapons to various factions, and giving diplomatic or military support to one group over another. Outside states have become involved in civil wars across the globe. Recent civil wars that have experienced outside intervention include those in Mali (intervention by France and the Economic Community of West African States), Somalia (intervention by the United States, Ethiopia, Kenya, and the African Union, among others), and Yemen (intervention by Iran on one side and by a multilateral coalition led by Saudi Arabia on the other).

Conventional War

Throughout most of human history, wars were fought by people—almost invariably male—who were chosen, trained, and authorized to attack or defend against their counterparts in other political communities. Almost all societies have also considered it off-limits to kill some groups, usually women, children, the elderly, and noncombatant civilians. The tools of war reflected this restriction. Weapons of choice have ranged from swords and shields to bows, guns, and cannons; to industrialized armies fielding infantry and riding in tanks; to navies sailing in specialized ships; and to air forces flying fixed-wing aircraft. Such weapons are used to defeat the enemy on a territorial battlefield. The key attribute of conventional weapons is that their destructive effects can be limited in space and time to those who are the legitimate targets of war. Conventional wars are won or lost when the warriors of one group, or their leaders, acknowledge defeat following a clash of arms.

World War I and World War II challenged conventional war as the standard way of fighting war. World War I saw the first large-scale use of chemical weapons on the battlefield. Near the Flemish (Belgian) town of Ypres, in 1915, German forces unleashed 168 tons of chlorine gas against French positions. French troops suffered 6,000 casualties in just a few minutes as prevailing winds carried the poisonous gas across the fields and into the trenches. But German forces were unable to exploit the four-mile-wide gap in French lines that opened as a result. Many German troops had been wounded or killed in handling the gas or by moving through areas still affected, and they were unable to exploit the temporary advantages gained. In addition, the effects of the weapons proved difficult to restrict to combat. Chemicals leached into the soil and water table, affecting agriculture for months afterward. After the war, winners and losers signed a Geneva Protocol outlawing the use of chemical weapons in war.

World War II added two additional challenges to the use of conventional weapons as the standard tools of war. First, the advent of strategic bombing led to the possibility of large-scale harm to noncombatants and to a reexamination of who or what a "noncombatant" actually was. Prior to the war, there was general agreement that civilians were to be protected from intentional harm. But the belligerents possessed large fleets of ships, armored vehicles, and planes, all of which required civilians to build and maintain them. Were those civilians to be protected, too? What about the farmers who fed the soldiers, airmen, and sailors? As the war intensified, the dividing line between those who were to be protected from deliberate harm and those who could be legitimately targeted broke down. By the war's end, both sides had taken to using massive air strikes to deliberately target civilians. In March 1945, bombers from the U.S. Eighth Air Force targeted Japan's capital, Tokyo, with incendiary bombs. The ensuing flames killed over 100,000 Japanese in a single raid, most of them civilians. Second, World War II saw the development of a nuclear weapon—a weapon that clearly could not be limited to combatants, as the bombings of Hiroshima and Nagasaki in August 1945 demonstrated. Around 200,000 people died from the attacks.

Unconventional Warfare

Unconventional warfare, which is as old as conventional warfare, is distinguished by a willingness to flout restrictions on legitimate targets of violence or refuse to accept the traditional outcomes of battles—say, the destruction of a regular army, loss of a capital, or capture of a national leader—as an indicator of victory or defeat.

Two major changes moved unconventional war from a side role to a prominent feature of war. The first is the idea of *nationalism*—a sense of national consciousness placing primary emphasis on one's own nation's culture and interests over those of other nations. Nationalism became an important feature of war during the French Revolution. French nationalism was highly prevalent when the French army under Napoleon Bonaparte was at war with other European states in the 1790s. The French army was a national one, composed of troops with nationalist pride. They felt that they were citizens fighting for their own cause. This intense devotion made the French army a formidable opponent, especially when contrasted with the general indifference of the opposing troops, who did not feel a sense of membership in their own political systems. However, nationalism can be a double-edged sword. While nationalism helped motivate Napoleon's army, the source of greatest defeats lay in nationalist-inspired resistance in Russia and Spain.

The second major change was the growth in the use of guerrilla warfare (the term comes from a Spanish word meaning "small war"). Guerrilla warfare is an old idea, but a strategic innovation by Mao Zedong led to the spread of its use and increased its effectiveness. Mao Zedong's strategy was first called "revolutionary guerrilla warfare." It was specifically designed to counter a technologically advanced and well-equipped industrial adversary by effectively reversing the conventional relationship between soldiers and civilians. In conventional war, soldiers risk their lives to protect civilians. In guerrilla warfare, civilians risk their lives to protect the guerrillas, who hide among them and who cannot easily be distinguished from ordinary civilians when not actually fighting.

Using revolutionary guerrilla warfare during the Chinese Civil War (1927–37, 1945–49) and in China's resistance to Japanese occupation during World War II (1937–45), Mao's People's Liberation Army was able to survive many setbacks. Eventually, it defeated the well-armed and U.S.-supplied Nationalist armies of Jiang Jieshi (Chiang Kai-shek), whose forces fled to the island of Formosa, now Taiwan. This unexpected outcome left Mao with a vast storehouse of captured weapons and, more importantly, led to the spread of revolutionary guerrilla warfare as a template for other insurgents, particularly in Asia.

Revolutionary guerrilla warfare is often used when one party in a conflict is significantly more powerful than the other. This type of conflict between a more powerful party and a significantly weaker party is referred to as **asymmetric conflict**. Asymmetric conflict is also a challenge to a conventional understanding of war. It undercuts an important proposition of both conventional warfare and nuclear war: that conventional weapons and nuclear confrontations are more likely to occur among states having rough equality of military strength and using similar strategies and tactics. If one party is decidedly weaker, the proposition goes, fear of defeat makes that party unlikely to resort to war. Asymmetric conflicts, in contrast, are conducted between parties of very unequal strength. The weaker party attempts to exploit the opponent's weaknesses.[4]

The second half of the twentieth century witnessed a string of unexpected defeats in such asymmetric conflicts for the major advanced industrial powers, each of which lost wars against "weak" or "backward" adversaries. Britain was forced to grant independence to India. France was defeated in Indochina and Algeria; Portugal in Mozambique and Angola; the United States in Vietnam; the Soviet Union in Afghanistan; and Israel in Lebanon. In each case, well-equipped, industrialized militaries had sought to overcome smaller, nonindustrial adversaries and lost.

Like any strategy, however, revolutionary guerrilla warfare itself has weaknesses. In two asymmetric conflicts following World War II, the strong actors— Britain during the Malayan Emergency (1948–60) and the United States in the Philippines (1952–53)—devised a counterinsurgency strategy that effectively defeated revolutionary guerrillas. That strategy aimed not at insurgent armed forces (terrorists and guerrillas), or even their leaders, but instead at the real strength of successful guerrilla warfare: the people. As Mao recognized in his early writings, incumbent governments can defeat a well-led, well-organized guerrilla resistance in only two ways: either change the minds of the people (via a conciliation, or "hearts and minds," strategy) or destroy them utterly. In either case, the social support of a guerrilla resistance is destroyed, and that resistance will collapse. Mao was confident that his "Western" and democratic adversaries were too arrogant in their own power to attempt to change minds and too squeamish in their ethical conduct to pursue a genocidal counterinsurgency. Yet in both Malaya and the Philippines, incumbent governments, supported by Britain and the United States, sought to redress the grievances that had led many of the country's poor or disaffected either to active support of the guerrillas or to political apathy. Since World War II, "hearts and minds" strategies have proven the most effective method of counterinsurgency on the ground, but they are costly in political terms because they take a long time to work and, in most cases, they demand large numbers of troops.[5]

Guerrilla warfare is only one of several strategies a combatant might use to overcome a more materially powerful incumbent and its allies. Another such strategy is nonviolent resistance. Like revolutionary guerrilla warfare, nonviolent resistance deliberately places ordinary people at grave risk of harm in the pursuit of political objectives. Unlike guerrilla warfare or terrorism, however, nonviolent resistance avoids the use of violence as a means of protest. Prominent examples of nonviolent resistance include Mohandas Gandhi's resistance to British rule in the 1940s and the Reverend Dr. Martin Luther King Jr.'s civil rights movement of the 1960s.

Terrorism

Another strategy for overcoming a materially more powerful adversary is terrorism. **Terrorism**, a particular kind of asymmetric conflict, is increasingly perceived as a serious international security threat in the world today. It is particularly seen as a threat because terrorist attacks are often unconventional and highly unpredictable.[6] Scholars of terrorism disagree on a universal definition of terrorism, but most definitions share three key elements:

1.   Terrorism is *political* in nature or intent.

2.   Perpetrators of terrorism are *nonstate* actors.

3.   Targets of terrorism are *noncombatants*, such as ordinary citizens, political figures, or bureaucrats.

Terrorism has often been called the strategy of the weak, but this argument begs the question of what "power" actually is. Is power only the material power to kill, or can it reside in the power of ideas? Gandhi, for example, did not overcome the British and win India's independence by means of violent revolution. The power of ideas proved decisive. Terrorists also hope to harness the power of ideas: they invariably justify their violence by using immortality imagery. This imagery tends to take one of three forms: nationalist, Marxist, or religious. In each case, terrorists intend their violent acts to preserve the nation, the proletariat, or the faithful and ensure its immortality. In the Irish Republican Army's long struggles with British rule in Ireland, all three immortality images came into play, as predominantly nationalist, socialist, and Catholic terrorists sought to coerce Britain into abandoning Ireland's Protestant minority, among other things.

Terrorism involves physical harm, but the essence of terrorism is psychological, not physical. Whatever the aims of the individual terrorist, killing is a by-product of terrorism as a strategy. The real aim of terrorism is to call attention to a cause, while at the same time calling into question the legitimacy of a target government by highlighting its inability to protect its citizens. For example, during the 1972 Summer Olympic Games in Munich, Germany, a group of Palestinian Arab terrorists styling themselves "Black September" took 11 Israeli athletes hostage in the Olympic Village. Two of the hostages were murdered immediately. During a botched rescue attempt by the surprised and ill-prepared Germans, the remaining nine hostages were murdered by their captors. Black September was a part of the Palestinian Liberation Organization (PLO), a group founded by Yasser Arafat in 1964 to advance the cause of Palestinian Arab statehood by means of violence. But until Munich, few outside the Middle East had ever heard of the PLO. After the games, the PLO (and "terrorists" more broadly) became a widespread topic of conversation and state action.

Much recent terrorist activity has its roots in the Middle East—in the ongoing quest of Palestinian Arabs for self-determination and their own internal conflicts over strategy, in the hostility among various Islamic groups toward Western forces and ideas (in particular, what they perceive as Western support of Israel's persecution of Palestinian Arabs and the education and independence of women), and in the resurgence of extremist Islamic fundamentalism. Among terrorist groups with roots in the Middle East are Hamas, Hezbollah, and Palestine Islamic Jihad. After September 11, 2001, Al Qaeda was the most publicized of these groups. A shadowy network of extremist Islamic fundamentalists from many countries, including some outside the Middle East, Al Qaeda, originally led by the late Osama bin Laden, is motivated by the desire to install strict Islamic regimes in the Middle East, support radical Islamic insurgencies in Southeast Asia, and punish the United States for its support of Israel. When the United States and its allies began to seriously hurt Al Qaeda—as they did from 2009 to 2012—its leadership adapted by dispersing and forming new affiliates, such as Al Qaeda in Iraq and Al Qaeda in Yemen. With the growth of the IS, Al Qaeda has largely faded from the international scene, except in Afghanistan, where the group remains active.

The roots of the IS formed during the 1979 Shiite revolution in Iran and the 2003 U.S.-led invasion of Iraq. That invasion by the United States gave Shiites power over the Arab Sunni minority, and the IS has taken up the radical Sunni cause. The IS uses social media to broadcast its terrorist acts: the beheadings of Westerners and Muslim opponents; mass executions; rapes of non-Muslim women like members of the Yazidi minority; the sexual enslavement of non-Sunni Muslims; the taking of hostages for ransom; and the destruction of cultural antiquities. The IS differs from most terrorist organizations in important respects, too. It seeks to control territory and has done so in parts of Syria and Iraq, and finances itself by controlling oil assets. The IS claims religious authority centered in the proclamation of a caliphate—an area under the leadership of an Islamic steward considered to be a religious successor to the Prophet Muhammad and the leader of the entire Muslim community. Many of its estimated 15,000 foreign recruits, from as many as 80 countries, are attracted by its utopian goals. As one scholar explains, the IS seeks to "create a 'pure' Sunni Islamist state governed by a brutal interpretation of *sharia* [religious Islamic law] to immediately obliterate the political borders of the Middle East that were created by Western powers in the twentieth century; and to position itself as the sole political, religious, and military authority over all of the world's Muslims."[7] Yet the very use of terror, as well as its religious fundamentalism, has isolated the IS from virtually all of its neighbors, most Muslims, and the rest of the international community.

Terrorism also has a long history outside the Middle East, reflecting diverse, often multiple, motivations. Some groups adhere to extreme religious positions, such as the Irish Republican Army, the protector of Northern Irish Catholics in their struggle against Protestant British rule. The Hindu-Muslim rivalry in India has also led to many terrorist incidents. Other groups seek or have sought territorial separation or autonomy from a state. The Basque separatists (ETA) in Spain, the Tamil Tigers in Sri Lanka, the Abu Sayyaf Group in the Philippines, and Chechen groups in Russia have all tried to achieve this goal.

Since the 1990s, terrorism has taken a new turn.[8] Terrorist acts have become more lethal, even as the groups responsible have become more dispersed. In the 1970s, about 17 percent of terrorist attacks killed someone, whereas in the 1990s, almost 25 percent of terrorist attacks resulted in deaths. Until 2000, the worst loss of life was the 1985 bombing of an Air India flight, in which 329 people were killed. That statistic changed dramatically on September 11, 2001, when over 3,000 civilians died and $80 billion in economic losses were incurred. Increasingly, terrorists have made use of a diverse array of weapons, including AK-47s, sarin gas, shoulder-fired missiles, anthrax, backpack explosives, truck bombs, and airplanes

Despite the widespread violence caused by IS militants and sympathizers, recent efforts to counter their territorial dominance have been successful. In 2016, Iraqi forces were able to reclaim the crucial city Fallujah from the grips of the IS.

used as guided missiles. Yet their actions can also be very simple to carry out, such as driving cars or trucks into crowds of people, as in the 2016 attacks in Nice, France, where at least 80 people were killed and many others injured. The infrastructure that supports terrorism has also become more sophisticated. It is financed through money-laundering schemes and illegal criminal activities. Training camps attract not just young, single, and uneducated potential terrorists but also older, better-educated individuals who are willing to commit suicide to accomplish their objectives. Terrorist groups have also made increasingly effective use of the Internet and social media as a recruitment tool.

The groups practicing terrorism are ideologically wide-ranging, from nationalists and neo-Nazis to religious, left-wing, and right-wing militants. (See Table 6.1.) State-sponsored terrorism, the support of terrorist groups by states, remains common. The United States and many of its allies (for example, Britain, Germany, and France) have repeatedly accused North Korea, Iran, Iraq, Syria, Libya, Sudan, and Cuba of having lent support to terrorist groups. Yet, while strong evidence of state complicity exists in each case, the accusing states are apt to overlook their own sponsorship of groups others might call "terrorists." For example, U.S. support of *contras*—groups opposing communist rule in Nicaragua in the 1980s—could easily count as state-sponsored terrorism because the *contras* did not limit their targets to Nicaraguan police and soldiers, but also attacked civilians.

TABLE 6.1

Selected Terrorist Organizations

GROUP	LOCATION	CHARACTERISTICS AND ATTACKS
Al Qaeda	Formerly in Afghanistan; now dispersed throughout Afghanistan, Pakistan, Iran, Indonesia, and Yemen	Formed by Osama bin Laden in the late 1980s among Arabs who fought the Soviets in Afghanistan; responsible for bombings in Africa (1998), Yemen (2000), United States (2001), Spain (2004), Great Britain (2005), India (2006), Pakistan (2008, 2009), Algeria (2010).
Hamas (Islamic Resistance Movement)	Israel, West Bank, Gaza Strip	Its leader signed bin Laden's 1998 *fatwa* calling for attacks on U.S. interests; elected in 2006 as governing authority in Gaza.
Hezbollah (Party of God)	Lebanon	Also known as Islamic Jihad; often directed by Iran and suspected in the bombing of the U.S. embassy and marine barracks in Beirut in 1983; dominates Lebanon politically; fights against Israel.
Boko Haram (Western Ways Are Forbidden)	Northern Nigeria and neighboring countries; pushed into a final stronghold in the 23,000-square-mile Sambisa Forest in northeastern Nigeria in 2015 by coalition of Nigeria and the African Union	Salafi jihadists who violently pursue the establishment of a strict version of Sharia law throughout Nigeria. Kidnapped 276 schoolgirls in Chibok, Nigeria, in April 2014. Some were released in mid-2017, but about 100 are still believed to be in Boko Haram custody.
Haqqani Network	Pashtunistan (eastern Afghanistan and western Pakistan)	Insurgent Islamist group; supported by U.S. CIA during Soviet occupation of Afghanistan; now allied with Taliban and tacitly supported by Pakistan; fought against ISAF in Afghanistan until 2010.

TABLE 6.1 (continued)

GROUP	LOCATION	CHARACTERISTICS AND ATTACKS
The Islamic State	Formerly centered in Syria and northern Iraq, but actively franchising to Yemen, Afghanistan, Egypt, Libya, and possibly Chechnya	An outgrowth of Al Qaeda in Iraq, currently led by Abu Bakr al-Baghdadi, a former senior officer in Saddam Hussein's Iraqi army and the self-proclaimed caliph; the world's wealthiest terrorist group; aims to establish an "Islamic" caliphate (no territorial boundaries) and is responsible for thousands of murders, including beheadings, as well as rapes and sexual slavery; it targets any who oppose its restrictive interpretation of Sharia law.

Preventing terrorist activity has become increasingly difficult because most perpetrators have networks of supporters in the resident populations. Protecting populations from random acts of violence is an almost impossible task, given the availability of guns and bombs in the international marketplace. Pressure on governments is very strong because people worry disproportionately about terrorism, even though it kills a relatively small number of people, and because many people believe a violent response by state security forces will help protect them. Despite advances in detection technology like face-recognition software, committed individuals or groups of terrorists are difficult to preempt or deter. Indeed, such individuals may be seen as heroes in their community.

The international community has taken action against terrorists by creating a framework of international rules dealing with terrorism. The framework includes 12 conventions that address such issues as punishing hijackers and those who protect them; protecting airports, diplomats, and nuclear materials in transport; and blocking the flow of financial resources to global terrorist networks. Individual states have also taken steps to increase state security (the United States' controversial USA Patriot Act is one example), to support counterintelligence activities and to promote cooperation among national enforcement agencies in tracking and apprehending terrorists. States have sanctioned other states they view as supporting terrorists, or as not taking effective enforcement measures. Libya, Sudan, Afghanistan, Syria, Iran, and Iraq are prominent examples. But it is important to recall that even developed states such as the United States, Belgium, and France have had difficulty in taking effective enforcement measures against terrorists, although each has shut down many terrorist financial networks and enhanced security in airports and ports. After all, the terrorists who attacked New York's World Trade Center and the Pentagon on September 11, 2001, learned to fly commercial airplanes in Florida. And some of the terrorists responsible for the Paris bombings in 2015 were French citizens or were living in Belgium.

Cyberwarfare

In the past several decades, a new type of threat to national security has arisen—threats stemming from cyberspace. **Cyberspace** is more than just the Internet. As defined by Ronald Deibert, cyberspace includes "the entire spectrum of networked information and communication systems and devices" and now pervades all aspects of society, economics, and politics.[9] Given its central role in individual, national, and international relations, cyberspace is now considered to be a critical infrastructure by most state governments, transforming it into a central focus of national security. The goal is to protect the state from cyberwarfare. **Cyberwarfare** refers to state actions taken to penetrate another state's computers or networks for the purpose of causing damage or disruption. Nonstate actors can also engage in such cyberattacks—either on their own or in conjunction with state governments. The threats stemming from such attacks are as widespread as cyberspace itself.

Cyberwarfare has become increasingly common in state relations. China is thought to operate one of the most extensive cyberattack operations in the world against both government and corporate targets. It is believed that one of the first major cyberwarfare attacks—a series of coordinated attacks (labeled Titan Rain by the U.S. government) that began in 2003 and persisted for at least three years—was a Chinese operation. Russia is also a significant perpetrator of cyberattacks. In 2007, Estonia's state banking and public administration systems were frozen when millions of computers were hijacked and connected together as a "botnet" to flood the country's central computer systems. The attacks coincided with a disagreement between Estonia and Russia. Similarly, during the war over the territory of South Ossetia between Russia and Georgia, the Georgian government ministries were subject to a major denial-of-service attack (in which machines and network resources are rendered unavailable due to a disruption of servers connected to the Internet). In June 2017, a major cyberattack hit Ukraine and quickly spread worldwide. The attack was designed to hit the day before a holiday celebrating the adoption of Ukraine's first constitution after achieving independence from the Soviet Union. While some Russian industries were hit, Ukraine argued that Russia was behind the attack. In 2017, the United States implicated Russia in cyberattacks designed to influence the outcome of its 2016 presidential election.

One of the most prominent cyberwarfare attacks (using the Stuxnet worm) was an attack on Iranian nuclear enrichment facilities that is believed to have been organized by the United States and Israel. The attackers used multiple strategically exploitable vulnerabilities in software (zero-day exploits) and spent numerous months and millions of dollars on research and advance preparation. Although the attack brought Iranian nuclear enrichment programs to only a limited halt, it is widely seen as the first act of sabotage undertaken in cyberspace and it significantly advanced the evolution of cyberwarfare. In 2017, the United States was known to be actively pursuing this same type of cyberattack against the North Korean missile program in hopes of sabotaging test launches.

Because of the growing frequency and impact of cyberattacks, cybersecurity has become a central feature of states' strategic actions to protect themselves at the international level. The United States has placed cyberspace as equal in importance to land, air, sea, and space in its strategic doctrine and has established a special U.S. military command dedicated solely to cyberspace. Similarly, in 2010 China announced the creation of its own military unit dedicated to the investigation and prevention of cyberattacks on its own computer systems. Many states have taken similar steps.

While most actions in the realm of cybersecurity have been unilateral actions taken by individual states, some cooperative agreements have been forged. For example, the Council of Europe's Convention on Cybercrime (CEC) was created in 2001. The agreement requires states to pass laws criminalizing certain behaviors in cyberspace and providing police with the authority to enforce these laws. In 2008, the Shanghai Cooperation Organization (SCO), made up of China, Russia, Kazakhstan, Kyrgyzstan, Tajikistan, and Uzbekistan, adopted an "action plan" with principles similar to the law enforcement approach of the CEC. Bilateral agreements have also been created, and in some cases, these agreements involve states that have been highlighted as important sources of cybercrime. For example, in 2015 a breakthrough agreement on cybersecurity was signed between the United States and China. They agreed that they should increase communication and cooperation to investigate and prevent cybercrimes emanating from their territory. They also agreed that neither would knowingly conduct or support cyber-related theft of intellectual property. Both sides promised to establish a high-level joint dialogue on fighting cybercrime and related issues, as well as to identify, develop, and promote international norms of acceptable cyberspace behavior.

Cooperation at the global level, however, has been limited. In 2006, the UN General Assembly called for the establishment of a Group of Governmental Experts (GGE) on information and communications technology (ICT). Its purpose was to study existing and potential threats to states' information security and to develop possible cooperative measures to address them. By mid-2017, the GGE had met in five sets of sessions, publishing after each session a report providing advice on how states can begin to cooperate in the field of information and communications technology. The 2015 report called for states not to allow their territory to be used for internationally wrongful acts using ICT. Most importantly, it pushed for the establishment of a number of voluntary "confidence building measures." These measures are designed to increase a state's confidence that other states will not exploit its own cooperative actions in order to better prepare an attack against it. While such measures could pave the way for increased transparency and cooperation, the 2017 GGE failed to produce a report receiving consensus support. This failure has opened up questions about the future of the GGE and cooperation in cybersecurity.

Nevertheless, almost all aspects of cybersecurity have a transnational component, as users throughout the world are often affected by actions taken in cyberspace. One response to this reality has been the creation of computer emergency response teams (CERTs), groups of nonstate experts that are designed to manage computer security incidents and are located all around the world. These nationally based teams have begun to coordinate in the Forum of Incident Response and Security Teams (FIRST). FIRST was formed in 1990; its goals are to promote information sharing among its members, to assist in rapid reaction to incidents, and most importantly, to foster cooperation and coordination in working to prevent incidents in the first place. By the beginning of 2018, FIRST had more than 300 member groups.

There are many different types of war, and all can be devastating to a state's security. Given that war is so important, we should try to understand the causes of war and examine possible ways to prevent it. The three main perspectives of international relations provide some insights.

THE CAUSES OF WAR

In an analysis of any war, we will find more than one cause for the outbreak of violence. This multiplicity of explanations can seem overwhelming. How can we study the causes of war systematically, when the causes often seem idiosyncratic? Theories of international relations highlight different factors that might help explain why wars occur.

Realist Interpretations of the Causes of War

If one key issue distinguishes realists from their critics, it is that for realists, war is a natural, inevitable feature of interstate politics. As discussed in Chapter 3, realists see the problem of war as stemming from the fact that the international system is anarchic—in the international system there exists no hierarchically superior, coercive authority that can create laws, resolve disputes, or enforce law and order. War therefore breaks out because no authority exists to prevent it. As long as there is anarchy, there will be war. War, in such a system, might even appear to be the best course of action a state can take. War and conquest can help a state acquire resources that it can use to increase its power. Moreover, for offensive realists, war is a way to enhance a state's reputation by demonstrating its willingness to engage in conflict. Doing so can help a state get other states to join with it (bandwagon) in an effort to prevent themselves from being attacked as well.

The anarchic international system also has no legitimized authority to help peacefully resolve contending claims that states may have. John Mearsheimer calls this the "911 problem"—there is no hotline, or "central authority, to which a threatened state can turn for help."[10] One of the most common contending claims over which violence breaks out between states involves contested territory. For almost all of the previous century, the Arab-Israeli dispute rested on competing territorial claims to Palestine; in the Horn of Africa, the territorial aspirations of the Somali people remain disputed; in the Andes, Ecuador and Peru have competing territorial claims; and in the South China Sea, Japan, China, Taiwan, the Philippines, and Vietnam are all struggling over conflicting claims to offshore islands. Ukraine and Russia both view Crimea as part of their own territory. For realists, without an arbiter to resolve these disputes, a state might resort to violence to win the territory it claims as its own. For example, violence regularly takes place over claims to Palestine, violence has broken out on several occasions regarding the conflicting territorial claims over the Spratly Islands in the South China Sea, and in 2014 Russia sent military troops to take Crimea from Ukraine.

Likewise, there is also no effective arbiter of competing claims to self-determination made by groups within states. Tibetans, Chechens, Catalonians, Kurds, and Quebecois all express a desire for their own state. Who decides whether their claims for self-determination are legitimate? Without an internationally legitimized arbiter, authority rests with the states themselves—with the most powerful ones often becoming the decisive, interested arbiters. The groups seeking self-determination thus often resort to force against the state. For example, the struggle between Chechnya and Russia over Chechen independence regularly involves armed conflict. It has even broken out into all-out war. In 1999, Russia invaded Chechnya after it had declared independence and succeeded in returning it to Russian control. Violence has continued to break out regularly ever since.

In January 2003, U.S. President George W. Bush alerted the American people to intelligence that suggested Iraq was developing nuclear weapons, causing the United States to enter war with Iraq to maintain the balance of power. Those claims were later revealed to be inaccurate.

In addition to affirming the importance of anarchy for understanding why we see war, some realists attribute war to other facets of the international system, such as the distribution of power. For example, Kenneth Organski advances a realist argument referred to as "power transition theory." This theory posits that it is not only mismatched material power that tempts states to war, but also the *anticipation* of shifts in the relative balance of power. War occurs because states believe that more power leads to expectations of more influence, wealth, and security. A power transition can therefore cause war in one of two patterns. In the first pattern, a rising power might launch a war to solidify its position. For example, ten to twenty years before the beginning of World War II, Germany's power relative to that of France and the United Kingdom was extremely small, as Germany had just been defeated in World War I. Germany's power rose significantly over those decades and had almost reached parity with that of France and the United Kingdom by the start of the war. The prediction of power transition theory that Germany would act militarily to help secure its new position in the international system played out in this case, and World War II broke out.[11] In the second pattern, the currently most powerful state(s) might launch a preventive war to keep a rising challenger down. For example, one of the United States' reasons for going to war against Iraq in 2003 was that Iraq was developing nuclear weapons and its nuclear program needed to be dismantled before it acquired the capability to use such weapons, significantly increasing its power. Whichever pattern occurs, according to the theory, power transitions increase the likelihood of war.

Liberal Interpretations of the Causes of War

While realists focus significant attention in their analyses of war on characteristics of the international system, liberals tend to focus more on characteristics of the state and institutions (both domestic and international). State and societal explanations for war are among the oldest. Plato, for example, posited that war is less likely where the population is cohesive and enjoys a moderate level of prosperity. Since the population would be able to thwart an attack, an enemy is likely to refrain from launching such an attack. Many thinkers during the Enlightenment, including Immanuel Kant, believed that war was more likely in aristocratic states. Kant goes farther, arguing in his book *Perpetual Peace* (1795) that three factors help to foster peace—democracy, economic interdependence, and international institutions. These factors are central in liberal theories about why we do (or do not) see war.

In the liberal perspective, democratic peace theory holds that democracies rarely (if ever) go to war with other democracies. There are several reasons why this is the case. First, some theorists argue that democracies share norms of compromise and cooperation. At the domestic level, democracies offer citizens who have grievances a chance to deal with these complaints by nonviolent means. This norm is projected by democracies to the international level. Thus, two democracies who share this norm of nonviolent resolution of conflicts are both likely to pursue peaceful means to resolve their disputes. War is therefore less likely between them.

Second, some theorists argue that institutional constraints exist in democracies that help to prevent them from going to war with one another. One important institutional characteristic of democracies is transparency in the decision-making process. Transparency provides leaders on the other side with trust that commitments made in negotiated agreements will be upheld, as they can observe the process by which those decisions were made. If leaders in democracies back down from their commitments, they can also face audience costs—costs that stem from negative public opinion about leaders' actions. If states negotiate an agreement, it is thus believable that democracies will uphold their end. Nondemocracies have more difficulty in building trust and decreasing uncertainty, due to the nontransparent nature of their regimes. Two democracies that can each trust the other side to uphold its commitments are therefore more likely to be willing to negotiate a solution to a dispute than to go to war. If a state faces a nondemocracy, and thus cannot trust that it will uphold a negotiated solution, that state is more likely to turn to violence. A lack of transparency, and a lack of audience costs at the domestic level, can therefore also be reasons why we see war when nondemocracies are involved.

Another theory from the liberal perspective—"commercial peace theory"—focuses on interdependence between states. This theory posits that states that are more interdependent, particularly through trade and investment, are less likely to go to war. Peace maintains the prospect for continued economic benefits, something both states desire. War interrupts trade and blocks profits. Thus, states that are more interconnected by commercial institutions—and thus more dependent on one another for trade and other economic gains—are less likely to go to war with one another. A lack of interdependence and connections between states can therefore be a reason why we see states resort to violence to resolve their disputes. There is significantly less cost to doing so than there is for states that are interdependent and share these connections.

Some liberal theories also highlight how international institutions might influence the outbreak of conflict. First, international institutions help build positive connections between states, and economic institutions, in particular, foster interdependence. In this way, institutions can therefore help promote peace. The lack of shared membership in such institutions might thus increase the possibility that conflict could break out between states. Second, states that are left out of institutions might feel threatened by the connections forged between states within those institutions, potentially adding to the possibility of conflict. For example, as discussed in Chapter 3, the possibility that Ukraine might join NATO and sign an association agreement with the EU was seen by Russia as a threat to its interests, as membership in these institutions would bring Ukraine closer to the West. Theorists coming from a liberal perspective might argue that Russia's misgivings helped fuel the conflict that broke out between Russia and Ukraine in 2014.

Constructivist Interpretations of the Causes of War

Constructivists focus significant attention on the role of identities in international relations. Identities shape a state's interests, and thus influence its foreign policy goals and the tactics and strategies it uses to advance those goals. In this way, identities can influence whether a state is likely to be more aggressive or more restrained in how it pursues its foreign policy. For example, contrast the foreign policies of Switzerland and North Korea. Switzerland does not focus on military might or aggression. It identifies itself as a neutral actor in the international system, and its policy pursuits reflect this. Switzerland remained neutral in both world wars and has chosen not to join many international institutions. It did not even join the United Nations until 2002. In contrast, North Korea identifies itself in the post–Cold War period as the key "anti-imperialist, socialist bulwark" standing in opposition to the United States.[12] Its aggressive foreign policy, which centers on the defiance of international norms and development of nuclear weapons, is directly connected to this belligerent identity.[13] These contrasting identities make the likelihood that these states would become involved in a war quite different.

There is also a relational aspect to identities. The way one state views another state is shaped in important ways by the interactions that they have had. These interactions create perceptions of similarities and differences between states. Rather than pure military power, these perceptions and the identities they create influence the potential for war between different states. One state could be seen as an ally and not a threat, even if it is a militarily powerful state. Another state could be seen as an adversary even if it has fewer capabilities. For example, Canada might fear that North Korea is more of a threat than the United States, even though the United States has greater relative power than North Korea has, possesses nuclear weapons, and actually shares a border with Canada, which would make an invasion relatively simple. The difference in identities is what makes one state seem more threatening than another. So where do these identities come from?

Ideas are an important component in the construction of identities. The idea of the right to self-determination—the right of a people to determine its own future political status—contributes to the formation of common and conflicting identities and the outbreak of war. This is most clearly evident in the wars to end colonial rule in the mid-twentieth century. Examples include the 1945–50 Indonesian struggle for independence from the Netherlands and the 1945–54 Vietnamese war against France. Conflicts over self-determination have continued long since decolonization. For example, South Sudan fought a civil conflict with Sudan for over two decades, gaining its independence in 2011. Some conflicts for self-determination even continue today, as is the case with Chechnya in Russia.

Nationalism provides another example of the role ideas play in influencing war. The idea of nationalism has led to the creation of conflicting identities among nations throughout history. These conflicting identities have contributed to many wars. Ideas and identity can also be manipulated by elites to pursue their own individual goals through violence (i.e., war). Adolf Hitler used nationalism as a key motivating factor in Germany's actions in World War II. Slobodan Milošević used nationalism to create a sense of common identity among ethnic Serbians from the various republics of Yugoslavia, as well as a sense that their identity stood in contrast to the identities of other ethnicities. This nationalism fueled war and even, arguably, genocide. As one U.S. ambassador described Milošević's manipulation of nationalist sentiments among Serbs, "He is very successful in manipulating Serbian nationalism to stay in power. If there was serious peace and prosperity, he would not survive very long."[14] Overall, ideas and identities can play a central role in instigating conflict.

PREVENTING WAR AND MANAGING STATE SECURITY

With an understanding of the causes of war, we can begin to discuss how to prevent war. The different international relations perspectives offer different analyses of how war might be prevented.

Realist Approaches to Preventing War

Realist approaches to managing security stem from the fact that for realists, war is a necessary condition of interstate politics: it can be managed but never eradicated.

Classical realists, ranging from Thucydides to Hobbes to Hans Morgenthau, argued that human nature made transcending war unlikely. Neorealists replaced the emphasis on human nature with an emphasis on structure, arguing that war will be a permanent feature of interstate politics so long as anarchy persists. While approaching the issue from different angles, neorealists effectively share the pessimism of classical realists: as a prominent feature of interstate politics, war can never be transcended.

Although realism imagines war as an enduring feature of international politics, realists advance important arguments about how to decrease the frequency of war, as well as the intensity of war when it does break out. Power balancing and deterrence are two such approaches.

Power Balancing

In Chapter 3, we saw that a balance of power is a particular configuration of the distribution of power in the international system. But theorists use the terms in other ways as well. *Balance of power* may refer to an equilibrium between any two parties, and *balancing power* may describe an approach to managing power and state security. The latter usage is relevant here.

The core logic of power balancing is simple: when power is unbalanced, stronger states will be tempted to use their advantage to go to war with weaker states in order to secure more power. The greater the imbalance, the greater the stronger state's temptation to do so. For the stronger actor, the costs and risks of war seem low in comparison to potential gains, thus making war a rational strategy. But when aggressive, insecure, power-seeking states face others with relatively equal power, they are likely to be more hesitant to go to war because the costs of war are more likely to exceed the expected benefits.

Balance-of-power theorists therefore posit that states make rational and calculated evaluations of the costs and benefits of particular policies that determine the state's role in a balance of power. All states in the system are continually making choices to maintain their position vis-à-vis their adversaries, thereby maintaining a balance of power.

Alliances are the most important institutional tool for enhancing one's own security and balancing the perceived power potential of one's opponent. If an expanding state seems poised to achieve a dominant position, upsetting the current balance of power, threatened states can join with others against the expanding state. For example, when Germany's power rose in the lead-up to World War II, the United States and United Kingdom allied with Russia to balance against it, despite the rivalry between them.

Going Nuclear: A View from North Korea

For decades, North Korean leaders have been developing a nuclear weapons program. By 2017, the program had produced a hydrogen bomb and an ICBM that North Korea argued was capable of reaching U.S. territory. The international community has reacted with condemnation, placing increasing levels of sanctions on North Korea. Why, if the program has such negative consequences, do North Korean leaders continue?

The development of North Korea's nuclear program has raised several problems for its leaders. The program is expensive, requiring North Korean leaders to spend a significant portion of the state's budget on it. From 2004 to 2014, North Korea spent almost 25 percent of its GDP on the military—the highest percentage of military spending relative to GDP of any country. With spending so focused on the military, few funds have been dedicated to providing food aid for the people, despite the country facing a critical food shortage.

This problem has been exacerbated by the increasing levels of economic sanctions that have been placed on North Korea in response to its nuclear program. These sanctions have hit the lower class the hardest. As this class already faces extreme poverty, their growing discontent with ruling elites who have remained wealthy despite these sanctions has forced the leaders of North Korea to strengthen their control and surveillance over the population, as well as to increase oppression and crackdowns.

The sanctions have also spurred the growth of an illicit economy in North Korea, with many residents beginning to support themselves through smuggling. The regime has reacted to the growth of the illicit economy by strengthening the penalties against acts associated with them. North Korean leaders even attempted a currency reform to wipe out the capital of the traders participating in the illicit economy. However, the reform unsettled the lives of many North Koreans and contributed to a surge in inflation. Overall, a growing number of people believe they are paying the price for a nuclear program that does not benefit them in any way. Why, then, do North Korean leaders continue to pursue their nuclear ambitions, given that the program is creating these domestic problems?

North Korean leaders face two other problems that have led them to continue their nuclear program despite its negative effects. First, in the face of the severe food shortage, North Korean leaders have been able to leverage their nuclear program to obtain food aid, helping them deal with the crisis without having to spend their own funds. On several occasions, North Korean leaders have stated that they would give up their nuclear ambitions in return for such aid. For example, in 2012, it announced that it would suspend its nuclear activities and stop its missile tests in exchange for food aid. This action, however, was quickly reversed once North Korea received the aid it desired. Its nuclear program remains a bargaining chip that North Korean leaders can continue to use in the future to obtain food aid and other possible types of concessions.

Second, and more importantly, North Korean leaders want to remain in power, and current geopolitics threatens their ability to do so. For North Korean leaders, the 2003 U.S.-led invasion of Iraq and the 2011 NATO inter-

North Korean leader King Jong–Un inspects nuclear machinery.

vention in Libya against Muammar Qaddafi demonstrated the United States' willingness to invade enemy states and overthrow their governments. North Korean leaders are highly concerned about this problem. Their choice is to either bandwagon or balance, or else face the possibility of being invaded and deposed.

North Korea's leaders cannot bandwagon with the United States without sacrificing their political legitimacy. Indeed, they frame their image as leading North Korea to be an important socialist barrier standing up in opposition to U.S. "imperialism." This political image would lose credibility if they were to bandwagon. The alternative, therefore, is to balance. According to one expert, "The lesson North Koreans learned from the [U.S.] invasion of Iraq was that if Saddam Hussein really possessed those weapons of mass destruction, he might have survived."[a] In other words,

balancing could have worked for Saddam. Because North Korea's nuclear program serves to balance against U.S. power with a credible threat to use nuclear weapons against the United States or its allies, North Korean leaders believe the program helps deter military invasion.

Despite the costs, North Korean leaders' continued development of their nuclear program is rational. The effectiveness of their balancing efforts is illustrated by U.S. President Donald Trump's willingness to meet with North Korean leader Kim Jong-Un in June 2018 after almost a decade of no contact between the two countries' leaders. Whether North Korea will abandon its nuclear program in return for U.S. assurances of North Korean security remains to be seen. Some observers say that even if North Korea continues its nuclear program, the Kim-Trump meeting elevated Kim and North Korea in the eyes of the world.

a. John Delury, quoted in Stephen Evans, "Is North Korea's Leader Kim Jong-un Rational?" BBC News, March 18, 2017, www.bbc.com/news/world-asia-39269783 (accessed 12/11/17).

FOR CRITICAL ANALYSIS

1. Do you think North Korea's pursuit of nuclear weapons is rational? Why or why not?

2. What would liberal theorists recommend states do to stop North Korea's nuclear program? Do you think that solution would work? What about a realist solution?

3. Do you think that the geopolitical reasoning underlying North Korea's pursuit of nuclear weapons is justified? Why or why not?

the Security Council consider that measures provided for in Article 41 [measures not involving the use of armed force to attempt to resolve the dispute] would be inadequate or have proved to be inadequate, it may take such action by air, sea, or land forces as may be necessary to maintain or restore international peace and security. Such action may include demonstrations, blockade, and other operations by air, sea, or land forces of Members of the United Nations." For example, in the 1991 Gulf War, the UN Security Council passed a resolution allowing a joint, multicountry force (led by the United States) to use military means to remove Iraq from Kuwait after it had invaded the country.

Jus in Bello

The just war tradition also addresses legitimate conduct in war (known as *jus in bello*). Such legitimate conduct requires several qualifications, each an important pillar of just war theory. First, combatants and noncombatants must be differentiated, with noncombatants protected from harm as much as possible—hence the principle of noncombatant immunity. Second, the means of violence used must be proportionate to the ends to be achieved—the principle of proportionality. Finally, unnecessary human suffering should be avoided at all costs. This third qualification led to the banning of the use of particularly heinous weapons.

Many of these central norms of the just war tradition were codified into legally binding treaties. In 1899 and 1907 the Hague Conventions were created to regulate methods of warfare, and in 1949 four Geneva Conventions (and their two subsequent protocols in 1977) were created to regulate the protection of noncombatants, including civilians, prisoners of war, and injured soldiers. Many other treaties have followed, targeting new and more specific aspects of just war norms. For example, because mustard gas caused especially cruel deaths during World War I, its use was subsequently outlawed, paving the way for future chemical and biological warfare conventions. Together these treaties provide the basis for international humanitarian law.

Contemporary debates surround the question of how newer killing technologies—nuclear weapons, land mines, cluster munitions, fuel air explosives, and drone strikes—affect our assessments of moral and ethical conduct during war. This question arises because in many cases, these new technologies challenge our ability to uphold the norms of the just war tradition. For example, the use of nuclear weapons has been viewed as a just war concern for two reasons. First, unlike with most conventional weapons, the destructive effects of nuclear weapons are impossible to restrict in time and space. The Japanese government estimates that over 250,000 deaths, mostly of civilians, can be directly attributed to the bombings of Hiroshima and Nagasaki. This violates the first pillar of just war theory—the principle of noncombatant immunity. Second, the destructive potential of

Israeli drone strikes in Palestine have destroyed the homes and lives of many noncombatants. Should drones be used for warfare when they often harm civilian communities?

contemporary thermonuclear weapons is unprecedented. No one can say for certain what the impact of even a limited exchange of such weapons might be on the global ecosystem. An all-out exchange, in which hundreds of such weapons were deliberately detonated, might end all life on the planet, damage the atmosphere, or plunge the earth into an extended "nuclear winter." Thus, the proportionality of means and ends—the second pillar of just war theory—would be violated.

Other weapons have also come under fire under the "nondiscriminatory nature" theory of unjust war. Two of particular note include antipersonnel land mines and cluster munitions. Although land mines were originally viewed as legitimate weapons, the International Campaign to Ban Landmines (ICBL) has succeeded in shifting perceptions of these weapons by emphasizing—as with other weapons of mass destruction—the indiscriminate effect of their capacity to harm. They pose a threat to the safety of civilians long after a war has ended. In 2008, the Convention on Cluster Munitions was signed, banning and providing assistance for clearing weapons with a high potential to harm noncombatants. The campaigns against antipersonnel land mines and cluster munitions reflect growing pressure to restrict or eliminate the use of various weapons and practices in accordance with just war principles. Constructivists can rightly cite the power of norms and socialization to alter the behavior (and identity) of both state and nonstate actors in this regard.

Another recent debate regarding morals and ethics in war has surfaced due to advances in the use of drones and drone strikes. Initially, drones were used to provide surveillance over combat areas without risking pilots and expensive aircraft. But the tactics they are used for have changed radically in recent years.

Jus in Bello (Legal Requirements When Engaged in War)

- ▶ Combatants and noncombatants must be differentiated.
- ▶ Noncombatants must be protected from harm as much as possible (noncombatant immunity).
- ▶ The means of violence used must be proportionate to the ends to be achieved (proportionality).
- ▶ Unnecessary human suffering should be avoided at all costs.

Many U.S. drones are armed with missiles that operators can aim and launch from thousands of miles away, sometimes killing civilians as well as combatants. In July 2016, the United States estimated that outside conventional war zones, 2,372 to 2,581 combatants and 64 to 116 civilians have been killed in its drone strikes since 2009. These numbers are debated, however, and several independent organizations have estimated that anywhere from 200 to 800 civilians have been killed.[20]

Drone strikes thus raise the questions of noncombatant immunity and proportionality. Most of those targeted do not wear uniforms, nor do they formally serve a state, and the process by which U.S. intelligence agencies determine targets remains classified. Also, is the harm caused by drone missile strikes controlled so that noncombatant immunity is ensured to the greatest degree possible?

Cyberwarfare and Just War

Cyberwarfare has added a new dimension to the question of "just" war. In particular, the question is whether a cyberattack is prohibited under international law and under what conditions a cyberattack can justify legal retaliation in self-defense. First, the UN Charter's general prohibition on war is framed in terms of a prohibition on the "threat or use of force." Second, the UN Charter allows for retaliation in self-defense when "an armed attack occurs" against a state. Does a cyberattack constitute a "use of force" or an "armed attack?" Are there certain conditions when it does and certain conditions when it does not? If so, what are those conditions? The centrality of this debate in international politics today was evident when a prominent legal scholar was asked to testify before the U.S. Senate Armed Services Committee in March 2017 "to address some of the international law questions most relevant to cyber threats and U.S. strategy. These include whether and when a cyber-attack amounts to an 'act of war,' or, more precisely, an 'armed attack' triggering a right of self-defense."[21]

Three main positions have been put forward in the debate about cyberattacks and the right of self-defense under international law.[22] On one extreme, the "instrument-based" approach argues that a cyberattack will almost never be an armed attack because it does not have the physical characteristics of "traditional military coercion." A cyberattack can therefore only count as an armed attack if it uses military weapons. Such attacks might include bombings of computer servers or cables, but not attacks actually arising in cyberspace. On the other extreme, the "target-based" approach classifies any cyberattack that targets a sufficiently important computer system as an armed attack. In other words, a cyberattack counts as an armed attack when it penetrates any critical national infrastructure system. It would thus count as an armed attack regardless of whether it caused any physical destruction or casualties. This opens up a wide range of cyberactions that could trigger the use of force against a state acting in self-defense, and this approach is often criticized because following it could make war more likely. Falling between these two extreme positions, the "effects-based" approach classifies a cyberattack as an armed attack based on the "gravity" of its effects. This is the most mainstream of the three approaches. Debate, however, continues. The main issue is how to define what types of effects trigger the right to act in self-defense before an attack has occurred, and how to do so in a way that can be applied consistently. These questions remain unanswered, and debates are widespread among international relations scholars, legal scholars, and foreign policy makers. Indeed, disagreement regarding how cybersecurity fits in international law with regard to the use of force is the central reason why the UN Group of Governmental Experts could not reach an agreement in its 2017 meeting. These debates about cyberwarfare and *jus ad bellum* will likely continue for years to come.

Cyberwarfare also adds complications to the question of legal actions with regard to permissible conduct during war—*jus in bello*. First, a debate exists about cyberwarfare and noncombatant immunity. On the one hand, cyberattacks need to be spread to be effective. This creates a risk of affecting noncombatants, even though they might not be targeted. Moreover, because government and civilian networks are so interconnected, restricting attacks to military targets may not always be possible. For example, the Stuxnet worm was intended to target Iranian nuclear processing facilities but spread far beyond its intended targets. Some cyberattacks are even specifically designed to attack civilians and civilian industries and facilities. Cyberattacks are also known to have psychological effects. They cause significant anxiety and often influence rational political thinking, so much so that some argue that even if they do not cause physical harm, cyberattacks inevitably violate the principle of noncombatant immunity. On the other hand, others argue that cyberattacks can actually decrease the casualties suffered by noncombatants because they put noncombatants at less risk than physical wars do. Collateral damage may be decreased because cyberattacks can be more discriminatory than physical war. Using cyberwarfare instead of physical warfare may therefore save more noncombatants than it harms. For example, John Arquilla argues that during the Russo-Georgian War in 2008, "while there was little doubt about who would win that war, the Georgians would almost surely have fought longer and harder than the five days the conflict lasted had their command capabilities not been so seriously disrupted [by the Russian cyberattacks]." The attack therefore helped avoid greater physical violence.[23]

Second, cyberwarfare also raises the issue of proportionality. In cyberwarfare, as we have seen, the results are often unpredictable. Ensuring proportionality of an attack is therefore difficult. Moreover, because it is difficult to know what the actual effects of an attack are, and even harder to assess an attack's intended effects and the actual source of an attack, it is also difficult to judge the level of response to a cyberattack that would be proportional. Is a military attack in response to a cyberattack a proportional response? What if the attack was not carried out by a government? If so, is responding with an attack against a state proportional? Cyberwarfare raises many new questions and debates about how a "just war" can be fought today.

IN SUM: INTERNATIONAL AND STATE SECURITY TODAY

National security and conflict between states (of various forms) is a principal topic in the study of international relations today. Conflicts can occur between states, within states, and even in cyberspace. Understanding the causes of these conflicts, as well as the steps that can be taken to ensure national security, is therefore of central importance to policy makers and international relations scholars.

However, states are not always engaged in conflict. They can (and often do) cooperate. They sign treaties, they create and work together in institutions, and they negotiate ends to conflict. In addition to focusing on conflict, studying *cooperation* between states is therefore also important in the study of international relations. We turn to this issue in the next chapter.

Discussion Questions

1. How can we identify an aggressor in international conflicts? Is such identification important? Why or why not?

2. Cybersecurity raises interesting questions regarding just war. Do you think a cyberattack constitutes the use of force, and thus gives a state the right to respond in self-defense? Or are cyberattacks different than conventional attacks? What if they are not perpetrated by states? How should state leaders respond?

3. An American decision maker charged with U.S.–Russian Federation policy requests policy memos from realists (an offensive realist and a defensive realist), a liberal, and a constructivist. How might their respective recommendations differ?

4. Realists, liberals, and constructivists pose different "solutions" to the problem of war. Which of these approaches do you think is likely to be most effective? Why?

Key Terms

arms control (p. 220)

asymmetric conflict (p. 197)

cyberspace (p. 204)

cyberwarfare (p. 204)

disarmament (p. 220)

interstate wars (p. 191)

intrastate wars (p. 193)

jus ad bellum (p. 224)

jus in bello (p. 224)

national security (p. 188)

terrorism (p. 198)

unconventional warfare (p. 196)

war (p. 191)

One of the greatest successes that has emerged from states cooperating with one another is the dismantling of nuclear weapons across the world. While the threat of nuclear force still exists, it is at a much smaller scale than once predicted. Here, an aircraft equipped to launch nuclear missiles is dismantled in Ukraine.

7

International Cooperation and International Law

In 1970, the Nuclear Nonproliferation Treaty (NPT) came into force. In the treaty, states without nuclear weapons agreed not to acquire them, and states with nuclear weapons agreed to further the cause of disarmament. In many ways, the treaty can be considered a success. Of all arms control treaties, the NPT has the widest adherence. One hundred ninety states are parties to the treaty, and almost none have developed nuclear weapons programs. Even states that already had nuclear weapons or weapons development programs such as South Africa, Ukraine, Brazil, and Argentina dismantled their weapons and/or halted their development programs upon joining the treaty.

But the NPT is clearly not a complete success. Joining is voluntary, and the NPT itself cannot force compliance. So some states have chosen not to join the treaty, and some states have joined but not cooperated. India and Pakistan never joined the treaty, choosing instead to develop their own nuclear weapons capabilities and build up significant arsenals. North Korea continued its nuclear weapons program even after joining the treaty, and eventually withdrew from the treaty in 2003.

Why have most states cooperated, joining the NPT and choosing to comply with it while others have not? In fact, given that all states are concerned about their own security, and nuclear weapons are the most powerful of weapons, why have any cooperated at all? Why would a state not develop a nuclear program, which could help it build up its power and thus better protect itself? And even if a state did not want to develop nuclear weapons, if the treaty could not stop other states from doing so, why did states bother to make the treaty in the first place?

In this chapter, we seek to better understand initiatives like the NPT and the questions they raise: How and why do states cooperate instead of escalating conflict? And why do they (often) agree to follow laws that govern the world outside their own borders? Wars might get the biggest headlines, but international cooperation is happening every day. Understanding its dynamics is crucial to understanding international relations today.

LEARNING OBJECTIVES

▶ **Define international cooperation and explain why realists argue that achieving it can be difficult.**

▶ **Describe how the theoretical perspectives explain instances of cooperation.**

▶ **Define international law and describe its various sources.**

▶ **Explain the reasons why states comply with international law.**

In addition to state security, cooperation between states is a central topic in the study of international relations. The standard definition used in the international relations literature treats cooperation as a situation in which actors mutually adjust their behavior to accommodate the actual or anticipated preferences of others in the pursuit of common goals. Those preferences can neither be identical (or there would be no behavioral adjustment required) nor irreconcilable (as no adjustment of behavior could ever accommodate both sides).[1] **International cooperation** therefore exists when states adopt behavior that is consistent with the preferences of other states in order to achieve common objectives. Those common objectives are widespread, making cooperation an important issue to investigate.

This chapter focuses on two key aspects of the study of international cooperation: (1) the problem of cooperation and how it might be solved, and (2) the creation and enforcement of international law, which codifies rules to help govern international cooperation.

INTERNATIONAL COOPERATION

While conflicts occur between states, war is not the norm. We see a significant amount of cooperation between states. Given that states are sovereign actors and that there is no world government forcing cooperation or preventing states from attacking each other, why do states cooperate with one another? The various theories of international relations have different approaches to answering this question. Realists point out the difficulties underpinning international cooperation, while liberals provide insights into how states overcome those difficulties. Constructivists are largely agnostic as to whether states will cooperate or not, but highlight certain conditions under which we can expect one versus the other.

Realism and the Cooperation Problem

Realists recognize that international cooperation is difficult to achieve. Two key problems contribute to this difficulty—the relative gains problem and what they call the "prisoner's dilemma."

According to realists, the first problem is that states focus on relative gains. As discussed in Chapter 3, relative gains refers to how much more one state gains over another from a given interaction. States focus on relative gains because the anarchic international system creates a self-help world. A state can only truly rely on its own power to defend itself from coercion by others. Its ability to do so depends on how much power it has relative to other states. A gain in power for one state relative to another means it is better able to coerce that other state. In an effort to prevent this from happening, states focus on relative gains.

Because they focus on relative gains, states are likely to be hesitant to engage in cooperation, as the benefits of cooperation are likely to be unevenly distributed among participating states. For example, if two states are trading partners, and after each trade one gains $3 million and the other gains $1.5 million, both gain in absolute terms. However, over time the former will accumulate significantly more wealth than the latter. It can then use that advantage to coerce the other. In a realist world where state survival depends on having more power relative to other states, and where it is almost never (if ever) the case that states gain in exactly the same way from cooperation, it is likely to be difficult for states to cooperate even if they both can benefit from cooperation in absolute terms.

As an example of how cooperation can be hindered by relative gains concerns and the security dilemma, consider an arms race. Arms races are costly. They require states to develop and maintain expensive military arsenals. However, if one state increases its military armaments while another does not, it gains militarily relative to that other state. This increases the first state's ability to coerce or attack the second. Fearing this possibility, the second state will therefore increase its armaments as well. In doing so, it gains militarily relative to the first state, which then spurs the first state to further increase its armaments, and so on. Recognizing states' concerns with relative gains can therefore help us understand why we see states engaging in costly nuclear arms races. For example, following World War II, the United States had a monopoly on nuclear weapons. However, the Soviet Union was actively pursuing the technology in order to catch up with U.S. capabilities. At the beginning of the Cold War, it demonstrated its own acquisition of nuclear weapons, detonating its first nuclear bomb in 1949. Recognizing that the Soviet acquisition of nuclear weapons had changed the states' relative capabilities, the United States then began to pursue the development of an even stronger weapon, detonating its first hydrogen bomb in 1952. The Soviet Union responded by developing its own hydrogen bomb, detonating its first in 1953. In 1954, the United States detonated an even larger hydrogen bomb. This back-and-forth continued throughout the Cold War, as the United States and the Soviet Union developed intercontinental ballistic missiles, planes, and submarines capable of delivering nuclear bombs to the other side and steadily increased their weapons stockpiles. By 1981, the United States had about 8,000 intercontinental ballistic missiles and the Soviet Union had about 7,000. The United States had about 4,000 planes capable of delivering a nuclear bomb, and the Soviet Union had 5,000. By the end of the Cold War, the Soviet Union was estimated to be spending over 25 percent of its GDP on the military, and U.S. defense spending was over $350 billion.[2] Both would have benefited in absolute terms if they did not have to pay the costs of increasing and maintaining their nuclear arsenals. However, if one had cooperated in this way, it would have faced the risk that the other side would not do so, thus increasing the other side's relative military power. The risk associated with adopting cooperative behavior is high when relative gains are on the line. Realists therefore argue that getting states to cooperate is difficult.

The second problem that makes cooperation difficult, according to realists, is the problem of cheating by the other state. If you are being nice, someone else can potentially exploit that niceness in order to gain more, and you will be hurt in the process. This is often described as a "prisoner's dilemma."

The **prisoner's dilemma** is the story of two prisoners who are interrogated separately for an alleged crime. The police have enough evidence to convict both prisoners on a minor charge but need testimony from one in order to convict the other for a suspected major charge. An interrogator tells each prisoner that if one testifies against the other while the other stays silent, the one who testifies will go free—the sentence for the minor charge will be reduced for helping the police. The one who stays silent, however, will get a one-year prison term—the sentence for the major charge. If both testify, both will get six-month prison terms—the punishment for the major charge will be reduced for helping the police. If both stay silent, they will both receive one-month prison terms for the minor charge. Staying silent is referred to as "cooperating" with the other prisoner, while testifying against the other prisoner is referred to as "defecting."

In this "prisoner's dilemma" situation, each prisoner has an individual incentive to defect. If Prisoner A stays silent, Prisoner B is best off testifying and going free rather than staying silent as well and facing a one-month prison term. If Prisoner A testifies, Prisoner B is still best off testifying and receiving only the six-month prisoner term instead of the one-year term. Regardless of what Prisoner A does, Prisoner B is better off testifying. Prisoner A faces the same incentives. The outcome of the interaction is therefore that both will choose to testify against the other (defect).

Consider President Trump's decision in 2017 to withdraw the United States from the Paris climate change agreement. One of the central arguments for doing so was that adhering to the agreement would require the United States to impose costly regulatory requirements on its industries. If the United States then "cooperated" and did so, while states such as China and India "defected" from the agreement and did not, U.S. industries would become less able to compete against industries from those states. The potential loss of economic competitiveness was an important concern that contributed to the decision to withdraw from the cooperative agreement.

The "dilemma" of these prisoner's dilemma situations is that both sides end up defecting but would have been better off if they both had cooperated. If both prisoners had cooperated, they would each have received only a one-month sentence instead of the six-month sentence they received because they both defected. If all states cooperated and adopted regulatory policies to combat climate change, they would further their environmental goals. Yet achieving cooperation is difficult because each side has an incentive to cheat rather than uphold its side of the cooperative outcome. Cheating while the other side cooperates allows a prisoner to go free and a state to have more competitive industries. Knowing that this incentive to cheat exists, each side is driven away from the choice to cooperate in the first place. Mutual defection results even if mutual cooperation is more beneficial.

The Cooperation Problem

▶ Cooperation is difficult.

▶ States face the relative gains problem.

▶ The cooperation problem reflects the realist view of cooperation.

▶ States face the cheating problem (prisoner's dilemma).

For realists, then, the cooperation problem persists in international relations because the international system is anarchic. No authority exists to force states to cooperate. Without such an authority, states are left to make their choices based solely on their own self-interest. Realists argue that these self-interested choices point away from cooperation—either because of concerns for relative gains or because of concerns that other states will cheat and exploit cooperative efforts. Yet while we do see many instances of noncooperation in the international system, we also see cooperation. States sign arms control and arms reduction agreements. They negotiate trade and environmental protection agreements. Most importantly, they often uphold those commitments. Why, if cooperation is so hard, do we see these types of actions?

Neoliberal Institutionalism and Cooperation

The branch of liberal theory referred to as neoliberal institutionalism addresses the cooperation problem posed by realists most directly. Like realists, neoliberal institutionalists accept the fact that the international system is anarchic, that states are unitary actors that pursue their own self-interest in a rational way, and that no authority can force states to cooperate. Although neoliberal institutionalists begin at the same starting point as realists do, they expect that states will often cooperate, arguing that it is often in their own self-interest to do so. This self-interest in cooperation stems from the fact that states interact continuously, meaning that they have the opportunity to reciprocate cooperation or noncooperation.

As shown above, if the prisoner's dilemma is played only once, it is in each prisoner's self-interest to defect. However, if the prisoner's dilemma is played repeatedly, the likelihood of reciprocity (referred to as a "tit-for-tat" strategy) makes it rational for each prisoner to cooperate rather than defect.[3] If either prisoner testified against the other in a first round, then in a second round that prisoner could expect retaliation. That prisoner would receive the short-term gain of going free in the first round, but would face at least a six-month sentence when the other prisoner retaliated in the next round. Over time, the six-month sentences would add up, making the prison term, overall, significantly longer than it would have been if the prisoners had cooperated and only received the one-month sentence in each round. The expectation of reciprocity across repeated interactions makes it rational for the prisoners to cooperate rather than defect. The long-term benefits of cooperation outweigh the short-term benefits of defecting.

States in the international system have the same type of repeated interaction. They are not faced with a one-time round of "play": they confront each other repeatedly across a wide range of issues. Across these interactions, reciprocity can therefore be an effective strategy for eliciting cooperation. In early 2017, the United States wanted to entice China to cooperate with its efforts to put pressure on North Korea to cease its nuclear weapons program. So the United States promised China cooperation on other issues in return: the United States offered to relax its stance against China's increased power in the South China Sea and to soften its position in trade negotiations. Cooperation on these issues was offered in order to secure cooperation from China on the issue of North Korea. But while China and the United States interact on a variety of issues, some issues may be more salient to one state than the other. China is stalling on trying to change the behavior of North Korea, probably because it views its own national security interests as more vital than reciprocity on an issue vital to the United States. China may also be stalling because there are no international institutions that include all the relevant actors— China, the United States, and North Korea.

According to neoliberal institutionalists, international institutions—a term that, as defined in Chapter 3, refers to both international organizations and international law and treaties—play an important role in fostering the reciprocity between states that can sustain cooperation. First, institutions provide a guaranteed framework of interactions, and thus increase states' expectations that they will continue to interact far into the future. In other words, they lengthen the **shadow of the future**, creating a powerful expectation for states that they will have repeated interactions. The North Atlantic Treaty Organization and the European Union's Common Foreign and Security Policy provide expectations about consistent future interactions regarding security and defense policy among their member states. The North American Free Trade Agreement and the treaties of the European Union create expectations about consistent future interactions regarding trade among their member states. The expectation of repeated future interactions created by these institutions increases the potential for cooperation between their member states in these various issue areas by helping create the expectation that reciprocity can and will be used.

Second, international institutions—international treaties, in particular—enable states to align their expectations about what cooperative behavior looks like. As

Realists would likely highlight the actions of the United States at the G7 conference in June 2018 as an example of the prevalence of noncooperation, even on non-security issues such as trade. Here President Trump sits defiant against other G7 leaders.

James Morrow describes it, international law creates a "bright line" of a behavioral standard.[4] This is important because reciprocity can only be an effective strategy if both states know that their cooperative behavior will be met with the same in return. It may not always be clear, however, what behavior is cooperative in nature. For example, states might agree to treat their prisoners of war humanely. But what treatment of prisoners of war is cooperating (or not cooperating) with such an agreement? Is forcing them to provide information cooperating with the agreement or not? What about using them for labor? Institutions like the treaties that make up international law regarding conduct during war help make cooperative and noncooperative behavior easier to identify. The 1929 Geneva Convention lays out specific rules for what constitutes acceptable and unacceptable behavior toward prisoners of

IN FOCUS

Neoliberal Institutionalist Approach to Cooperation

- ▶ The cooperation problem can be overcome.

- ▶ Repeated interactions and reciprocity can help overcome the prisoner's dilemma.

- ▶ International institutions can lengthen the shadow of the future.

- ▶ International institutions provide information on cooperation and defection.

- ▶ International institutions can provide information about cooperation and defection of others.

war. These rules allow states to more easily identify instances when another state is acting cooperatively, and reciprocate accordingly.

Third, and finally, international institutions—international organizations, in particular—can provide states with information about the behavior being adopted by other states that is critical for reciprocity to be effective. States cannot reciprocate actions that they do not or cannot observe. Yet states cannot always tell whether or not other states are reducing carbon emissions, refraining from erecting barriers to free trade, or developing nuclear weapons. How can states reward cooperation and punish defection if they do not know what other states are doing? Institutions can monitor state actions and provide states with this type of information. The Kyoto Protocol established a verification system to monitor states' carbon emissions and share that information with the rest of the world. The World Trade Organization has a dispute settlement procedure that collects information and evaluates whether state actions are in violation of international trade laws. The International Atomic Energy Agency investigates state behavior regarding the use of nuclear technology. The information provided by these types of institutions helps states know when other states are cooperating and when they are defecting, allowing them to respond in turn. Overall, international institutions play a central role in fostering cooperation in neoliberal institutionalist theory.

Other Liberal Explanations of Cooperation

While neoliberal institutionalism provides the most direct answer to the realists' cooperation problem, other liberal theories also provide explanations for why states cooperate. Classical liberal thinkers put forth a positive conception of human nature to help understand why states are likely to cooperate. Liberals believe humans can learn from history and can thus achieve social progress. In other words, humans are willing and able to construct a more peaceful society. Individuals will thus naturally cooperate out of innate characteristics of humanity.

Other liberal theories provide more rational explanations for why states cooperate. As famously put forth by Immanuel Kant in his book *Perpetual Peace* (1795), liberals highlight three important factors that discourage states from engaging in conflict and foster international cooperation: democracy (Kant's reference to a "republican constitution"), economic interdependence (Kant's reference to a "commercial spirit of trade"), and international institutions (Kant's reference to a "federation of free states"). Together, these factors are labeled the "Kantian triangle of peace," and their existence can help explain the prevalence of cooperation between states.[5]

First, liberal theorists argue that democracy facilitates cooperation. Democratic political processes not only help prevent conflict (as discussed in Chapter 6) but also foster cooperative interactions. In a democracy, other states can observe the internal deliberation processes, promoting greater trust in the sincerity of leaders' public statements and increasing the ability of other states' leaders to monitor the democratic leaders' actions. Democratic leaders also face domestic audience costs if they defect from their international commitments, decreasing their incentive to do so. These factors reduce the fear of cheating—a key factor that realists argue makes cooperation difficult. When the fear that the other will cheat is mitigated for states on both sides, cooperation is more likely. Democracies are therefore more likely to engage in cooperative interactions than other pairs of states are.

Second, liberal theory highlights the central role of **economic interdependence** in fostering cooperation. Being economically interdependent means that states rely on one another for goods and/or economic gain. But as Norman Angell argued in *The Great Illusion*, war inevitably generates economic losses in business and trade. The territorial gains that can be achieved through war cannot compensate for these economic losses.[6] The more interdependent states are, the greater the economic losses they will experience from war, and thus the less likely they are to engage in conflict with one another. Economic interdependence, which is ever increasing with globalization, can therefore help explain why we see cooperation rather than conflict between states.

Third, international institutions—both formal organizations and treaties—play an important role in liberal explanations for cooperation. In addition to the role they play in facilitating cooperation in the context of neoliberal institutionalist arguments, liberals also argue that institutions reduce **transaction costs** (the costs of making an exchange). This facilitates states' ability to negotiate cooperative agreements. For example, the General Agreement on Tariffs and Trade (GATT) created a forum for multilateral trade negotiations. Without the GATT, states would have had to negotiate a large network of bilateral or smaller multilateral agreements liberalizing trade between them. Not only would doing so have created a fragmented trading system with different rules and standards across a large number of different agreements, but it also would have been extremely costly because of the resources required for such a large number of negotiations. In the institutional context of the GATT, states only had to participate in one negotiation and secure one agreement covering their trade relationship with a large number of other states.

International institutions not only facilitate the negotiation of agreements by lowering transaction costs, but also play a role in fostering cooperation after those agreements have been reached. In particular, they help coordinate their member states' behavior in order to bring about outcomes that are in their collective and individual long-term interests. Liberal theorists recognize that states are sovereign actors. However, they argue that states are often willing to respect the principles

Other Liberal Approaches to Cooperation

- ▶ The cooperation problem can be overcome.
- ▶ Sharing similar democratic institutions and values can foster cooperation.
- ▶ International institutions facilitate negotiations that can lead to cooperation.
- ▶ International institutions make commitments more credible.

- ▶ Classical liberal theorists argue that individuals will naturally cooperate out of innate characteristics of humanity.
- ▶ Economic interdependence can foster cooperation.
- ▶ International institutions coordinate cooperative behavior.

of international institutions in order to fulfill their long-term interests, even at the cost of forgoing short-term individual gains.

Institutions also help make states' commitments more credible. Becoming a party to a treaty or international organization makes the commitment embodied in that institution public and formal, which adds transparency to the process. A state is therefore likely to face reputational costs at both the domestic and international level if it violates that commitment. Raising the costs of violation makes it more likely that other states will believe the commitment will be upheld.[7] A commitment to reduce greenhouse emissions is likely to be seen as more credible when a state signs an environmental agreement. Other international actors are more likely to believe that states are committed to adopting liberal economic policies when they join trade agreements that formalize that commitment and make it public. Realists might respond to the liberal arguments by highlighting cases like U.S. actions after the G7 conference in June 2018. The United States refused to sign the joint communique that resulted from the conference, which sought to safeguard free trade between the G7 states. U.S. President Donald Trump threatened to raise trade barriers if the current cooperative agreements governing trade remained, which he viewed as unfair to the United States. Liberals would likely respond by highlighting the tit-for-tat threats to defect made by its G7 trade partners in response to U.S. defection in the hope that this would deter the United States from carrying out its threat in the first place. They would also likely cite the very creation of the joint communique, which provided an opportunity for the other G7 states to solidify their own cooperative relationships. With both realists and liberals able to draw on different aspects of cases like the G7 conference to defend their approach to cooperation, the debate between them is likely to continue.

Constructivism and Cooperation

While realists anticipate a general lack of cooperation between states, and liberals anticipate considerable amounts of cooperation, constructivists are largely agnostic as to whether conflict or cooperation is more likely. As Alexander Wendt put it, "Anarchy is what states make of it."[8] Whether we see cooperation or conflict between states depends on a variety of factors, including states' identities, the nature of their shared understandings, and norms that are in place.

Identities play a central role in constructivist accounts of international cooperation. Just as divergent identities can help us understand why we might see conflict between states, convergent identities can help us understand why we might see cooperation. Constructivists often point to the shared identity of democracies, in particular, to help explain cooperation. Democratic decision-making processes are governed by a norm of establishing nonviolent and compromise-oriented resolutions to conflict. The norms that regulate their domestic processes shape the identity of democracies, and are thus expected to regulate their interactions at the international level as well. This creates for democracies a mutual expectation of nonviolent and compromise-oriented interactions between them. This, in turn, fosters cooperation.

Liberals also highlight the role that norms associated with democracies can play in fostering cooperation. The main difference between liberal and constructivist explanations for cooperation is that constructivists view democracy as an identity, rather than a mere characteristic of states, as liberals view it. For constructivists, having a democratic identity (and sharing that identity) is what influences cooperation.

The North Atlantic Treaty Organization (NATO) provides an illustrative example. At the end of World War II, the United States had a monopoly on advanced military power and an economy that outweighed the economy of the Soviet Union, as well as the economies of all of Western Europe together. Despite the United States' superior power, France and Britain did not perceive the United States as threatening. Their shared identity as democracies, and the peaceful interactions that shared identity was expected to create, fostered a mutual sense of an "us" in which cooperative interactions were expected—an identity that stood in contrast to the Soviet Union, "them," whose nondemocratic identity did not foster an expectation of cooperative interactions. Rather than allying with the Soviet Union to balance against the United States, France and Britain chose to cooperate with the United States, forming a security alliance with it (NATO).[9]

The continuation of NATO after the end of the Cold War similarly points to the importance of this shared democratic identity in sustaining cooperation. Instead of disintegrating after the collapse of the Soviet Union, NATO has continued to exist. While the shared enemy, the Soviet Union, disappeared, the shared identity and values of the NATO democracies did not change with the end of the Cold War. NATO, which embodied those values, therefore did not become obsolete. In fact, democracy actually spread into Eastern Europe, and the expansion of NATO to include these new countries reflects the desire of democracies, with their shared identity, to work together in the international system. This shared identity, which is reinforced at meetings of NATO members, is considered critical. Hence, in 2017 when President Trump failed to confirm those shared values, he was widely criticized for betraying the foundation of the agreement.

In addition, for all states—even states that are not democracies—shared understandings that create expectations about the nature of their interactions can foster cooperation. As Wendt describes, in the international anarchic environment, states will begin to engage in interactions. These interactions can be amicable, such as the adoption of positive, cooperative reciprocal moves, or they can be conflictual. If the interactions are conflictual, cooperation between the states is less likely to develop. If the interactions are positive, however, mutual expectations that the other side will adopt cooperative behavior can arise over time. What began as spontaneous cooperative reciprocity can transform into mutually expected habits (norms). The norm of cooperation between the states thus drives further cooperation.[10] While liberals argue that strategic reciprocity sustains cooperation throughout time, constructivists argue that a norm of cooperation that has developed between certain states over time best explains cooperation between them today. For constructivists, not every move is a strategic calculation. Cooperation is often driven simply by states' shared expectations that their interactions will be cooperative.

For constructivists, not only can existing norms foster cooperation, but states can also become socialized to new norms that shape their interests in a way that fosters cooperation. For example, a norm exists today that medical personnel should be granted immunity during war and should be allowed to treat the wounded from both sides. This was not always a norm, however. The Red Cross had to work to

IN FOCUS

Constructivist Approaches to Cooperation

- ▶ The cooperation problem can be overcome.
- ▶ Cooperation is most likely between states with convergent identities.
- ▶ States can be socialized to norms of cooperation.
- ▶ Shared democratic identities and norms can foster cooperation.
- ▶ A norm of cooperation can develop.

persuade states that medical personnel and resources should not be captured as spoils of war and should be allowed to care for victims on both sides. Without immunity, medical personnel were disincentivized to come to the battlefield to treat the sick and wounded. States began to recognize that it was not in their interests to take actions that discouraged medical personnel from treating their wounded. Moreover, they recognized that it was in their overarching interests to have their own wounded soldiers cared for on the enemy's battlefield. In order to get cooperation from other states, they would have to grant immunity to medical personnel on their own territory, as well as allow them to treat wounded enemy combatants. States' interests, which had previously been focused on seizing medical personnel and preventing them from treating enemy combatants, shifted. As states' interests shifted, the norm of immunity for the wounded and medical personnel spread. States began to cooperate and protect medical personnel on their own territory, and opposing states did so as well. As this example illustrates, not only can norms of behavior foster cooperation, but states can also be socialized to accept new cooperation-inducing norms.

Overall, there are many possible explanations for why we see cooperation among states. Institutions, in particular, play an important role in this process. One of the most critical institutions for facilitating cooperation is international law.

INTERNATIONAL LAW

International law consists of a body of rules and norms regulating interactions among states, between states and IGOs, and, in more limited cases, among IGOs, states, and individuals. It is an important type of international institution that codifies methods of cooperation and provides a mechanism for settling disputes between states. It also serves a variety of other functions: setting a body of expectations, providing order, protecting the status quo, and legitimating the use of force by a government to maintain order. In addition, international law serves ethical and moral functions, aiming in most cases to be fair and equitable and delineating what is socially and culturally desirable.

International law developed thousands of years before contemporary international organizations. Treaties between city-states and communities can be found in Mesopotamia; the Greeks and the Romans differentiated among different kinds of law, including international law; and during the Middle Ages, the authority of the Catholic Church developed canon law applying to all believers internationally. Yet international law is largely a product of Western civilization. The man dubbed the father of international law, the Dutch scholar Hugo Grotius (1583–1645), elucidated a number of fundamental principles that serve as the foundation for modern international law and international organization. For Grotius, all international relations are subject to the rule of law—that is, a law of nations and the law of nature, the latter serving as the ethical basis for the former. Grotian thinking rejects the idea that states can do whatever they wish and that war is the supreme right of states and the hallmark of their sovereignty. Grotius, a classic idealist, believed that states, like people, basically are rational and law abiding, capable of achieving cooperative goals.

The Grotian tradition holds that order in international relations is based on the rule of law. Although Grotius himself was not concerned with an organization for administering this rule of law, many subsequent theorists have seen an organizational structure as a vital component in realizing the principles of international order. The Grotian tradition was challenged by the Westphalian tradition, which established the notion of state sovereignty within a territorial space (see Chapter 2). A persistent tension arose between the Westphalian tradition, with its emphasis on sovereignty, and the Grotian tradition, with its focus on law and order. Did affirmation of state sovereignty mean that international law was irrelevant? Could international law undermine, or even threaten, state sovereignty? Would states join an international body that could challenge or even subvert their own sovereignty?

These questions of sovereignty are especially important because international law demands obedience and compels behavior. Compliance by states is not flawless, but in many cases we do see states cooperating and acting in accordance with international law. Why do sovereign states do so? To answer this question, it is important to consider the various sources of international law and the ways it might be enforced in the international system.

Sources of International Law

In individual states, domestic laws are made by legislatures, adjudicated by a judiciary, and enforced by an executive. In the international system, however, there is no world government, no legislature, and no executive. Where does international law come from? Two of the most important sources are customs and treaties.

Customs

International law, like domestic law, comes from a variety of sources. Virtually all law emerges from custom. Either a hegemon or a group of states solves a problem in a particular way; these habits become ingrained as more states follow the same custom, and eventually the body codifies the custom into law. For example, Great Britain and later the United States were primarily responsible for developing the law of the sea. As great seafaring powers, each state adopted practices— establishing rights of passage through straits, methods of signaling other ships, conduct during war, and the like—that became the customary law of the sea and were eventually codified into treaties. The laws protecting diplomats and embassies likewise emerged from long-standing customs.

But customary law is limited. For one thing, it often develops slowly since multiple cases are needed to demonstrate the existence of a new customary practice. British naval custom evolved into the law of the sea over several hundred years. Sometimes customs become outmoded. For example, the three-mile territorial extension from shore was established because that was the distance a cannonball could fly. Eventually, law caught up with changes in technology, and states were granted a 12-mile extension of territory into the ocean. But even then, a period of conflict between advocates of the new and supporters of the old often follows. Occasionally, customs change more rapidly. The norms and prohibition against genocide developed in just one generation, as discussed in Chapter 10. Furthermore, not all states participate in the making of customary law, let alone assent to the customs that have become law through European-centered practices. And the fact that customary law is initially uncodified leads to ambiguity in interpretation.

Treaties

International law also arises from treaties, the dominant source of law today. **Treaties** (sometimes called conventions, covenants, or protocols) are explicitly written agreements among states that lay out rights and obligations. Their creation and enforcement today are governed by the Vienna Convention on the Law of Treaties (the "treaty on treaties") that was adopted in 1969. Over 25,000 treaties have been created covering myriad issues, including peace, arms control, trade, refugees, and the environment. Even issues like air, land, and water transport and space exploration have dedicated treaties. In all of these issues areas, treaties are legally binding on states: only major changes in circumstances give states the right not to follow treaties they have ratified.

Treaties are created by states themselves through a process of negotiation and acceptance. The International Law Commission drafts some, and states then negotiate and change them. Almost all, however, are both drafted and negotiated by states. First, states meet (sometimes across multiple sessions) and work out the details of the treaty. The "adoption" of a treaty signifies that negotiations over the text have come to an end. As specified by the Vienna Convention on the Law of Treaties, the adoption of a treaty is typically done either by consensus or by at least a two-thirds majority vote of the states participating in the negotiations. Once a treaty has been adopted, it is opened for signature. States can then choose to sign or not sign, regardless of whether they participated in the negotiations. For example,

Treaties are crucial in establishing law across all areas of the international system. In 1963, representatives from the United States, the United Kingdom, and the Soviet Union signed the Outer Space Treaty, which provided a framework for the international laws of space travel and exploration.

the United States participated in the negotiation of the Law of the Sea Treaty but never signed it.

Some treaties specify that a signature is all that is needed for a state to become legally bound by the treaty. Once these treaties enter into force, they are legally binding on the states that have signed them. However, most treaties require more than just a signature. Most require an additional process of ratification, as many states have domestic requirements that mandate legislative approval of treaties. Only if states ratify these types of treaties through their domestic process will they be legally bound by them. Signature in these cases is not enough. Many states have signed treaties that they did not ratify and are therefore not bound by those treaties' obligations. For example, the United States signed but not did not ratify the Kyoto Protocol, the Convention on the Elimination of All Forms of Discrimination against Women, and other major human rights treaties.

Even after ratification, a state is not legally bound to a treaty until it enters into force. Treaties usually enter into force at a time specified in the treaty itself, sometimes with specific requirements. For example, the Kyoto Protocol (1997) could not enter into force until at least 55 parties ratified it, with those ratifiers including industrialized countries that accounted for at least 55 percent of carbon dioxide (CO_2) emissions in 1990. These types of provisions sometimes cause interesting problems for states. For example, despite having signed the Kyoto Protocol, the United States (which accounted for about 36 percent of CO_2 emissions in 1990) made clear in the 2000s that it would not ratify it. This meant that even though over 120 states had ratified the protocol, the 55 percent CO_2 emissions requirement would not be met and it could therefore not enter into force. The ratifiers thus had to go to Russia and agree to not require any emission reductions on its part if it participated. The treaty entered into force, but without U.S. participation and without emissions reduction requirements for Russia.

Once a treaty enters into force, the states that have ratified it are legally bound by its provisions. States can also join a treaty even after it has entered into force and even if it is no longer open for signature. This is the same as a ratification process, but it is referred to as "acceding" to the treaty. States that have acceded are legally bound once they have done so, just like the states that ratified it. For example, in 2002 the United Kingdom acceded to the Law of the Sea Treaty. The treaty had entered into force in 1994. Once the UK acceded in 2002, it was legally bound by the treaty, though from 1994 until 2002 it had not been.

Overall, both customs and treaties are important sources of international law. The question, then, is when and why states comply with them.

Enforcement Mechanisms and State Compliance

States are sovereign actors, and compliance with international law is clearly not absolute. Russia violated the treaty banning American and Russian land-based intermediate-range missiles when it deployed such a weapon in 2017. Syria violated the treaty prohibiting the use of chemical weapons when it employed such weapons in Khan Sheikhoun in 2017. Portugal violated the Law of the Sea Treaty in 2004 by refusing entry into the country and the right of innocent passage through its territorial waters to a ship that fulfilled all the requirements. The United States violated the UN Charter by going to war with Iraq in 2003 without approval by the UN Security Council. There are many other examples of such violations. Yet these violations are exceptions. Most of the time, most states do comply with international law. When and why do they do so? Several mechanisms exist that help to produce state compliance (see Table 7.1).

Vertical Enforcement

Vertical enforcement is a legal process whereby one actor works to constrain the actions of another actor over which it has authority in order to secure its compliance with the law. This is the way that domestic law is enforced. If someone violates domestic law, the government of that state has the authority to punish that individual through its police and judicial system. The threat of this punishment motivates citizens to comply with the law. While there is no world government and no world police to enforce international law in the same way, some mechanisms for

TABLE 7.1

Enforcement of International Law

TYPE OF ENFORCEMENT	METHOD	EXAMPLES
Vertical enforcement (top-down)	An international institution with authority over a state secures compliance.	In 2016, the European Court of Justice fined Greece 10 million euros upon request from the European Commission for breaking EU laws regarding the disposal of waste.
Vertical enforcement (bottom-up)	National and local courts can enforce international law.	In 2015, the Spanish Constitutional Court found that a court had breached the right to a fair trial of an interim public employee by refusing to apply clear and consistent EU law.
Horizontal enforcement	States secure compliance from other states.	In 2015, coercive economic sanctions on Iran helped get it to agree to halt its nuclear program.
Self-interest	States benefit from the cooperative behavior resulting from the treaties they sign; they want to continue to foster that beneficial behavior.	The U.S. Department of Transportation passed an order that came into effect in 2008 requiring all standards and recommended practices put forth by the International Civil Aviation Organization to be implemented by the Federal Aviation Administration, recognizing that the United States has an interest in safe, secure, and efficient air navigation services in domestic and international airspace.
Norms and ethics	States follow international rules because they are seen as legitimate and doing so is the "right thing to do."	In 2015, recognizing the legitimacy of the International Court of Justice (ICJ) and its rulings, Nicaragua agreed to abide by the ICJ's decision that Costa Rica had sovereignty over a disputed territory.

vertical enforcement do exist in the international system. In particular, states have created certain international institutions designed to help ensure state compliance with international law.

The most prominent example is the European Union (EU). As discussed in more detail in Chapter 9, the EU consists of several institutions. The European Parliament and the Council of the European Union are tasked with legislating EU law, the European Commission is tasked with proposing new EU legislation and executing EU law, and, along with member states themselves, the European Court of Justice is tasked with interpreting and enforcing EU law. These different organs of the EU are all above the level of the member states, and European law supersedes national laws in many issue areas. The EU institutions help enforce state compliance with the EU laws. The European Court of Justice rules on whether or not national laws are compliant with EU law in virtually every topic of European integration, and can require states to change their national laws if they are found out of compliance. The European Court of Justice can even authorize the European Commission to sanction a state found out of compliance. This method of enforcement of EU law is a prime example of vertical enforcement of international law.

Beyond the EU, states have created a wide array of international courts tasked with interpreting international law and ruling on cases regarding state compliance. The International Court of Justice (ICJ) is the most prominent example. The ICJ is an organ of the United Nations established by the UN Charter. It has two key roles. It settles legal disputes between states in accordance with international law ("contentious cases") and it gives advisory opinions on legal matters referred to it by UN organs. It has ruled on a number of cases covering issues including territorial disputes, maritime disputes and questions regarding the law of the sea, state jurisdiction, diplomatic and consular law, and even allegations regarding the unlawful use of force. In many cases, states abide by the ICJ's rulings. In 1994, the court ruled on a dispute between Libya and Chad about territory over which they have had multiple armed conflicts. The court ruled in favor of Chad, and a few months later, Libya withdrew its troops from the territory. In 1999, the court ruled on a dispute between Botswana and Namibia over an island located in the Chobe River. The court ruled that the island belonged to Botswana, and Namibia announced it would abide by the decision. In 2015, the court ruled on a dispute between Costa Rica and Nicaragua over the sovereignty of a patch of wetlands on the San Juan River. It ruled that Costa Rica had sovereignty over the disputed territory, and that by digging channels in the area and establishing military presence on what was Costa Rican territory, Nicaragua had violated Costa Rica's territory and sovereignty. Nicaragua's deputy foreign minister said Nicaragua would abide by the verdict.

Although the ICJ has been responsible for some significant decisions, it is a fairly weak institution for several reasons. First, the court actually hears very few cases;

between 1946 and 2017, the ICJ has had 141 contentious cases brought before it and has issued only 26 advisory opinions, although since the end of the Cold War, its caseload has increased. Ever since the small developing country of Nicaragua won a judicial victory over the United States in 1986, developing countries have shown greater trust in the court. Although procedures have changed to speed up the lengthy process, the court's noncompulsory jurisdiction provision still limits its caseload. Both parties must agree to the court's jurisdiction before a case is taken. This stands in stark contrast to domestic courts, which enjoy compulsory jurisdiction. A person accused of a crime is compelled to judgment. No state is compelled to submit to the ICJ.

Second, when cases are heard, they rarely deal with the major controversies of the day, such as the war in Vietnam, the invasion of Afghanistan, or the unraveling of the Soviet Union or of Yugoslavia. Those controversies are generally political and outside the court's reach, although interstate boundary disputes are major issues on the court's agenda. These have included cases concerning maritime disputes, including delimitation of the North Sea continental shelf, fisheries jurisdiction in the Gulf of Maine, and the maritime boundary between Cameroon and Nigeria. The court has also ruled on the legality of nuclear tests, environmental protection, and genocide, among other issues. Advisory cases, though they do not enjoy the force of law, have been on some consequential issues, including Israel's construction of the barrier wall in the occupied Palestinian territories (opinion issued in 2004) and Kosovo's unilateral declaration of independence (opinion issued in 2010). Both of these were highly political issues.

Third, only states may initiate proceedings; individuals and nongovernmental actors such as multinational corporations cannot. This stipulation excludes the court from dealing with contemporary disputes involving states and nonstate actors, such as terrorist and paramilitary groups, NGOs, and private corporations.

The ICJ may not be a strong enforcer of international law, but with greater legalization of international issues, there has been an increase in the number of international courts and an increased willingness by developing countries to use international judicial bodies, especially since the Cold War's end. These new courts, some 20 permanent judicial institutions and more than 70 other international institutions that exercise judicial or quasi-judicial functions, are part of a group of "new-style" courts.[11] These courts enjoy compulsory jurisdiction and allow nonstate actors to litigate. They not only resolve disputes but also assess state compliance with international law and review the legal validity of state and international legislative and administrative acts. There has been a significant increase in the volume of binding rulings issued by this growing number of international courts. About 37,000 such rulings have been issued, with more than 90 percent of those occurring since 1990. Thus, even without a central enforcer, they can have a significant impact.

Vertical enforcement can also occur from the bottom up; national and even local courts can be enforcers of international law. Such courts have broad jurisdiction: they may hear cases occurring on their territory in which international law is invoked, or cases involving their own citizens who live elsewhere; they may hear any case to which the principle of universal jurisdiction applies. Under **universal jurisdiction**, states may claim jurisdiction if an individual's conduct is sufficiently heinous to violate the laws of all states. Several states claimed such jurisdiction for the genocide in World War II and, more recently, for war crimes in Bosnia, Croatia, Rwanda, and Sierra Leone, among others. In the European Union, national and local courts are a vital source of law. A citizen of an EU country can ask a national court to invalidate any provision of domestic law found to be in conflict with provisions of the EU treaty. A citizen can also seek invalidation of a national law found to be in conflict with self-executing provisions of community directives issued by the Council of the European Union. Thus, in the European system, national courts are both essential sources of European community law and enforcers of that law.

At the same time, however, it is important to note that without enforcement mechanisms, international courts are limited in their ability to enforce international law against sovereign states. When the ICJ ruled against the United States in its 1986 *Nicaragua v. United States* decision, the United States simply withdrew its acceptance of ICJ jurisdiction and refused to pay the reparations awarded to Nicaragua in the decision. Similarly, the Permanent Court of Arbitration (an international tribunal in the Hague) ruled against China in 2016, arguing that its claims to sovereignty over islands in the South China Sea had no legal basis and that the harm it caused to the marine environment through the construction of artificial islands in the area was in violation of international law. China simply refused to abide by the decision, stating that it neither accepted nor recognized it. While vertical enforcement mechanisms do exist, the effectiveness as a method of enforcement is spotty. Other enforcement mechanisms have proven more effective, as illustrated in the issue of human rights described in Chapter 10.

Horizontal Enforcement

Horizontal enforcement is a process whereby states work to elicit compliance with international law by other states; state interactions foster compliance. Two main factors drive such horizontal enforcement—power and reciprocity.

Realists highlight the important role that state power plays in eliciting compliance with international law. States do not simply choose to comply with international law. Instead, they comply because more powerful states make them. The powerful, however, are not constrained in this same way, and therefore we are most likely to see compliance by weaker states that are forced to comply by more powerful ones. This argument dates back to Thucydides, who wrote in *History of the Peloponnesian War* that "the strong do what they can and the weak states suffer what they must."

Several mechanisms exist that more powerful states can use to elicit compliance by other states, including diplomacy, economic statecraft, and use of force, as discussed in Chapter 5. Why did Iran sign an agreement in 2015 to halt its nuclear program? It did so because it was coerced into doing so by the economic sanctions placed on it by powerful states acting through the UN Security Council. Why did Iraq leave Kuwait after invading it in the early 1990s? It did so because more powerful states coerced it into doing so by using military force against it. For realists, actions by powerful states help explain why we see compliance by others.

Liberals also highlight the role these tools of statecraft play in helping to foster state compliance with international law. But they contend, rightly in many cases, that the use of these mechanisms by one state alone is apt to be ineffective. A diplomatic protest from a single state is likely to be ignored, although diplomatic sanctions from a group can be more effective. Economic boycotts and sanctions by one state will be ineffective as long as the transgressor state has multiple trading partners that it can turn to. For enforcement to be most effective, all states must join together in collective action against the violator of international law. In the view of liberals, states find protection and solace in collective action and collective security. The economic sanctions against Iran that helped get it to agree to end its nuclear program and the military actions against Iraq were carried out not by a single powerful state but by many states coordinating their efforts through the UN. Multilateral action, according to liberals, is essential.

Liberals—neoliberal institutionalists, in particular—also highlight the importance of reciprocity in eliciting compliance. In the anarchic system where the prisoner's dilemma exists, states can help elicit cooperation by engaging in tit-for-tat interactions. If you do not cooperate with me, I will not cooperate with you; if you do cooperate with me, I will cooperate with you. Compliance with international laws, which codify these cooperative interactions, is one way this cooperation is manifested. The desire to reap the gains that stem from reciprocal cooperative actions incentivizes states to comply with the laws codifying those cooperative interactions. For example, despite incentives that might exist to harm or extort information from prisoners of war, states cooperate with the 1929 Geneva Convention in order to secure cooperation from other states in return.

Self-Interest

Both realists and liberals agree that compliance relies generally on states and their individual self-interest. States benefit from participating in making the rules through treaties, or else they would not participate in making or ratifying them. They can ensure, through participation, that those rules will be compatible with

Bodies of International Law

International law deals with many different issue areas, including war, trade, human rights, and the environment. There is even international law governing conduct regarding the seas, the Arctic, and outer space. Chapter 6 discussed international law regarding war, covering laws on entering into war (*jus ad bellum*) as well as laws on acceptable conduct during war (*jus in bello*). Chapter 8 discusses issues of international law regarding trade and investment. Chapters 10 and 11 discuss international law in the realm of human rights, health, the environment, and migration. While these are some of the most commonly discussed types of international law, there are other important issue areas in which international law plays a central role in state interactions today: international criminal law and the law of the sea.

International Criminal Law

States have negotiated many treaties related to criminal law, addressing both procedural issues (information sharing, evidence gathering, and extradition) and substantive transnational issues (terrorism, drug trafficking, human trafficking, organized crime, and cybercrime).

Mutual legal assistance treaties regularize cooperation between governments in the gathering of evidence. They require actions such as sharing information about a crime, searching and seizing evidence, tracking suspects or witnesses, and taking written testimony. Such treaties are numerous. The United States alone has more than 60 mutual legal assistance treaties; its partners range from neighboring states such as Canada and Mexico to countries in Europe, Asia, Africa, Australia, and South America. Many other pairs of states have negotiated such treaties. Argentina and Panama, South Africa and India, Indonesia and Australia, and Thailand and Canada are just a few. Together, over 400 mutual legal assistance treaties exist today, creating a large network of cooperation in criminal matters.

International criminal law also deals with issues of extradition. **Extradition** refers to the process of delivering an individual from the territory of one state to another state for prosecution or to serve a sentence. Extradition treaties are just as prevalent, if not more prevalent, than mutual legal assistance treaties. The United States alone has over 100 such treaties in place. Extradition treaties vary widely, but often include three types of provisions. The offense being charged against the individual must be a crime in both states, the individual may only be tried for the crime used to justify the extradition, and the offense cannot be "political" in nature.

Many substantive treaties have also been negotiated dealing with various transnational crimes. Over the last two decades, transnational crime has emerged as a major issue of international relations. As Moisés Naím wrote, "Global criminal activities are transforming the international system, upending the rules, creating new players, and reconfiguring power in international politics and economics."[15] Drug trafficking is an important example. Over 20 multilateral treaties and their various protocols have been negotiated at both the bilateral and regional level to deal with the issue. However, a key problem in preventing drug trafficking across state borders is that the production, refinement, and shipment of narcotics contribute substantially to the gross national product of many countries, including those that supply the raw materials for illegal narcotics (like Colombia and Afghanistan) and those that are transit routes for narcotics (like Tajikistan and Guinea-Bissau). Thus, destroying poppy fields in Afghanistan or coca fields in Colombia would be tantamount to destroying the economies of each of these states. Afghanistan, for example, produces an estimated 70 percent of the world's heroin, most of which is consumed in the Russian Federation. The economic value to Tajikistan of heroin smuggling from Afghanistan to the Russian Federation is equivalent to 30 to 50 percent of its gross domestic product. A similar fate has affected the West African state of Guinea-Bissau, whose offshore islands and miles of coastland have been too costly for the relatively poor country to police adequately. Drug traffickers in Guinea-Bissau, with the complicity of some in the national military, have established a collection and distribution base that may be responsible for the transit of

After a failed coup in Turkey in July 2016, the responsible Turkish officers fled to Greece. Though Turkey requested extradition of the perpetrators to return and stand trial, the Supreme Court of Greece denied their request and granted asylum to the Turkish officers.

2,200 pounds of cocaine per night. The existence of international law dealing with the issue does not guarantee compliance.

Another important criminal issue that has garnered attention under international law is terrorism. There is no single treaty that deals with terrorism overall, as states differ in whether or not they consider various types of groups and various types of actions "terrorist." Various terrorist actions are therefore dealt with across several different multilateral treaties, including hijacking, the taking of hostages, terrorist bombings, and the financing of terrorism. The multilateral treaties dealing with these various issues require that these actions be criminalized under national law and that alleged offenders be either extradited or prosecuted in the state's own courts. Many states are parties to these treaties, but not all. Recognizing the central importance of these crimes in the world today, the UN Security Council and UN General Assembly have called on states that are not already parties to these treaties to become parties "as soon as possible."

While it might seem like there should be significant agreement on policing international crime, working together to deal with these issues is often highly politicized. Even an issue as seemingly mundane as extradition has been a source of disagreement and tension between states. In particular, the EU and individual states including Mexico, Italy, Switzerland, and South Africa argue that they will not extradite an individual if the death penalty could be used. Rulings by international institutions and international courts have backed up this argument, citing various international laws. In *Soering v. United Kingdom* (1989), the European Court of Human Rights ruled that the United Kingdom's extradition of an individual to face capital murder charges in Virginia would violate obligations under the European Convention on Human Rights, which prohibits cruel, inhuman, or degrading treatment or punishment. Similarly, in *Judge v. Canada* (2003), the UN Human Rights Committee found that Canada violated the International Covenant on Civil and Political Rights by deporting an individual to the United States to face a death sentence.

National courts have even weighed in on this argument. National courts in Mexico, Switzerland, South Africa, and the Netherlands have ruled that assurances that the state requesting extradition would not impose the death penalty were necessary before they would extradite an individual. The Italian Constitutional Court even ruled that extradition was not allowed even if such assurances were given. Italy would not extradite an individual to any country where the death penalty was used.

The United States strongly disputes these arguments, maintaining that the use of the death penalty does not violate international law and that requests made under negotiated extradition treaties should therefore be honored. This issue is significant for two reasons. First, whether or not to use the death penalty in the United States is left up to the individual states. An overall prohibition of the death penalty at the federal level would therefore violate states' rights—an issue of central importance to many U.S. leaders and citizens. Second, U.S. states use the death penalty in cases involving serious crimes—cases in which extradition is especially vital.

The politicization of the issue is an important source of conflict between the United States and others. For example, a special assistant to the prosecutor in Arizona argued of Mexico's extradition requirements, "We find it extremely disturbing that the Mexican government would dictate to us, in Arizona, how we would enforce our laws. . . . That's an interference of Mexican authorities in our judicial process."[16] And Bob Baker, president of the Los Angeles Police Protective League, argued in 2005 that the court rulings requiring assurances that the death penalty would not be used are an "unwarranted intrusion on the criminal justice system in the United States and an infringement on U.S. sovereignty."[17] Cooperation regarding criminal law—even on an issue as seemingly mundane as extradition—is not as straightforward as it may seem.

Law of the Sea

In the late 1950s through the early 1970s, the United Nations held several conferences in order to codify the law of the sea, which until that time had been governed by customary law. The treaty that resulted is the UN Convention on the Law of the Sea, and this treaty still governs the law of the sea today. It deals with many different issues related to the law of the sea, including the establishment of maritime zones around state borders, as well as functional issues such as fishing and management of mineral resources in the seabed.

The establishment of maritime zones around coastal borders is a key issue in international law. In particular, states have certain rights in the sea depending on how close it is to their coastal borders, and other states have limited rights in those various types of waters. A baseline is drawn on each state's coast at the low-water line marked in sea charts from which the various maritime zones are defined (see Figure 7.1). This includes the coast of islands. Any water landward of the baseline is considered a state's "internal waters," which are treated just as if they were a state's territorial land. The coastal state has full sovereignty in these waters, and its criminal and civil laws apply to actions taken within them.

Outward from the baseline up to 12 nautical miles are a state's territorial waters. A state still has sovereignty over these waters and rights over all the natural resources within the seabed of those waters, but there are some limitations on its actions. A state cannot impede the "innocent passage" of foreign vessels in its territorial waters or levy taxes on vessels engaged in such innocent passage. Foreign vessels not engaged in innocent passage may be excluded from the territorial sea.

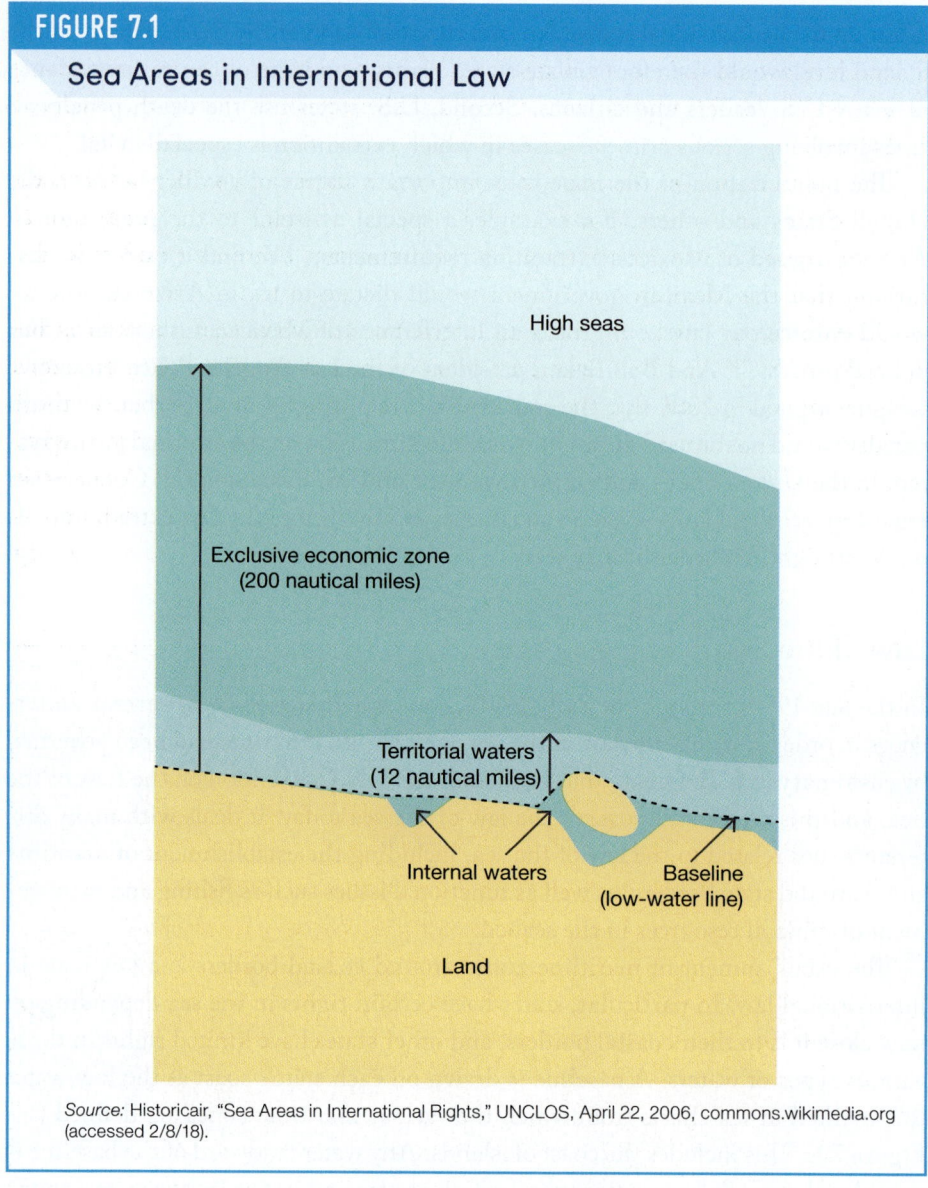

FIGURE 7.1

Sea Areas in International Law

High seas

Exclusive economic zone
(200 nautical miles)

Territorial waters
(12 nautical miles)

Internal waters

Baseline
(low-water line)

Land

Source: Historicair, "Sea Areas in International Rights," UNCLOS, April 22, 2006, commons.wikimedia.org (accessed 2/8/18).

States also agreed to allow a coastal state to declare an "exclusive economic zone" within 200 nautical miles of its baseline. Within the exclusive economic zone, the coastal state has full sovereign rights for purposes of exploring, exploiting, conserving, and managing the living things and nonliving things within its waters and seabed. This covers activities like fishing and using natural resources within the seabed. However, foreign vessels have all the other freedoms within the exclusive economic zone that they have on the high seas. The high seas are open to all states for a wide variety of activities, including navigation, fishing, and mining natural resources. All waters beyond the exclusive economic zone are considered the high seas.

These boundaries are of central importance for states because they affect their sovereignty, as well as economic activities such as fishing and mining natural resources. Maritime boundaries are also an important source of conflict in the international system today.

All land territory including islands can generate territorial waters and an exclusive economic zone. Conflict has therefore been rampant over the control of islands in the South China Sea. An important part of the reason why control over these islands is a major source of conflict has to do with the law of the sea. Sovereignty over these islands would create territorial waters and an exclusive economic zone the sovereign state would have in its control. Not only is fishing an important part of the economy of many of the states that claim sovereignty over the islands (fishing

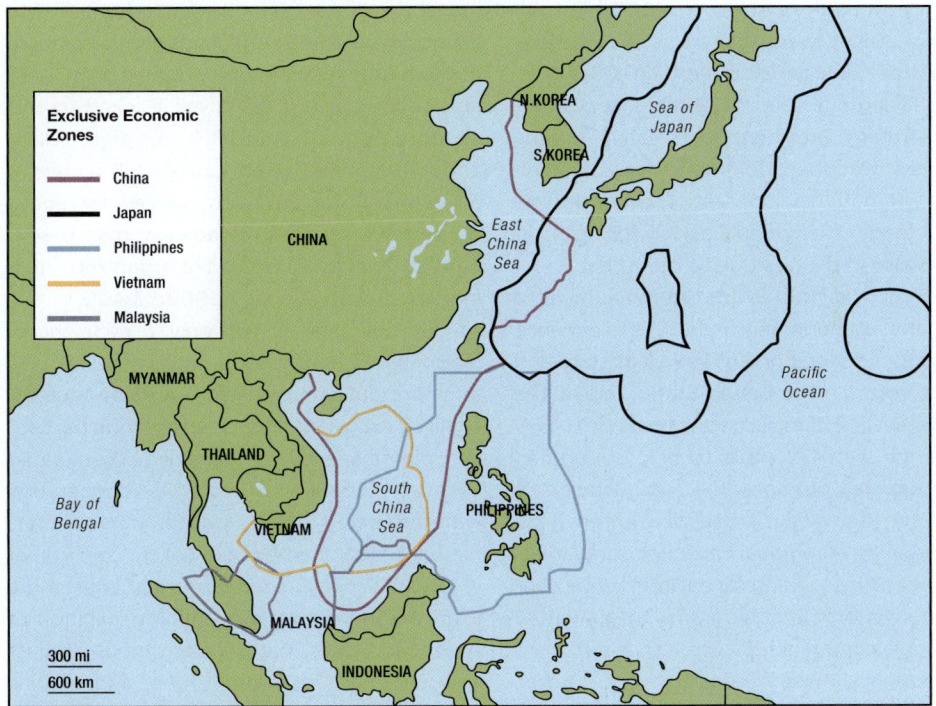

Maritime boundaries, East Asia

Source: Stratfor, "Cooperation as a Means to All Ends in the South China Sea," *RealClearDefense*, September 26, 2016, realcleardefense.com (accessed 2/8/18).

Triangular Cooperation: A View from Colombia

Cooperation in the international system is a complex network of interactions. Colombia's position within that network is an intriguing case study, as it receives assistance from more developed states while also providing assistance to other developing states. This "triangular cooperation" model, touted by the Organization for Economic Cooperation and Development (OECD), is becoming increasingly popular as a mechanism for assisting developing countries.

Colombia's place in the ever-expanding triangular cooperation network in the international system represents an important change in Colombia's capacity to engage internationally, since for over 50 years (the mid-1960s through the mid-2010s) the country was in civil war—a war that took an estimated 220,000 lives. When laying out Colombia's national cooperation strategy, President Juan Manuel Santos Calderón described Colombia's new position in the international cooperation network: "We are no longer the country asking for help but we are also in the position to offer help."[a]

Colombia is, first, an important recipient of international cooperation initiatives to enhance its economic development as well as state and human security. The United States, Japan, the EU, and several European states outside the EU cooperate with Colombia to help strengthen infrastructure, promote the productivity of medium and small businesses, and improve the quality of life in regional cities and rural areas. It even receives funding for environmental conservation efforts and programs to guarantee vulnerable communities' access to water.

Through these cooperation efforts, Colombia has made significant progress on the path of development. From 2008 to 2016, unemployment dropped from 11.3 percent to 9.9 percent and poverty levels dropped dramatically, from 72 percent to 28 percent.

International cooperation has been particularly effective in the area of state and human security. From 2000 to 2008 alone, Colombia received over $6 billion in military and economic aid from the United States. The two countries have also engaged in multiple coordinated security operations and military and police training initiatives. Backed by this support, from 2008 to 2016 homicides fell by about 15 percent. Kidnappings fell by about 50 percent, terrorist attacks fell by about 60 percent, seizures of coca leaf rose 17 percent, and persons accused of organized crime increased from almost 2,500 to 3,400.[b]

But Colombia is not only a recipient of international cooperation initiatives. It is also an important provider. In the area of addressing illicit drugs and organized crime, in particular, Colombia sees itself as having accumulated valuable experiences from its cooperation with the United States. Supported by an international legal framework—which consists of resolutions dealing with transnational crime from the United Nations, the Organization of American States, the UN Convention against Transnational Organized Crime, and various bilateral and multilateral agreements dealing with transnational crime—and backed by aid from the United States, Colombia has begun to provide technical and legal assistance in the security sector to other states. It has advised

Drug-sniffing dogs inspect packages in Medellin, Columbia.

of complementary strengths. Both Colombia and its partners benefit in important ways. As Colombian president Santos stated, "Greater and improved cooperation—going both ways—is a conducive way to further strengthening the prosperity and security in our country and in our region."[c]

a. Quoted in Gobierno de Colombia, *National Strategy of International Cooperation, 2012–2014*, www20.iadb.org/intal/catalogo/PE/2013/11768en.pdf (accessed 12/15/17).
b. United Nations Office on Drugs and Crime, "The 2017 United Nations Survey of Crime Trends and Operations of Criminal Justice Systems (2017 UNCTS)," www.unodc.org/unodc/en/data-and-analysis/statistics/crime/cts-data-collection.html (accessed 1/17/18); Mindefensa (Ministry of National Defense of Colombia), *Logras de la Política de Defensa y Seguridad Todos por un Nuevo País*, December 2017, www.mindefensa.gov.co/irj/go/km/docs/Mindefensa/Documentos/descargas/estudios_sectoriales/info_estadistica/Logros_Sector_Defensa.pdf (accessed 1/17/18).
c. Quoted in Gobierno de Colombia, *National Strategy of International Cooperation*.

on police reform in Honduras, Guatemala, and the Dominican Republic and has established agreements to reproduce its national model against drug trafficking throughout Central America. Overall, between 2009 and 2013 it provided police and military training to 21,949 people from 47 different countries in the Caribbean, Central America, and West Africa.

This type of cooperative process—in which a state both receives cooperation assistance from more developed countries (North-South cooperation) and also provides it to other developing states (South-South cooperation)—is known as "triangular cooperation." Colombia has taken significant steps in managing its triangular cooperation in order to benefit from international assistance as well as to offer its own experience and skills to others. For Colombia, triangular cooperation is seen as an avenue to bridge North-South and South-South cooperation, creating partnerships characterized by sharing, learning, and the exploration

FOR CRITICAL ANALYSIS

1. Do you think South-South cooperation is a viable path to development? Is the North-South cooperation that accompanies South-South cooperation in the triangular model necessary?

2. Colombia argues that it benefits from providing security assistance to other states. Do you think this is true of assistance beyond the security realm?

3. How has international law facilitated Colombia's cooperation strategy?

4. How would a realist analyze the idea of triangular cooperation? How would a liberal analyze it?

rights are governed by the law of the sea), but also the seabed of these islands is believed to have significant amounts of natural resources.

More importantly, the creation of territorial waters around the islands would limit the activities of foreign vessels within them. The United States keeps military vessels in this area that it uses to help maintain control over the Pacific. If China had sovereignty over the islands, these vessels would not be allowed to remain. In an effort to gain control over the waters, China has even begun to construct its own artificial islands in order to further expand its territorial waters and exclusive economic zone. Recognizing this, and in defiance of China's claim over the islands, the United States in 2015 sailed a guided missile destroyer within 12 nautical miles of the artificial islands China had created. China accused the United States of making an "illegal incursion" into its waters.

In July 2016, the Permanent Court of Arbitration rejected China's argument that it has sovereign rights over the South China Sea islands. The tribunal ruled that China had violated international law by causing "irreparable harm" to the marine environment, endangering Philippine ships, and interfering with Philippine fishing and oil exploration. The decision is legally binding, but China has claimed it does not recognize the decision as legitimate and will not abide by it. With no international enforcement mechanism to impose the law on China, China continues its actions in the South China Sea. The law of the sea, and the rights it confers to coastal states, plays a key role in international relations today.

IN SUM: THE CENTRALITY OF COOPERATION

International cooperation and international laws designed to solidify that cooperation are of central importance in the world today. Though wars and intense conflicts receive the most attention, cooperation and respect for international law are more prevalent. Treaties are regularly forged on a wide variety of issue areas, ever expanding the volume of international law. Multilateral trade happens every day, and states' treaty obligations in many other issue areas are upheld. Conflict exists, but so does cooperation. Subsequent chapters examine in more detail a variety of substantive issue areas in which we see conflict but also a wide range of cooperation.

Discussion Questions

1. Choose an issue area in which there is a body of international law. Which type of enforcement mechanism do you think best explains why states largely comply with treaties in this issue area? Why?

2. Think of an example of noncooperation between states. In this case, why do we not see cooperation? Why have the mechanisms liberal and constructivist theorists argue can help bring about cooperation not worked?

3. Think of an example of cooperation between states. Why do we see cooperation regarding this issue? Which mechanisms highlighted by liberal and constructivist theories are at work in fostering this cooperation?

Key Terms

economic interdependence (p. 242)

extradition (p. 258)

horizontal enforcement (p. 254)

international cooperation (p. 234)

international law (p. 246)

legitimate (p. 257)

prisoner's dilemma (p. 237)

shadow of the future (p. 239)

transaction costs (p. 242)

treaties (p. 248)

universal jurisdiction (p. 254)

vertical enforcement (p. 250)

Thousands across the world protested the signing of the Trans-Pacific Partnership in 2016. Protesters in Latin America specifically cited the trade deal as harmful to laborers and exploitative of indigenous lands and communities. What does this mean for the future of economic globalization?

8

International Political Economy

Thousands of Argentinian workers and labor union members marched in protest in 2016, angered by the loss of 154,000 state and private-sector jobs. In the same year, Peruvian citizens protested against the government's entry into the Trans-Pacific Partnership, as well as mining companies' exploitation of indigenous lands. And in Chile, protesters in coastal villages marched in defiance of government-imposed fishing bans, believing those bans were designed to protect salmon exporters. Each of these protests was spurred by the perception that economic globalization founded in economic liberalism has led to job loss and exploitation by big business. Despite the promises of economic liberals, all people have not been lifted out of poverty and their standard of living has not improved.

These actions stand in contrast to expectations expressed decades before: that economic liberalization and new technologies were stimulating not only the increasing flow of capital and trade but also the decreasing territorialization of economic life, at both global and regional levels. That optimism led to Thomas Friedman's observation in *The Lexus and the Olive Tree*: Globalization is the "inexorable integration of markets, nation-states and technologies to a degree never witnessed before in a way that is enabling individuals, corporations and nation-states to reach around the world further, faster, deeper and cheaper than ever before."[1]

How does the international economy work, and who does it work for? Why is economic globalization so controversial? And why in the last decade have we seen a reaction against globalization generally and economic liberalism specifically?

LEARNING OBJECTIVES

▶ Understand the core concepts of economic liberalism.

▶ Analyze the roles the major economic institutions play in the international political economy.

▶ Describe how the views of mercantilists/economic nationalists and radicals differ from those of economic liberals.

▶ Explain how the international economic system has become globalized in key areas: international finance, international monetary policy, international trade, and international development.

▶ Show how the global economic crisis and the Eurozone crisis are connected and have led many to question the tenets of economic liberalism.

▶ Explain how critics of international economic liberalism and economic globalization reflect differences in ideologies.

THE EVOLUTION OF THE INTERNATIONAL ECONOMY: IDEAS AND INSTITUTIONS

The era from the late Middle Ages through the end of the eighteenth century saw a number of key changes in technology, ideas, and practices that altered the international economy. Spurred by advances in ship design and navigation systems, European explorers opened up new frontiers in the Americas, Asia, and the Middle East to trade and commerce. Although Greek, Phoenician, and Mesopotamian traders had preceded them, the British East India Company, the Hudson's Bay Company, and the Dutch East India Company facilitated trade in goods (and people as slaves); provided capital for investments in the agricultural development of the new lands; and transported cotton, tobacco, and sugar to Europe. Settlers increasingly moved to these lands; linked to the motherland by economics, politics, and culture, they formed a nascent transnational class pursuing individual economic interests.

Writing during this time was the eighteenth-century British economist Adam Smith. As we noted in Chapter 2, Smith began with the notion that human beings act in rational ways to maximize their self-interest. When individuals act rationally, markets develop to produce, distribute, and consume goods. These markets enable individuals to carry out the necessary transactions to improve their own welfare. When there are many buyers and sellers, market competition ensures that prices will be as low as possible. Low prices result in increased consumer welfare. Thus, in maximizing economic welfare and stimulating individual (and therefore collective) economic growth, markets epitomize economic efficiency. Those markets need to be virtually free from government interference; only through a free flow of commerce will efficient allocation of resources occur. That is the rationale underpinning the theory of economic liberalism.

Yet the policies of many European governments at the time reflected an alternative view, **mercantilism**. The goal of a mercantilist government was to build economic wealth as an instrument of state power. Drawing on the views of the Frenchman Jean-Baptiste Colbert (1619–83), an adviser to Louis XIV, the mercantilist view held that states needed to accumulate gold and silver to guarantee power. A strong central government was needed for efficient tax collection and maximization of exports, both geared toward guaranteeing military prowess. Such governments encouraged exports over imports and industrialization over agriculture, protected domestic production against competition from imports, and intervened in trade to promote employment. The United States' first secretary of the treasury, Alexander Hamilton (1757–1804), advocated **protectionism**, policies that included high tariffs to protect the growth of the new nation's manufacturers. In his "Report on Manufactures" to Congress in 1791, he supported high tariffs and encouraged investment in inventions. Mercantilist policies thus included protectionist measures and discouraged foreign investment in the name of achieving national self-sufficiency.

From the beginning of the nineteenth century through World War I, the expansion of colonialism and the Industrial Revolution occurred as the result of major technological improvements in communications, transportation, and manufacturing processes. The European states needed the raw materials found in the colonies, so international trade expanded, as did international investment; capital moved from Europe to the Americas as investors searched for higher profits. Often the creation of those economic links led to political and cultural domination. Britain was the center of the Industrial Revolution, the major trading state and source of international capital, as well as a political and cultural hegemon, contested only by France. Britain facilitated trade by lowering its own tariffs and opening its markets, policing the sea to provide safer transit, and encouraging investment abroad. It is no wonder that this period has been labeled the "Pax Britannica," when the hegemonic power of Great Britain, under the guise of economic liberalism, expanded so that "the sun never set on the British empire."

The excesses of that period gave rise to another perspective—**economic radicalism**—drawing on the body of Marxist and neo-Marxist writings. Having seen the harsh living conditions of the working class during nineteenth-century industrialization and imperialist expansion, and cognizant of the economic chasm between the developed and the developing worlds during the twentieth century, economic radicals blamed the capitalist system under liberalism. Although interpretations vary, the core belief found in Marxist and neo-Marxist writing is that society basically is conflictual. Conflict emerges from the competition among groups of individuals—namely, the owners of wealth and the workers—for scarce resources. The state tends to support the owners of the means of production. Finally, the owners of capital are determined to expand and accumulate resources at the expense of the working class and those in the developing world. As Marx himself argued, the constant expansion of capitalist markets leads to crises; dangerous speculation by those holders of capital only exacerbates these crises.

The worldwide depression of the 1930s saw a major decline in trade and investment, made worse by "beggar thy neighbor" policies, in which states seeking to protect themselves from the effects of the economic crisis, by increasing domestic employment, tended to worsen the economic problems of neighboring countries, reducing employment in those countries. Thus, at the end of World War II, the goal of the Western victors was to promote openness of trade and stimulate international capital flows while establishing a stable exchange-rate system. States, multinational corporations (MNCs), and the institutions of the Bretton Woods system are to play a major role in realizing the more open economy of the twenty-first century.

Economic Institutions

The Role of States

States exercise key roles in influencing domestic and international economic policy. States have available two major **macroeconomic policies**: fiscal and monetary policies. **Fiscal policies** affect a government's budget, including the level of government spending and the tax rates. To stimulate the economy, the government may choose to increase government spending and/or decrease tax rates. To slow the economy down or balance the budget, states may select to cut government spending or increase tax rates. **Monetary policies** include increasing or decreasing the money supply, generally through manipulation of short-term interest rates. Such policies influence broad conditions in the economy, including employment and inflation rates. Finally, states select **microeconomic policies**—policies on regulation, subsidies, competition, and antitrust actions. In all cases, governments undertake a balancing act—too much of one instrument can have consequences in other areas and can also have unintended consequences.

In a globalized world, a state's actions do not occur in a vacuum; what one state decides affects other states, which are confronted with their own choices. The price of money depends on **exchange rates**, the price of one currency in relation to another. That rate facilitates the exchange of goods and services and has an immediate impact on the price of a country's goods and assets. Under floating exchange rates, the market—individuals and governments buying and selling currencies—determines the actual value of one currency compared with other currencies. Under a fixed exchange rate, a government keeps its money at an established value, in terms of gold or another currency. Sometimes central banks intervene to manage the value of the exchange rate. Some states have adopted a common currency, using the currency of another state or a group of states. A weaker domestic currency stimulates exports and makes imports more expensive, whereas a stronger domestic currency curtails exports, making imports cheaper.

International trade is a key economic driver in a globalized world. States make a variety of decisions affecting the amount and level of trade, depending on the amount of protection they desire from the effects of the international market. Among the key trade policies are the level of **tariffs**—the taxes on goods and services crossing borders—and the kind of **nontariff barriers**—the restrictions on international trade designed to protect health, safety, or national security. Such policies may be used to protect the domestic economy, the consumer, new industries, and even national security. For example, Japan and South Korea impose tariffs on American beef, justifying the action in terms of protecting its population from disease. This has the effect, intended or not, of bolstering their own domestic beef producers.

Because of the interconnectedness of the world economy, a state's economic policy decisions affect the economies of other states. Economists have developed methods to measure these relationships. **Current accounts** measure the net border flows between countries of goods, services, governmental transfers, and income on capital investments. **Capital accounts** measure the flows of capital between countries, including foreign direct investment and portfolio investment in and out. Together, those two measures compose the **balance of payments**—a country's current and capital account balances. The balance of payments is either positive (or in surplus) or negative (or in deficit). In a surplus balance of payments, like in the German economy, the value of exported goods, services, and investment income is greater than the value of imported goods, services, and investment income. In contrast, many developing countries have a balance of payments deficit: the value of their imported goods, services, and investment income exceeds the value of their exported goods, services, and investment income. The United States carries both current accounts and balance-of-payments deficits.

In economic liberalism, markets are the major determinant of a state's policy, with states providing market rules and a level playing field. But other actors, namely multinational corporations and international governmental organizations, also play key roles.

The Role of Multinational Corporations

MNCs, defined in Chapter 3 as corporations that span state borders, either through their actual presence in several countries or through investment in and trade with other corporations within them, are not new institutions.[2] They have a long history, with forerunners in the British East India Company, the Hudson's Bay Company, and the Dutch East India Company in the seventeenth and eighteenth centuries. Before World War II, most MNCs were in manufacturing—like General Motors, Ford, Siemens, Nestlé, and Bayer, among others. Since the 1990s, there has been not only an expansion of the number and complexity of MNCs but also an increase in their size. Today, there are about 60,000 MNCs. They account for 50 percent of worldwide trade; they constitute up to 40 percent of the value of the stock markets in the West; and they own the lion's share of intellectual property. Just 10 percent of these MNCs generate 80 percent of all profits. Of the largest, 60 percent have their headquarters in the United States, Canada, or western Europe, and about 34 percent are headquartered in Asia. Large MNCs include such well-known names as Walmart, ExxonMobil, Royal Dutch Shell, Toyota, and General Motors, but also less well-known companies, like Sinopec, HSBC Holdings, Carrefour, Royal Bank of Scotland, Gazprom, and Tesco. But since the global economic crisis of 2008, there has been some diminution in the power of MNCs. Sales of Western firms outside their home country have declined and MNC profits are falling, in part due to the decline in commodity prices and in the profits of oil companies.[3]

Multinational corporations play a key role as engines of economic growth, providing international finance and items to trade. In liberal economics, MNCs are the vanguard of the international order. They are, in the words of Robert Gilpin, the "embodiment par excellence of the liberal ideal of an interdependent world economy. [They have] taken the integration of national economies beyond trade and money to the internationalization of production. For the first time in history, production, marketing, and investment are being organized on a global scale rather than in terms of isolated national economies."[4] To supporters of economic liberalism, MNCs are a positive development: economic improvement happens through the most efficient mechanism. MNCs invest in capital stock worldwide, they move money to the most efficient markets, and they finance projects that industrialize and improve agricultural output. MNCs are the transmission belt for capital, ideas, and economic growth. MNCs prefer to act independently of states; the market itself will regulate behavior. Any MNC abuses can be best corrected by other market actors, or at worst by government regulation.

MNCs take many different forms and engage in many different activities, such as investing in foreign countries, importing and exporting goods and services, negotiating licenses in foreign markets, and opening facilities abroad. Whatever form their business takes, MNCs participate in international markets for a variety of reasons. They seek to avoid tariff and import barriers, as many U.S. firms did in the 1960s when they established manufacturing facilities in Europe. They may seek to reduce transportation costs by moving facilities closer to consumer markets. Some MNCs are able to obtain incentives such as tax advantages or labor concessions from host governments; these incentives can cut production costs and increase profitability. Others go abroad so they can meet the competition and the customers, capitalize on cheaper labor markets (e.g., Chinese firms may move production to Vietnam or Laos), or obtain the services of foreign technical personnel (e.g., computer firms may relocate to India). These reasons are based in economics, but rationales based on the political policies of the host state may also play a role. MNCs may move abroad to circumvent tough governmental regulations at home, such as banking rules, currency restrictions, or environmental regulations. In the process, MNCs become not only economic organizations but also political ones, potentially influencing the policies of both home and host governments.

Some scholars go further, extolling the virtues of MNCs in promoting peace. Norman Angell, recipient of the 1933 Nobel Peace Prize, argued that through trade, national differences would vanish and interdependence would be enhanced, leading to world peace.[5] Although not all scholars agree with Angell, economic liberalism advocates open markets, free trade, and the free flow of goods and services—with government playing a limited role in protecting property rights and providing a functioning legal system. MNCs are key institutions in the post–World War II international political economy.

The Role of the Bretton Woods Institutions

At the end of World War II, policy makers established a set of intergovernmental organizations to support economic liberalism. The so-called Bretton Woods institutions—the World Bank, the International Monetary Fund (IMF), and, to a lesser extent, the General Agreement on Tariffs and Trade (GATT), now the World Trade Organization (WTO)—have all played, and continue to play, key roles in the expansion of economic liberalism (see Figure 8.1).

FIGURE 8.1

The International Economic Institutions

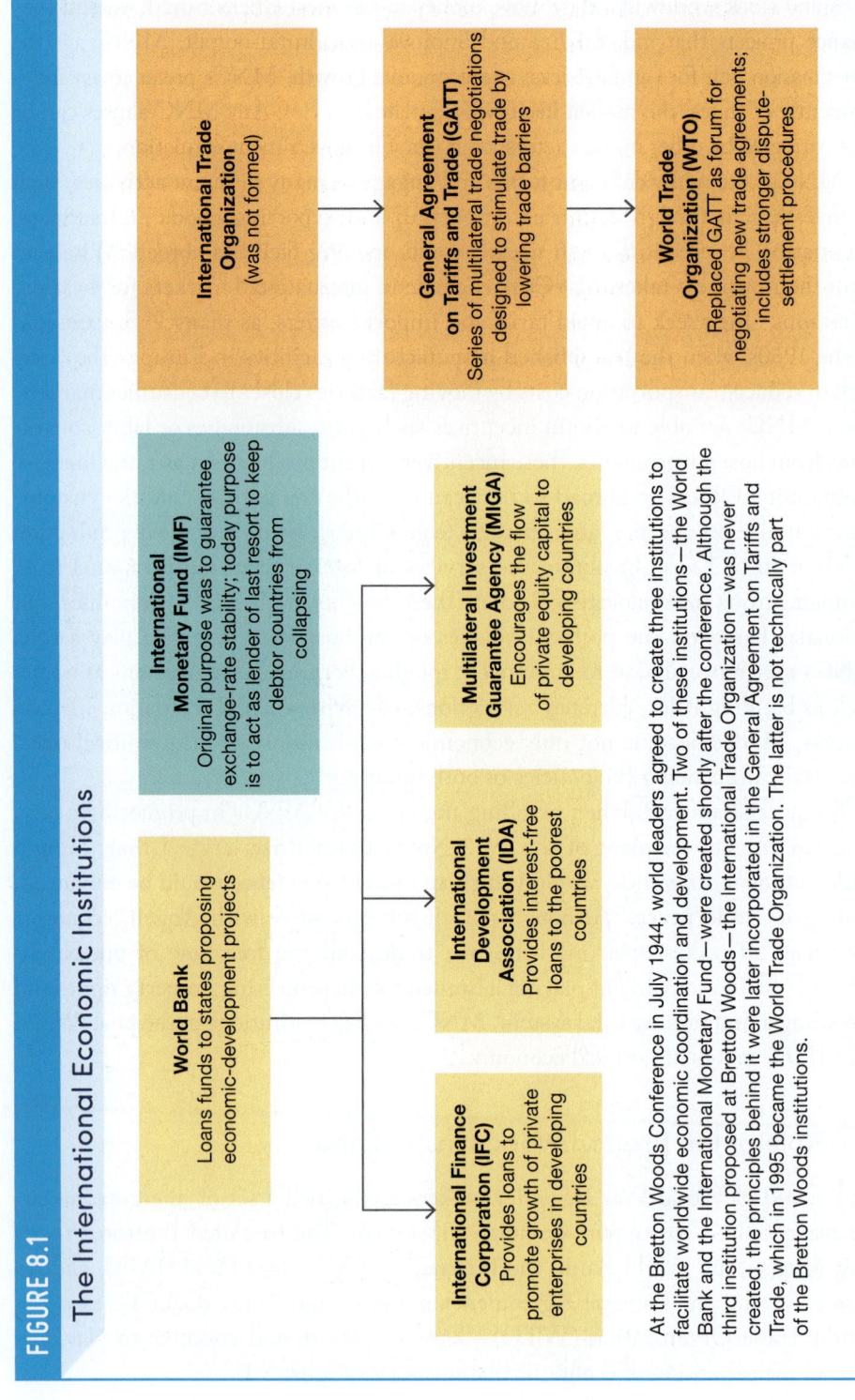

World Bank
Loans funds to states proposing economic-development projects

International Monetary Fund (IMF)
Original purpose was to guarantee exchange-rate stability; today purpose is to act as lender of last resort to keep debtor countries from collapsing

International Trade Organization
(was not formed)

International Finance Corporation (IFC)
Provides loans to promote growth of private enterprises in developing countries

International Development Association (IDA)
Provides interest-free loans to the poorest countries

Multilateral Investment Guarantee Agency (MIGA)
Encourages the flow of private equity capital to developing countries

General Agreement on Tariffs and Trade (GATT)
Series of multilateral trade negotiations designed to stimulate trade by lowering trade barriers

World Trade Organization (WTO)
Replaced GATT as forum for negotiating new trade agreements; includes stronger dispute-settlement procedures

At the Bretton Woods Conference in July 1944, world leaders agreed to create three institutions to facilitate worldwide economic coordination and development. Two of these institutions—the World Bank and the International Monetary Fund—were created shortly after the conference. Although the third institution proposed at Bretton Woods—the International Trade Organization—was never created, the principles behind it were later incorporated in the General Agreement on Tariffs and Trade, which in 1995 became the World Trade Organization. The latter is not technically part of the Bretton Woods institutions.

The **World Bank** was initially designed to facilitate reconstruction in post–World War II Europe, hence its formal name: the International Bank for Reconstruction and Development. During the 1950s, the World Bank shifted its primary emphasis from reconstruction to development. It now generates capital funds from member-state contributions and from borrowing in international financial markets. As with any bank, its purpose is to loan these funds, with interest, for economic-development projects. Its lending is designed not to replace private capital but to facilitate the use of private capital. While a high proportion of the World Bank's funding has been used for infrastructure projects—hydroelectric dams, basic transportation needs such as bridges and highways, and agribusiness ventures—the bank funds governments and the private sector to carry out a wide array of economic-development activities, including those in the social sector.

THEORY IN BRIEF

Contending Perspectives on the International Political Economy

	Economic Liberalism	Mercantilism/ Economic Nationalism	Economic Radicalism
View of Human Nature	Individuals act in rational ways to maximize their self-interest	Humans are aggressive; conflictual tendencies	Naturally cooperative as individuals; conflictual in groups
Relationship among Individuals, Society, State, Market	When individuals act rationally, markets are created to produce, distribute, and consume goods; markets function best when free of government interference	Goal is to increase state power, achieved by regulating economic life; economics is subordinate to state interests	Competition occurs among groups, particularly between owners of wealth and laborers; group relations are conflictual and exploitative
Relationship between Domestic and International Society	International wealth is maximized with free exchange of goods and services; on the basis of comparative advantage, international economy gains	International economy is conflictual; insecurity of anarchy breeds competition; state defends itself	Conflictual relationships because of inherent expansion of capitalism; seeks radical change in international economic system

The **International Monetary Fund (IMF)** was designed to provide stability in exchange rates. Originally, the fund established a system of fixed exchange rates, with the United States guaranteeing currency convertibility. From the 1940s to the 1970s, the United States guaranteed the stability of this system by fixing the value of the dollar against gold at $35 an ounce. In 1972, however, this system collapsed when the United States announced that it would no longer guarantee a system of fixed exchange rates. This decision was revised in 1976 when the International Monetary Fund formalized the system of floating exchange rates, relying on market forces to define currency prices. At that time, monetary cooperation became the responsibility of the **Group of 7 (G7)**, composed of the United States, Japan, Germany, Great Britain, France, Italy, and Canada. The IMF was to provide short-term loans for member states confronting temporary balance-of-payments deficits. But, as it became increasingly apparent, "temporary" difficulties were rarely temporary. States needed to undertake structural changes, and the IMF expanded its functions to include policy advice on macroeconomic issues and economic restructuring.

The third part of the liberal economic order was the **General Agreement on Tariffs and Trade (GATT)**. This treaty enshrined important liberal principles:

- support of trade liberalization, because trade is the engine for growth and economic development

- the **most-favored-nation (MFN) principle**—nondiscrimination in trade whereby states agree to give the same treatment to all other GATT members as they give to their best (most-favored) trading partner

- preferential access in developed markets to products from the less developed countries to stimulate economic development

- support for "national treatment" of foreign enterprises—that is, treating them in the same way that domestic firms are treated

The GATT established these trade principles as well as procedures for moving toward free trade. Multilateral negotiations among countries sharing major interests in an issue (major producers and consumers of a product, for example) were hammered out and then expanded to all GATT participants. Individual states could claim exemptions (called *safeguards*) to accommodate any domestic or balance-of-payments difficulties that might result from existing trade agreements. A weak dispute-resolution process was developed, allowing states that believed GATT principles were being violated by another state to file complaints. Backed by U.S. hegemonic leadership, the Bretton Woods system led to postwar recovery and economic prosperity.

For 20 years after the end of World War II, economic growth occurred much as liberal economic theory had predicted. Growth rates in the developed and the developing world averaged more than 4 percent. Trade volume increased over sevenfold, and poverty rates fell dramatically worldwide. And the volume of international finance exploded, as the communication revolution expanded the possibilities for international financial transactions. The groundwork of economic globalization had been laid.

The international political economy is viewed differently by the major economic theories. The majority of academics and policy makers in the Western world are supporters of economic liberalism. They believe that internationalization of finance and free unfettered trade is positive, leading to greater economic welfare for all. Order, they say, is achieved by international market competition. Economic nationalists, the old mercantilists, are not so sure. Historically, their goal has been the accrual of individual state power; economic gain by one results in a diminution of power in others. Hence finance, trade, and investment are all arenas in the struggle for national power. Order is achieved when there is a balance of power or when there is a clear dominant power or a hegemon. Economic radicals see internationalization as leading to domination by a few and thus to underdevelopment and exploitation of the poorer classes and states. They see that capitalism has resulted in overconcentration of economic resources and that the domination by finance has led to increasing crises in the international political economy.

So which theory best explains the international political economy? To answer this question, we first examine how the international economy functions in the twenty-first century. We examine four issues: international finance, international monetary policy, international trade, and international development. Then we turn to two major challenges in the contemporary political economy—the persistence of crises and the arguments articulated by the critics of international economic liberalism.

HOW THE GLOBALIZED ECONOMY WORKS TODAY

International Finance

Capital movements played a key role in earlier phases of the international political economy, as they do today. International capital traditionally moves through international private finance, including MNCs, other private companies, pension funds, investors, and other nongovernmental sources. This occurs through **foreign direct investment (FDI)**—construction of factories and investment in the facilities for extraction of natural resources by MNCs—and through **portfolio investment**—investment in another country's stocks or bonds, either short or long term, without taking direct control of those investments. International capital also moves through currency manipulations (discussed below).

Indeed, between the 1960s and the 1980s, private international capital provided essential lending to the successful Asian "tigers," including Taiwan and South Korea. In fact, the infusion of private investment in emerging economies—China, Brazil, Argentina, Chile, South Korea, Mexico, Singapore, Turkey, and Thailand—has played a major role in their economic success. Yet the volatility of private capital flows makes them unreliable for sustained development in some parts of the world, and private capital alone cannot explain economic outcomes in these countries.

The poorest states have more difficulty attracting private investment. Until recently, African countries typically have received the least. Separate institutions within the World Bank were established to provide capital to states that were unable to attract private investment alone. The International Finance Corporation (IFC) and the International Development Association (IDA) were created in 1956 and 1960, respectively, for that purpose. The IFC provides loans to promote the growth of private enterprises in developing countries. The IDA provides capital to the poorest countries, usually in the form of interest-free loans. Repayment schedules of 50 years theoretically allow the developing countries time to reach economic takeoff and sustain growth. Funds for the IDA need to be continually replenished by major donor countries. In 1988, the Multilateral Investment Guarantee Agency (MIGA) was added to the World Bank group. This agency meets its goal—augmenting the flow of capital to developing countries—by insuring investments against losses. Such losses may result from expropriation, government currency restrictions, or civil war or ethnic conflict. Even with these changes, since the mid-1980s, the flows from both multilateral institutions (the World Bank institutions, regional development banks) and official bilateral donors (the United States, Germany, Japan) have declined as a percentage of total capital flows; at the same time, private capital flows from MNCs and other private sources have expanded, except for a relatively brief time in 2008 during the international financial crisis.

The scale of activity in international private finance is massive. Each day roughly \$4.5 trillion crosses international borders, including \$110 billion in the form of loans and \$150 billion in the form of portfolio investments, and between \$50 and \$100 billion in purely speculative currency exchanges. Tens of thousands of financial institutions are involved in these transactions.

Beginning in the 1980s, international financial flows accelerated through several other mechanisms. New economic actors, **sovereign wealth funds**—state-controlled investment funds composed of financial assets, including stocks, bonds, precious metal, property, or other financial instruments—formed in capital-surplus countries such as China and in the major petroleum exporters such as Kuwait, the United Arab Emirates, Norway, Russia, and Canada. Those wealth funds have been able to move capital quickly across national boundaries, taking advantage of currency differentials and buying and selling new financial instruments to maximize long-term economic return. Such investments are designed to cushion states that have relied on a declining natural resource. Markets also developed new financial instruments, such as **derivatives**, whereby investors bet on the future prices of package asset classes, including loans and mortgages. Such instruments are packaged and sold around the world, spreading risk and accelerating the flow of capital. Finally, economic liberalism has led to the emergence of **offshore financial centers**, such as the Cayman Islands, Bermuda, and the British Virgin Islands. These jurisdictions have low taxation and little or no regulation. Capital can move in and out rapidly via electronic transfers.

The Asian financial crisis of the 1990s illustrates the possible outcomes of the globalization of finance. Beginning in Thailand in 1997, in a relatively short period, investors left Thailand, fearing that the government was no longer credible in its commitments; 2 percent of gross domestic product fled that country. Within weeks, the crisis spread to Indonesia, Malaysia, the Philippines, and beyond. Many countries were unable to adjust to the rapid withdrawal of capital. Exchange rates plummeted to 50 percent of pre-crisis values, stock markets fell 80 percent, and real GDP dropped 4 to 8 percent. Individuals lost their jobs as companies went bankrupt or were forced to restructure. Millions of people were forced into poverty. In Thailand, then spreading to South Korea and Taiwan, and eventually, to Brazil and Russia, those economies that had previously depended on external trade experienced an unparalleled sense of economic vulnerability. Fueled by instantaneous communication, the capacity to move trillions of dollars daily, and the power of MNCs and financial entrepreneurs, economic globalization quickly displayed its pitfalls. The market had melted down, and states and individuals appeared helpless.

The IMF responded to the social and political upheaval with large, controversial bailout packages to three of the affected countries (Thailand, $17 billion; Indonesia, $36 billion; and South Korea, $58 billion); lengthy sets of conditions that each country was supposed to follow; and monitoring devices to ensure compliance. Extensive structural reforms would transform their economies to more market-oriented ones. In South Korea, for example, the government lifted restrictions on capital movements and foreign ownership, permitted companies to lay off workers, and adopted measures to restructure the country's financial institutions. Budget cuts eliminated more social services and pushed more families below the poverty line, leading to a backlash against governments and the IMF. Solutions that the international financial institutions implemented in one country proved counterproductive in others, and marginalized groups suffered. Dissatisfaction with IMF policies led many in developing countries to conclude that these institutions were captive to the interests of the developed world.

Yet following two years of economic stress and the wounded credibility of the IMF, none of the countries involved retreated from globalization or the international financial markets, and all resumed a path of strong economic growth. States did change their behavior, and that had consequences.

International Monetary Policy

Like goods and services, national currencies are generally bought and sold in a free market system. The prices of each currency adjust continually in response to market supply and demand.

But the system has not always operated this way. Historically, gold was the linchpin of the world currency system. During the 1920s the value of the U.S. dollar was linked to gold, and after World War II the U.S. dollar returned to the gold standard, although since it was the only currency to do so, other countries attempted to "peg" their currencies to (or establish their currencies' value in relation to) the U.S. dollar. The dollar-gold standard helped consolidate the role of the United States as the world's creditor and the manager of the international financial system, but in 1971 the U.S. dollar was taken off the gold standard. With currencies allowed to rise and fall with fluctuations in the major economies, traders in currency exchange markets and in MNCs could capitalize on buying and selling currencies. Such currency transactions averaged more than $3 trillion a day. These fluctuations can be a source of international finance.

There is no global institution addressing monetary policy—the IMF has rather limited powers in this regard and the United States' relative indifference toward the institution has weakened it. Rather, there are a variety of different ways the international system "manages" the international monetary system, with the United States playing a key role. Approximately 60 percent of the world's output and its people reside within the de facto dollar area, where currencies are pegged to the dollar and adjust to it. More than 60 percent of foreign-exchange reserves held by banks are in U.S. dollars; 45 percent of all foreign-exchange market transactions involve the dollar, including all transactions in the petroleum markets. America's Wall Street sets the global rhythm and the U.S. Federal Reserve facilitates the dollar payment system worldwide. Yet in the words of *The Economist*, "America is at the centre of the global monetary disorder."[6]

There are other contenders for the role the dollar plays. In 2016, the IMF added the Chinese currency, the renminbi, to the basket of currencies that make up the special drawing rights, the reserve asset in which the IMF denominates loans. These currencies include the U.S. dollar, the British pound, the Japanese yen, and the euro. The IMF decision was largely symbolic—a recognition that China had become a world economic power (the second largest after the United States), with a GDP of $11 trillion, making up 15 percent of the world GDP. The country holds about 30 percent of global foreign-exchange reserves. But the renminbi represents only about 2 percent of cross-border payments internationally. China wants to free itself from dependence on the U.S. dollar in part because the system gives the United States extensive leverage over the international payments system and enables the United States to impose financial sanctions, as it has done over Russian, Iranian, and North Korean banks. Thus, China has taken a number of steps to try to increase the internationalization of its currency, but there is opposition from domestic interests. Chinese exporters fear that currency appreciation would make their exports less competitive in foreign markets. Whether the renminbi will become an internationally important reserve currency depends, then, on domestic reforms in China—on China's ability to open up financial markets while still maintaining its "socialism with Chinese characteristics."[7]

Many economists argue that although the international monetary system has major flaws, there does not appear to be a successor system. "The global monetary system is unreformed, unstable and possibly unsustainable," *The Economist* reports. "What it needs is an engineer to design smart ways to tame capital flows, a policeman to stop beggar-thy-neighbor policies, a nurse to provide a safety net if things go wrong, and a judge to run the global payments system impartially. If America's political system makes it hard to fill those vacancies, can China do better?"[8]

International Trade

Economic growth is fueled by both financial and trade flows. This idea was the key contribution of liberal economic theorists beginning with Adam Smith. Liberal economics recognizes that states differ in their resource endowments of land, labor, and capital. Under these conditions, worldwide wealth is maximized if states engage in international trade. International trade is a win-win situation.

The British economist David Ricardo (1772–1823) developed a theory that states should engage in international trade according to their **comparative advantage**. Because each state differs in its ability to produce specific products—because of differences in natural resource bases, labor force characteristics, and land values—each state should produce and export that which it can produce most efficiently and import goods that other states can produce more efficiently. Thus, states maximize gains from trade. However, individual actors can be hurt in this process, necessitating periodic government intervention to ensure that all people gain.

Although China used to thrive on its ability to provide cheap labor to foreign countries, it has begun to outsource its cheap labor elsewhere. Ethiopia has become a popular destination for Chinese companies to set up factories, as pictured here.

Consider the production of cars and trucks in the United States and Canada. The United States can produce both cars and trucks using fewer workers than Canada would use, making production less expensive in the United States. Under the principle of *absolute* advantage, the United States would manufacture both cars and trucks, and then export both to Canada. However, under *comparative* advantage, each country should specialize; the United States should produce the car, for which it has a relative advantage in production, and Canada, the truck. By trading cars for trucks, each country gains by specialization. Each state minimizes its opportunity cost, the benefit given up to achieve another goal. The United States gives up the production of trucks to gain car production; Canada gives up the production of cars to gain more truck production. Each country gains by shifting resources to manufacture more of the commodity it produces more efficiently and by trading for the other commodity. Both countries can consume more than they would have if they had remained in isolation, consuming only what they produced domestically. Liberal economics posits that under comparative advantage, production is oriented toward an international market. Efficiency in production is increased, and worldwide wealth is maximized.

Two economists in the 1920s clarified comparative advantage. The **Heckscher-Ohlin theory** posits that countries will export goods that use the most intensive endowments of the state. A land-rich state will export agricultural products, while a state with an abundance of low-skill labor will export products that use this labor.

Furthermore, states will import products that use factors of production (land, labor, or capital) that are scarce. This explains why the United States will be a major agricultural and high-tech product exporter while it is an importer of clothing from labor-abundant states like Bangladesh and India.

While international trade based on comparative advantage may result in economic growth of the collectivity, individual states also have other policy objectives. They want to maintain domestic employment levels and minimize unemployment. They want to enforce their own domestic labor and environmental standards. They may want to help subsidize emerging sectors to enable them to be competitive. They often view some economic sectors as vital for national security reasons and thus seek to protect domestic production. Therefore, negotiations over trading arrangements must consider not only the anticipated economic gains from opening up the economy to competition from others, but also the costs of achieving the other objectives. No wonder trade negotiations have been so contentious.

International Trade Negotiations

The negotiating parties in the GATT, the forerunner of the World Trade Organization, sought to expand international trade by lowering trade barriers. That work occurred over the course of eight negotiating rounds, with each round progressively cutting tariffs, giving better treatment to the developing countries, and addressing new problems (subsidies and countervailing duties). Overall, between 1946 and the mid-1990s, tariffs were reduced in the major trading countries from an average of 40 percent to 5 percent on imported goods.

The final round, the Uruguay Round, began in 1986 and concluded in 1994. That round covered new items such as telecommunications, financial services, insurance, intellectual property rights (copyrights, patents, trademarks), and, for the first time, agriculture. Previously, agriculture was seen as too contentious an issue, complicated by both U.S. agricultural subsidies and the European Union's protectionist Common Agricultural Policy (CAP). In late 1994, the most comprehensive trade agreement in history was finally reached, a 400-page document covering everything from paper clips to computer chips. Tariffs on manufactured goods were cut by an average of 37 percent among members. The developing countries that participated in these tariff cuts—the liberalizers—enjoyed a full percentage point per year boost in growth compared with the nonliberalizers.[9]

In 1995, the GATT became a formal institution, renaming itself the **World Trade Organization (WTO)**. The WTO incorporated the general areas of the GATT's jurisdiction and expanded jurisdiction in services and intellectual property. Regular ministerial meetings gave the WTO a political prominence that the GATT lacked. Representing states that conduct over 90 percent of the world's trade, the WTO has the task of implementing the Uruguay Round, serving as a forum for trade negotiations and providing a venue for trade review, dispute settlement, and enforcement.

Two important procedures were initiated in the WTO. First is the Trade Policy Review Mechanism (TPRM), which conducts periodic surveillance of the trade practices of member states. Under this procedure, there is a forum where states can question each other about trade practices. Second is the Dispute Settlement Body, designed as an authoritative panel to hear and settle trade disputes. With the power to authorize affected states to sanction violators (for example, by raising tariffs on certain goods) and not be found in violation of WTO rules, this body is more powerful than earlier GATT arrangements.

Getting global participation in the WTO has proved a painstaking task. China's accession to the WTO in 2001, after 15 years of negotiations, illustrates the long process and the significant concessions made, as well as the benefits ultimately gained. For example, China revised its laws to permit foreign ventures in previously restricted areas, leading to a significant inflow of foreign investment in telecommunications, tourism, insurance, and banking. Today, China continues to dismantle barriers to trade, relaxing tariffs and quotas. In addition, special domestic courts in China hear WTO-related disputes. China is also now proactive in the WTO itself. By the beginning of 2017, China had initiated 15 cases, been a respondent in 39, and been a third party in 135, even though it has lost a majority of the cases. But China has difficulties complying with WTO rules. Its laws are still rudimentary and its security markets are ill prepared for economic liberalization. China still lags on intellectual-property-rights issues, long a source of contention. Yet many of the reforms that China has made can be attributed to WTO membership. Vietnam, which joined the WTO in 2007, is undergoing some of the same reforms. In 2012, Russia joined as well, following 18 years of contentious negotiations, largely over industrial subsidies. In each case, disentangling the government from the economy has proven to be a difficult task.

The WTO process remains contentious, as illustrated by the Doha Round, launched in 2001. The negotiations ended in stalemate, pitting the United States and the EU against India, Brazil, and China. The main sticking point has been the liberalization of agricultural markets. Neither the United States nor the EU was willing to reduce farm subsidies significantly, which would have made agricultural products from developing countries more competitive in international markets. India and China, in particular, sought, if not an end to farm subsidies, then special safeguard mechanisms for their own poor farmers to ensure food security. In 2013 and 2014, negotiators finally broke the impasse. That agreement paved the way for a trade-facilitation agreement to streamline customs procedures and upgrade border and port infrastructure. But the developing countries continue to seek more advantages in the politically sensitive areas of agriculture and other labor-intensive sectors.

The United States is increasingly dissatisfied with the WTO. The WTO permits developing countries to impose higher tariffs than the industrialized countries do. China was designated as a developing country when it joined the WTO in 2001; at that time, China's average income was 20 to 25 percent of that of the United States. Yet today China is the world's second-largest economy and the biggest producer of cars and steel. But it is estimated that China imposes an average tariff of 27 percent on imported goods. The WTO also permits developed countries like the European Union states of Germany and France to include the equivalent of its value-added tax in their tariffs. That tax on imports currently averages 25 percent across a number of goods. In contrast, the United States imposes an average tariff of 9 percent.[10] U.S. policy makers wonder, why should China still be classified as a developing country? Why should China be allowed to have average tariffs three times as high as those of the United States? Why should the EU states be permitted their high tariffs? The expectation was that tariffs would be lowered further during the Doha Round of WTO negotiations. But that did not happen. As *The Economist* reports, "The WTO is still good at enforcing existing trade agreements, but has not managed to bring in a comprehensive new deal for two decades."[11]

Negotiating agreements among 161 countries at varying levels of development and with diverse national objectives is a challenge. Those challenges have been made even more difficult by the procedure adopted by negotiators: "Nothing is agreed until everything is agreed." These barriers are one reason why the United States, the European Union, the Association of Southeast Asian Nations (ASEAN), and others are pursuing regional and bilateral trade agreements and renegotiating the terms of those already in force.

The Regionalization of Trade and Beyond

Despite the efforts of the World Trade Organization and multinational corporations to support internationalization of the economy, regionalization has seen a resurgence, especially in trade. In 1994, there were but 47 bilateral free-trade agreements; in 2016, there were over 260 such agreements. The United States, the EU, China, and Japan, as well as South Korea, Chile, Mexico, and Singapore, have all negotiated multiple bilateral agreements, many with political and strategic objectives in mind. And many more regional economic arrangements have been negotiated, from roughly 50 in 1990 to more than 400 in 2016, with many more still being negotiated, including an agreement between between ASEAN members and six other WTO members in Asia; and the Pacific Alliance between Chile,

Colombia, Mexico, and Peru in Latin America. Those already operational have been strengthened; others have suffered setbacks. No regional economic agreement has been as strong, or as copied, as the European Union.

European Economic Integration

European economic integration was predicated on the notion that a larger market, along with the free movement of goods and services, would permit (1) economies of scale (providing goods for a larger market would lower the fixed cost per unit) and (2) specialization to stimulate growth, competition, and innovation. Both goals are compatible with economic liberalism. The European Union (EU) has generally proven successful in achieving some of these objectives, creating a single market and developing a monetary union, although Great Britain's exit from the EU threatens that success.

The impetus for expanded European economic integration lay in part in Europe's sluggish economy in the 1970s and 1980s, a time when the United States and Japan were increasingly competitive. To stimulate Europe's growth, and hence its international competitiveness, the Single European Act of 1987 accelerated the integration process, setting the goal of achieving a single market by 1992. That effort involved removing physical, fiscal, and technical barriers to trade and harmonizing national standards by adopting more than 300 community directives. Some parts of the goal—such as the elimination of customs barriers—were quickly achieved; other areas—such as labor mobility—have proved more problematic. Although most countries eliminated passport controls and adopted similar visa rules, recognition of education and professional qualifications has proven a thorny issue. Abolishing technical barriers to trade has been difficult because of differing health and safety standards, but the process is ongoing, as is the effort to break state monopolies and eliminate state aid to specific sectors.

The overall results have been positive, with the growth of all types of economic transactions across state borders deepening integration among the national economies of the 28 member states. Exports of goods and services constitute more than one-third of the GDP for the average EU member. More than 70 percent of total trade in goods is conducted with other EU members. Not only is trade integrated, but so are capital flows; cross-border mergers and acquisitions have accelerated. The broad consensus is that European integration has resulted in greater trade creation and has had a positive welfare effect on member and nonmember states.[12]

The EU is more than a regional trading area or a single market. During the discussions for the single market, the outlines of a monetary union were also negotiated. With monetary stability and a single currency, the union would grow and prosper even more. The European Monetary Union, set forth in the Maastricht Treaty in 1992, called for the establishment of a single currency, the euro; it became the unit of exchange for businesses in 1998 and for consumers in 2002. Thereafter, the individual 17 members of the Eurozone could no longer use monetary policy like exchange rates or interest rates as instruments of economic policy. Most observers agree that the euro has facilitated business transactions and eliminated the uncertainty caused by fluctuations in exchange rates. But the euro has come under unprecedented pressure since 2009, creating a financial crisis, and may jeopardize the European integration project.

Very early, the European Union recognized that agriculture was different from other economic sectors. First, agricultural prices dramatically fluctuate with weather and disease, so there has long been a strong incentive to moderate the price fluctuations caused by supply volatility. Second, foodstuffs are viewed as vital for national security; in emergencies, no state wants its population to depend on others for food. Third, in many countries, the well-organized farm sector enjoys disproportionate political power. For all these reasons, the EU adopted the Common Agricultural Policy (CAP). The CAP has changed over time, moving gradually away from a production-oriented policy in which the EU purchases surplus crops from farmers at guaranteed prices and then either stores the surplus, anticipating higher prices in the future, or donates it to food aid programs, absorbing the losses. Since the 2003 reforms, the EU has moved toward a Single Payment Scheme, wherein each country chooses whether the EU payment goes to the farm or the region. Farmers themselves choose to produce any commodity, except fruit, potatoes, or other vegetables. Price interventions by the EU are limited to wheat, butter, and types of milk. Large farmers are being phased out of the program. Rural development is promoted.

The CAP's total budget was 39 percent of the EU budget in 2015, down from 73 percent in 1985. The CAP has proved to be one of the most controversial EU policies. Not only has it been a major issue for states seeking membership and wanting their share of the agricultural budget, but it is also a critical issue in multilateral negotiations because nonmembers pay more for EU agricultural products than members do.

Have the EU's policies contributed to economic globalization or proved an impediment? Most economists agree that the openness of the European markets has benefited most Europeans and become increasingly compatible with the goals of the multilateral global system. Indeed, the EU has developed a web of preferential agreements with its neighbors in the Mediterranean area and with former colonies having shared histories in Africa, as well as with other geographic regions, including North America and Latin America. In general, the EU has enhanced

Europe's global economic power, making Europe more competitive with both the United States and China.

But Britain's unexpected exit from the European Union, discussed in the next chapter, poses a number of questions. What will be Britain's economic and trade relationship with the EU, with its member states, and with other states having preferential arrangements with the EU? (In Chapter 9, see "'Brexit'" on pp. 348–349 and the Global Perspectives box on pp. 350–351).

The North American Free Trade Agreement (NAFTA)

The free-trade area negotiated by the United States, Canada, and Mexico in 1994 differs substantially from the European Union and other regional schemes. Mexico's and Canada's combined economic strength is one-tenth that of the United States. The driving force behind NAFTA was not political elites but business interests seeking larger market shares than their Japanese and European competition, as well as free-trade advocates in all countries. The subsequent phasing out of many restrictions on foreign investment and most tariff and nontariff barriers, as well as the many restrictions on foreign investment, has allowed MNCs to shift production to low-wage labor centers in Mexico and to gain economically by creating bigger companies through mergers and acquisitions.

Cooperation in trade and investment is not intended to lead to the free movement of labor. The goal is quite the opposite; the United States expected that Mexican workers would *not* seek employment in the United States, because economic development in Mexico would provide employment opportunities. And in NAFTA, economic cooperation never implied political integration. With NAFTA, economic integration is to remain just that—cooperation confined to specific economic sectors.

The phased elimination of tariff and nontariff barriers in NAFTA has resulted in expansion of trade. Trade among the three partners has tripled since 1994; today over 14 percent of world trade in goods occurs under NAFTA rules and regulations. Most noticeable are the proliferation of cross-border supply chains, making the participating MNCs more competitive and profitable. Agriculture and manufacturing in general may well be the winners. Agricultural markets are better integrated, and consumers enjoy lower prices because virtually all agricultural tariffs have been eliminated. Both Canada and Mexico are now large markets for U.S. agricultural exports. Similarly, the share of Canadian exports absorbed by the United States has expanded, and agricultural exports from Mexico have boomed. Tariffs on manufactured goods have also been almost entirely eliminated. Most analysts find that the agreement has had a positive impact on U.S. GDP, adding $80 billion to the U.S. economy, with much of that concentrated in auto manufacturing. In addition, an estimated 14 million U.S. jobs now rely on trade with Mexico and Canada, paying up to 20 percent more than the jobs lost. Foreign direct investment among the three countries has increased tenfold.

Why, then, has NAFTA been so controversial? After all, isn't freer trade a positive-sum game, a win-win situation for all? The fact is that there are some winners and some losers, especially over the shorter term. Labor unions in the United States estimate that hundreds of thousands of workers have lost their jobs to Mexico—by one estimate, over 600,000 U.S. jobs have been lost to Mexico over the last two decades, though there are several other explanations, including gains in labor productivity. In addition, environmental groups point to firms in the United States that have relocated to Mexico to take advantage of weak environmental regulations. And while the United States posted a trade surplus with Mexico in 1993 of $1.7 billion, 20 years later there was a $63.2 billion deficit. Why is that beneficial to the United States, critics ask?

Canada and Mexico also have NAFTA supporters and critics. Canada has had a threefold surge in cross-border investment and is a leading importer of U.S. agricultural products. But Canadian labor contends that the country is becoming too dependent on natural resource exports. Mexican supporters point to some major increases in jobs, including a fourfold increase in the number of Mexican autoworkers, while critics point to the slide in real manufacturing wages due to the movement of lower-skilled jobs to China. And as Jorge Castañeda, Mexico's former foreign minister reported, "If the purpose of the agreement was to spur economic growth, create jobs, boost productivity, lift wages, and discourage emigration, then the results have been less clear-cut."[13] Mexico has failed to develop backward linkages in its export sector; ancillary services and other manufacturing facilities have not developed, in part because of foreigners' unwillingness to invest in Mexico. While foreign investment in Mexico has increased from $4.4 billion in 1993 before NAFTA to about $22 billion annually, that figure is below foreign investment in Brazil, Chile, and Colombia, non-NAFTA countries. And wages have been relatively stagnant in Mexico, with poverty remaining at about the same level as in 1994. To radical opponents, NAFTA is yet another example of U.S. expansionism and of the exploitation of the Mexican workforce by, on the one hand, both the United States and Canada and, on the other hand, the Mexican government, whose redistribution policies have failed to raise the standard of living for all.[14]

During his presidential campaign Donald Trump called NAFTA the "worst trade deal," but later officials in his administration acknowledged that withdrawing from it could be complicated and costly. Hence, in the fall of 2017 negotiations began on a number of key issues. To achieve the goal of reducing the trade deficit, the United States seeks changes in the rules of origin—the product-specific rules that stipulate what must happen to inputs from non-NAFTA countries for the final exported product to qualify for NAFTA benefits. The United States maintains that the percentage of production within a NAFTA country should be increased in order to shift some production from Asia to NAFTA countries, preferably the United States. The United States would also like Mexico and Canada to eliminate certain barriers to U.S. exports. Another issue is the dispute-settlement process. The U.S. view is that the panel established in NAFTA should be weakened, and the United States has disagreed strongly with a number of the panel's decisions.

Canada is pushing for a more "progressive" agreement in terms of more environmental and labor protections, including gender equality and indigenous rights. Canadians advocate opening up government procurement and making it easier for professionals to work across borders. Mexicans had wanted a quick time framework for renegotiation since Mexican presidential elections were scheduled for 2018. Negotiations, however, have been neither rapid nor smooth.

Not only do individual states' interests differ, but also sectors within each state have divergent interests. U.S. natural gas exporters want to continue to sell natural gas to Mexico, and Mexican demand keeps prices from collapsing. Agricultural interests want continuing favorable treatment because they are allowed under NAFTA to keep some of their markets closed. Other sectors with the most to lose or gain with renegotiation include automobiles, apparel, and medical devices because they are intertwined in global supply chains. In short, what begins as an economic issue quickly becomes a political one.

Believing that there will be more winners than losers in freer trade, other regions have developed regional trading arrangements. ASEAN in Asia and Mercosur in Latin America are two examples.

ASEAN Free Trade Area and Mercosur

Individual East Asian countries have experienced phenomenal economic growth through competitive exports; prior to the 1990s, most of the exports went to either the United States or European countries. In 1992, the Association of Southeast Asian Nations (ASEAN) established the ASEAN Free Trade Area (AFTA). Its goal is twofold: to attract foreign investment to the region, and to increase members' competitive edge in the global market by eliminating tariff and nontariff barriers within ASEAN. The exception to these reductions is rice—the food staple of the region—and certain other highly sensitive products. And like the EU, AFTA has also emphasized nontariff barriers, quantitative restrictions, and harmonization of customs rules. By the end of 2014, 70 percent of ASEAN intraregional trade incurred no tariffs, and the average tariff rate was less than 5 percent. Unlike in the EU, however, the goal is not to create a common external tariff. The hope is that closer regional economic integration will boost growth. Whether ASEAN members can bridge their large differences in levels of development and national

Leaders from Japan, India, China, the Philippines, Singapore, Australia, New Zealand, and the United States attend the ASEAN Summit to discuss economic, political, and security issues in the Southeast Asian region.

standards, however, remains to be seen. China has voiced interest in joining AFTA—a step certain to complicate regional economic integration.

Among the many subregional trade agreements in the 1990s was the Common Market of the South (Mercado Común del Sur) or Mercosur founded in 1991 by Brazil, Argentina, Uruguay, and Paraguay, with Venezuela joining in 2012.[15] With grand ambitions, Mercosur was not merely an economic response to the creation of NAFTA and the EU's single market, which its members feared would cost them markets and influence. It was also an attempt to reverse decades of authoritarianism, crises, and antagonism, especially between Argentina and Brazil. While trade increased among its members five times over during the 1990s, trade over the last 20 years has fallen compared to trade with nonmember states. Mercosur is a trading bloc with designated free-trade zones. Products made in those zones are treated more favorably in interstate commerce than those made in the states' own territories. But progress has been blocked by the absence of agreement on a common external tariff, by economic crises in both Brazil and Argentina, and by Venezuela's erratic government. In August 2017, Venezuela was suspended from membership because of President Nicolás Maduro's antidemocratic measures. In 2016, the presidents of Brazil and Argentina pushed for Mercosur to enter into negotiations with other Latin American countries as well as with the European Union.

Transregional Economic Arrangements

Interest in transregional economic arrangements such as those proposed by Mercosur leaders has accelerated. Under President Obama, the United States negotiated on trade and investment issues with both Asia and Europe. Agreement was reached in late 2015 among the United States, Japan, and ten Pacific Rim countries (including Canada, Chile, and Mexico) for the Trans-Pacific Partnership (TPP). The agreement, touted as a global trendsetter for commerce, included a phasing out of import tariffs on 18,000 U.S. products, like automobiles, machinery, technology, and agricultural products. Macroeconomic cooperation would be strengthened, and protections for labor, the environment, and copyrights and patents would be enhanced. But the election of President Trump halted America's participation in what he labeled a "horrible deal." Under the leadership of Japan, Australia, and New Zealand, negotiations resumed. In 2018, 11 states signed the Trans-Pacific Trade Accord, a revision of the proposed Trans-Pacific Partnership without the United States. The new agreement drops tariffs and establishes sweeping new trade rules.

Also on hold are negotiations between the United States and the European Union over new trade and investment agreements that would knit together their economies even more closely. The proposed Transatlantic Trade and Investment Partnership (TTIP) is intended to reduce obstacles to trade and investment, such as EU barriers to genetically modified foods, and empower U.S. firms to sue in local European courts. Some Europeans are concerned about granting more rights to U.S. firms, which could lead to weakened worker protections. But the future of that proposed agreement is unknown. A major stumbling block is President Trump's well-known antipathy to multilateral trade deals and his promise to reduce the U.S. trade deficit by imposing protectionist policies.

The Debate over Bilateral, Regional, and Transregional Trade Agreements

The proliferation of all types of trade agreements is controversial, leading one prominent opponent, Jagdish Bhagwati, to refer to the patchwork of agreements as "termites in the trading system."[16] Three questions regarding economic regionalization have emerged. First, do regional trade agreements actually improve the economic welfare of their members through trade creation, or is trade actually diverted to nonmember states and economic welfare reduced? With regional trade agreements, some trade is created in goods produced efficiently relative to the rest of the world. Trade is also diverted from efficient nonmembers because of the preferences member states grant to each other, and hence, state welfare is reduced.

Second, does economic regionalization enhance the position of labor and improve environmental arrangements? Or does economic regionalization force a downward pressure on wages and environmental standards as countries and regions actively compete for trade and foreign direct investment?

Third, are regional trade agreements a stepping-stone or a stumbling block to global trade arrangements? On the one hand, they clearly reduce the number of actors in international negotiations and enhance competitiveness of some domestic industries. On the other hand, under regional trade agreements, larger economies can impose their will and interest groups may find it easier to lobby for their interests. Regional agreements may make states less likely to agree to global tariff cuts. The answers to these questions continue to be debated. For developing countries, the answers are critical.

International Development

The end of colonialization following the end of World War II and through the mid-1960s led not only to geopolitical competition between the United States and the Soviet Union but also to the emergence of newly independent states that were poor and lacking the material resources and expertise to deliver economic goods to their citizens. Very quickly, international programs developed to begin to meet the needs of these states, including the World Bank's affiliates—the International Finance Corporation and the International Development Association. The GATT itself adopted the idea of more favorable treatment for developing countries. Even the Doha Round of the GATT was labeled a "development" round, although, as one cynic put it, the round "has not filled any bellies."[17]

Despite these efforts, the most developed countries in the Global North bask in relative wealth, with high consumption habits, high levels of education and health services, and social-welfare safety nets. In contrast, a few countries in the Global South struggle to meet basic needs, with poor educational and health services and no welfare nets. The Human Development Index (HDI) in Table 8.1 shows these stark contrasts across several indicators. Caused by many factors—colonialism, earlier industrialization of Europe, geography, poor government policies, unaccountable governments—this is the development gap, or for the poorest, the development trap.[18] In actuality, the divisions between the poor and the rich have become more complex since the 1990s. As exemplified during the latest round of trade negotiations, the G7 major economic powers are faced by both the **BRICS** (Brazil, Russia, India, China, and South Africa) and the Group of 20 collective of emerging powers, which includes the G7, the BRICS, and Australia, Mexico, South Korea, Turkey, Argentina, Indonesia, and Saudi Arabia.

Strategies to Achieve Economic Development

Ideas about how development occurs have evolved from the work of state policy makers, officials within the UN system, and analysts within institutions such as the World Bank. Most of the debates over the best approach have focused on variations or adaptations of the liberal economic model, but other critiques are more fundamental. As constructivists assert, there is a real conflict over ideas and those ideas keep changing.

During the 1950s and 1960s, the development institutions, including the World Bank and major donors such as the United States, adopted a strategy for development that emphasized financially large infrastructure projects—such as dams, electric power, and telecommunications—as necessary for providing the foundations of development. In the 1970s, realizing that not all groups were benefiting from such investments, the aid agencies began to fund projects in health, education, and housing, designed to improve the economic life of the poor. The 1980s saw a shift toward reliance on private-sector participation to meet the task of restructuring economies and reconstructing states torn apart by ethnic conflict. When areas of the economy are privatized, the government's fiscal burden is reduced, and state spending in education and health can then increase. This approach to economic growth has become known as the **Washington Consensus**, a version of economic liberalism. Its adherents hold that only with certain economic policies—including privatization, liberalization of trade and foreign direct investment, government deregulation in favor of open competition, and broad tax reform—will development occur. The Bretton Woods institutions have been the leaders in advocating these policies.

Although the IMF was not originally charged with development, its bureaucrats realized very quickly that many countries' seemingly temporary balance-of-payments problems were actually long-term structural problems that prevented those countries from developing, and the IMF's short-term loans could not address these problems. Thus, during the early 1980s, the IMF began to provide longer-term loans if states adopted **structural adjustment programs** consistent with the Washington Consensus. If a state adopted those policies—economic reforms (limiting money and credit growth, forcing currency devaluation, reforming the financial sector, introducing user fees, eliminating subsidies), trade liberalization reforms (removing tariffs, rehabilitating export infrastructure), government reforms (privatizing public enterprises), and private-sector policies (ending government monopolies)—then the IMF gave its stamp of approval, leading other multilateral lenders and bilateral and international private banks to lend as well.

In the 1990s, **sustainable development**, an approach to economic development that incorporates concern for renewable resources and the environment,

TABLE 8.1

Human Development Index, 2016

	LIFE EXPECTANCY AT BIRTH (YEARS)	MEAN YEARS OF SCHOOLING (YEARS)	EXPECTED YEARS OF SCHOOLING (YEARS)	GROSS NATIONAL INCOME PER CAPITA (2015 PPP$)[a]	HUMAN DEVELOPMENT INDEX VALUE[b]
Arab States	70.8	6.8	11.7	14,958	0.637
East Asia and the Pacific	74.2	7.7	13.0	12,125	0.720
Europe and Central Asia	72.6	10.3	13.9	12,862	0.756
Latin America and the Caribbean	75.2	8.3	14.1	14,028	0.751
South Asia	68.7	6.2	11.3	5,799	0.621
Sub-Saharan Africa	58.9	5.4	9.7	3,383	0.523
World	71.5	7.9	12.2	14,301	0.717

a. PPP is purchasing power parity. It is a way to compare levels of economic data cross-nationally, free of price and exchange-data distortions.

b. The HDI combines indicators for life expectancy, educational attainment, and income into a composite value, ranging between 0 (low development) and 1 (high development).

Source: United Nations Human Development Report, 2016.

became part of the World Bank's rhetoric, although that rhetoric did not always translate into its practices. During the 1990s, however, it became apparent that even under structural adjustment, some countries could not get out from under the weight of their debt and begin to develop. That debt had been escalating; developing countries owed $2.2 trillion in 2000 (20 years earlier, the debt had been $577 billion). There was also mounting pressure to adopt a more systematic approach to debt. Buoyed by Jubilee 2000, a social movement that promoted changes in the name of social justice and was supported by economic radicals and others who thought debt doomed states to permanent underdevelopment, a major policy shift occurred. Sponsored by the IMF, the World Bank, and the G7 economic powers, the Heavily Indebted Poor Countries (HIPC) Initiative was a historic one. Never before had foreign national debt been canceled or substantially rescheduled. While implementation of the plan and its attendant conditions has been slow and controversial, by mid-2017, 36 countries had received debt relief, 30 of them in Africa, amounting to over $76 billion in debt relief. Countries receiving such relief had to submit plans to channel debt savings into poverty-reduction programs.

Another change occurred in the international financial institutions beginning in 2009, following a study by the World Bank's Commission on Growth and Development. The institutions discontinued structural performance criteria for loans, even for loans to low-income countries, in response to both their critics and the 2008 global financial crisis. This represents a substantial overhaul of the lending framework. The amount of the loans can be greater than previously allowed, and loans are to be tailored according to the respective state's needs, a direct response to criticism of the "cookie-cutter" approach of structural adjustment lending. Monitoring of the loans will be done more quietly to reduce the stigma of conditionality. Also in response to previous criticism, the IMF has urged lending to programs that encourage social safety nets for the most vulnerable within the populations. Ideas that were previously unacceptable to the IMF—that capital flows may need regulation and that states might take a proactive role in coordinating economic development—became more acceptable in response to the market failures of the global financial crisis.[19]

A broad consensus has emerged among virtually all states on the utility of market-oriented economic policies that lead to sustainable economic development. Scarce natural resources cannot be exploited as in the past; sustainability means that growth can be ensured for future generations. There must also be more emphasis on human development, particularly education and health. In addition, the targets of development—the people—should have a say in how funds are allocated. And there is much more attention being paid to the political dimension of development. Daron Acemoglu and James Robinson, among others, argue that successful development demands strong economic and political institutions that protect private property, foster competition, and ensure the rule of law to prevent corruption. In short, the current thinking is that institutions play a more critical role in successful development than the liberal economic model suggests.[20]

NGOs organized at the grassroots level to carry out locally based projects play a critical role in this new approach. Involving NGOs in development was one approach for improving the accountability and effectiveness of both multilateral and bilateral donor programs. NGOs such as Catholic Relief Services, Oxfam, and Doctors Without Borders not only deliver food and medical assistance during emergencies but also distribute seeds, drill wells, and plan local-level projects that they hope will bring economic development. NGOs can also be an alternative channel for finance to individuals and small groups that are often neglected by the national or international banks; many of these programs are subcontracted to NGOs from national and international development institutions.

One well-publicized effort, now duplicated many times over, has been microfinance. Grameen Bank in Bangladesh, created in 1983 by an academic-turned-banker, Muhammad Yunus (2006 recipient of the Nobel Peace Prize), provides small amounts of funding for individuals and groups to invest in an economically productive enterprise. The Grameen Foundation has aided 23 million of the world's poor with the support of its national and local partners. Using a variety of funds, microloans, savings accounts, and other financial services, programs have been incubated in India, Indonesia, the Philippines, and Ethiopia, among others. The purpose is to empower women, who are typically ignored by multilateral institutions, by providing them with income that they are expected to use for productive purposes. In 2015–16, 94 percent of the foundation's clients were women.

Microfinance institutions have grown exponentially, becoming bigger, more competitive, and more diverse. Some are not-for-profit, such as the Grameen Bank, while others are for-profit institutions; some offer just credit, while, increasingly, others offer a variety of saving alternatives. But do microfinance institutions lift individuals out of poverty? Do they foster economic development and growth more generally, as the Grameen Bank has claimed?

Recent studies show a more nuanced result from microfinance's efforts to alleviate poverty. One study finds that microfinance had no overall impact on the borrower's household welfare after 18 months, measured by income, spending, or school attendance. However, when the borrower already owned a small business, then the new credit infusion improved income and spending. In other words, microcredit helps those who are already better off.[21] Another study of six

Development: A View from Rwanda

In 1994, Rwanda in central east Africa experienced a genocide in which one-eighth of its population, or 800,000 people, were killed. Rwandan leaders do not want that genocide to define the country. In 2000, with the democratic election of Paul Kagame as president and the launch of Vision 2020, the country adopted a new path of development, designed to lift it out of poverty.

That goal will not be easy to achieve. The mostly rural country is landlocked, with over 13 million people densely living on a gently rolling landscape. It has no natural resources, and 70 percent of the population is engaged in subsistence agriculture. According to the World Bank, almost 63 percent of the population still lives in extreme poverty, subsisting on less than $1.25 a day. In 2015, Rwanda received a .498 on the Human Development Index, placing it in the category of low human development.

Vision 2020 proposed a transformation of Rwanda from a low-income agricultural country to a knowledge-based, service-oriented, middle-income country by 2020. Between 2001 and 2015, GDP growth increased 8 percent annually. But even with these high growth rates, how can this goal be achieved? How successful has Rwanda been in achieving this goal?

Diversifying the agricultural sector continues to be a high priority. This includes improving the productivity of the subsistence agricultural sector by diversifying crops, employing better tools, and boosting its resilience to adverse weather shocks like droughts through insurance schemes. In addition, the export crops of coffee and tea must be continually upgraded and marketed internationally. And the size of farms needs to be increased in order to make them more efficient and take advantage of economies of scale.

While the industrial sector is almost 15 percent of the GDP, that sector is not given high priority. Instead, the service sector is given the highest priority, with the goal of making Rwanda the African hub for information and communications technology (ICT). Since 2012, Rwanda has devoted 5 percent of its spending to the development of science and technology, a high percentage compared to most countries. Mobile networks now cover 99.8 percent of the country, with 64 percent of the population participating.

Vision 2020 gives high priority to the health sector in order to improve human security. Ninety percent of the population is now covered by a near-universal health-care system, financed by tax revenues, foreign aid, and voluntary premiums scaled by income. The results have been impressive: life expectancy has increased from 55.2 years to 64.0 years. Mortality for children under five years old has dropped from 106.4 to 52.0 per 1,000 live births. By the end of 2015, most of the Millennium Development Goals have been met.

The strategy used to achieve these objectives combines strong support for domestic private investment with wooing and keeping international public and private investors. Support for private investment entails making it relatively easy to set up and run a business enterprise. Red tape has been cut. On the World Bank's index for ease of doing business, Rwanda ranks 32 out of 189 countries, and in another index, Rwanda is touted as the number two in Africa for the ease of conducting business.

Attracting and keeping foreign investment and aid is essential since the percentage of

Women wash and sort coffee beans near Kigali, Rwanda.

the annual budget covered by foreign donors fluctuates between 30 and 40 percent. Given Rwanda's dependence on other states and international institutions, Kagame's strategy is to build and utilize networks of powerful friends and allies to augment private and public investment. Councils of international advisers participate in this lobbying effort. A prominent example is the use of this network to persuade Costco to buy Rwanda's coffee.

Utilizing personal relationships to attract investment depends on marketing the Rwanda "brand." That brand emerges from Rwanda's successes: achieving political stability after a horrific genocide; cutting corruption and encouraging entrepreneurship; becoming a well-organized, safe, and clean country; and supporting the political participation of women (now a majority in the national parliament). No wonder tourism continues to flourish, making this industry Rwanda's major earner of foreign exchange. In 2017, Paul Kagame received 99 percent of the vote, winning his third term in office. He proclaimed, "This is another seven years to take care of issues that affect Rwandans and ensure that we become real Rwandans who are [economically] developing."[a] The Rwanda brand is strong.

a. Quoted in Jason Burke, "Paul Kagame Re-elected President with 99% in Rwanda Election," *Guardian*, August 5, 2017.

FOR CRITICAL ANALYSIS

1. What are the dangers of Rwanda's reliance on foreign aid and tourism for achieving economic development?

2. Is Rwanda's goal of being a hub for ITC activities realistic?

3. What other countries might market their brand to boost economic development?

met for a time by the establishment of the Organization of the Petroleum Exporting Countries in 1960 to try to manage production and hence stabilize prices.

The 2008–2009 Global Financial Crisis

Despite all the reforms undertaken during past economic crises, the Bretton Woods institutions did not include actual surveillance and temporary fixes for the richer countries or the economically strong United States. The 1980s and 1990s saw an explosion of unregulated, highly leveraged financial instruments, including oil futures and derivatives markets. U.S.-based financial institutions and governmental units at all levels were participating in those markets. Excess credit against insufficient equity prevailed across the housing market, the financial sector, and consumer-credit markets. That spending spree was accompanied by the importation of cheap goods from China, causing an unsustainable trade imbalance with China and the oil-exporting countries. By 2007, it was clear that the U.S. economy itself was exhibiting fundamental structural weaknesses, although few policy makers were ready to take action. First to feel the impact was the subprime mortgage market. Because financial companies and international banks were carrying unsustainable debt with no assets to back up the loans, defaults increased. Credit became more difficult to acquire. Private investment to build factories and produce goods dried up.

What began as a financial crisis centered in the United States rapidly became a global economic crisis. The U.S.-based financial instruments that had spawned the excess lending had been sold abroad to investors ranging from local communities in Norway to banks in Europe and East Asia and investors in Japan and China. What safer place to invest, they thought, than the United States? That proved not to be the case. Financial institutions were unable to meet their obligations. Credit became almost impossible to obtain in the United States and Europe. Businesses cut expenditures and workforces. Consumer demand plummeted. States such as China, South Korea, and Japan, dependent on exports to the United States and Europe, saw their markets shrink and export earnings fall. Oil prices dropped by 69 percent between July and December 2008, severely affecting such oil-exporting countries as Russia, Angola, and Venezuela. In emerging markets dependent on private foreign investment (especially Eastern Europe and states of the former Soviet Union), investment plummeted; in 2008, it was less than half that of a year earlier. In late 2008, Iceland became the first state victim when its banking system collapsed. In the Baltic states, Ukraine, and Eastern Europe, economies virtually collapsed. International trade declined. The crisis rippled outward to developing countries that faced the prospect of sharply reduced or negative growth and the erosion of gains from globalization-driven growth. The speed and depth of the collapse in global financial and international trade markets surprised even the experts; the self-correcting mechanisms were not working as economic liberals had theorized.

Both the United States and various EU member governments took unprecedented steps, bailing out banks and insurance companies to get credit markets functioning again and stimulate investor confidence. These same states, along with Japan and China, each responded with substantial economic stimulus packages to encourage economic growth. Some coordinated actions were taken among central bankers. The U.S. Federal Reserve, the European Central Bank, and the Bank of England engaged in currency swaps.

The IMF also responded to the crisis by making available almost $250 billion for credit lines. Iceland became the first Western country to borrow from the IMF since 1976. Substantial loans were made to Ukraine, Hungary, and Pakistan. The IMF, with an infusion of $750 billion, created the Short-Term Liquidity Facility for emerging-market countries suffering temporary liquidity problems. It reorganized the Exogenous Shocks Facility, designed to help low-income states by providing assistance more rapidly and streamlining conditions. Unfortunately, the IMF's capacity had already been weakened by those preferring market solutions over greater regulation and those wanting to abolish the Bretton Woods system itself. But the International Development Association was able to increase its resources during the crisis for loans to some of the poorest developing countries. Short-term responses were needed, as well as better long-term cross-border supervision of financial institutions, standards for accounting and banking regulations, and an early warning system for the world economy. But these were not yet in place for the subsequent Eurozone crisis.

The 2009 Eurozone Crisis

As growth within the states in the EU began to slow or reverse because of the global economic crisis, a crisis closer to home was magnified. In the early years of the new millennium, easy credit had ushered in a decade of risky borrowing from international banks and profligate spending by some EU countries. In Greece, high public-sector wages and long-term pension obligations fueled public-sector borrowing. In Ireland and Spain, private-sector borrowing accelerated, like it did in the U.S. housing bubble. Then, when the global economic crisis hit, households faced underwater mortgages, foreclosures, and even bankruptcy. Many individuals whose net worth had dramatically declined now faced unemployment and declining wages, only deepening the debt trap.

And governments dependent on borrowing in international markets were turned away, deepening their debt obligations.

But the crisis was not just a debt problem. It was also caused by an imbalance of trade. After the turn of the century, Germany's export trade grew, while that of the so-called PIGS (Portugal, Italy, Greece, and Spain) had worsening balance-of-payments positions. Wages rose faster than gains in productivity, making their exports uncompetitive, while Germany's wage restraint made German exports even more competitive. Today, Germany's trade surplus is the world's largest at $200 billion; 40 percent of that surplus comes from trade within the Eurozone.

The arrangements within the European monetary union and within the Eurozone itself made addressing the twin problems of unsustainable debt and trade imbalances even more difficult. As the Eurozone's critics wondered, how could the euro work with no fiscal union and no treasury? Individual states did not have the ability to manage their monetary policy: they could not print more money, and they could not devalue their currency to make their exports more competitive. Labor mobility was constrained, and there were no agreed-upon procedures for transferring funds between states.[28] When the banks, including German ones, that had lent money liberally during the credit explosion became stressed, they demanded higher interest rates from the PIGS, making it more difficult for those governments to finance budget deficits and service the existing debt, a problem compounded by low growth rates.

There were more than 25 summits to address the Eurozone crisis. In response, the PIGS undertook numerous reforms to reduce government debt, slashing expenditures, increasing the retirement age, promising to improve the tax collection system, and using financial transfers to avert bankruptcy. Greece was the government in the most severe crisis. Not only did that country have a debt problem, but also its worsening balance-of-payments problems and its high wages and low productivity made its exports uncompetitive. Greece was forced to take bailouts from the IMF, the European Central Bank, and the EU, totaling $380 billion by the middle of 2017. In return for the bailouts, the Greek government slashed public spending by cutting services, laying off workers, improving tax collection, renegotiating labor contracts, and ending subsidies. With that bailout, there has been increased pressure to ease the Greek debt burden for fear that the government will never be able to repay the loans. As in African developing countries, negotiations continue with the IMF for a debt-relief package.

Domestic constituencies suffered through the economic distress: Greeks stood in line at soup kitchens; Cypriot bank customers could not withdraw funds; Spanish youth faced an unemployment rate of 50 percent; Germans paid the bailout costs. These constituencies continue to pressure their democratically elected leaders for outcomes favorable to their own interests—in other words, there has been a resurgence of economic nationalism. Yet what is best for the national interest may undermine Eurozone stability or the viability of the EU.

As the European states continue to recover in the aftermath of the Eurozone crisis, the unexpected 2016 decision of Britain to exit the European Union (even though it had never joined the Eurozone) has sharpened the debate over the future of the EU. Just as economist C. Fred Bergsten predicted, tighter constraints imposed on government budgets have slowed down the integration project.[29] Discussions on widening European integration into other countries or deepening integration in particular policy areas are stalled. And until the terms of Brexit are hammered out and the specific economic arrangements negotiated between Britain and EU members become known, the future of the European project remains unknown.

Responses to Economic Crises

Crises do not affect all states equally and in the same way. While the Eurozone crisis adversely affected the PIGS, forcing them to take austerity measures, the global financial crisis did not have its anticipated effect in many countries of Africa. Prior to the crisis, many African economies had been experiencing a resurgence in terms of growth of real GDP, increases in private capital investments, unprecedented Chinese economic activity, and even several multilateral debt-relief initiatives.

Neither Ghana nor Kenya, for example, was directly affected by these crises at the time. Ghana, a longtime world leader in both cocoa and coffee production, had been increasing cocoa production, earning $2 billion annually from international trade, a 32-year high. Because Ghana was also a major gold producer, it benefited from higher prices as consumers moved into gold to protect themselves from declining currencies. In 2007 the country discovered a large petroleum field off its coast, and by 2011 the first oil flowed, helping to spur its 7.7 percent annual growth rate. Private equity was now investing in projects. Kenya, too, did not experience the dire effects of the economic crises. Kenya, like other east African states, benefited from international investments, including Chinese investment in railways that link East African states, tripling intraregional exports among these regional economies. Kenya has also emphasized education, building more schools and requiring compulsory education. And, more than in other countries, indigenous technology companies like M-Pesa in Kenya are bringing new communication devices to educational, agriculture, and service and banking sectors.

While investments from the United States, Europe, and MNCs declined during the global financial crisis, investments from China and other emerging economies like India were growing at an unprecedented rate. China alone increased foreign investment from $9.5 billion in 2005 to $86.3 billion in 2013. In Ghana, Chinese loans and investments have gone to roads, communications systems, rural electrification, and dam building. In Kenya, about one-third of Chinese investments are in manufacturing. Chinese companies are carrying out construction of roads, bridges, and airports. The World Bank optimistically predicted in 2011, "Africa could be on the brink of an economic take-off, much like China was 30 years ago and India 20 years ago."[30]

Much of this optimism assumes that China is the driver of world economic growth. That assumption is now being sorely tested not only in China itself but also in countries that have enjoyed Chinese investment. A recent *New York Times* headline reads, "'Africa Rising'? 'Africa Reeling' May Be More Fitting Now."[31] African growth may not have been as robust as reported—not in Ethiopia, one of the continent's fastest growing economies, where a state of emergency now exists; not in Nigeria, where petroleum prices are plummeting; and not in South Africa, where labor unrest is rampant.

Critics suggest the need for some reforms of the global economic system. But what is needed—a hatchet or a scalpel?[32] Or do we need alternative institutions? The theories introduced above and different policy makers have some responses to these problems.

The Future of Economic Liberalism and Globalization: Crisis, Continuity, or Reform?

Do these economic crises point to the end of economic globalization as now practiced? Can we continue to expect that individuals will act rationally and that markets will always be stable and efficient and will eventually recover? Are economic inequality and high levels of poverty in the developing world inevitable?

Many students of the international political economy view the crises and the problems in economic globalization as an opportunity to make "scalpel-like" reforms. In the immediate aftermath of both the global financial crisis and the Eurozone crisis, reforms were passed. The surveillance functions of the IMF to anticipate risks and threats were given new life. The G7 and G20, with their finance ministers, their central bank officials, and the leaders of their member states, became more active in trying to address the crises. Rules and regulations of the private financial institutions in many states were strengthened and made more transparent, although the latter has proven more difficult than anticipated. Reforms in the Eurozone states gave more authority to the European Central Bank to act as a regulator of banks in member countries and gave more authority to an IMF-like institution—namely, the European Stability Mechanism—to handle bailouts and work with the European Central Bank. Economic liberals believe that these rather incremental reforms can preserve the system, giving more transparency to market transactions. They point to the promising economic recovery after 2010 as evidence that equilibrium can reemerge.

Reformers both outside and within the international financial institutions question fundamental premises, governance, and specific policies.[33] Some reformers are skeptical that the **moral hazard** problem can be overcome. States that are rescued from the consequences of their reckless behavior have little incentive to change that behavior. So reforms designed to rescue states from their own bad decisions may not necessarily lead to better decisions in the future. In terms of governance, reformers propose altering the weighted voting system the IMF and the World Bank now use in favor of greater representation for the emerging economies. In the current system, the major donors are guaranteed voting power commensurate with their contributions. The largest shareholders in each institution—the United States, the European Union states, Japan, and Canada—hold about 60 percent of the total votes. Reformists believe a more representative voting structure might lead to a fairer system and one that promotes different policies. While incremental changes have been proposed, including giving more weight to China by increasing its weight-voting share from 3.66 percent to 6.06 percent, fundamental voting power has not shifted. Further, hiring a more diverse group of bureaucrats, instead of relying on the current group, which is dominated by economists trained in developed Western countries, might bring new, innovative solutions to development dilemmas.

Other reformers are critical of specific policies; here, the critics differ. On the one hand, some argue that both the IMF and the World Bank have strayed too far from their liberal economic foundations, taking on too many different tasks (e.g., trying to promote an environmental agenda or gender equality) and deviating from actions promoting market liberalization. In fact, some maintain that aid and loans themselves should be allocated by competition, creating a liberal market for aid funds. On the other hand, radical political economists claim the institutions promote the interests of private international capital, pointing to the economic returns for firms that provide services for dams and power plants. Other bank policies that have been rigidly developed without considering local conditions and local knowledge end up disproportionately affecting the disadvantaged sectors of the population: the unskilled, women, and the weak.

The World Trade Organization has also become a lightning rod for criticism from many countries. They feel that the WTO, a symbol of economic globalization, is usurping local decisions and degrading the welfare of individuals. NGOs are

Farmers in Manila protest the WTO's regulation of agricultural trade in advance of a speech by WTO director-general Roberto Azevêdo. The liberalization of agricultural markets has been a major point of contention between developed and emerging economies in recent rounds of trade negotiation.

some of the major critics of WTO activities. Some of them oppose the idea that the WTO has the power to make regulations and settle disputes in high-handed ways that intrude on or jeopardize national sovereignty. Still others fear that promotion of unregulated free trade undermines the application of labor and environmental standards; they believe that the WTO sets economic liberalization above other social values. In actuality, the WTO is relatively weak; its resources are stretched thin, constrained by its limit of 640 employees, and it has a slow dispute-settlement mechanism. In an age of protracted supply chains across countries and continents, the trade rules written for another era are no longer as useful or relevant.

Alternative Institutions: The Debate over Globalization Continues

Failing fundamental changes in the organizations discussed above, there is a movement to create alternative institutions that reflect changing power relations, with China playing a key role. Among these alternatives are two multilateral development banks, the Asian Infrastructure Investment Bank (AIIB) and the New Development Bank (NDB). The AIIB became operational in 2015. When first proposed in 2006, China's foreign-exchange reserves were reaching $4 trillion and the bank was a way to invest those funds through a new institution and in emerging-country markets. With a capitalization of $100 billion, the bank is designed to rapidly respond to loan requests that promote long-term growth, mainly through massive investment in infrastructure. The target is to lend $1.2 billion annually.

As of early 2018, 56 members have joined the AIIB, with 24 others pending. But the United States and Japan are not among the members. The United States has argued that the AIIB will not follow governance procedures and will not adhere to environmental standards. Furthermore, the United States sees the bank as a project to promote China's economic and geopolitical role in Asia. Despite pressure from the United States, American allies like Australia, South Korea, and the United Kingdom have joined the AIIB.

The NDB was founded by the BRICS states of Brazil, Russia, India, China, and South Africa and became effective in 2015. With an initial authorized capital of $100 billion, one-half of which were shares equally distributed among the founding members, the NDB grants equal voting power to each member. Its purpose is to support public and private projects through loans, guarantees, and equity participation. Projects are to focus on infrastructure and renewable energy. Loans are focused on BRICS member states themselves.

Are these two institutions rivals to the World Bank dominated by the United States, and the regional multilateral development banks like the Asian Development Bank dominated by Japan? Or are they partner institutions? In terms of resources available, they are not effective rivals. For example, the AIIB's capital is one-half of that of the World Bank and two-thirds of that of the Asian Development Bank. And experts in each of the banks point to their cooperation with other development institutions. Yet it is clear that these institutions are designed to stimulate cooperation among the BRICS and to serve China's economic and geopolitical objectives. Both are headquartered in China, and China is the major financial contributor, but it has no veto power.

Another alternative may be found in China's major economic and geopolitical initiative "One Belt, One Road." This initiative is designed to boost regional integration in Asia and beyond. In 2013, Chinese president Xi Jinping produced the notions of the Silk Road Economic Belt and the Maritime Silk Road. Combining these together as the "One Belt, One Road" Initiative, China is supporting massive infrastructure projects designed to connect China with Central and South Asia and to extend all the way to Istanbul, Moscow, and Venice, providing a conduit for Chinese imports and exports and serving later as production centers. With slowing growth at home, this plan provides an outlet for China's steel, cement, and machinery production, promising $1 trillion in infrastructure touching 60 countries and connecting them to China.[34]

As China expands this belt and projects are planned, strong national and local reactions are mounting. Affected communities and individuals displaced by the construction of new infrastructure like dams, highways, and airports have had their land confiscated, often with low remuneration, and their livelihood threatened. Such local-level reactions to economic globalization, as seen in Laos, Myanmar, and Kenya, are not new. In 1994, an army of peasant guerrillas seized towns in the southern Mexican state of Chiapas to protest against an economic and political system that they viewed as biased against them. The date of the protest coincided with the beginning of NAFTA. Feeling that economic decisions were beyond their control, the peasants protested against the structures of the international market, the state, and economic globalization. This rebellion alerted the world to the challenges of globalization. The protesters were able to tell their side of the story, ironically enough, through the Internet, one of the by-products of the globalization they opposed. Today's protesters have an even wider range of communication tools to get their message to the outside world.

A wider antiglobalization movement has grown in response to other issues as well, including the rise of labor mobility and the development of illicit markets arising from the more porous national borders. The movement of labor and peoples is examined in detail in Chapter 11. The rise of illicit markets represents an unanticipated effect of globalization. Arms and money earned from illicit enterprises, illegal drugs, human organs, or endangered species flow across borders. Both the movement of labor and the rise of illicit markets pose a threat to human security, the viability of the state, and state security.

Even in countries that seem to have benefited the most from economic globalization, groups and individuals are dissatisfied. Brexit in Great Britain was one response, a reaction to the perceived losses from membership in the European Union. The election of Donald J. Trump in the United States was another, with voters attracted to his emphasis on growing economic alienation from job losses and lower wagers caused by economic globalization. There are different ways to address globalization's shortcomings—better and higher-paying jobs, stronger (or weaker) environmental regulations, improved labor conditions, alternative energy strategies, greater (or less) control of big capital. But stimulated by unanticipated repercussions from the openness of economic markets, reform groups have forged unity in seeking more local control and more meaningful participation in economic governance. The global economic crisis of 2008 and the Eurozone crisis of 2009 were powerful stimuli for the antiglobalization movement and reformers seeking to avoid the pitfalls of economic globalization.

The View from Economic Theories

Most adherents of economic liberalism propose rather modest reforms to the system, as described above. Not surprisingly, economic radical theorists have a different take. They have always been critical of the liberal economic path, just as they were in the nineteenth century. Development has not occurred, they assert, and for dependency theorists in particular, MNCs and their facilitators are the culprit; they exploit the resources of the poor, and they perpetuate the dominance of the North and the dependency of the South. Radicals detest instruments of dependency, exploitation, and imperialism. They argue that decisions made in the economic and financial centers of the world—Tokyo, London, New York, Frankfurt, Seoul—create an inherently unequal and unfair international economic system. And it was those decisions and policies that were responsible for the global financial crisis. Radicals believe that political power must be altered and international regulations aimed at redistributing wealth must be enacted. Thus, radicals recognize that delivering the hatchet to economic globalization would be necessary to achieve their goals of a more just and equitable international economic system.

Mercantilists and economic nationalists have their own take. Having acknowledged that the state has a national interest in determining economic policy and that it sees other states' growing economic prowess as a threat to its own, economic nationalists might applaud the return to state-level policies protecting a state's own citizens and the rise of state-controlled enterprises. After all, as they did in the seventeenth and eighteenth centuries, old-style mercantilists, with their interpretation of economic nationalism, argue that economic policy should be subservient to the state and its interests; for them, politics determines economics. This mercantilist thinking dominated explanations of the economic success of several East Asian states. Those governments harnessed the power of MNCs in the state's interest. Setting national economic and political objectives above international economic and political objectives, statists see MNCs as economic actors to be controlled. They suggest imposing national controls on MNCs, including denying market entry to some of them, using the power of taxation to control repatriation of profits, and imposing currency controls. Mercantilists, like economic nationalists, believe that the international system is dominated by competition among states for power; to economic nationalists, the global economy is a struggle over relative gains. States will take any action necessary to survive, protecting their self-interests. In the aftermath of crises and the consequences of economic globalization, economic nationalists support more policies favorable to individual states.

IN SUM: FROM THE ECONOMY TO OTHER INSTITUTIONS OF COOPERATION

Globalization characterizes not only the international political economy but also, as we have hinted at here, intergovernmental organizations and nongovernmental organizations. We discuss those important institutions and groups in the next chapter.

Discussion Questions

1. You are an economist in the Mexican government. What policies can you suggest to influence economic policy?

2. Economic liberals, mercantilists/economic nationalists, and economic radicals see multinational corporations in different ways. What are those differences?

3. How are the international financial system and the international monetary system more complex than they were in the past?

4. Does economic regionalization lead to globalization? Why or why not? Provide evidence.

5. How has your belief in the economic liberal model been modified by the global economic crises?

Key Terms

balance of payments (p. 273)

Beijing Consensus (p. 302)

BRICS (p. 295)

capital accounts (p. 273)

comparative advantage (p. 283)

current accounts (p. 273)

derivatives (p. 281)

economic radicalism (p. 272)

exchange rates (p. 273)

fiscal policies (p. 272)

foreign direct investment (FDI) (p. 279)

General Agreement on Tariffs and Trade (GATT) (p. 278)

Group of 7 (G7) (p. 278)

Heckscher-Ohlin theory (p. 284)

International Monetary Fund (IMF) (p. 278)

macroeconomic policies (p. 272)

mercantilism (p. 271)

microeconomic policies (p. 273)

monetary policies (p. 273)

moral hazard (p. 311)

most-favored-nation (MFN) principle (p. 278)

nontariff barriers (p. 273)

offshore financial centers (p. 281)

portfolio investment (p. 280)

protectionism (p. 271)

sovereign wealth funds (p. 280)

structural adjustment programs (p. 296)

sustainable development (p. 296)

tariffs (p. 273)

Washington Consensus (p. 296)

World Bank (p. 277)

World Trade Organization (WTO) (p. 285)

U.S. President Donald Trump addresses the UN General Assembly using uncharacteristically aggressive language to acknowledge North Korean nuclear aggression. How does this kind of behavior influence how an intergovernmental organization like the UN operates?

9

Intergovernmental Organizations and Nongovernmental Organizations

Every September, the opening sessions of the United Nations General Assembly are widely anticipated around the world. Which leaders will appear? Whom will they meet? What issues will be discussed? The year 2017 was no different. Russia's Vladimir Putin and China's Xi Jinping were notably absent. So was Myanmar's Aung San Suu Kyi. Both Israeli prime minister Benjamin Netanyahu and Palestinian president Mahmoud Abbas gave speeches that had been heard before. But American president Donald Trump's speech generated the most anticipation. Would he exhibit the customary diplomatic restraint during the General Assembly? What would he say about the UN? What would the president say to the organization that a few months earlier he had called a "club for people to get together, talk and have a good time" and denounced for its "utter weakness and incompetence"? What reforms to the budget would be proposed? (That is always a key question since the United States contributes 22 percent to the regular budget and 28 percent to peacekeeping.)

Diplomatic niceties were not heard. Rather than giving the perfunctory speech promising peace and goodwill, President Trump lashed out at North Korean leader Kim Jong-Un, calling him "rocket man" and describing his regime as "depraved" and on a "suicide mission." Trump also threatened to "totally destroy" North Korea should it fail to comply with the international community.

President Trump's speech in the 2017 General Assembly illustrates that although the U.S. relationship with the UN has always been ambivalent, the coming years may be even more rocky. This rockiness raises important questions about the UN and other international governmental organizations (IGOs). What are the possibilities and limitations of these organizations, given that the members of these organizations are states? Who are these organizations for? What roles can international nongovernmental organizations (NGOs) play in addressing key world problems? Can they provide new forms of cooperation and offer resistance to both states and IGOs?

LEARNING OBJECTIVES

▶ **Explain why intergovernmental organizations form.**

▶ **Describe what intergovernmental organizations, such as the United Nations, have contributed to international peace and security.**

▶ **Trace how the European Union changed over time.**

▶ **Describe the roles nongovernmental organizations play in international relations.**

▶ **Analyze the contending perspectives international relations theorists bring to their analysis of intergovernmental organizations and nongovernmental organizations.**

INTERGOVERNMENTAL ORGANIZATIONS

The Creation of IGOs

Why do states organize themselves collectively? In Chapter 7, we learned the liberal and neoliberal institutionalist response. International institutions, both formal organizations and rule-making international treaties, are the arenas where states

Functionalism

▶ War is caused by economic deprivation.

▶ Economic disparity cannot be solved in a system of independent states.

▶ New functional units should be created to solve specific economic problems.

▶ People and groups will develop habits of cooperation, which will spill over from economic cooperation to political cooperation.

▶ In the end, economic disparities will lessen and war will be eliminated.

interact and cooperate to solve common problems. And, as the liberal institutionalists during the 1970s described, "even if . . . anarchy constrains the willingness of states to cooperate, states nevertheless can work together and can do so especially with the assistance of international institutions."[1] Multiple interactions lead to greater possibilities for cooperation. This continuous interaction among states provides the motivation for states to create international institutions like international law that provide a framework for interactions, establish mechanisms to reduce cheating by monitoring others and punishing the uncooperative, and facilitate transparency for state actions. These institutions are the focal points for coordination and make state commitments more credible, specifying expectations and establishing reputations for compliance.

International institutions are particularly useful for solving two sets of problems. One set of problems arises from the need to cooperate on technical, often nonpolitical, issues that states are not the appropriate units for resolving. As the scholar David Mitrany writes in *A Working Peace System*, units (states, subnational actors) need to "bind together those interests which are common, where they are common, and to the extent to which they are common."[2] This *functional* approach advocates building on and expanding the habits of cooperation nurtured by groups of technical experts outside formal state channels. This notion explains why international cooperation began in specific, technical-issue areas such as health and communications during the nineteenth century. Solving problems in these technical areas (e.g., curbing epidemics, facilitating international mail and telegraphic services) would inspire cooperation or spill over into political and military affairs, and new international organizations would form.

International institutions also form around collective goods, the second set of problems. In "The Tragedy of the Commons," biologist Garrett Hardin tells the story of a group of herders who share a common grazing area. Each herder finds it economically rational to increase the size of his own herd, allowing him to sell more in the market. Yet if all herders follow what is individually rational behavior, then the group loses: too many animals graze the land and the quality of the pasture deteriorates, leading to decreased output for all. As each person rationally attempts to maximize his own gain, the collectivity suffers, and, eventually, all individuals suffer.[3]

What Hardin describes—the common grazing area—is a **collective good**. The grazing area is available to all group members, regardless of individual contribution. The use of collective goods involves interdependent activities and choices. The ozone layer is a collective good, providing a protective shield from the sun's rays for all. The production and sale of chlorofluorocarbons makes refrigeration possible, a major benefit. Yet the use of these chemicals by everyone harms the collectivity, by depleting the ozone layer over the long term. States and individuals suffer negative consequences because of the actions of others. What can be done to manage this unintended effect?

Hardin proposed several possible solutions to this tragedy of the commons. First, use coercion. Force nations or peoples to control the collective goods. States, for example, could force people to limit the number of children they have in order to curb the use of resources that harm the environment. Second, restructure the preferences of states through rewards and punishments. Offer positive incentives for states to refrain from engaging in the destruction of the commons; tax, or threaten to tax, those who use chlorofluorocarbons or fail to cooperate. Third, alter the size of the group. Smaller groups can more effectively exert pressure on their members because violations of the commons will be more easily noticed. Close monitoring is more likely to lead to compliance. These alternatives can also be achieved through international institutions. For many, they are the preferred way to address problems of the commons—the sea, space, the environment.

While all international problems are not collective-goods problems, most international issues involve continuous interactions among parties. Hence, over the long term, states find it mutually beneficial to cooperate, especially if the costs

IN FOCUS

Collective Goods

▶ Collective goods are available to all members of a group, regardless of individual contributions.

▶ Some activities of states involve the provision of collective goods.

▶ Groups need to devise strategies to overcome problems of collective goods caused by the negative consequences of the actions of others—the "tragedy of the commons."

▶ Strategies include coercion, altering preferences by offering incentives, and altering the size of the group.

of ensuring transparency, reducing cheating, and punishing the uncooperative are relatively low. For this, formal international organizations are useful.

The Roles of IGOs

Intergovernmental organizations, such as the United Nations, the World Bank, and the International Civil Aviation Organization, can address major problems at each level of analysis.[4] In the international system, IGOs contribute to habits of cooperation; states become socialized to regular interactions, such as through the United Nations. Some programs of IGOs, such as the International Atomic Energy Agency's nuclear-monitoring program, establish regularized processes of information gathering, analysis, and surveillance. Some IGOs, such as the World Trade Organization, develop procedures for making rules, settling disputes, and punishing those who fail to follow the rules. IGOs may also play key roles in international bargaining, facilitating the formation of transgovernmental and transnational networks, sometimes leading to common expectations of states' behavior. By bringing states together, IGOs reduce the incentive to cheat and enhance the value of a good reputation.

For states, IGOs both enlarge the possibilities for foreign policy making and add to the constraints under which states conduct and, in particular, implement foreign policy. States join IGOs to use them as instruments of foreign policy. IGOs may legitimate a state's viewpoints and policies—thus, the United States sought the support of the Organization of American States during the Cuban missile crisis in 1962. IGOs increase available information about other states, thereby enhancing predictability in the policy-making process. Some IGOs, such as the UN High Commissioner for Refugees and UNICEF, may conduct specific activities that are compatible with, or augment, state policy.

But IGOs also constrain member states by setting international, and hence national, agendas and forcing governments to make decisions or develop new ways to implement those decisions. Both large and small states may have to align their policies if they wish to benefit from their membership.

IGOs also affect individuals by providing opportunities for leadership. As individuals work with or in IGOs, they, like states, may become socialized to cooperate internationally.

Not all IGOs perform all of these functions, and the manner in and extent to which each carries out particular functions varies. Sometimes, the failure of one organization to perform its functions leads to its replacement by another organization that tries a different approach. The United Nations, for example, reflects the successes and the failures of its predecessor organization, the League of Nations.

To deliver aid in hard-to-reach regions, UNICEF is testing a drone pilot program that drops aid packages in rural areas. Here, a drone-delivered aid package from Japan is presented to a mother in Malawi.

The United Nations

The United Nations is a product of a historical process; it reflects processes that occurred during the nineteenth century when the European powers experimented with the Concert of Europe, as described in Chapter 2. European leaders met together at least 30 times between 1815 and 1878 to solve problems. The UN also developed out of the experience of public international unions, organizations designed to address problems stemming from international commerce, communication, and shipping. Finally, the UN is the product of the Hague conferences held between 1899 and 1907. In those conferences, representatives met to develop techniques to prevent war—arbitration, conciliation, and international adjudication. But, most of all, the United Nations is a product of the League of Nations experience.

Founded following World War I, the goal of the League was to end all wars; indeed, half of the League Covenant's provisions focused on preventing war. If dispute resolution failed, sanctions would follow, and should they fail, states would act against an aggressor by using force if necessary. The expectation was that if all states acted together, the aggressor would be deterred, or failing that, all states would join in to punish the aggressor. This is the idea of collective security explained in Chapter 6.

The League did enjoy a number of successes, many of them on territorial issues. It conducted votes in contested areas of Poland and Germany to gauge the will of the population; it demarcated the German-Polish border; it settled territorial disputes between Lithuania and Poland, Finland and Russia, and Bulgaria and Greece. However, the League failed to act decisively against the aggression of Italy and Japan in the 1930s. The voluntary sanctions imposed carried little effect. Britain and France had other more pressing interests. The absence of great-power support for the League was evident in its failure to attract the United States to join the organization. The League could not prevent the outbreak of World War II. The United Nations built on the League's successes and tried to correct some of its weaknesses.

Basic Principles and Changing Interpretations

The United Nations, like the League of Nations, was founded on three fundamental principles. Yet, over the life of the United Nations, changing realities have significantly challenged each of these principles.[5]

First, the United Nations is based on the notion of the sovereign equality of member states, as is consistent with the Westphalian tradition. Each state—the United States, Lithuania, India, or Suriname, irrespective of size or population—is legally the equivalent of every other state. This legal equality is the basis for each state's having one vote in the General Assembly. However, the actual inequality of states is recognized in the veto power given to the five permanent members of the Security Council and the special role reserved for the wealthy states in budget negotiations.

Second is the principle that only international problems fall within the jurisdiction of the United Nations. Indicative of the Westphalian influence, the UN Charter does not "authorize the United Nations to intervene in matters which are essentially within the domestic jurisdiction of any state" (Article 2, Section 7). Over the life of the United Nations, the once-rigid distinction between domestic and international issues has weakened, leading to a reinterpretation, or an erosion, of sovereignty. Global telecommunications and economic interdependencies, international human rights, election monitoring, and environmental regulation all infringe on traditional areas of domestic jurisdiction and hence on states' sovereignty. War is increasingly civil war, which is not legally under the purview of the United Nations. Yet because international human rights are being abrogated, because refugees cross national borders, and because weapons are supplied through transnational networks, such conflicts are increasingly viewed as international, and the United Nations is viewed by some as the appropriate venue for action. These changes have led to a growing body of precedent for humanitarian intervention without the consent of the host country (a phenomenon discussed in more detail in Chapter 10).

The third principle is that the United Nations is designed primarily to maintain international peace and security. This principle has meant that member states should refrain from the threat or the use of force; settle disputes by peaceful means, as detailed at the Hague conferences; and support enforcement measures, namely sanctions or use of force.

Although the founders of both the League of Nations and the United Nations focused on security in the realist, classical sense—protection of national territory and sovereignty—the United Nations is increasingly confronted with demands for action to support a broadened view of security. UN operations to feed the starving populations of Somalia and Niger, or to provide relief in the form of food, clothing, and shelter for Haitians and Nepalese forced out of their homes by natural disasters, are examples of this broadened notion of security—**human security**. (These issues are examined in Chapter 11.) Expansion into these newer areas of security collides head on with the domestic authority of states, undermining the principle of state sovereignty. The United Nations' founders recognized the tension between the commitment to act collectively against a member state and the affirmation of state sovereignty. But they could not foresee the dilemmas that changing definitions of security would pose.

Structure

The structure of the United Nations was developed to serve the multiple roles assigned by its Charter, but incremental changes in that structure have accommodated changes in the international system, particularly the increase in the number of states. There are six central UN organs, as Table 9.1 shows.

The power and prestige of these various organs have changed over time. The **Security Council** was kept small to facilitate swift decision making in response to threats to international peace and security. Its five permanent members—the United States, Great Britain, France, Russia (successor state to the Soviet Union in 1992), and the People's Republic of China (replacing the Republic of China in 1971)—are key to council decision making. Each permanent member enjoys veto power on substantive issues; on procedural issues, a supermajority is required, usually nine permanent and nonpermanent members. Until the mid-1970s, the Security Council became deadlocked by the Soviet Union's frequent use of the veto, which it used 113 times. Since that time, the United States has used its veto more times than any other permanent member, over 70 times. The majority of these vetoes have been used in defense of Israel on votes concerning the Arab-Israeli-Palestinian conflict. During the 1990s China generally chose to abstain, but since 2007 China, in cooperation with Russia, has exercised its veto more often.

TABLE 9.1

Principal Organs of the United Nations

ORGAN	MEMBERSHIP AND VOTING	RESPONSIBILITIES
Security Council	15 members: five permanent with veto, ten rotating members elected by region	Peace and security: identifies aggressor; decides on enforcement measures
General Assembly	193 members; each state has one vote; members work in six functional committees	Debates any topic within Charter's purview; admits states; elects members to special bodies
Secretariat, headed by Secretary-General	Secretariat of 44,000; secretary-general elected for five-year renewable term by General Assembly and Security Council	Secretariat: gathers information, coordinates and conducts activities; secretary-general: chief administrative officer, spokesperson
Economic and Social Council (ECOSOC)	54 members elected for three-year terms	Coordinates economic and social welfare programs; coordinates action of specialized agencies (FAO, WHO, UNESCO)
Trusteeship Council	Originally composed of administering and nonadministering countries; now made up of five great powers	Supervision has ended; proposals have been floated to change function to that of forum for indigenous peoples, NGOs, or nation building
International Court of Justice	15 judges	Noncompulsory jurisdiction on cases brought by states and international organizations

Since the end of the Cold War, the Security Council has regained power because of the drop in the use of the veto. The number of annual official meetings has risen, the number of resolutions passed has increased with consensus voting, and informal meetings among the permanent members have been more frequent. With greater cooperation among the permanent powers—especially since 1990, when the council authorized force against Iraq after its invasion of Kuwait—the Security Council has taken on more armed conflicts, imposed more types of sanctions in more situations, created war crimes tribunals to prosecute war criminals, authorized protectorates in Kosovo and East Timor, and, after 9/11, expanded involvement in antiterrorism activities and coped with the disruptions from the Arab Spring.

Although the Security Council has enormous formal power, it does not have direct control over the means to use that power. It depends on states for funding, personnel, enforcement of sanctions, and military action. A state's willingness to contribute depends on whether it perceives the council as legitimate. The issue of legitimacy has spawned a vigorous debate: Do most states accept the right of the council to make hard decisions even when some members disagree, or does the council's failure to do so on key issues, like Palestine, Darfur, Iraq, and Syria, delegitimize the organization?[6]

The **General Assembly** is the main deliberative body of the United Nations and permits debate on any topic under its purview. All member states are represented in the General Assembly, which has grown in membership from 51 in 1946 to 193 in 2017. The bulk of the work of the General Assembly is done in six functional committees: Disarmament and Security; Economic and Financial; Social, Humanitarian, and Cultural; Political and Decolonization; Administrative and Budgetary; and Legal. Debate on resolutions emerging from the committees is organized around regionally based voting blocs, with member states using their one vote to coordinate positions and build support for them.

The resolutions of the General Assembly often provide the basis for new international law by articulating new principles, including the common heritage of humankind and sustainable development. As these principles are repeated, they have become the basis for soft law—norms that have generated international consensus.

Since the end of the Cold War, however, the General Assembly's work has been increasingly marginalized, as the epicenter of UN power has shifted back to the Security Council and a more active Secretariat. This marginalization has happened much to the dismay of various caucusing groups, including the **Group of 77**, the coalition of developing states; regional groups (Africa, Asia, Latin America); and some members of the **Group of 20**, a coalition of the emerging economies. Occasionally, the work of the General Assembly attracts public attention, as it did during the 2011, 2012, and 2017 debates over the status of Palestine, but generally, it provides a forum for member states to express positions and conduct the UN's housekeeping functions.

The Secretariat has expanded to employ a global staff of around 44,000, with about one-quarter located at UN headquarters. The role of the secretary-general has expanded significantly. Having few formal powers, the secretary-general depends on persuasive capability and an aura of neutrality for authority. With this power, the secretary-general, especially in the post–Cold War era, can potentially forge an activist agenda, as Secretary-General Kofi Annan did until his retirement in 2006. In 1998, he negotiated a compromise between Iraq and the United States over the authority, composition, and timing of UN weapon inspections in Iraq; he mediated between Iraq and the rest of the international community; and he also implemented significant administrative and budgetary reforms and worked hard to establish a better relationship with the U.S. Congress. Annan used the office to push other initiatives, including the international response to the AIDS epidemic and the promotion of better relations between the private sector and the United Nations. A highly visible secretary-general, he was awarded the Nobel Peace Prize in 2001.

His successor, Ban Ki-moon of the Republic of Korea, served two terms, tackling initiatives on climate change, Darfur, preventive diplomacy, violence against women, and LGBT rights. In pressing for management reform, he appointed more women to top positions, eliminated patronage jobs, instituted internal competition for jobs, and reorganized major departments. However, he was generally viewed as a weak leader, lacking in key communication skills and preferring to operate below the radar. But, as one journalist acknowledged, "The fact is that when the great powers squabble, there's little that anyone in the organization can accomplish, be they competent or not."[7]

In 2017, António Guterres became the ninth secretary-general. A former Portuguese politician and diplomat and former UN High Commissioner for Refugees, Guterres ran in a vigorously contested election for the secretary-general position. For the first time, all eight candidates appeared before the General Assembly to present platforms and answer questions, including those from civil society. Despite strong pressure to elect its first ever female secretary-general and for an Eastern European candidate, Guterres prevailed.

Throughout the United Nations, when one organ has increased in importance, others have diminished, most notably the Economic and Social Council (ECOSOC) and the Trusteeship Council, albeit for very different reasons. ECOSOC was originally established to coordinate the various economic and social activities within the UN system through a number of specialized agencies. But the expansion of those activities and the increase in the number of programs has made ECOSOC's task of coordination a problematic one. In addition to covering such broad issues as human rights, the status of women, population and development, and social development, ECOSOC is charged with coordinating the work of the family of specialized UN institutions (discussed later). In contrast, the Trusteeship Council has worked its way out of a job. Its task was to supervise decolonization and to phase out trust territories placed under UN guardianship during the transition of colonies to independent states. Thus, the very success of the Trusteeship Council has led to its demise.

Key Political Issues

The United Nations has always reflected what is happening in the world, and, in turn, the United Nations and its organs have shaped the world. The United Nations played a key role in the decolonization of Africa and Asia. The UN Charter endorsed the principle of self-determination for colonial peoples, and former colonies such as India, Egypt, Indonesia, and the Latin American states seized on the United Nations as a forum in which to push the agenda of decolonization. By 1960, a majority of the United Nations' members favored decolonization. UN resolutions condemned the continuation of colonial rule and called for annual reports on the progress toward independence of all remaining territories. The United Nations was instrumental in the legitimation of the new international norm that colonialism and imperialism are unacceptable state policies. By the mid-1960s, most former colonies had achieved independence with little threat to international peace, and the United Nations had played a significant role in this transformation.

The emergence of the newly independent states transformed the United Nations and international politics more generally. These states formed a coalition of the South, or Group of 77—developing states whose interests lie in economic development, a group often at loggerheads with the developed countries of the North. The North-South conflict continues to be a central feature of world politics and of the United Nations, although the coalitions have become more fluid with the rise of the emerging economies.

Peacekeeping

Of the many issues the United Nations confronts, none is as vexing as peace and security. A new approach, labeled *peacekeeping*, evolved as a way to limit the scope of conflict and prevent it from escalating into a Cold War confrontation. Peacekeeping operations fall into two types, or two generations. In **traditional peacekeeping**, multilateral institutions such as the United Nations seek to contain conflicts between two states through third-party military forces. Ad hoc military units, drawn from the armed forces of nonpermanent members of the UN Security Council (often small, neutral members), have been used to prevent the escalation of conflicts and to keep the warring parties apart until the dispute can be settled. Invited in by the disputants, the troops operate under UN auspices, supervising armistices, trying to maintain cease-fires, and physically interposing themselves in a buffer zone between warring parties. Table 9.2 lists some of these traditional UN peacekeeping operations.

Whereas traditional peacekeeping activities primarily address interstate conflict, in the post–Cold War era UN peacekeeping has expanded to address different types

TABLE 9.2

Traditional Peacekeeping Operations, Representative Cases

OPERATION	LOCATION(S)	DURATION	STRENGTH
UNEF I (First UN Emergency Force)	Suez Canal, Sinai Peninsula	Nov. 1956– June 1967	3,378 troops
UNMEE (UN Mission in Ethiopia and Eritrea)	Ethiopia/ Eritrean border	Sept. 2000– July 2008	3,940 troops; 214 police
UNFICYP (UN Peacekeeping Force in Cyprus)	Cyprus	March 1964– present	833 troops; 69 police; 152 civilians
UNIFIL (UN Interim Force in Lebanon)	Southern Lebanon	March 1978– present	10,340 troops; 814 civilians

Source: United Nations.

of conflicts and to take on new responsibilities. **Complex (or multidimensional) peacekeeping** activities respond to civil war and ethnonationalist conflicts within states. And in some cases the UN may not have been invited in by the established authorities. To deal with these new conflicts, peacekeepers have taken on a range of both military and nonmilitary functions. On the military side, they have aided in the verification of troop withdrawal (the Soviet Union from Afghanistan) and have separated warring factions until the underlying issues could be settled (Bosnia). Sometimes, resolving underlying issues has meant organizing and running national elections, as in Cambodia, Namibia, and Afghanistan; sometimes, it has involved implementing human rights agreements, as in Central America, the Democratic Republic of Congo, and Mali. At other times, UN peacekeepers have tried to maintain law and order in failing or disintegrating societies by aiding in civil administration, policing, and rehabilitating infrastructure, as in Somalia, East Timor, and Afghanistan. (This is often called **peacebuilding**.) And peacekeepers have provided humanitarian aid, supplying food, medicine, and a secure environment as part of an expanded conception of human security in Africa, most recently in Somali, Mali, and South Sudan. Table 9.3 lists some representative cases of complex peacekeeping operations.

TABLE 9.3

Complex/Multidimensional Peacekeeping Operations, Representative Cases

OPERATION	LOCATION(S)	DURATION	STRENGTH
UNPROFOR (UN Protection Force)	Former Yugoslavia (Croatia, Bosnia and Herzegovina, Macedonia)	Feb. 1992–Dec. 1995	35,599 troops; 4,632 civilians
UNAMIR (UN Assistance Mission in Rwanda)	Rwanda	Oct. 1993–March 1996	5,500 troops; 320 military observers; 90 police
Monusco (UN Organization Stabilization Mission in the Democratic Republic of Congo); Renamed from MONUC in 2010	Democratic Republic of Congo	Nov. 1999–present	16,215 troops; 660 military observers; 1,441 police
UNAMID (African Union/United Nations Hybrid Operation in Darfur)	Darfur	July 2007–present	15,845 troops; 3,403 police
UNMISS (UN Mission in Republic of South Sudan	South Sudan	July 2011–present	12,241 troops; 186 military observers; 1,587 police; 2,196 civilians

Source: United Nations.

Complex peacekeeping has had successes and failures, as illustrated by Namibia, Rwanda, Sudan, and the Democratic Republic of Congo. Namibia (formerly South-West Africa), a former German colony, was administered by South Africa following the end of World War I. Over the years, pressure was exerted on South Africa to relinquish control of the territory, but as long as Soviet-backed Cuban troops occupied neighboring Angola, South Africa refused to consider a change, citing security concerns. Finally, in 1988, Cuba and Angola agreed to withdraw Cuban troops as part of a regional peace settlement that included Namibian independence. The UN peacekeeping operation supervised the cease-fire, monitored the withdrawal of South African forces, supervised the civilian police force, secured the repeal of discriminatory legislation, and created conditions for free and fair elections. The UN Transition Assistance Group (UNTAG) in Namibia became the model for UN complex peacekeeping and nation building in Cambodia in the early 1990s and in East Timor in the late 1990s.

But not all UN peacekeeping operations have been successful. Rwanda is an example of a situation wherein a limited UN peacekeeping force proved to be insufficient and genocide subsequently escalated as the international community watched and did nothing. Rwanda and neighboring Burundi have seen periodic outbreaks of devastating ethnic violence between Hutus and Tutsis since the 1960s. In the 1990s, intermittent fighting once again broke out. A 1993 peace agreement called for a UN force (the UN Assistance Mission for Rwanda, or UNAMIR) to monitor the cease-fire. Yet less than a year later, large-scale violence erupted following the death of the Rwandan president in a plane crash, with Hutu extremists in the Rwandan military and police slaughtering minority Tutsis, resulting in 750,000 Tutsi deaths in a ten-week period. UNAMIR was not equipped to handle the crisis, and despite its commander's call for more troops, the UN Security Council failed to respond until it was too late. Although UNAMIR did establish a humanitarian protection zone and provided security for relief-supply depots and escorts for aid convoys, peacekeeping failed disastrously.

The UN's response to the crisis in Darfur, Sudan, has also proven problematic. When in 2003 thousands of people fled their villages to escape attacks from the government-based Arab militias (the Janjaweed), the UN system and NGOs responded with humanitarian aid, setting up refugee camps and providing emergency food and health care. The Security Council, however, issued only weak warnings to Sudan since both China and Russia opposed coercive measures, despite evidence that Darfur was witnessing a genocide. Between 2003 and 2008, estimates report that more than 300,000 were killed, 2.5 million were displaced within the country, and another 250,000 fled to neighboring Chad. Eventually, Sudan did accept a small African Union (AU) monitoring force and, in 2007, a stronger UN-AU peacekeeping force, just as the crisis became more complex, with the number of factions increasing. By 2012, the worst of the mass killings had eased: the situation in Darfur stabilized; the Sudan-Chad border was relatively secure; and 100,000 refugees returned to an increasingly urbanized Darfur. But the Sudanese government continues to be hostile to the UN-AU peacekeeping forces, limiting their theater of operation and their ability to protect civilians. Thus, since 2014, more reports have surfaced about Sudanese troops engaged in more systematic killings and rape. Despite the independence of the Republic of South Sudan, permanent cessation of violence has come to neither the Darfur region nor South Sudan.

Most problematic has been the UN's complex peacekeeping operation in the Democratic Republic of Congo, introduced in Chapter 6. Despite being one of the largest UN forces ever mounted, the organization has been unable to craft an overall strategy, since the strategic interests of key member states and organizations diverge. And the logistical and operational difficulties are enormous due to the size of the country, the lack of transportation infrastructure, the inability to protect the civilian population, the lack of preparedness of UN troops, and the difficulty in managing the behavior of the UN troops who, themselves, have been accused of sex crimes and corruption. This operation has clearly tarnished the UN's reputation, leading many to wonder whether, in the absence of the will and resources for a robust operation, it is perhaps better to refrain from any operation than to undertake a weak operation.[8]

These issues have also arisen in the UN's more recent operations in Mali and the Central African Republic. These robust stabilization operations have often meant

The UN has undertaken more than 70 peacekeeping missions since 1946. Here, UN peacekeepers monitor peace in the Abyei Area on the border of Sudan and South Sudan.

protecting the government against insurgents or aggressors, including engaging in offensive operations while trying to protect civilians. The UN cannot simultaneously neutralize some nonstate actors and protect civilians, while using force only selectively. There are critical unintended effects: civilians are caught in the cross fire, the safety of UN peacekeepers is jeopardized, and the activities of humanitarian organizations are undermined as their neutrality and impartiality is sacrificed.

Enforcement and Chapter VII

Since the end of the Cold War, the Security Council has intervened in situations deemed threatening to international peace and security, as authorized in Chapter VII of the UN Charter. That provision enables the Security Council to take enforcement measures (economic sanctions, direct military force) to prevent or deter threats to international peace or to counter acts of aggression. Previously, the council had invoked Chapter VII only twice before the 1990s because the UN could only muster support for the more limited, traditional peacekeeping route.

The 1990s, however, became known as the "sanctions decade" for the numerous times targeted sanctions were imposed. The disarmament provisions overseen by the UN Special Commission for the Disarmament of Iraq and the International Atomic Energy Agency (IAEA), one of the United Nations' specialized agencies, and the economic sanctions against Iraq during the 1990s were enforcement actions under Chapter VII.

Sanctions have been the major approach used by the UN, the European Union, and the United States to try to prevent Iran from developing nuclear weapons, because its program is seen as a threat to international peace and security. From 2006 to 2012, UN-based resolutions kept expanding the reach of the sanctions, while tightening monitoring and inspections. These sanctions isolated Iran from the international banking system and progressively targeted individuals, companies, and organizations for asset freezes. Estimates show that the sanctions resulted in a 25 percent decline in Iran's GDP between 2012 and 2014. But getting agreement on when to impose sanctions, especially multilateral sanctions like those imposed on Iran, can be difficult, as explained in Chapter 5. In this case, those sanctions appeared to be a major factor leading Iran to the negotiating table with the P5+1 and EU in 2014 and 2015, culminating in the Joint Comprehensive Plan of Action announced in 2015.

Taking military action is another enforcement mechanism. The 1991 Gulf War was an enforcement action under Chapter VII. The Security Council authorized members "to use all necessary means"—a mandate that led to direct military action by the multinational coalition under U.S. command. In 2002, the United States went to the Security Council seeking Chapter VII enforcement against Iraq

TABLE 9.4

Representative International and Regional Organizations

UN SPECIALIZED AGENCIES	INDEPENDENT ORGANIZATIONS
World Health Organization	Organization of the Petroleum Exporting Countries
Food and Agriculture Organization	World Trade Organization
International Labour Organization	Organisation of Islamic Cooperation
International Atomic Energy Agency	North Atlantic Treaty Organization
World Bank Group	Organization for the Prohibition of Chemical Weapons

REGIONAL ORGANIZATIONS	SUBREGIONAL ORGANIZATIONS
European Union	European Free Trade Association
African Union	Economic Community of West African States
Organization of American States	Mercosur
Arab League	Gulf Cooperation Council

The European Union—Organizing Regionally

Regional organizations also play an increasingly visible role in international relations. But none has been as visible, as strong, or as copied as the **European Union (EU)**. The idea of a united Europe goes back centuries. Both Immanuel Kant and Jean-Jacques Rousseau presented plans on how to unite Europe.[15] After World War I, idealists dreamed that a united Europe could have forestalled the conflict. World War II only intensified these sentiments. Hence, after the conclusion of World War II, vigorous debate ensued over the future organization of Europe. On the one hand were the federalists: drawing on the writings of Rousseau, they believed that because sovereign states instigated wars, peace was possible only if states gave up their sovereignty and invested in a higher federal body. States eventually could eliminate military competition, the root cause of war, if they joined with other states, each one surrendering some pieces of sovereignty to a higher unit. The proposed European Defense Community would have placed the military under community control, thus touching the core of national sovereignty.

On the other hand were the functionalists: their principal proponent, Jean Monnet, believed that the forces of nationalism, in the end, could be undermined by the logic of economic integration. He proposed cooperative ventures, beginning with the European Coal and Steel Community (the predecessor of the European Economic Community, or EEC), in nonpolitical issue areas. It was anticipated that these ventures would spill over eventually from the economic arena to issues of national security. The European Defense Community was defeated by the French Parliament in 1954, and the functionalists' logic prevailed. No one at the time could have envisioned a union that in 2017 would bring together more than 508 million citizens in 28 countries, many of them able to travel freely with a burgundy EU passport. Nor could anyone have imagined the union enjoying an economy of more than $15 trillion (or 18 percent of the world's GDP) and 19 of its countries using a common currency, the euro.

Historical Evolution

The impetus for the creation of the European Union grew not only from the devastation of the wartime experience but also from the security threat that remained. Urged on by the United States, an economically strong Europe (made possible by the reduction of trade barriers) knew it would be better equipped to counter the Soviet threat if it integrated. Europe also understood that if the Germans were enmeshed in such agreements, they would pose a lesser threat to other states. Of course, U.S.-based multinational corporations would also benefit from an expanded market. Thus, security threats, economic incentives, and a postwar vision all played a role in the drive of political elites for European integration.[16]

The European Coal and Steel Community, placing French and (West) German coal and steel production under a common "High Authority," was the first step toward realizing this idea. Although Germany was treated as an equal, its key economic sector supporting the arms industry was brought into a community with France, Italy, and the Benelux countries (Belgium, Netherlands, and Luxembourg). This functionalist experiment was so successful in boosting coal and steel production that the member states agreed to expand cooperation under the European Atomic Energy Community and the European Economic Community. Thus, the Treaties of Rome, signed in 1957, committed the six states to create a common market—removing restrictions on internal trade; imposing a common external tariff; reducing barriers to the movement of people, services, and capital; and

Expansion of the European Union, 1952–2017

establishing a common agricultural and transport policy. By 1968, two years ahead of schedule, most of these goals had been achieved.

New policy areas were gradually brought under the umbrella of the community, including health, safety, and consumer standards. As success in these areas waxed and waned, and economic stagnation hindered progress, action was taken. The first initiative was expanding the size of the community in the so-called widening process. Successive enlargements followed, resulting in today's 28-state membership (see map, above), a process that increased the organization's influence but complicated its decision making.

In 1986, the most important step was taken in deepening the integration process—the signing of the Single European Act (SEA), which established the goal of completing a single market by the end of 1992. Achieving this goal meant a complicated process of removing the remaining physical, fiscal, and technical barriers to trade; harmonizing national standards of health; varying levels of taxation; and eliminating the barriers to movement of peoples. The process also addressed new environmental and technological issues. Three thousand specific measures were needed to complete the single market.

Even before that process was completed, the Maastricht Treaty was signed in 1992. The European Community became the EU. Members committed themselves not only to an economic union but also to a political one, including the establishment of common foreign and defense policies, a single currency, and a regional central bank. Five years later, in 1997, the Amsterdam Treaty was signed, making some changes to the previous treaties, including granting more power to the European Parliament but generally putting more emphasis on the rights of individuals, citizenship, justice, and home affairs.

The increased power of the EU has not been without its opponents. As several national votes have illustrated, while the European public generally supports the idea of economic and political cooperation, it also fears a diminution of national sovereignty and is reluctant to surrender democratic rights by placing more power in the hands of bureaucrats and other nonelected elites. The debate over the proposed European Constitution brought that issue to a head. Pushed forward by elites, the European Constitution was signed by the heads of state in 2004, only to be rejected in two national referendums a year later. In its stead, in 2007, the Treaty of Lisbon replaced the Constitution. This treaty is another attempt to enhance the efficacy of the EU by creating the offices of president of the European Council and High Representative for Foreign Affairs (who leads a more united policy) and increasing the use of qualified majority voting in place of unanimity. The treaty is also aimed at improving the democratic legitimacy of the EU by increasing the authority of the European Parliament. The treaty became law on December 1, 2009 (see Table 9.5).

Structure

Table 9.6 provides the basic information about the EU's decision-making bodies, membership, voting, and responsibilities. Just as power has shifted among the UN organs, so, too, has power shifted in the EU. Initially, power resided in the European Commission, which represents the interests of the community as a whole. Although each state is entitled to one member, Commission members, who are not national representatives, must be impartial. Each is responsible for a particular policy area, known as a directorate-general, which, in turn, is divided into directorates that cover specific parts of that policy area. For much of its history, the EU Commission has played this engine role, with the Council of Ministers ratifying, modifying, or vetoing proposals, even though the Commission formally reports to the Council. Over time, the Council has accrued more power, using a qualified majority voting system. Each member is given a certain number of votes, weighted by size and population; so currently, a positive vote requires 55 percent

TABLE 9.5

Significant Events in the Development of the European Union

YEAR	EVENT
1952	European Coal and Steel Community created by Belgium, France, Italy, Luxembourg, Netherlands, and West Germany.
1954	French National Assembly rejects proposal to form the European Defense Community.
1957	Treaties of Rome establish the European Economic Community (EEC) and the European Atomic Energy Community, comprising same six members.
1968	Customs Union is completed; all internal customs, duties, and quotas are removed; and common external tariff is established.
1975	Lomé Convention between the EEC and 46 developing countries in Africa, the Caribbean, and the Pacific signed.
1979	High-level negotiations on European Monetary System are completed; first direct elections to the European Parliament.
1986	Signing of the Single European Act designed to ensure faster decisions; more attention to environmental and technological issues; list compiled of measures that need to be taken before achieving single market in 1992.
1992	Maastricht Treaty completed, committing members to political union, including the establishment of common foreign and defense policies, a single currency, and a regional central bank; name changed to European Union (EU); controversial referendums held in several countries.
1997	Treaty of Amsterdam extends competence on issues of justice and home affairs and defines European citizenship.
1999	Common monetary policy and single currency (the euro) launched.
2002	Euro in circulation.
2004	European Constitution negotiated.
2005	French and Dutch publics reject the proposed constitution; ongoing discussions.
2009	Lisbon Treaty authorizes institutional reforms.
2009–Present	Eurozone crisis.
2014–Present	Refugee crisis.
2016	Great Britain votes to leave the EU—"Brexit."

TABLE 9.6

Principal Institutions of the European Union, 2017

INSTITUTION	MEMBERSHIP AND VOTING	RESPONSIBILITIES
European Commission	28 members; four-year terms, approved by member states; plus 23,000 support staff (Eurocrats)	Initiates proposals; guards treaties; executes policies; responsible for common policies
Council of Ministers	Ministers of member states; unanimity or qualified majority voting depending on issue	Legislates; sets political objectives; coordinates; resolves differences
European Parliament	751 members, elected for five years by voters in member states; allocated by size of population; organized around political parties	Legislates; approves budget and the laws with the Council of Ministers
European Council	Heads of government; Commission president; High Representative for Foreign Affairs; summit meetings quarterly; elects president to represent EU to world	Defines policy agenda and priorities
Court of Justice of the European Union	Includes European Court of Justice (judges) appointed by states for six-year terms; General Court; Civil Service Tribunal	Adjudicates disputes over EU treaties; ensures uniform interpretation of EU laws; renders preliminary opinions to states

of the member states, representing 65 percent of the EU's total population. A few policy decisions in foreign and security affairs, immigration, and taxation may require unanimous support.

The increasing power of the European Parliament is another change. Since the mid-1980s, the parliament has gained a greater legislative and supervisory role. Because members are elected by universal suffrage every five years, this body has an element of democratic accountability not found in the other institutions. The relatively low turnout in the 2014 parliamentary elections (43 percent) indicates that the legitimacy of the institutions remains a problem.

So, too, has the power increased of the Court of Justice of the European Union (CJEU), an institution that includes three courts: the European Court of Justice (ECJ), the General Court, and the Civil Service Tribunal. The General Court considers new cases, especially on issues regarding the single market, while the ECJ acts as a court of appeals. Virtually every member state has been brought before the court at some point for failing to fulfill its obligations; disputes have involved diverse topics such as customs duties, tax discrimination, elimination of nontariff barriers, agricultural subsidies, environmental law, consumer safety issues, and mobility of labor. The court's wide-ranging responsibilities for interpreting and enforcing EU law include ruling on the constitutionality of all EU law; interpreting treaties; providing advisory opinions to national courts; and settling disputes among member states, EU institutions, corporations, and individuals. Member states are obligated to uphold EU law. If they fail to comply, the European Commission may undertake infringement proceedings that may include fines or imposition of sanctions.

The ECJ has a very heavy case load, hearing annually over 900 cases, although completing fewer. Generally, three to five judges hear any one case, depending on its complexity. Playing a role greater than its founders ever envisioned, the ECJ plays a major institutional role in European regionalism and the new legal order that is embodied in EU law. EU law represents pooled sovereignty, wherein states agree to combine resources with partner states, making the EU very different from other IGOs.

Policies and Problems

The EU has moved progressively into more policy areas, from trade and agriculture to transport, competition, social policy, monetary policy, the environment, justice, and common foreign and security policy. Among the many controversial issues are the problems of trade, agriculture, and the euro, discussed in Chapter 8. The difficulties forging a common European foreign and security policy, the problem of immigration and asylum, the disputes over membership, and the crisis generated by the vote of Britain to leave the EU are addressed below.

The functionalist aspiration was that the EU eventually would be able to forge a common foreign and security policy. But that has proven difficult. Indeed, on several major foreign policy issues, members of the EU were split. During the 2003 Iraq War, Great Britain, Spain, and Poland strongly supported the United States, sending in their military, while Germany and France opposed the policy, mainly because the UN Security Council had not given authorization. After Russia annexed Crimea in 2014, European Union leaders again were divided over punishing Russia. Great Britain's prime minister, David Cameron, called for tough new sanctions to punish Russia, while Germany's Angela Merkel argued that Russia would have to send its military into eastern Ukraine to trigger stronger measures. Britain, Sweden, and East European members pushed for halting arms sales to Russia; France opposed the measure. Differences in the countries' positions tend to reflect economic ties. France has military contracts with Russia. Germany and Italy depend on imports of Russian gas and oil; Great Britain does not. While the record of unity on foreign policy is weak, the EU did negotiate in unity at the Iran nuclear negotiations, with the High Representative for Foreign Affairs playing a prominent role.

The difficulties in security policy have had repercussions in other arenas as well. The Amsterdam Treaty elevated the issue of the movement of persons and all border-management issues, including illegal immigration and asylum. But the ongoing refugee crisis, discussed in Chapter 11, has bitterly divided EU members. The framework articulated in the 2015 European Agenda on Migration in response to the crisis has not resolved the issue. While the agenda provided for more funding for rescuing refugees at sea, relocating refugees, and aiding refugee-swamped Italy and Greece, member states are divided. Germany and Sweden, two of the most generous countries toward the influx, want burden sharing, with other countries taking in a "fair share" of refugees. Central European members have refused to accept refugee quotas, with Hungary, Slovakia, and the Czech Republic the most vehemently opposed. And the terrorist acts committed in Paris, Brussels, Nice, Manchester, and London by people with ties to the Middle East and, in some cases, to the Islamic State have made every state more cautious about accepting large numbers of refugees without closer vetting and better security cooperation. In 2017, the European Court of Justice overruled Hungary and Slovakia's objections to a compulsory fixed-quota scheme, suggesting the difficulty of arriving at an enforceable consensus on this issue.

Equally problematic are the issues surrounding membership. Should the EU continue to expand its membership by reaching out to the newly democratic states of Eastern Europe and the former Soviet Union like Ukraine, or to those in need such as Iceland? How rapidly can new members come to adhere to the 80,000 pages of EU law and regulations currently in effect? How will the special concessions these countries won affect the functioning of the union? Although new members such as Croatia, which joined in 2013, have been given extra time to phase in EU law, they also need to wait before receiving full benefits that range from agricultural subsidies to free movement of labor. Can Turkey, the first candidate state with a majority-Muslim population, eventually meet the criteria for membership: stable democratic institutions, a functioning market, and a capacity to meet union obligations? Until recently, Turkey had made enormous improvements in its human rights record and minority protection, but its record has been tarnished since the 2016 coup attempt against President Recep Tayyip Erdoğan. Will candidate member Serbia be accepted more rapidly? Will the EU governing institutions be able to change? Or have Turkey and Serbia lost their enthusiasm for membership?

"Brexit"

These issues, and indeed, the future of the EU itself, have been called into question by the British public's vote to leave the EU in 2016, commonly referred to as Brexit. Prime Minister David Cameron sought a mandate to restructure the country's relationship with the EU, but in a dramatic turn, the public voted 52 percent to 48 percent to exit.

Supporters of Brexit voiced two major lines of argument. First, the EU had provided the false promise of increasing wealth, but the electorate was not seeing the anticipated economic or political rewards. People were poorer, with migrants from other EU members taking jobs and undermining wage growth. Many sectors, like fishing, were captive to regulations from the EU that again slowed growth. While the EU had promised to promote democracy, certain central European EU members were instead flirting with authoritarianism and a closer relationship with Russia. The promises were not being fulfilled.

Second, advocates for Brexit wanted a return to complete sovereignty, in which the British Parliament controlled trade relationships and established rules for control of the borders. No longer were they content to be governed by faceless bureaucrats in EU institutions—either the Eurocrats in Brussels or the European Court of Justice judges in Luxembourg. The EU, they said, suffered from its own democratic deficit, with its lack of transparency and accountability. The only alternative was to withdraw and renegotiate new arrangements with Europe and the rest of the world.

The process for exit is complicated. In March 2017, the British government invoked Article 50 of the Treaty of Lisbon, announcing its intention to withdraw and thus beginning a two-year period of negotiations about the terms of the "divorce." Any agreement specifying the future relationship between Great Britain and the European Union requires votes in all the relevant legislatures in Europe and in Great Britain. If there is no agreement within the two years, then the country is ejected with no agreement. And agreement may be difficult to forge even among the interests in Great Britain.

In the aftermath of Brexit, there is extended speculation on what Brexit means for international relations more generally. Will Russia and China enjoy greater leverage vis-à-vis a weakened EU? What will Britain's exit mean for other European agreements like NATO? And does the Brexit vote mean that the EU itself is an "endangered species"?

Other Regional Organizations: The OAS, the AU, and the Arab League

For many years, the critical question was whether other regions would follow the European Union model. Clearly, others would be unlikely to duplicate precisely the circumstances surrounding the development of the European Union, despite the attempts by such subregional groups as the Economic Community of West African States and the Caribbean Community. Most Asian leaders thought the European model inappropriate for their region.

Two continent-wide regional organizations, the Organization of American States (OAS) and the African Union (AU), have followed independent paths. At its establishment in 1948, the OAS adopted wide-ranging goals: political (promotion of democracy), economic (enhancement of development, preferential treatment in trade and finance), social (promotion of human rights), and military (collective defense against aggression from outside the region and peaceful settlement of disputes within). No other regional organization includes such a North-South split between a hegemonic member such as the United States (and Canada) on the one hand and a "southern constituency" on the other. With that division, the OAS has adopted many of the foreign policy concerns of the hegemon, such as the defeat of communist/leftist factions during the Cold War and an emphasis on democracy promotion. In 1985, the OAS resolved to take action should an irregular interruption of democracy occur, declaring that a member should be suspended if its government is overthrown by force. The OAS has acted against coups or countercoups nine times, including, for example, in Haiti (1991–94), Peru (1992), Paraguay (1996, 2000), and Venezuela (1992, 2002). It instituted sanctions against Haiti and, in 2009, suspended Honduras from membership after that country's coup, lifting the suspension in 2011. But the organization has been deadlocked over Venezuela and its president Nicolás Maduro's authoritarianism and economic mismanagement. Despite intense debates and Venezuela's threat to withdraw from the organization, OAS ministers have repeatedly failed to issue a formal declaration condemning that government's handling of economic and political issues.

The overall record in achieving its political, economic, and social goals is mixed, however, as the OAS has been constrained by a dearth of economic resources and political will. Unlike the EU, the OAS has played a limited role in economic development of the region. In recent years, the OAS has devoted more attention to transnational criminal threats like drugs, terrorism, money laundering, and human trafficking.

Brexit: A View from Great Britain

The popular vote to exit the European Union in 2016 shocked both Great Britain and the world. Public-opinion polling had predicted a Remain victory, and the idea of a member state withdrawing was anathema. Yet the unexpected happened.

Disentangling Great Britain from its economic, social, and legal commitments involves complex negotiations at multiple layers: among domestic groups, the remaining 27 EU members, and the rest of the world. After notifying the EU of its impending departure on March 27, 2017, Great Britain had a two-year deadline for disentangling its commitments and determining its future relationship with the EU. Until 2019, Great Britain remains an EU member.

In Great Britain, the Remain and Leave positions are coalitions of conflicting domestic interests under weak leadership. Some Remain supporters seek renegotiation on certain issues, while others are enthusiastic supporters of the EU. The victorious Leave supporters are likewise divided. Supporters of a "hard exit" seek to sever the single market, allow Britain to determine its own tariffs and duties, reassert national control over immigration, terminate European Court of Justice jurisdiction, and demand full membership in the World Trade Organization. In short, they seek to reclaim sovereignty and return rule-making to London. Supporters of a "soft exit" prefer terms that give priority to following the EU-determined rules of the single market, they accept limited European Court of Justice (ECJ) jurisdiction and some limitations on control over borders, and are willing to pay into the EU budget. Clearly, there are different expectations of what leaving the EU means.

Further complicating domestic politics is the fact that Great Britain is composed of England, Northern Ireland, Scotland, and Wales, and the latter three have parliaments that will have to ratify any future agreement. Northern Ireland and Scotland, however, voted to Remain in the EU. Northern Ireland and the independent state of Ireland share a 300-mile border, where goods and peoples can flow unimpeded due to EU membership. Fears that the border would become regulated have been alleviated as all sides have agreed that there will be no hard border between Ireland and Northern Ireland. Scots also voted to Remain, seeing the economic benefits of EU membership. Scotland already has a strong nationalist political party that advocates breaking away from the United Kingdom and exiting the EU may be the impetus to do so. Voters in the city of London also strongly supported staying in the EU. As the center of European finance, London has benefited economically from EU membership. In the wake of withdrawal, financial institutions are moving out of London and setting up operations in other EU member cities, like Frankfurt, Dublin, and Paris, jeopardizing the vitality of the booming metropolis.

If Britain withdraws from the single market, what special deal with EU members can be negotiated? Would Britain stay in some kind of customs union, in which members could trade freely while charging a tariff on some goods from nonmember states? Or would a free trade deal be renegotiated? These arrangements would have to be approved unanimously by all EU members and ratified by national and regional parliaments. The EU also has existing free-trade pacts with 53 states. What would happen to these agreements, given that some were negotiated with the understanding that Great Britain was a member? Would Britain decide to renegotiate new terms bilaterally with all these states?

Also to be negotiated are the rights of 3.2 million EU citizens living in Britain and

Protesters wave British and EU flags to express support for Great Britain remaining in the European Union.

1.2 million British citizens living in EU countries. Britain has already announced that the rights of those living in Great Britain would be respected. But because immigration from EU states into Great Britain was already controversial, and for many the key reason for the Leave vote, a new approach to immigration would need to be negotiated.

Finally, because Great Britain is a major source of EU funding, it is already obligated to pay EU staff pensions and honor other long-term liabilities. In negotiations finalized at the end of 2017, Britain agreed to pay between $47 billion and $76 billion in the "divorce" settlement. Additional EU commitments involve the sharing of intelligence, policing, and counter-terrorism information, those new arrangements need to be negotiated. Britain has made it clear that it wants to continue in those mutually beneficial agreements. But will the EU members agree? The fear is that if EU members give away too many principles, then other member states may follow the British example, leading to a weakening of the EU or its ultimate demise.

With so many divisive issues, Great Britain appears ill prepared for this two-level game among both domestic groups and between the state and other states. As *The Economist* notes, Brexit is "a process, not a single event."[a]

a. "The Tories and Brexit: Mind Your Step," *The Economist*, October 8, 2016, 53.

FOR CRITICAL ANALYSIS

1. If you were the lead Brexit negotiator for Great Britain, what would be your priorities?

2. The difficulties in Brexit reflect how embedded the EU has become in British laws and institutions. How did that happen?

3. If you represented one of the other major EU states, such as France or Germany, what kind of deal would you accept for the departure of Britain from the EU?

By taking purposeful and public actions, NGOs can direct media attention to their cause, which in turn can create pressure on politicians to change policy. Here, Greenpeace activists highlight the environmental degradation of palm oil production in Indonesia.

media. Occasionally, NGOs have chosen direct action—organizing demonstrations, disrupting actions of offending groups, and even breaking laws to make positions clear.

Nowhere has the impact of NGOs been felt more strongly than at the 1992 UN Conference on the Environment and Development (UNCED) in Rio de Janeiro. NGOs played key roles in both the preparatory conferences and the Rio conference itself, adding representation and openness (or transparency) to the process. They made statements from the floor; they drafted informational materials; they scrutinized working drafts of UN documents; they spoke up to support or oppose specific phrasing. They networked. These activities paid off. Agenda 21, the official document produced by the conference, recognized the unique capabilities of NGOs and recommended their participation at all levels, from policy formulation and decision making to implementation. But later conferences have been disappointing, as illustrated by the Rio+20 conference in 2012. Neither NGOs nor some states were able to generate enough consensus to move the agenda ahead. As one scholar observed, there were "no targets, no timelines, or specific objectives."[18]

NGOs play unique roles at the national level. In a few unusual cases, NGOs take the place of states, either performing services that an inept or corrupt government is not providing or stepping in for a failed state. Bangladesh hosts one of the largest NGO sectors in the world, a response in part to that government's failure and the failure of the private for-profit sector to provide for the poor. Thus, NGOs have assumed responsibility in education, health, agriculture, and microcredit— originally all government functions. Other NGOs work to change various countries' public institutions, as illustrated by the Muslim Brotherhood in Egypt. Dating back to 1928, the Brotherhood had a long, confrontational relationship with the Egyptian government until its political party successfully competed in the 2011 parliamentary elections and assumed the presidency. A year later, it was overthrown during mass protests, its leaders were killed or imprisoned, and it was declared a terrorist organization. In 2013, the government shut down over 1,500 religiously affiliated charities, accusing them of supporting the Brotherhood. In 2014, the government banned groups receiving foreign funding for any activity harming Egyptian national interests. Human rights organizations are being investigated for violations, leading to asset freezes and detentions for members.

Egypt is not the only government to crack down on NGOs. Between 2014 and 2016, over 60 states have restricted civil society NGOs, in part because the process of democracy has stalled in many of these countries. Russia and other states of the former Soviet Union, including Uzbekistan and Tajikistan, have limited the actions of international NGOs. Similarly, Ethiopia and Kenya have issued regulations that have weakened NGOs, decreased their funding, and limited their programs. In Kenya, NGOs have played a prominent role in augmenting state capacity and providing services and programs under the direction of international donors, who have provided resources worth an estimated $1.2 billion. However, Kenya has shuttered many NGOs in the name of national security, because they have allegedly raised funds for terrorism. And in Israel in 2016, the Knesset passed a law forcing human rights groups that receive more than half of their funding from abroad to disclose their sources to officials. The law applies to left-wing groups campaigning for Palestinian rights but excludes right-wing pro-settlement NGOs, which are not required to report. These actions have led international NGOs to change how they operate: they have curbed their engagement in politically sensitive areas, reduced in-country international personnel, operated more remotely with new technologies, and built on the capacity of local funding partners.[19]

Yet NGOs seldom work alone. The communications revolution has linked NGOs with each other. These networks and coalitions create multilevel linkages among different organizations, enhancing each other's power. These networks have learned from each other, just as constructivists would have predicted.

We usually associate NGOs with humanitarian and environmental groups working for a greater social, economic, or political good, but NGOs may also be formed for malevolent purposes—the Mafia, international drug cartels, and even Al Qaeda being prominent examples. The Mafia, traditionally based in Italy but with networks in Russia, Eastern Europe, and the Americas, is engaged in numerous illegal business practices, including money laundering, tax evasion, and fraud. International drug cartels, many with origins in Colombia, function with suppliers in states such as Peru, Venezuela, Afghanistan, and Myanmar, while maintaining links with middlemen in Nigeria, Mexico, Guinea, and the Caribbean to deliver illegal drugs to North America and Europe. What these NGOs share is a loose series of networks across national boundaries that move illicit goods and services in international trade. Their leadership is dispersed and their targets are ever-changing, making their activities particularly difficult to contain.

Al Qaeda, too, is such an NGO—decentralized and dispersed, with individuals deeply committed to a cause, even at the price of death, and able and willing to take initiatives independent of a central authority. The organization has changed and expanded its goals over time, which has enabled it to recruit members willing to die for diverse causes. Osama bin Laden had forged broad links and alliances with various groups until his death in 2011. Like all NGOs, Al Qaeda has benefited from new communications technologies, using the Internet to collect information and train individuals and using e-mail to transfer funds and communicate messages, all virtually untrackable. Opponents of Al Qaeda and these other NGOs are waging a different battle: a war on organized crime, a war on drugs, and a war against terror.

The Power of NGOs

What gives NGOs the ability to play such diverse roles in the international system? What are their sources of power? Most NGOs rely on soft power, trying to persuade others to change their behavior without using coercion, as explained in Chapter 4. This requires NGOs to have certain resources and capabilities, including an independent donor base, links with grassroots groups that enable them to operate in different areas of the world, and the flexibility to move staff rapidly depending on need. This very flexibility enables them to create networks to increase their power potential, banding together with other like-minded NGOs and forming coalitions to promote their respective agendas. New communication technologies have facilitated this networking and coalition-building source of NGO power.

NGOs have distinct advantages over individuals, states, and intergovernmental organizations. They are usually politically independent from any sovereign state, so they can make and execute international policy more rapidly and directly, and with less risk to national sensitivities, than IGOs can. They can participate at all levels, from policy formation and decision making to implementation, if they choose. Yet they can also influence state behavior by initiating formal, legally binding action; pressuring authorities to impose sanctions; carrying out independent investigations; and linking issues together in ways that force some measure of compliance.

The International Campaign to Ban Landmines (ICBL) is an outstanding example of the power of an NGO network. Beginning in 1992, nine NGOs were eventually joined by more than 1,000 other NGOs and local groups in more than 60 countries. They used electronic media to frame the message that land mines are a human rights issue and have devastating effects on innocent civilians. Leaders formed a network, the Ottawa Process, bolstered by the death in 1997 of Diana, Princess of Wales, one of its vocal supporters. Jody Williams, a founder of the ICBL and the winner of the 1997 Nobel Peace Prize for her efforts, coordinated the process, and Canada's foreign minister pushed the issue, hosted the conference, and provided financial support. The Convention to Ban Landmines was ratified in 1999. But not every attempt to forge such networks has been successful, as illustrated by the failure of the movement to curb small arm sales and the stillborn effort to stop killer robots. NGOs have limits.

The Limits of NGOs

NGOs often lack material forms of power. Except for some of the malevolent groups, they do not have military or police forces as governments do, and thus they cannot command obedience through physical means.

Most NGOs have very limited economic resources because they do not collect taxes, as states do. Thus, the competition for funding is fierce; NGOs that share the same concerns—for example, human rights organizations—often compete for the same donors. They have a continuous need to raise money, leading some NGOs to find new causes to widen their donor base. To expand their resources, NGOs increasingly rely on governments, an alternative that comes with its own set of limitations. If NGOs choose to accept state assistance, then their neutrality and legitimacy are potentially compromised. They may be forced continually to report "success" to renew their financing, even though success may be difficult to prove or even be an inaccurate description of reality. In short, NGOs are locked in a competitive scramble for resources.[20]

Do most NGOs succeed in accomplishing their goals? This question is difficult to evaluate, because the NGO community is itself diverse; it has no single agenda, and NGOs often work at cross-purposes, just as states do. Groups can be found on almost any side of every issue, resulting in countervailing pressures. In a world that is increasingly viewed as democratic, are NGOs appropriate? To whom are NGOs accountable if their leaders are not elected? How do they maintain transparency when they have no publicly accountable mechanism? Do NGOs reflect only liberal values?

Incomplete or unsatisfactory answers to these questions have led scholars to suggest that NGOs may be more like other actors and less altruistic than supposed—self-interested, self-aggrandizing, concerned with their own narrow agendas, hierarchical rather than democratic, more worried about financial gains than achieving progressive social purposes. This suggestion has led some critics to refer to NGOs as "wild cards" and "benign parasites."[21] Some case studies have found that NGOs' actions have led to unintended and detrimental consequences. In refugee camps in Rwanda run by NGOs such as Doctors Without Borders and the International Rescue Committee, the leaders of the genocide were actually being protected. When NGOs are active in war zones, are they becoming more like "force multipliers," expanding the capabilities of the military?[22]

To still others, NGOs are not just "benign parasites"—they have emerged from Western capitalist state experiences to serve the interests of the dominant capitalist classes. After all, NGOs are largely based in the North and are dominated by members of the same elite that run the state and international organizations. These critics see NGOs as falling under the exigencies of the capitalist economic system and as captive to those dominant interests. Too few NGOs have been able to break out of this mold and develop networks that could enable mass participation and change the fundamental rules of the game.

The roles NGOs play and the legitimacy they may or may not have depend in part on how they answer critical questions of accountability and transparency. Whether they are accountable and transparent or not, NGOs increasingly work with states, IGOs, and regional organizations.

DO IGOs AND NGOs MAKE A DIFFERENCE?

The Realist View

Realists are skeptical about intergovernmental organizations and nongovernmental organizations, though they do not completely discount their place. Under anarchy, each state must act in its own self-interest and rely on self-help mechanisms. Realists doubt that collective action is effective and believe states will refuse to rely on the collectivity for the protection of their individual national interests. Realists can point to both the failures of the League of Nations and the weaknesses of the UN, especially during the Cold War era. The failure in 2003 of the United Nations to enforce Security Council resolutions against Iraq and its ineffectiveness in addressing the Syrian crisis are additional reminders of the organization's weakness and irrelevance.

In the state-centric world of the realists, NGOs are generally not on the radar screen at all. After all, most NGOs exist at the pleasure of states; states grant them legal authority, and states can take away that authority. To realists, NGOs are not independent actors.

The Liberal View

Liberals are convinced that IGOs and NGOs do matter in international politics. To liberals, these organizations and institutions do not replace states as the primary actors in international politics, although, in a few cases, they may be moving in that direction. They do provide alternative venues, whether intergovernmental, private, or domestic, for states to engage in collective action and for individuals to join with other like-minded individuals in pursuit of their goals. They permit old issues to be seen in new ways, and they provide both a venue for discussing new transnational issues and an arena for action that is repeated over time. Such continuous interaction is apt to lead to more cooperative behavior, just as the neoliberal institutionalists hypothesized.

The Constructivist View

Constructivists place critical importance on institutions and norms.[23] Both IGOs and NGOs can be norm entrepreneurs that socialize states and teach them new norms. Over time, those norms are internalized by states themselves, they change

THEORY IN BRIEF

Contending Perspectives on IGOs and NGOs

	Realism/ Neorealism	Liberalism/ Neoliberal Institutionalism	Constructivism
IGOs	Skeptical of their ability to engage in collective action	Important independent actors for collective action; neoliberals see as forums	Both IGOs and NGOs can be norm entrepreneurs and can socialize states, leading to changes in state behavior
NGOs	Not independent actors; power belongs to states; any NGO power is derived from states	Increasingly key actors that represent different interests and facilitate collective action	Both IGOs and NGOs may lead to dysfunctional behavior, but may also represent new ideas and norms

state preferences, and they shape behavior. A number of key norms are of particular interest to constructivists—for example, multilateralism, the practice of joining with others in making decisions. Both outside and within formal organizations, participants learn the value of this norm. Through multilateral participation, states have also learned other norms, including the emerging prohibition against the use of nuclear weapons, the norm of humanitarian intervention, and the increasing attention to human rights norms. Those norms may be contested, as we have seen in the struggle over adoption of norms over violence against women and rights of sexual minorities. Through contestation, states participate in shaping norms.

Constructivists offer a warning, too, about the potential dangers of international institutions. Michael Barnett and Martha Finnemore argue in *Rules for the World* that international organizations may act in ways that are contrary to the interests of their constituency. They may pursue particularistic goals, creating a bureaucratic culture that tolerates inefficiency and lack of accountability. International institutions may become dysfunctional, serving the interests of international bureaucrats.[24] Supporters must beware of what IGOs and NGOs may bring.

IN SUM: IGOs AND NGOs RESPOND TO NEW ISSUES OF THE TWENTY-FIRST CENTURY

IGOs and NGOs have acted in conjunction with states to address traditional international relations issues such as state security and the international political economy, as illustrated in this chapter. But in nontraditional issues like human rights and human security—including migration, health, and the environment—IGOs and NGOs have played a more independent and catalyzing role, as we see in the two next chapters.

Discussion Questions

1. Everyone agrees that reform of the UN Security Council is necessary. What proposal for reform would you support? Why?

2. Do IGOs and NGOs threaten state sovereignty, or do they not? Substantiate your position.

3. What is the relationship between NGOs and the state?

4. What problems arise when NGOs take over the tasks of states?

Key Terms

collective good (p. 322)

complex (or multidimensional) peacekeeping (p. 331)

European Union (EU) (p. 340)

General Assembly (p. 328)

Group of 77 (p. 328)

Group of 20 (p. 328)

human security (p. 326)

intergovernmental organizations (IGOs) (p. 323)

peacebuilding (p. 331)

Security Council (p. 326)

traditional peacekeeping (p. 330)

In January 2017, protesters from #BringBackOurGirls marched on the capital of Nigeria to mark 1,000 days since Boko Haram kidnapped 200 girls. Although some of the girls have been released since their capture, the fight to bring the remainder home to their families continues.

10

Human Rights

Since 2009, over 10,000 people have been killed and 1.5 million people displaced due to Boko Haram–related violence in northern Nigeria. Boko Haram, whose name means "Western ways are forbidden," is a radical Islamist guerrilla group fighting the Nigerian government. Since 2014, the group has kidnapped more than 2,000 women and children from towns and villages. World attention was drawn to the situation when more than 270 girls were kidnapped from one boarding school in 2014, leading to an international media campaign, #BringBackOurGirls, that drew the support of activists worldwide. The campaign dominated the airwaves and social media for several months, only to die a slow death as the girls remained in captivity, more were kidnapped, and the Nigerian military floundered in its efforts to right the wrong. Twenty girls were released in 2016 and another 82 in May 2017, but nearly 100 girls remain in captivity, three years after the abduction. The estimated 9,000 Boko Haram fighters live to terrorize civilians another day.

What should the world do about these atrocities, if anything? For several centuries after the Treaties of Westphalia, state sovereignty remained unchallenged. How states treated individuals and groups within their own jurisdiction was their own responsibility. In the twenty-first century, that is no longer true. What happens in Asian cities, African towns, European streets, and American halls of government is not only heard around the world but also watched carefully. State authorities that take coercive actions against individuals and groups are widely condemned by other states and the media, even if no others choose to act. Even what happens within the family (e.g., violence against spouses, children, and people of a different sexual orientation) is now viewed as a public issue.

The actions of Boko Haram and other groups committing such atrocities are no longer viewed as acceptable during war or civil conflict, any more than using child soldiers, torturing prisoners of war, or targeting groups because of their ethnicity or race is viewed as acceptable. And in peacetime, trafficking of people and illicit goods by states and criminal organizations and perpetuating violence against women either in the public or private sphere are actions no longer deemed to be defensible.

International human rights has emerged as another key issue in world politics. But while these issues have only relatively recently risen to a prominent place on the international agenda, the ethical treatment of individuals and groups of individuals— or human rights—has a long historical genesis. Over the ages, both philosophers and theologians have waxed eloquent over proper treatment of individuals and groups, while novelists and essayists have called attention to the evils of slavery, forced servitude, and the degradation of women and children. Individuals who have been prevented from freely expressing themselves or practicing their religion have emigrated, finding new homes far away from offending authorities. Civil wars are fought over acceptable treatment of individuals and groups. The principle that people care about other people comes from religious, philosophical, and historical traditions. We briefly explore those traditions and then trace how the notion of responsibility for protection of rights of individuals and groups has become internationalized.

LEARNING OBJECTIVES

▶ Describe the religious, philosophical, and historical foundations of human rights.

▶ Explain the roles that states, IGOs, and NGOs perform in the protection and monitoring of human rights.

▶ Identify what human rights have been protected under international law.

▶ Analyze why the international community has so often failed to respond to allegations of genocide.

▶ Analyze why women's human rights in the private sphere are so difficult to address.

▶ Explain the strengths and weaknesses of the R2P norm.

RELIGIOUS, PHILOSOPHICAL, AND HISTORICAL FOUNDATIONS

All of the world's great religions—Hinduism, Judaism, Christianity, Buddhism, Islam, and Confucianism—assert the dignity of individuals and people's responsibilities to fellow human beings. Different religions emphasize different facets: Confucianism, the social group; Judaism, the responsibility to help those in need; and Buddhism, the rejection of government policies that cause suffering.[1] But do these religions assert the inalienable rights of human beings to a standard of treatment? Or are these merely duties or responsibilities of the faithful? Who protects these rights and enforces these duties? Who acts on behalf of those whose rights are violated? Do these religions support human rights for all? The answers are not clear.

Like the world's religions, philosophers and political theorists have also conceptualized the rights of humans, each with different emphases. Liberal political theorists assert individual rights that the state can neither usurp nor undermine. John Locke, for example, wrote that individuals are equal and autonomous beings whose natural rights predate both national and international law. Public authority is designed to secure these rights. Key historic documents such as the English Magna Carta in 1215, the French Declaration of the Rights of Man in 1789, and the U.S. Bill of Rights in 1791 lay out these rights. Political and civil rights, including freedom of speech, religion, and press, deserve protection. Neither authoritarian governments nor arbitrary actions should deprive individuals of these freedoms, known as political and civil human rights.

Theorists in the radical tradition, heavily influenced by Karl Marx and other socialist writers, identify social and economic rights for individuals, which they believe the state should provide. Individuals, according to this view, enjoy material rights—rights to education, decent work, an adequate standard of living, housing—that are critical for sustaining and improving life. Socialist theorists believe that without these guarantees of socioeconomic rights, political and civil rights are meaningless.

What is included as a human right has continually been reconceptualized in the last two centuries, expanding into the realm of group rights. These include both group rights for marginalized peoples and collective rights. Group rights include protection for indigenous peoples, the disabled, and those of different sexual orientations. Collective rights include rights necessary for the collectivity to survive—namely, the right to development and the right to live in a democracy. These rights are highly contested within states and in the international arena. Yet the question is germane: Does the expansion of what is included as a fundamental human right actually dilute the very rights that others are trying to protect?

The Dharavi neighborhood is one of the biggest slums in Mumbai, India. Many of its residents lack decent work, education, housing, and health. Although human rights are often debated in lofty terms, the absence of socioeconomic rights protections has real consequences for people.

Four major debates emerge from these foundations. First, are such issues really human rights? That is, are they inalienable—fundamental to every person? Are they necessary to life? Are they nonnegotiable—that is, are the rights so essential that they cannot be taken away? If human rights are inalienable, are they not, by definition, universal rights?

Second, if human rights are universal, are they applicable to all peoples, in all states, religions, and cultures, without exception? Or are rights dependent on culture? Some scholars have argued for **cultural relativism**, the idea that some rights are culturally determined, and hence, that different rights are relevant in specific cultural settings. Particularly sensitive have been the debates on women's status, child protection, and practices such as female circumcision, practices that have divided Muslims from other religions (and have even divided some within the faith). Some scholars, like political scientist Jack Donnelly, argue for both universal and contextual elements, which he calls "relative universality."[2] The Vienna Declaration adopted at the 1993 World Conference on Human Rights stated, "All human rights are universal, indivisible and interdependent and interrelated." But the same document qualified the statement, saying "the significance of national and regional particularities and various historical, cultural and religious backgrounds must be borne in mind."

Third, should some rights be prioritized over others? Just because political-civil rights have a longer historical genesis, are those rights more important than others? Some writers from East Asia, for example, argue that advocating the rights of the individual over the welfare of the community as a whole is unsound and potentially dangerous.[3] The socialist states of the former Soviet bloc, as well as many European social-welfare states, rank economic and social rights as high priorities, even higher than political and civil rights. Other states in the West prioritize political-civil rights. And, indeed, many of the international initiatives in articulating and enforcing rights have been on behalf of political-civil rights. Yet, to many, human rights are interdependent or linked; the purpose of each type of human right is to treat people with respect and dignity.

Fourth, who has the responsibility and the "right" to respond to violations of human rights? And is this response an absolute obligation or merely an opportunity? Traditionally, it has been the state's responsibility to protect its citizens, but if the state is the abuser, who should and can respond? How? Does state sovereignty trump protection of human rights?

The first global human rights movement, the antislavery movement, illustrates the long struggle in responding to these questions.[4] Beginning in the late eighteenth century, abolitionists (including religious groups, workers, housewives, and business leaders) in the United States, Great Britain, and France organized to advocate for an end to the slave trade. In 1815, when the Final Act of the Congress of Vienna was signed, it stated that the slave trade was "repugnant to the principles of humanity and universal morality." The act was framed in terms of morality, not in human rights language. The act did not declare that slavery was illegal, nor did it provide mechanisms for supporting that aspiration. At that point, states did not view freedom as an inalienable right, fundamental to every person.

Nor did the right apply universally to all states and cultures. States responded individually to the actions of what were generally domestic constituencies: letter writing, petition signing, and public advocacy, among other actions. Responding to these pressures, both the British and American governments banned the slave trade in their territories in 1807 (i.e., new slaves could not be imported from abroad). But it was not until a half century later that the U.S. Civil War was fought to free the slaves. Elsewhere, Spain abolished slavery in Cuba in 1880, and Brazil ended the practice in 1888. The International Convention on the Abolition of Slavery was not ratified until 1926. The antislavery movement suggests that political-civil rights and social-economic rights are intertwined. Since slaves were owned by other humans as property, they had no rights, indeed no human dignity at all. Even after political and civil rights were won, the former slaves and their descendants had, and still have, a long struggle to acquire full social-economic rights, rights often denied because of discrimination and racism.

Recently, the Islamic State seems to have revived the institution of slavery. In 2014, the group forced Yazidi women by the thousands into sex slavery. Contrary to prevailing norms, the IS claims that the practice is a religious one approved by the Koran, even as other Muslim scholars refute that association and affirm the universal consensus that slavery is both morally repugnant and illegal. But the practice continues. The International Organization for Migration reports that young North African males migrating to Libya in hopes of reaching Europe are being auctioned off for labor in a new slave trade. They are being held in bondage or imprisoned in Libya and forced to work. And African women are being bought by private Libyans and used as sex slaves. The Global Slavery Index, compiled by an NGO, finds that in 14 states, over 1 percent of the population is enslaved; half of these states are Muslim states.[5] More generally, slavery has been reconceptualized in contemporary terms. In 1990, Anti-Slavery International included as part of its agenda the prohibition of human trafficking, child labor, and forced labor, each representing contemporary notions of slavery. In 2017, an estimated 20 million people remained in bondage. Over time, the notion of who is human expanded to include slaves and others in economically enforced servitude.

Recognition of who should take responsibility to protect rights has also expanded over time. States remain primarily responsible. But since World War II, the notion of an international community responsibility to protect human rights has developed.

HUMAN RIGHTS AS EMERGING INTERNATIONAL RESPONSIBILITY

Human rights only gradually became an international issue. While NGOs propelled the antislavery initiatives, it was one individual, Henry Dunant, a French medic working in the Battle of Solferino in 1859, who pushed for ways to protect those on the battlefield. Working in conjunction with a nongovernmental group, the Geneva Public Welfare Society, later to become the International Committee of the Red Cross, states codified that protection in 1864 in the first Geneva Convention for the Amelioration of the Condition of the Wounded and Sick in Armed Forces in the Field.

Four Geneva Conventions (1949) and three protocols together form the core of **international humanitarian law** with virtual universal approval. These include Geneva I for protection of the wounded in the armed forces; Geneva II for protection of the wounded and sick shipwrecked at sea; Geneva III for protection of prisoners of war; and Geneva IV for protection of civilians at the time of war. These also form the basis for war crimes and crimes against humanity, now spelled out in Articles 7 and 8 of the Rome Statute (see below). Most of the norms regarding armed conflict apply only to interstate wars and to states, not to nonstate actors, though one of the protocols does apply to victims of noninternational conflicts.

Internationalization of human rights in other sensitive areas was slower to evolve. At the Congress of Versailles, which ended World War I, the Japanese government tried to convince other delegates, principally U.S. president Woodrow Wilson, to adopt a statement on human rights. As a victorious and economically advanced power, Japan felt it had a credible claim that such basic rights as racial equality and religious freedom would not be rejected. Yet the initiative was blocked, with the U.S. representatives recognizing that such a provision would doom Senate passage of the peace treaty.

The League of Nations Covenant made little explicit mention of human rights, although it noted protection of certain groups. For example, the Mandates Commission was authorized to protect the treatment of dependent peoples with the goal of self-determination, but it could not carry out independent inspections. Likewise, the 1919 Minorities Treaties required states to provide protection to all inhabitants, regardless of nationality, language, race, or religion. The League also established principles for assisting refugees, the precedent for the protected status of refugees under the 1951 Convention Relating to the Status of Refugees.

President Franklin Roosevelt's famous "Four Freedoms" speech in 1941 called for a world based on four essential freedoms. However, that new moral order would not take shape until after World War II, when the full extent of the Holocaust was shockingly revealed. With that recognition came the demand for international action. Thus, at the conference founding the UN, civil society groups, churches, and peace societies successfully pushed for inclusion of human rights in the charter. In the end, the UN Charter (Article 55c) gave a role to the organization in "promoting and encouraging respect for rights and for fundamental freedoms for all without distinction as to race, sex, language, or religion."

Drawing on the religious, philosophical, and historical foundations discussed earlier, the UN General Assembly approved the Universal Declaration of Human Rights in 1948, a statement of human rights aspirations. The statement identified 30 principles incorporating both political and economic rights. These principles were eventually codified in two documents, the International Covenant on Economic, Social, and Cultural Rights and the International Covenant on Civil and Political Rights, approved in 1966 and ratified in 1976. Together, the three documents are known as the **International Bill of Rights**. The conflict between Western and socialist views blocked conclusion of a single treaty.

Subsequently, the UN and its agencies have been responsible for setting human rights standards in numerous areas, as Table 10.1 shows. But, while the Charter gave human rights a prominent place and the states that ratified the conventions a standard to follow, the Charter (Article 2[7]) acknowledges the primacy of state sovereignty: "Nothing contained in the present Charter shall authorize the United Nations to intervene in matters which are essentially within the domestic jurisdiction of any state." So who protects human rights and how?

TABLE 10.1

Selected UN Human Rights Conventions

CONVENTION	OPENED FOR RATIFICATION	ENTERED INTO FORCE	RATIFICATIONS (AS OF 2017)
GENERAL HUMAN RIGHTS			
International Covenant on Civil and Political Rights	1966	1976	169
International Covenant on Economic, Social, and Cultural Rights	1966	1976	166
RACIAL DISCRIMINATION			
International Convention on the Elimination of All Forms of Racial Discrimination	1966	1969	179
International Convention on the Suppression and Punishment of the Crime of Apartheid	1973	1976	109
RIGHTS OF WOMEN			
Convention on the Elimination of All Forms of Discrimination against Women	1979	1981	189
HUMAN TRAFFICKING AND OTHER SLAVE-LIKE PRACTICES			
UN Convention for the Suppression of the Traffic in Persons and of the Exploitation of the Prostitution of Others	1949	1951	82
International Convention on the Abolition of Slavery and the Slave Trade (1926), as amended in 1953	1953	1955	123

TABLE 10.1 (continued)

CONVENTION	OPENED FOR RATIFICATION	ENTERED INTO FORCE	RATIFICATIONS (AS OF 2017)
UN Convention against Transnational Organized Crime: Protocol to Prevent, Suppress, and Punish Trafficking in Persons, Especially Women and Children	2000	2003	188

REFUGEES AND STATELESS PERSONS

Convention Relating to the Status of Refugees	1951	1954	145

CHILDREN

Convention on the Rights of the Child	1989	1990	196

PHYSICAL SECURITY

Convention on the Prevention and Punishment of the Crime of Genocide	1948	1951	149
Convention against Torture and Other Cruel, Inhuman, or Degrading Treatment or Punishment	1984	1987	161
Convention for the Protection of All Persons from Enforced Disappearance	2006	2010	58

OTHER

Convention Concerning Indigenous and Tribal Peoples in Independent Countries	1989	1991	22

TABLE 10.1 (continued)

CONVENTION	OPENED FOR RATIFICATION	ENTERED INTO FORCE	RATIFICATIONS (AS OF 2017)
International Convention on the Protection of the Rights of All Migrant Workers and Members of Their Families	1990	2003	51
Convention on the Rights of Persons with Disabilities	2007	2008	175

Sources: University of Minnesota Human Rights Library and UN High Commissioner for Human Rights.

STATES AS PROTECTORS OF HUMAN RIGHTS

States, as the Westphalian tradition and realists posit, are primarily responsible for protecting human rights standards within their own jurisdiction. Many liberal democratic states have based human rights practices on political and civil liberties. The constitutions of the United States and many European democracies emphasize freedom of speech, freedom of religion, and due process. And those same states have tried to internationalize these principles. That is, it has become part of their foreign policy agenda to support similar provisions in newly emerging states. U.S. support for such initiatives is evident in both Iraq and Afghanistan, where specific human rights guarantees were written into the new constitutions. And the European Union has made candidate members show significant progress toward improving political and civil liberties records before granting them membership in the EU. These actions may represent subtle coercion—funding and membership are contingent on human rights protection. But in the long run, constructivists might anticipate that states become gradually socialized into these new norms of international behavior.

Why do democratic states support political and civil rights in their foreign policy? One explanation is based on self-interest: states sharing these values are better positioned to trade with one another and will, according to the democratic peace theory discussed in Chapters 3 and 6, be less likely to go to war with one another. The second explanation is based in liberalism: democracies believe strongly in the protection of individuals from unsavory governments and desire those values and beliefs to be projected abroad.

Some European socialist states have taken up the mantle of protecting economic and social rights because they hold that the government should play a positive role in providing those rights. In this view, governments need to do as much as possible to ensure access to education, adequate health care, and employment. But how much should the government actually do? What is an adequate level? Economic and social rights are achieved only gradually, and thus the crux of the discussion is whether the state is acting in good faith and doing enough to protect the economic and social welfare of its citizens.

State Tactics to Protect Human Rights

What can states do if they believe that the human rights of individuals in another state are not being protected? A number of instruments are available. States may use diplomacy to try to improve human rights. They do this by tying other benefits—usually related to the economy or security—to an improvement in the state's human rights. For example, a state may be granted trade concessions if human rights abuses decline. These kinds of diplomatic agreements might have additional benefits for human rights as well: better economic relations and a more open economic system can create domestic pressure for less offensive human rights practices. With Cuba, the Obama administration expressed the same hope. For over six decades, sanctions had not stopped Cuba's abusive human rights practices and its imposition of socialism. The Obama administration felt that perhaps opening diplomatic relations and engaging with Cuba economically and culturally would result in the desired outcome. But the reversal of that opening by the Trump administration in 2017 suggests that negative sanctions will continue to be used to punish Cuba for its human rights abuses.

In addition to using economic incentives, the United States and European donor states can also tie better human rights policies to more foreign or military aid, or reduce aid if a state's human rights record is particularly egregious. In 1976, under pressure from Congress, the U.S. Department of State began writing annual country reports on human rights. Over time, these reports have become increasingly comprehensive. Along with annual reports from NGOs like Amnesty International and Freedom House, they are used in the process of deciding whether the United States should allocate foreign aid to a country or engage in a relationship. Just hours before then secretary of state John Kerry left for Vienna to conclude the Iran nuclear deal in 2015, the U.S. Department of State released a negative assessment of Iran's human rights record. However, these reports are not the only criteria, and sometimes major human rights violators do receive aid or win significant concessions because of other overriding strategic or political interests.

Human Rights and Human Security:
A View from Canada

"Good international citizens," "the world's conscience," "the moral superpower of the Americas"—these words identify Canada and are often used by Canadians to describe themselves. Canada's policies reflect, in part, distinct values in terms of human rights and human security.

During the early years of the United Nations, Canada and the Nordic countries began to identify as middle powers. Such countries have, in the words of Canadian and Australian scholars, the "tendency to pursue multilateral solutions to international problems, tendency to embrace compromise positions in international disputes, and tendency to embrace notions of 'good international citizenship.'"[a] That expression of good citizenship was seen early in the actions of Canadians working multilaterally. John Humphrey, a legal scholar and human rights supporter, was instrumental in drafting the Universal Declaration of Human Rights and was the first director of the UN Centre for Human Rights. Lawyer Philippe Kirsch headed the conference establishing the International Criminal Court, served as a judge, and was that court's first president.

Canada has been an international leader in promotion of women's rights, the rights of the child, and rights of sexual minorities. The state was one of the first to ratify the Convention on the Elimination of Discrimination against Women. Canadians also played a critical role in UN women's conferences in which women's rights were recognized as human rights. In 2017, the minister of foreign affairs announced the first Feminist International Assistance Policy on behalf of women's rights and sexual and reproductive rights. In the words of one Canadian official, "Part of being Canadian is to feel obligated to defend human rights."[b]

Reflecting its strong support for multilateral institutions, Canada sent peacekeeping troops to every UN operation during the Cold War. But during the 1990s, as its military budget declined, Canada turned to niche diplomacy, concentrating its resources in a few specialized areas, including developing measures to reduce abuses against civilians during conflict.

That support for the protection of civilians provided a bridge from human rights to human security. That link was made during the Ottawa Process in 1996–97, when Canada spearheaded an innovative approach leading to the outlawing of land mines. Under the leadership of foreign affairs minister Lloyd Axworthy, the negotiators made elimination of these weapons, which kill and maim innocent people years after their deployment, a human rights issue. Canada's NGO community led the campaign on behalf of the ban and, after the negotiation, for ratification.

Canada's successful international leadership in promotion of human rights and human security issues would not be possible without its strong NGO sector. The umbrella organization Rights and Democracy lobbies Parliament and the prime minister. It also works to help implement Canadian government programs overseas. Other NGOs are key actors in mobilizing domestic constituencies at the provincial level. And Canada is a major funder of international NGOs like Human Rights Internet and groups like Child

Protesters reaffirm Canada's commitment to refugees despite some public concern after the Paris terrorist attack.

Promotion of international human rights and human security is one way Canada is distinguished from its neighbor. But, just like the United States, Canada is revisiting its past policies toward its indigenous population. Sir John A. Macdonald, Canada's first prime minister and architect of the confederation agreement, was an avowed racist, promoting what is now labeled cultural genocide: mandatory white schooling for indigenous children. As one Canadian admitted, "Sometimes we like to hold ourselves up as this perfect, inclusive, nonracist society, but we're not. . . . But I'm confident we're heading to a better place."[c]

a. Andrew F. Cooper, Richard A. Higgott, and Kim Richard Nossal, *Relocating Middle Powers: Australia and Canada in a Changing World Order* (Vancouver: University of British Columbia Press, 1993), p. 19.

b. Quoted in Alison Brysk, *Global Good Samaritans: Human Rights as Foreign Policy* (New York: Oxford University Press, 2009), p. 92.

c. Arthur Milnes, quoted in Ian Austen, "In Canada, a Reckoning over a Racist Founding Father," *New York Times*, August 29, 2017, A4.

Soldiers International, as well as a willing partner in their activities.

Canada's generous spirit is also seen in its refugee policy. Peoples fearing persecution—the Hungarians in 1956, the Vietnamese in 1979–80, and the Iraqis and Syrians in 2016–17—were admitted as refugees. And gender discrimination and sexual violence are now considered in making the refugee determination, a pathbreaking development. After the election of President Donald Trump, persons residing in the United States with irregular immigration status were invited to Canada by Prime Minister Justin Trudeau. But by the middle of 2017, with Canada so swamped with these persons that the government lacked the capacity to process their resettlement, the invitation no longer held.

FOR CRITICAL ANALYSIS

1. If Canada's support for human rights varies according to the political party in office, how can one say that commitment to human rights forms an integral part of Canadian culture?

2. Canada seeks to separate itself from the United States. Canada supported the United States in the war in Afghanistan, but not in the war in Iraq. Did human rights play a role in that decision?

3. Can Canada be a world leader if it focuses only on human rights and human security? What would a realist say?

Punishing states through sanctions, as Table 5.1 (p. 161) shows, is another tactic states use to push for stronger human rights policies. Following China's crackdown on dissidents and the Tiananmen Square massacre in June 1989, the United States instituted an arms embargo against China and canceled new foreign aid; it was joined by Japan and members of the European Union. Some estimate that the coercive action may have cost China over $11 billion in aid over a four-year period. But imposing sanctions to try to pressure a state to reverse its egregious policy (or policies) often punishes the population more than the state, impinging further on individual rights. Reports suggest that the international community's economic sanctions against Iraq after the first Gulf War resulted in a lower standard of living for the population and an imposition of real economic hardship on the masses, while the targeted elites remained unaffected. The purpose of the sanctions was to secure the elimination of Iraq's weapons of mass destruction—the chemical weapons that it did have and the nuclear weapons it did not possess.

In cases of particularly severe violations, like genocide or mass atrocities, states may choose to target an offending state using unilateral action. And sometimes states may justify sanctioning or employing force in the name of responding to human rights violations, even though they are really acting to protect other interests. Sanctioning is most effective if implemented multilaterally. But using force is less often a multilateral endeavor. In either case, using coercive measures to address human rights violations is selective and often controversial.

States as Abusers of Human Rights

States are also violators of human rights. Both regime type and forms of real or perceived threats to the state are explanations for state abuse. In general, authoritarian or autocratic states are more likely to abuse political and civil rights, while less developed states, even liberal democratic ones, may be unable or unwilling to meet basic obligations of social and economic rights due to scarce resources or lack of political will.

All states, including democratic ones, threatened by civil strife or terrorist activity are apt to use repression against foes, domestic or foreign. State security usually prevails over individual rights. In fact, the International Covenant on Civil and Political Rights acknowledges that heads of state may revoke some political-civil liberties when national security is threatened.

Nowhere is the potential clash between human rights and national security more focused than in the issue of torture, prohibited in the Convention against Torture and Other Cruel, Inhuman, or Degrading Treatment or Punishment. May states, fearing imminent attack or grave harm, use torture to coerce those they believe have relevant knowledge? If states restrain themselves and avoid coercive interrogations, some citizens may die. Which, then, is the greater harm—violation of the rights of the detained, or loss of the lives of innocent citizens? In 2009, former U.S. vice president Dick Cheney argued publicly that political leaders had a greater responsibility to the nation's security, an argument reprised by candidate Donald Trump in 2016 during the U.S. presidential campaign. Others, including prominent American military leaders, responded by questioning whether less violent methods might not have achieved the same results. Still others, like U.S. senator John McCain—himself a victim of torture during the Vietnam War—have consistently argued that Americans should not use torture because it is wrong and violates what it means to be an American.[6] Indeed, the Convention against Torture is clear: freedom from torture is a right never to be revoked. But what acts are considered torture remains controversial.

Economic conditions also influence a country's adherence to human rights standards. Poor states or states experiencing deteriorating economic conditions are apt to repress political-civil rights, in an effort by the elite to maintain authority and divert attention from economic disintegration. But even economically developed states may have difficulty meeting the demands of economic and social rights for all members of their population. Even a country as rich as the United States cannot provide access to basic medical care for certain rural sectors of its population. In some cases, those rights may be deliberately undermined or denied due to discrimination based on race, creed, national origin, or gender.

Finally, culture and history affect a state's human rights record. Where there is a long history of communal violence and ethnic hatred, human rights are more apt to be abused. High degrees of factionalization along ethnic, religious, or ideological lines also bring out the worst abuses.

THE ROLE OF THE INTERNATIONAL COMMUNITY—IGOs AND NGOs

What can the international community do to protect human rights? What can the United Nations and other intergovernmental organizations do when they are themselves composed of the very sovereign states that threaten individual and group rights?[7]

IGOs in Action

The human rights activities of the United Nations and other intergovernmental organizations (IGOs) involve, first and foremost, setting the international human rights standards articulated in the many international treaties. (See Table 10.1.)

With standards set, even though some may be aspirational, the IGOs can then move on to problems connected with implementing those standards.

Second, the United Nations and the Council of Europe's European Court of Human Rights have worked to monitor state behavior by establishing procedures for complaints about state practices, compiling reports from interested and neutral observers about state behavior, and investigating alleged violations. Monitoring state behavior is a sensitive undertaking. Special bodies have been established to examine, advise, and publicly report on the human rights situation in a given country or on worldwide violations. In 2017, a group of United Nations experts, in advance of a UN Human Rights Council meeting, voiced public concern over China's repression of Buddhist cultural practices in Tibet. But for China as well as for other states, intensive scrutiny of a government's behavior in its own country impinges on state sovereignty.

Beginning in 2006, the UN Human Rights Council initiated a new approach, the Universal Periodic Review, wherein every member state participates in evaluating the strengths and weaknesses of its own human rights record every four years. Based on that assessment, other states make recommendations, such as calling for the state to request assistance in a particular area, offering new approaches, suggesting that the state share its best practices with others, or even taking specific actions. For example, both Cuba and Burkina Faso have been pressured to abolish the death penalty. Empirical data suggests that almost two-thirds of recommendations have been accepted. But reforms occur slowly.[8]

The third area in which IGOs have operated is in taking measures to improve levels of state compliance. In the UN system, that responsibility rests with the office of the High Commissioner for Human Rights. Among the most visible of those promotional activities is ensuring fair elections. Since 1992, the United Nations has provided electoral assistance in over 100 countries. The role of the UN varies, from certifying the electoral process in Côte d'Ivoire in 2010 to providing expert monitoring—sometimes sharing that responsibility with states, as in Afghanistan in 2004 and 2005 and in the Republic of South Sudan in 2011. In 2014, the UN oversaw the counting of votes in the contested Afghanistan election. While not eliminating cheating and fraud, states gain legitimacy by having external monitors. Enforcement actions by IGOs for human rights violations are also possible, but rare. In the case of apartheid—legalized racial discrimination against the black majority in South Africa and a comparable policy in Southern Rhodesia (now Zimbabwe)—the international community took coercive economic measures. But the South African government did not immediately change its human rights policy, nor was the government immediately ousted from power.

In a few cases, states may use IGOs to respond to egregious humanitarian emergencies. So-called humanitarian intervention was used in the crisis in Somalia in 1992, in Kosovo by NATO in 1999 to halt large-scale ethnic cleansing by Serbian forces, and in Libya in 2011 to halt what many predicted to be a widespread slaughter of people. In each case, the UN Security Council explicitly linked human rights violations to security threats. In some cases, the UN undertook coercive action without the consent of the states concerned; in other cases, NATO became the instrument of the intervention. Yet the cases wherein IGOs intervene are few. Many states are suspicious of strengthening international organizations' power to intervene in what they still regard as their domestic jurisdiction.

The International Criminal Court provides the means to prosecute leaders accused of crimes under international humanitarian law. Its record is discussed below. Other courts, mostly regional in membership, work to enforce human rights law. Both the European Court of Human Rights and the Inter-American Court of Human Rights respond to cases brought by states and individuals claiming that human rights norms have been violated. In 2016, the European Court alone sat in judgment in almost 2,000 cases. But while these courts make a legal determination, it is ultimately states that enforce decisions.

NGOs' Unique Roles

NGOs have been particularly vocal and sometimes very effective in the area of human rights. Of the hundreds of human rights organizations with interests that cross national borders, a core group has been the most vocal and attracted the most attention, including Amnesty International (AI) and Human Rights Watch (HRW). These organizations publicize issues, put pressure on states (both offenders and enforcers), and lobby international organizations. Furthermore, these organizations have often formed coalitions, leading to advocacy networks and social movements.[9]

NGO campaigns on a particular issue take time. During the 1970s, disability rights groups formed first in Europe and North America, generally organizing along lines of disability type. Activists were fragmented, and there was no overarching approach. Over time, these various groups adopted a rights-based approach. By 1992, seven of the groups had merged into a loose network, the International Disability Alliance. As new communication technologies were becoming mainstream, disability activists began to elicit the support of established NGOs like HRW and AI. With the backing of HRW and AI, and funding from the Open Society Institute, a disability convention was brought to the UN General Assembly. In 2006, the Convention on the Rights of Persons with Disabilities was adopted.[10] By the end of 2017, 175 states had become parties to the treaty, obligating them to prohibit all discrimination on the basis of disability. This example illustrates how concerted NGO action over time can result in substantive international law.

The use of social media, Twitter, and the Internet has proven particularly effective for shaping discourse surrounding an issue and generating interest among multiple constituencies. One example of a media-driven effort illustrates both the promise and the problems of the approach. For over two decades, the Lord's Resistance Army and its leader, Ugandan Joseph Kony, have kidnapped more than 20,000 children in northern Uganda and used them as child soldiers and sex slaves, creating fear and intimidation among the population. In 2005, the International Criminal Court issued a warrant for Kony's arrest for war crimes and crimes against humanity. Invisible Children, founded in 2004, was originally an NGO organized to call attention to this abuse through film and organized political activity, presenting a simplistic but graphic message aimed at Western audiences. In 2012, its half-hour video called "Kony 2012" went viral, attracting 80 million hits. While all agree that the abuse represents an egregious violation of human rights, not everyone agreed with Invisible Children's approach of advocating military force, even as the U.S. military collaborated with the organization in the region until President Trump suspended the activity in 2017. Eventually, as funds became scarce in 2015, the NGO changed tactics, emphasizing intelligence gathering by providing radios to villagers to track the movement of Kony and his rebels, which were estimated to number 100 in 2017.

So, in constructivist discourse, NGOs can both aid in the spread of ideas and sometimes distort the message or oversimplify a complex problem. But NGOs, too,

Students in Seattle distribute a poster in support of controversial group Invisible Children's Kony 2012 campaign. The campaign was designed to bring Joseph Kony, leader of the Lord's Resistance Army, to justice.

have the power to transform themselves to develop new approaches and tackle new problems. Remember, they have no independent legal standing, have few material resources compared to states, and exist at the discretion of the states in which they are operating.

Evaluating the Efforts of the International Community

How effective are the efforts of the international community in the area of human rights? Setting the standards in treaties is critical—without a standard, there is no benchmark for assessment. But of the various activities discussed, perhaps none is as effective as monitoring. NGOs have also been particularly useful in monitoring activities. Amnesty International, founded in 1961, has become perhaps the most effective human rights monitor. AI was involved in efforts to end the abuse of human rights in Uruguay and Paraguay in the 1970s. Using its research and publicity expertise, AI was instrumental in bringing international attention to the Argentinian military abuses involving abductions and disappearances in the early 1980s. While the organization originally emphasized the protection of individual political prisoners, its agenda has now broadened to include multiple issues, including systematic abuses of economic and social rights, women's rights, and LGBT rights. AI and organizations like it provide information for the UN's own monitoring activities and for the United States.[11]

Does monitoring by IGOs or NGOs through investigations, reports, resolutions, and naming and shaming ultimately make a difference for rights protection? The evidence is mixed. One study of over 400 human rights organizations on shaming governments between 1992 and 2004 found that states targeted by NGOs do improve their human rights practices. But shaming is not enough. Shaming is effective when both domestic NGOs on the ground and advocacy by other third parties and individuals are present.[12] Another study of monitoring by the UN, NGOs, and the media between 1975 and 2000 found that governments identified as violators often "adopt better protections for political rights afterward, but they rarely stop or appear to lessen acts of terror."[13] Only when NGOs actively took up issues did practices improve. Thus, IGO and NGO monitoring over time, as well as the Universal Periodic Review, is not necessarily enough to alter practices.

All of these activities on behalf of human rights are fraught with difficulties. A state's ratification of a treaty is no guarantee of its willingness or ability to follow the treaty's provisions. Monitoring state compliance through self-reporting systems presumes a willingness to comply and be transparent, a major caveat to be sure. Taking direct action by imposing economic embargoes may not achieve the objective—a change in human rights policy—and may be harmful to those very individuals whom the embargoes are trying to help.

International and national actions on behalf of human rights objectives remain a very tricky business. This idea becomes all the more apparent when we delve into specific human rights problems.

SPECIFIC HUMAN RIGHTS ISSUES

Generally, international human rights treaties address separate issues, each of which is worthy of study. In this section, we first turn to a study of genocide and mass atrocities, since it was the reaction to the atrocities of World War II that led to the internationalization of human rights. Then we take up the issue of protection of women. That issue is instructive, as it involves the expansion of rights across time and space and it involves protection of rights in the public and private sphere.

The Problem of Genocide and Mass Atrocities

The twentieth century saw millions of deaths from deliberate acts of warfare, ethnic cleansing, crimes against humanity, and physical violence against individuals. Yet the word to describe one kind of physical violence—**genocide**—did not even exist

Armenians rally outside the Turkish consulate in 2017 to commemorate the 102nd anniversary of the Armenian genocide by Turkish forces during World War I. The claim of genocide is still contested, and some countries do not formally recognize the genocide.

during the first half of the century. A Polish lawyer, Raphael Lemkin, became so incensed by the destruction of Armenians in 1915 that he devoted his life to the human rights cause, penning the word *genocide* and then traveling around the world in support of an international law prohibiting it.

It took the genocide of Jews and other "undesirables" during World War II to finally make the international community ready to act. In 1948, the Convention on the Prevention and Punishment of the Crime of Genocide was adopted. Genocide is defined in the convention (see Box 10.1). While the convention was signed, ratified, and recognized as an advance in international human rights, like most legal conventions, it is both precise on some questions and vague on others. Such ambiguity often reflects disagreement among the parties during the negotiating process or an inability of the negotiators to reach a compromise. From one perspective, the convention is precise in terms of defining what constitutes genocide. The perpetrator of the genocide must have the intention to kill; the killing or maiming is not an unintended

BOX 10.1

The Genocide Convention

ARTICLE 1 The Contracting Parties confirm that genocide, whether committed in time of peace or in time of war, is a crime under international law which they undertake to prevent and punish.

ARTICLE 2 In the present convention, genocide means any of the following acts committed with intent to destroy, in whole or in part, a national, ethnical, racial or religious group, as such:

(a) Killing members of the group;

(b) Causing serious bodily or mental harm to members of the group;

(c) Deliberately inflicting on the group conditions of life calculated to bring about its physical destruction in whole or in part;

(d) Imposing measures intended to prevent births within the group;

(e) Forcibly transferring children of the group to another group.

ARTICLE 3 The following acts shall be punishable:

(a) Genocide;

(b) Conspiracy to commit genocide;

(c) Direct and public incitement to commit genocide;

(d) Attempt to commit genocide;

(e) Complicity in genocide.

result of violence or a random act. The targets of the violence must be a national, ethnical, racial, or religious group. But from another view, the convention is vague. It does not specify how many people must be killed to be considered genocide. Nor does it specify what evidence is necessary to prove intentionality. The convention provides no permanent body to monitor potential genocides or any system for early warnings. How the international community should respond is vague, but respond it should.

Despite the convention and the good intentions of the popular slogan "never again" in reference to the Holocaust, the international community has failed to act decisively in cases of purported genocide. One million Bangladeshis were killed in the 1970s; India intervened but did not stop the carnage. Two million Cambodians were killed in the same era, but Vietnam's intervention, undertaken for different reasons, was too late and the rest of the world was silent.

In the 1990s, over 800,000 Rwandans were killed while the small UN contingent on the ground sat back and watched. In the states of the former Yugoslavia, including Bosnia-Herzegovina, Croatia, Serbia, and Kosovo, people of one ethnic group were forced to move, were sometimes killed or placed in concentration camps, and were raped, but the reaction by the United Nations and NATO proved ineffective in stopping the carnage. In Darfur in the early 2000s, it is estimated that between 100,000 and 400,000 people were killed and millions were forced to move. While the NGOs provided humanitarian relief, states failed to act decisively. A UN/African Union peacekeeping force was approved later, but it had a narrow mandate.

In the Rwanda and Darfur cases, major states adopted a concerted policy not to use the word *genocide*, cognizant that admitting these cases were genocide would necessitate international responses. Instead, at the outset these were framed as "ordinary" ethnic conflicts. In retrospect, it is clear they were anything but ordinary. Even when the NATO-backed coalition was organized to stop the ethnic cleansing of Serbs in Kosovo, NATO never used the word *genocide* to describe what was happening. Neither is the word *genocide* used by many states, including the United States, for the killing of 1.5 million Armenian Christians in Turkey in 1915 because of fear of offending Turkey. A century later, the dispute continues today over what to call the abuse suffered by the minority group Rohingya in Myanmar. Is that crisis only a refugee crisis, as described in Chapter 11? Or do the actions approach a genocide?

Along with the prohibition against genocide came the codification of other crimes against humanity and crimes committed during warfare. These **crimes against humanity** are now incorporated in Article 7 of the Rome Statute of the International Criminal Court (see Box 10.2).

The former Yugoslavia illustrates the dilemmas associated with these terms and the different conclusions found after investigation of the events. During the war in the early 1990s, the term *ethnic cleansing* was coined to refer to systematic efforts by Croatia and the Bosnian Serbs to remove peoples of another group from their territory. During 1992 and 1993, the UN Commission on Human Rights concluded

Crimes against Humanity

ARTICLE 7 of the Rome Statute of the International Criminal Court reads as follows: For the purpose of this Statute, "crime against humanity" means any of the following acts when committed as part of a widespread or systematic attack directed against any civilian population, with knowledge of the attack:

(a) Murder;

(b) Extermination;

(c) Enslavement;

(d) Deportation or forcible transfer of population;

(e) Imprisonment or other severe deprivation of physical liberty in violation of fundamental rules of international law;

(f) Torture;

(g) Rape, sexual slavery, enforced prostitution, forced pregnancy, enforced sterilization, or any other form of sexual violence of comparable gravity;

(h) Persecution against any identifiable group or collectivity on political, racial, national, ethnic, cultural, religious, gender as defined in paragraph 3, or other grounds that are universally recognized as impermissible under international law, in connection with any act referred to in this paragraph or any crime within the jurisdiction of the Court;

(i) Enforced disappearance of persons;

(j) The crime of apartheid;

(k) Other inhumane acts of a similar character intentionally causing great suffering, or serious injury to body or to mental or physical health.

that there were "massive and grave violations of human rights" and that Muslims were the principal victims. The Security Council Commission of Experts found that all sides were committing war crimes, but only the Serbs were conducting a systematic campaign of genocide. But some states and many NGOs disagreed. In 2007, the International Court of Justice ruled that Serbia neither committed genocide nor conspired or was complicit in the act of genocide. The judges pointed to insufficient proof of intentionality to destroy the Bosnians. In 2015, the same court ruled that both Serbia and Croatia committed crimes, but the intent to commit genocide had not been proven.[14] Labeling events an ethnic cleaning, a crime against humanity, or a genocide is not straightforward, yet the label has consequences, triggering a response should genocide be identified.

Cases of possible genocide and war crimes continue to occur. In 2015, the UN High Commissioner for Human Rights reported that the Islamic State may have committed genocide and war crimes against the Yazidi community in Iraq and called for the Security Council to refer the case to the International Criminal Court. When celebrity human rights lawyer Amal Clooney took on the case of a possible genocide and war crimes in the middle of 2016 and appeared before the UN Security Council in 2017, the issue received wide public exposure. But so far the issue has stalled. International efforts to prevent or stop mass human rights abuses have been fitful. When prevention is not possible, for practical or political reasons, the next issue is whether and how to punish the individuals responsible.

Punishing the Guilty Individuals

A key trend in the new millennium is that individuals responsible for genocide and crimes against humanity should be held accountable. This idea is not new. After World War II, the Allies convened trials to punish German and Japanese leaders for their wartime actions. However, because these trials were the victor's punishment, they were not seen as legitimate precedents. Following the atrocities in Yugoslavia and Rwanda, the United Nations established two ad hoc criminal tribunals, the International Criminal Tribunal for the Former Yugoslavia, in 1993, and the International Criminal Tribunal for Rwanda, in 1994. These tribunals, approved by the UN Security Council, developed procedures to deal with the issues of jurisdiction, evidence, sentencing, and imprisonment. Because of the need to establish procedures and the difficulty in finding the accused, the trials proceeded very slowly. By the end of 2017, the Yugoslav tribunal had indicted 162 individuals, with convictions for 84 persons and acquittals for 19, at a price of more than $2 billion. In late 2017, the last trial concluded. Ratko Mladić (the Butcher of Bosnia), accused of orchestrating ethnic cleansing and the slaughter of 7,000 Bosnian Muslim men and boys in 1995, was found guilty of genocide. The Rwanda tribunal led to 62 convictions and 14 acquittals, at a cost of $1–$2 billion.

In light of the costs and inefficiencies of these ad hoc tribunals, states under UN auspices negotiated the Rome Statute for the International Criminal Court (ICC), establishing an innovative international court having both compulsory jurisdiction and jurisdiction over individuals.[15] The Rome Statute covers four types of crimes: genocide, crimes against humanity, war crimes, and crimes of aggression. No individuals (save those under 18 years of age) are immune from jurisdiction, including heads of states and military leaders. The ICC functions as a court of last resort, hearing cases only when national courts are unwilling or unable to deal with prosecuting grave atrocities.

In 2003, the work of the ICC began; by the beginning of 2018, it had opened preliminary examinations in eight cases, was investigating 11 cases, and had issued 25 arrest warrants, many of which are still outstanding, including those for Sudanese president Omar Hassan al-Bashir and Joseph Kony of the Lord's Resistance Army. Four of the cases have ended in convictions. Most of these cases involve crimes committed in African countries. Few have been given extensive attention in the Western media, but the 2014 arrest and trial of Congolese warlord Bosco Ntaganda for war crimes of rape, murder, and use of child soldiers is a prominent exception.

While many supporters see the court as essential for establishing international law and enforcing individual accountability, the ICC is widely criticized. The United States asserts that the ICC infringes on U.S. sovereignty. Believing that the United States has "exceptional" international responsibilities as a hegemon, U.S. leaders feel that they, along with the American military, should be immune from the ICC's jurisdiction, and hence the United States has not ratified the treaty. While the controversy continues, the United States, as a member of the UN Security Council, voted in favor of referring Libya to the ICC in 2011. In 2016, Russia withdrew its support of the ICC after a preliminary investigation of alleged crimes committed by Russian and Georgian forces during the 2008 war. Most critically, African states, once supporters of the ICC, are increasingly skeptical of its neutrality since so many cases on the court's docket target African leaders. As a result, states like Gambia and South Africa withdrew, but they subsequently revoked their withdrawal, not wanting to be viewed in the same light as pariah states. Others like Namibia, Kenya, and Uganda continue to threaten withdrawal. In the fall of 2017, Burundi became the first state to actually withdraw. Such actions seriously jeopardize the court's legitimacy.

Has the ICC deterred would-be abusers, punished perpetrators, and fostered peace? On the first question, one study of the ten-year period before the ICC and the ten-year period after it finds that "actors who are concerned with their legitimacy in the eyes of domestic publics and/or the international community are much more likely to be deterred by the possibility of ICC prosecution than those who are not."[16] On the second question, a few perpetrators have been punished, but not many and at a high cost. On the third question, some critics contend that bringing individuals to justice might jeopardize the long-term peace because those facing future prosecution may try harder to stay in power. The ICC's indictments of Sudan's al-Bashir for war crimes and his "essential role" in murder and atrocities in Darfur and of Kony for his war crimes in Uganda illustrate the dilemma. Would the conflicts have ended sooner had these cases not been referred to the ICC by the Security Council? Did the indictments complicate any potential political settlements? Has al-Bashir's open defiance of the court, buttressed by the noncooperation of many African states, including South Africa's refusal to arrest al-Bashir when he visited South Africa, undermined the court's legitimacy? For some, there needs to be a better way to proceed.

Reconciling and Rebuilding: Truth Commissions and Hybrid Arrangements

Truth commissions are another approach that has gained popularity since their use in South Africa following the end of apartheid. The idea behind such commissions is to examine in an open forum what happened during the time of crisis, in order to uncover the truth and, in the process, move forward with the reconciliation process. This approach is seen as appropriate in countries emerging out of civil war where violence is widespread, where blame is apportioned to all sides, and where all parties must now live side by side. Increasingly, truth commissions are used in conjunction with other legal mechanisms, such as local courts (as in Rwanda and Bosnia) or hybrid courts (as in Sierra Leone or Cambodia).

The hybrid court in Cambodia is a typical case. It has come under intense scrutiny for the price tag of $300 million for three convictions. Law professor Philippe Sands, in discussing that case, expressed a more general, but not widely shared, sentiment: "I don't think it's a fair sign of success or failure just to look at dollar signs and convictions. The bigger question is, to what extent has this tribunal contributed to beginning the process of embedding the idea of justice, the absence of impunity, into public consciousness, to help Cambodians transition to a better place?"[17] In 2017, procedures were established in Kosovo, with funding by the European Union, to build a body of law to address abuses during that conflict.

WOMEN'S RIGHTS AS HUMAN RIGHTS: THE GLOBALIZATION OF WOMEN'S RIGHTS

The case of women's rights illustrates how human rights have moved from the national to the international agenda, how different types of rights have become interconnected, and how women's human rights touch directly on cultural values and norms. Demonstrating that women's rights have gradually become a global issue, a UN poster prepared for the Vienna Conference in 1993 was headlined: "Women's Rights Are Human Rights." But this view has not always been the case.

From Political and Economic Rights to Human Rights

Women first took up the call for political participation within national jurisdictions, demanding their political and civil rights in the form of women's suffrage. Although British and U.S. women won that right in 1918 and 1920, respectively, women in many parts of the world had to wait until after World War II. Then the immediate priority of the UN and its Commission on the Status of Women following the 1949 Universal Declaration of Human Rights was getting states to grant women the rights to vote, hold office, and enjoy legal rights. More than a decade later, the 1979 Convention on the Elimination of All Forms of Discrimination against Women (CEDAW) further articulated the standard, positing that discrimination against women in political and public life is illegal.

During the 1960s and 1970s, states paid more attention to economic and social rights for women. The development community had believed for many years that all individuals, including women, could participate and benefit equally from the economic-development process. Yet as experts began to examine statistics on economic and social issues relevant to women, they found that not to be the case. Men benefit disproportionately from the introduction of technology, whether bicycles or tractors, appropriating it for themselves. Women need policies specifically aimed at them.

The result was the women in development (WID) movement—a transnational movement concerned with systematic discrimination against women and the failure of development to make an impact on the lives of the poor. The movement gained steam through four successive UN-sponsored world conferences on women, where women mobilized and networks developed enabling them to set a critical economic agenda affecting women, including equal pay, maternity protection, and nondiscrimination in the workplace. Under WID, the World Bank and virtually the entire UN system initiated programs for women's economic enhancement. Today, the WID agenda is well integrated in most international assistance programs.[18]

CEDAW addresses both political-civil rights and a wide range of socioeconomic rights. Although 189 states have become parties to the treaty, a number of states have added reservations that clarify how the states will implement the treaty commitments. Many of those reservations protect the right of states to impose their own domestic laws with respect to the rights of women. States like Algeria and Egypt, along with many others, noted conflicts between CEDAW and their own domestic and family law codes and prioritized domestic laws reflecting religious and cultural values.

Most controversial has been protection against human rights abuses in the private sphere. The latter includes violence against women in the family and domestic life and violence against women in war, namely rape and torture. In short, gender-based violence against women in all arenas was identified as a breach of both human rights and humanitarian norms.

Continuing Violence against Women

In 2015, the UN reported that violence against women and girls "persists at alarmingly high levels"—more than one in three have experienced physical violence. Two examples illustrate this widespread and often controversial problem.

During Taliban rule, Afghan girls were prohibited from attending school. Today, girls are allowed receive an education, but still face many difficulties in doing so.

Rape is a prime example of violence against women. Several contemporary events highlight this unique form of violence against women: the rape of 2,000 Kuwaiti women by Iraqi soldiers during the 1991 Gulf War; the rape of 60,000 Bosnian women in 1993 by Serb and Croat forces; the rape of 250,000 women in Burundi's and Rwanda's ethnic conflicts in 1993–94; the rape of an estimated 200,000 women during ongoing violence in the Democratic Republic of Congo; and the rape of over 200 women and girls in Darfur in 2014. In Nigeria, of the 234 women rescued by the military from Boko Haram in 2017, 214 were pregnant. And in 2017, the Islamic State is reported to have normalized widespread rape and torture of both Sunni Arab women and ethnic minorities like the Yazidis. Plus, the reports of rape committed by the Myanmar military on Rohingya women continue almost daily. At earlier wartime trials, rape was not brought up as a war crime, even though states systematically employed it as an instrument of war during World War II.

Is rape part of a deliberate strategy of war, part of a systematic state policy? At the tribunal for Rwanda, Jean-Paul Akayesu was accused of gang rape and genocide. In a controversial 1998 decision, the judges issued the unprecedented ruling that rape constitutes not only a crime against humanity but also genocide. Now the statute for the International Criminal Court includes rape, sexual slavery, and forced prostitution among crimes against humanity, when such actions are part of a widespread and systematic attack against a civilian population. Despite this finding, critical questions persist: Is rape a strategy to build group cohesion among militias? Alternatively, is rape a product of opportunity—a crime, to be sure, but not a wartime strategy? Dara Kay Cohen, in *Rape during Civil War*, discusses these possibilities, using interviews with both victims and perpetrators in three conflicts.[19]

Rape is not just a wartime issue. In South Asia and the Middle East, the problem is particularly acute even during peacetime. In some places, the rape of women may be seen as an acceptable act of revenge for a prior wrong. The raped women, being dishonored, may be subsequently killed. Or prosecution of the crime may be difficult, as in Pakistan, where a woman who has been raped may be convicted of adultery unless four male witnesses corroborate her rape story. The case of the gang rape of an Indian student in 2012 and her subsequent death brought the issue into the international limelight in a country where the definition of rape is vague, local police and government authorities fail to investigate, and prosecutors do not pursue cases vigorously. Under widespread public pressure, the Indian government fast-tracked the prosecution of that case and gave four death sentences.

Physical assault against women is a problem in many parts of the world, as well. Beginning in the 1990s, Ciudad Juárez, Mexico—across the border from El Paso, Texas—experienced a wave of attacks against women, about a third of which involved sexual assault, resulting in 304 deaths in 2010 alone. Like in Pakistan and India, Mexican authorities have been criticized for their lax investigations and failure to bring perpetrators to justice. In the U.S. military, rape of female soldiers by their male counterparts attracted widespread attention in 2012–13. While the military has taken measures to curb this abhorrent behavior, Congress left prosecution in the hands of the military itself, much to the dismay of those wanting civilian authorities to handle cases.

Increasingly, human rights NGOs like Human Rights Watch and Amnesty International bring violations of women's rights to the attention of the international community, and public pressure is brought to bear. If state authorities fail to take these cases seriously, then the state, too, becomes complicit. But given different cultural norms, private-sphere activities are much easier to hide and more resistant to change.

Trafficking in women and children is another form of gender-specific human rights violations. While prohibited under the CEDAW convention, the practice has become more prevalent, facilitated by open borders, pressures to keep labor costs low, and poverty that drives women and families to seek any kind of employment (including working in the sex trade). The number of women forced into bonded sweatshop labor and domestic servitude is unknown, ranging between 12 and 27 million persons; about one-quarter of these are trafficked, many for the sex trade. This problem is especially vexing, because unlike rape, in which consent is not given, women may choose to be trafficked for economic reasons. Yet the international community, speaking through several treaties, has made this kind of exploitation illegal (see Table 10.1).

Although international standards against trafficking in women and children exist, monitoring and enforcement remain difficult. First, despite the international agreements, disagreement remains on the local level about what constitutes trafficking. Second, the clandestine nature of the problem complicates enforcement. Furthermore, the issue has been framed as both a human rights problem and a transnational crime issue. Various UN-related groups responsible for monitoring and pressuring states, and anti-trafficking NGOs, are involved. They employ a variety of different strategies, including giving alternative employment opportunities to women, educating women on the dangers of trafficking, punishing the traffickers through incarceration, and providing stricter law enforcement across national boundaries.

In the long term, the solution to fully address discrimination against women, be it political, economic, or social, is to elevate women from their historically subordinate status to men. Liberal feminists see that progress has been made, as women have secured privileges that were once exclusively male prerogatives. The fact that both public and private abuses are the subject of media attention, concerted NGO activity, and state action also denotes progress. However, radical (socialist) feminists do not see as much progress as they point to the economic forces that continually place women in a disadvantaged position. Encouragingly, virtually all condemn the various forms of both public and private violence against women, though their remedies for relief vary.

While the legal stage has been set by various human rights treaties and international organizations, the mainstay of enforcement will continue to be at the state level. And there, women's rights international NGOs have proven critical. According to an empirical study of over 1,500 such organizations from the 1990s to 2005, NGO shaming improved women's economic and social rights but had less impact on women's political rights.[20] Such groups support specific policies—funding shelters, creating rape crisis centers, adopting legislation protecting vulnerable populations, and funding prevention programs.[21]

What is the linkage of the treatment of women at the individual level to the broader international relations questions? One prominent study that examined this micro-macro link finds that the best statistical predictor of state peacefulness is not democracy or wealth but the level of physical security for women. The higher the level of violence against women, the more likely the state is to be involved in interstate and intrastate conflict and the less likely the state is to be acting peacefully in the international system.[22]

THE DEBATE OVER HUMANITARIAN INTERVENTION AND R2P

Moving from articulating support for human rights in all their various manifestations to enforcing international human rights standards against abusers is fraught with difficulty. The just war tradition asserts that military action by states or the international community may be necessary to alleviate massive violations of human rights—such action is also known as **humanitarian intervention**. That position contradicts the Westphalian view of state sovereignty. Yet throughout history, states have applied military intervention on behalf of humanitarian causes, although they have done so on a selective basis. In the nineteenth century, Europeans used military force to protect Christians in Turkey and the Middle East, though they chose not to protect other religious groups. And European nations did not intervene militarily to stop slavery, though they prohibited their own citizens from participating in the slave trade.[23]

Since the end of World War II, the notion has emerged that all human beings—not just particular groups—deserve protection, and traditionally states have had the responsibility to protect their own people, free from external intervention, as an essential feature of sovereignty. But in the 1990s, after humanitarian crises in Somalia and Rwanda, and following widespread murder, rape, and devastation in Darfur, Sudan, the International Commission on Intervention and State Sovereignty, composed of scholars, high-level officials, and Canadian government personnel, changed the discourse. It maintains that if the state does not protect its own, then other states should do something, even using military force as a last resort, if authorized by the UN Security Council. That is the foundation argument of the **responsibility to protect (R2P)**.

R2P is the idea that in cases of massive violations of human rights, when domestic avenues for redress have been exhausted and actions by other states might reasonably end the abuse, these states have a *responsibility* to intervene in the domestic affairs of the state in which the abuse is occurring. As two UN officials described the development of R2P, "[This] marks the coming of age of the imperative of action in the face of human rights abuses, over the citadels of state sovereignty."[24]

Like many international institutions, the responsibility to protect comes with its own set of problems. Can intervention be a legitimate response if it is used only selectively, in some cases and not in others? In 2011, for example, why did the international community (the UN, NATO, and the Arab League) all voice support for military action against Libya's Colonel Muammar Qaddafi? Qaddafi's predictions of "rivers of blood" against his opponents and his threats to "cleanse Libya house by house" provided the justification for internationally sanctioned intervention.[25] But mass atrocities against the Syrian people since 2011 attributed to the Syrian regime of Bashar al-Assad have not led to the same response. Might the danger be that all interventions in another state's affairs can ultimately be justified by R2P? After all, the American government, when no weapons of mass destruction were found in Iraq, justified the invasion by pointing to the ruthless regime of Saddam Hussein. And Russian president Vladimir Putin invoked a version of R2P in his justification for annexing Crimea in 2014.

Putin argued that a military intervention was part of Russia's responsibility to protect the lives and property of ethnic Russians in Crimea and parts of eastern Ukraine. When does the use of the term become a justification for a state or group of states to act in its national interest on issues having nothing to do with protection of individuals or groups?

Indeed, states differ over interpretation of the norm. When the UN Security Council approved the resolution authorizing measures to protect Libyan civilians, Brazil, India, China, and Russia abstained. In particular, Russia and China place the highest priority on sovereignty and noninterference in the internal affairs of states. When NATO acted to end Qaddafi's four-decade rule, Brazil joined with Russia and China in expressing public outrage. As Brazil argued, the Libyan intervention acted against humanitarian purposes because it created conditions that accelerated the terrorist threat and resulted in more civilian deaths. Brazil later supported an alternative concept, "responsibility while protecting." They argued that a case-by-case assessment of the consequences of military actions was needed so that more civilians would not be put at risk.[26]

Questions about R2P remain. How massive do the violations of human rights have to be to justify intervention? The Geneva Conventions specify that "genocide" is not about how *many* people are killed, but about the *intent* to kill an entire group. Who decides when to respond to the abuses? Might some states use humanitarian intervention as a pretext for achieving other, less humanitarian goals? Should states have an obligation to intervene militarily in these humanitarian emergencies? Why are some interventions justified (e.g., Kosovo and Libya), while others, in which equally heinous abuse is taking place (e.g., Rwanda and Syria), are ignored?

Given their experiences under colonial rule, many Asian and African countries are skeptical about humanitarian justifications for intervention by Western countries. Other states, such as Russia and China, have insisted that for a claim of humanitarian intervention to be legitimate, it must be authorized by the UN Security Council, where Russia and China are among the powers possessing a veto. In practice, humanitarian interventions are often multilateral, although they do not always receive authorization by the UN. For instance, when Western states sought military intervention in Kosovo, Russia opposed the measure, so Western powers turned to the North Atlantic Treaty Organization (NATO) instead.

States that have supported humanitarian interventions in the past do not always support future interventions. This change in policy can occur for several reasons, including the perception of the success or failure of previous missions, as well as the nature of other interests at stake in the conflict. Having suffered a humiliating setback in Somalia in 1993, for instance, the United States (and the UN) opposed increased use of the military to protect civilians in Rwanda in 1994, despite clear evidence of genocide. Similarly, only a small military contingent from the

African Union was originally mobilized for the Darfur region, despite between 100,000 and 400,000 deaths and the culpability of the Sudanese government. In the Darfur case, other national interests were deemed more vital than support for humanitarian intervention: China cared about access to Sudanese oil; Russia cared about export arms markets; the United States was preoccupied with Iraq and the war on terrorism. In May 2012, a massacre of women, children, and even infants in Taldou, Syria, by the security forces of Syria's Bashar al-Assad caused an international outcry, but China and Russia opposed UN-sanctioned military intervention. Both countries issued statements asserting that any foreign military intervention would only make the situation in Syria, and the region, worse. Russia's and China's positions on intervention ultimately failed to halt international military intervention in the civil war in Syria (2012–present). This outcome may be why Russia later determined that its own military intervention in Syria was both necessary to reverse the chaos caused by U.S. and allied interventions, and just.

So although support for R2P is an emergent norm, it remains the subject of ongoing controversy. Because states do not intervene in all situations of humanitarian emergency, state sovereignty remains intact. But when gross violations of human rights are obvious, and when military intervention does not conflict with other national interests, states increasingly view humanitarian intervention as a justifiable use of force on behalf of human rights. Yet as Rosa Brooks reminds us, "Once you assert that every state can decide for itself that a military intervention inside another state's borders is justified, regardless of the Security Council, you're on a very slippery slope."[27]

CONTENDING PERSPECTIVES ON RESPONDING TO HUMAN RIGHTS ABUSES

What explains the lack of decisive action in responding to human rights abuses? Realists say that states have determined that it is not in their national interest to respond, since human rights abuses do not usually threaten a state's own national security. If genocide committed by one state does jeopardize another state's national interest, including intruding on its core values, then it could act. As former U.S. national security adviser Henry Kissinger has warned, a wise realist policy maker would be moved not by sentiment alone or by personal welfare, but by the calculation of the national interest.[28] How else can we explain the lack of a coercive international response to egregious violations of human rights, as occurred with the United States regarding Rwanda, China regarding Darfur, and Russia regarding Syria? For many realists, such as Rosa Brooks, R2P is "irrelevant or pernicious."[29]

While national interest is generally viewed in terms of security, it may be broader than that, encompassing historical tradition or domestic values. The United States has historically fought for human rights consistent with its domestic values. President Franklin Roosevelt in 1941 affirmed, "Freedom means the supremacy of human rights everywhere. Our support goes to those who struggle to gain those rights and keep them." After World War II, Americans advocated punishing the guilty and, at the UN's founding conference, there was strong American support for including human rights as a key area of responsibility. Yet other U.S. actions have not followed. During the Cold War, the United States supported anticommunist regimes, even those having abusive human rights records; the United States also supported the South African white regime. Furthermore, it failed to ratify many key human rights documents, including the statute on the International Criminal Court. The realist explanation is that these actions were in the national interest and consistent with protection of sovereignty.

Liberals would be more likely to advise state intervention in response not only to genocide but also to less dramatic abuses. Liberals' emphasis on individual welfare and on the malleability of the state makes such intrusions into the actions of other states more appealing to them. Like the realists, they may prefer that nongovernmental actors or humanitarian agencies take the initiative. Hence, sending in the UN humanitarian agencies is often their first response. But liberals generally see it as a state's duty to intercede in blatant cases of human rights abuse. However, that interest may conflict with other contending interests—preserving an alliance, hamstringing an enemy, or putting resources into domestic policy initiatives. For most liberals, humanitarian intervention or R2P is more legitimate if it is authorized and implemented by international institutions. Requiring multilateral approval makes it more difficult for a single state to intervene for purposes other than protection of others.

For constructivists, human rights represents a key test of the central tenet that ideas matter; ideas such as human rights can change and amplify over time. Constructivists try to explain the local, domestic, and international forces that propel the changes and how states' responses to human rights abuses may reflect these broader changes. Among those broader changes is the constructivist notion of sovereignty. Since sovereignty is not absolute in the Westphalian tradition, it is contingent and changing as new international issues emerge and states, internal organizations, and nongovernmental organizations respond to human rights abuses.

IN SUM: FROM HUMAN RIGHTS TO HUMAN SECURITY

While human rights may be, as former U.S. national security adviser Zbigniew Brzezinski noted, "the single most magnetic political idea of the contemporary time,"[30] other transnational issues are also emergent—and those issues, like human rights, impinge directly on human security.

Discussion Questions

1. Which rights do you think should have priority? Political-civil rights? Socioeconomic rights? Collective rights of groups? Why?

2. Find two newspaper articles that provide examples of state officials abusing the rights of their citizens. Do these citizens have any recourse?

3. Genocide is sometimes difficult to prove. Choose a specific case of state-sponsored violence (e.g., Turkey against the Armenians; Sudan against the Darfurians; or the Assad government in Syria against its citizens). Does the violence qualify as genocide? What evidence would you have to collect to answer that question?

4. If you were a woman whose human rights were being abused, what avenues of recourse might you use to make your case?

5. How can R2P be stated in more concrete terms so that it is clearer when the international community should intervene—and when it should not (in the name of preserving state sovereignty)?

Key Terms

crimes against humanity (p. 386)

cultural relativism (p. 368)

genocide (p. 384)

humanitarian intervention (p. 395)

International Bill of Rights (p. 371)

international humanitarian law (p. 370)

responsibility to protect (R2P) (p. 395)

After their boat was in distress, refugees from Syria, Eritrea, and Libya were rescued off the Libyan border by a ship headed for Italy. The increase in migration has resulted in heightened dangers for migrants on overcrowded boats.

11

Human Security: Migration, Global Health, and the Environment

In the first four months of 2017, almost 25,000 people landed in Italy, successfully completing a perilous journey across the Mediterranean Sea from Libya. This was a 30 percent increase from the previous year. Also increasing was the number of people dying in transit. In the first three months of 2017, one out of 30 persons died due to flimsy, overcrowded boats lacking in adequate provisions. Who were these travelers? They were mostly economic migrants fleeing from sub-Saharan African countries like Senegal, Sierra Leone, and Somalia, and refugees fleeing persecution in Eritrea and Sudan.

These people are but a small fraction of the estimated 65 million people displaced by war, internal conflicts, drought, or poor economic conditions. In a globalized world, we witness this human migration and the accompanying tragedies in a way never seen by

Conceptual Perspectives

Two conceptual perspectives help us think critically about the interrelation of environmental issues. These perspectives augment each other. First is the notion of collective goods. (See Chapter 9.) Collective goods help us conceptualize how to achieve shared benefits that depend on overcoming conflicting individual interests. How can individual herders in the commons be convinced to abridge their own self-interest (which is for each to increase the number of sheep he or she allows to graze on the commons) in the interest of preserving the commons for the collectivity? How can individual polluters of the global air and water commons be likewise convinced to abridge their self-interest to preserve these commons for the collectivity? One difficulty is that our most influential economic theories—rooted in Adam Smith's *Wealth of Nations*, published in 1776—had their origins at a time when the global air, sea, and natural resource commons seemed infinite. Yet by the close of the nineteenth century, this seemingly infinite supply of space and resources had become bounded. Since the end of World War II, we have come to understand that our planet itself is a commons, and as such, we must reassess the collective impact of our individual self-interests.

The second conceptual perspective is sustainability, or sustainable development, introduced in Chapter 8. Sustainability is a crucial perspective because it helps us think about advancing our survival and welfare without doing lasting damage to our environment and thereby abridging the health and welfare of our descendants. As a conceptual perspective, then, sustainability reminds us that it is possible, desirable, and even necessary to value the future quality of the earth's air, water, and land. Both perspectives underline the most fundamental problem facing those committed to slowing and ultimately reversing damage to the global ecosystem: because the costs of harm to the environment are diffused across both space and time, and the benefits of pollution and unsustainable resource consumption are concentrated, each individual state, corporation, or person has a strong incentive to enjoy a "free ride" and hope others will bear the costs of restraint. A pernicious logic takes root: if we install pollution controls, our competitors who did not will achieve a competitive edge. Furthermore, free-riding and cheating are very difficult to detect and monitor; worse still, the effects of cheating may last for years, even after it has been detected and halted, as explained in Chapter 7.

But, as in the example of the grazing commons, real-world evidence of harm has forced today's "farmers" to acknowledge an interest in acting to slow or halt further damage to our shared air, water, and land resources. The influence of this evidence is why principles and norms concerning the environment have evolved considerably in customary international law in the past few decades. One core principle is the *no significant harm principle*, meaning a state cannot initiate policies that cause significant environmental damages to another state. Another is the *good neighbor principle* of cooperation. Beyond these are soft-law principles, often expressed in conferences, declarations, or resolutions, which, although currently nonbinding, often informally describe acceptable norms of behavior. These include the *polluter pays principle* (those causing the pollution should be responsible for cleaning it up, or curtailing it), the *precautionary principle* (action should be taken based on scientific warning before irreversible harm occurs), and the *preventive action principle* (states should take action in their own jurisdictions). New emerging principles include sustainable development and intergenerational equity, both linking economics and the environment to future generations.

The level of attention accorded to the environment is reflected in the international treaties and agreements that have been ratified on a host of different issues. These include the protection of natural resources, such as endangered species of wild fauna and flora, tropical timber, natural waterways and lakes, migratory species of wild animals, and biological diversity in general, as well as protection against polluting in marine environments, on land, and in the air. Each of these treaties sets standards for state behavior, and some provide monitoring mechanisms. These treaties are controversial because they affect core political, economic, and human rights interests, and because, ultimately, individual states must guarantee them, even in circumstances wherein abiding by the treaty means a short-term cost or missed opportunity.

By studying three key environmental topics—pollution and climate change, natural resources, and population—we can see how interests in economic development, promoting human rights, and protecting the environment often conflict. Although each topic may be treated separately, and often is, they are all integrally related, and each affects human security.

Pollution and Climate Change

As pressures on the global commons mount, the quality of geographic space diminishes. In the 1950s and 1960s, several events dramatically publicized the deteriorating quality of the commons. The oceanographer Jacques Cousteau warned of the degradation of the ocean, a warning made prescient by the 1967 Torrey Canyon oil spill off the coast of England. Rachel Carson's best-selling 1962 book *Silent Spring* warned of the impact of pesticides and chemicals on the environment.[13] Carson highlighted the paradoxical effect of pesticides such as DDT—which could dramatically reduce the spread of diseases like malaria, but at the same time devastated the reproductive cycle of wildfowl and ultimately caused cancer in humans. Millions of Americans and many others worldwide, who had never thought about the links between pesticides, the ecosystem, and human health outcomes, were suddenly aware of these connections and became concerned about the damage. More people became aware that human activity associated with agricultural and industrial practices was degrading the natural world, and that humans do not exist separately from the natural world. They saw that economic development in agriculture and industry has **negative externalities**—costly unintended consequences—for everyone, as well as positive consequences like job and wealth creation.

China's rapid development provides an example of negative externalities. Its desire for energy has led to increased coal usage. Coal-burning power plants emit soot, toxic chemicals, and gases, which, with weather inversions, create air pollution not only over China, neighboring Korea, and Japan but also over the west coast of the United States. These sulfur dioxide emissions carry known health risks, including respiratory and heart disease and certain kinds of cancer. In addition, the small particle aerosols that come from the burning of coal are shown to produce haze, which scatters sunlight and affects rainfall, leading to frequent and more severe droughts. China and other countries are now taking critical initiatives to replace polluting power plants, but air pollution alerts in major Chinese cities are frequent and the hypothesized effects on rainfall may affect many countries in Asia and Africa that are dependent on rain-fed agriculture.

Nothing affects our globe more than the pollution issues of the twenty-first century: ozone depletion and global warming. Both concern pollution in spaces that belong to no single state. Both result from negative externalities associated with rising levels of economic development. Both pit groups of states against one another. Both have been the subjects of highly contested international negotiations. And both directly affect the quality of human life and the chances for human survival.

Ozone Depletion and Global Warming

Thrust onto the international agenda in 1975, the issue of ozone depletion is a relative success story of international cooperation. States recognized an environmental problem—that global emissions of chlorofluorocarbons (CFCs), concentrated in the polar regions, has led to a thinning of the ozone layer over the earth. Strong measures were needed. Both developed and developing countries became involved, with the latter receiving financial aid from the former to finance changes in technology. Substitutes for CFCs were developed, and multinational corporations eventually supported the prohibition of CFCs in the 1987 Montreal Protocol on Substances That Deplete the Ozone Layer. As a result, the depletion of the ozone layer was reversed. The story is in part a success story; consumption of ozone-depleting substances has dropped 75 percent since the Montreal Protocol. Outside the polar zones, the ozone layer is recovering, but at the poles, the loss is variable. Complete recovery could take decades after the harm has stopped. But that success has had an unintended consequence. CFCs were replaced with manmade hydrofluorocarbons (HFCs). While those do not deplete the ozone and last for only a short time, they do contribute to global warming.

The issue of global climate change has proved much more complicated. There are no inexpensive substitutes for agricultural, communications, and industrial processes that emit greenhouse gases; the costs of reducing emissions are high and must be paid now, while the benefits are diffuse and may only emerge after decades. But scientific facts are indisputable. The preponderance of greenhouse gas emissions comes from the burning of fossil fuels in the industrialized countries of the North, and increasingly from China and India's growing use of fossil fuels. Greenhouse gases are also emitted by the developing countries, most notably from deforestation of the tropics for agriculture and the timber industry (see Figure 11.3). These greenhouse emissions have consequences.

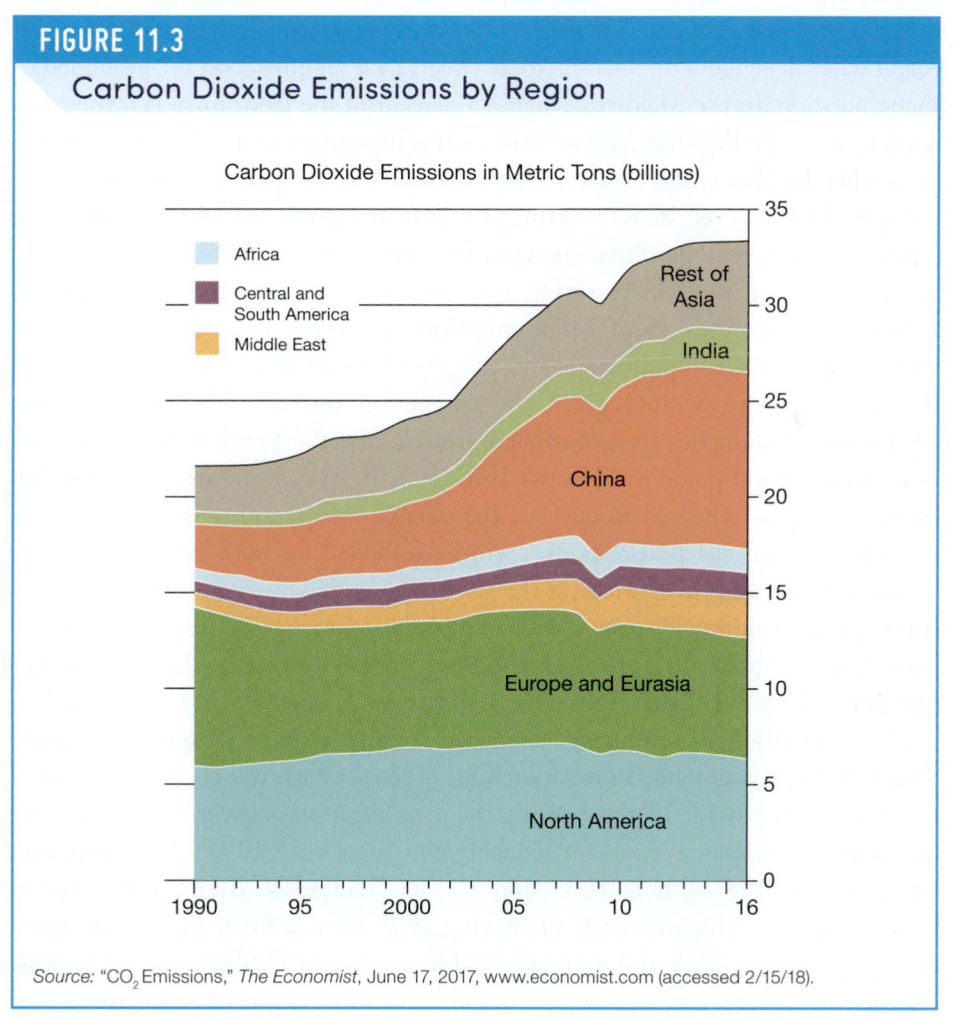

FIGURE 11.3

Carbon Dioxide Emissions by Region

Carbon Dioxide Emissions in Metric Tons (billions)

Africa
Central and South America
Middle East

Rest of Asia
India
China
Europe and Eurasia
North America

Source: "CO$_2$ Emissions," *The Economist*, June 17, 2017, www.economist.com (accessed 2/15/18).

The earth is warming, with an increase of between 1.9 and 3 degrees Celsius estimated by the end of the twenty-first century, relative to temperatures recorded between 1986 and 2005. "The atmosphere and ocean have warmed, the amounts of snow and ice have diminished, sea level has risen, and the concentrations of greenhouse gases have increased," the Intergovernmental Panel on Climate Change reported in 2013. A year later, the same group affirmed once again that the human influence on climate change is clear.[14] The scientific community finds the evidence compelling. Glaciers and sea ice are melting, oceans are becoming acidified, and unusual weather events like hurricanes and floods are occurring more frequently.

The scientific fact of climate change has a human cost. Small island states and states with low elevations near the seas already see their land subsiding and their national territory shrinking; their populations are experiencing higher rates of waterborne diseases, due to increased temperatures and changes in rainfall. For small island states dependent on tourism, these effects have an impact on the livelihood of the population. In the Maldives, where 95 percent of the labor force is involved in tourism, or in the Bahamas, where 70 percent is dependent on tourism, tourists stay away when beaches erode, coral reefs are polluted, and the quality of drinking water declines. And sea level rise is occurring at 1.22 inches per decade. At that rate, up to 2 billion people could be climate refugees from rising seas by 2100.

Although scientists increasingly agree on the problem—that contemporary industrial, agricultural, and communications processes have strongly accelerated global warming—politicians and economists struggle to find solutions. This struggle is not surprising, given the competing interests of various parties. Industrialized countries seek continued growth, and the South wants to become industrialized and enjoy the North's consumer lifestyle; both are made possible by converting oil and gas to energy. The parties disagree on whether voluntary restraints or market-based responses will be sufficient for both "worlds" to reach their economic objectives while at the same time reducing greenhouse emissions (that is, achieve *sustainable* growth). If the global response proves insufficient, might authoritative regulations be needed, and if so, what authority should be invoked to monitor and enforce them—international, state level, subnational, or even local?

The international community has made several attempts to respond to climate change through negotiated state action. One of those efforts was the Kyoto Protocol of 1997, which provided for stabilizing the concentration of greenhouse gases and delineated international goals for reducing emissions by 2010. The protocol came into force in 2005, without U.S. support. The George W. Bush administration argued that the economic costs of moving away from a fossil fuel–based economy would be too high and an unacceptable number of U.S. jobs would be lost. Furthermore, India and China were not obligated to cut greenhouse gases under

Kyoto, as they were classified as developing countries. In the Bush administration's view, this gave these states an unfair economic advantage. U.S. views, however, began to change as the private sector realized that climate change was affecting their operations and that the transition to a "green economy" could be economically beneficial as well as socially responsible. And the U.S. military has acted to cut greenhouse emissions, in recognition of the growing security threats that rising sea levels pose for the vulnerability of people and critical food supplies. Some kind of new approach was necessary.

European states and Japan did sign the Kyoto Protocol and established the EU Emissions Trading System as a way to reduce industrial greenhouse gas emissions. States that use less than their allowance may sell credits to others that are not meeting their obligations. However, with the economic recession and the Eurozone crisis, demand for the permits has dropped, and there is oversupply in the carbon market.

Three lines of thinking have emerged from difficulties with Kyoto. First, perhaps by seeking a comprehensive global treaty, the individuals, groups, states, and coalitions of states seeking to slow, halt, and reverse global warming have aimed too high. As Robert Keohane and David Victor have argued, perhaps what is needed is a kind of middle ground that focuses on key parts of the climate change problem rather than the whole.[15] Many have concluded that the process of trying to accomplish many goals simultaneously is impractical and dysfunctional. Thus, negotiators have examined issues in a piecemeal fashion for about a decade. Forests were the priority in 2008, with states agreeing to get credit for saving forests; a fund was established to help poor countries adapt. Technology and financing were the topics in 2009, when the parties agreed to focus on new technologies and increase financing to mitigate the effects of climate change.

A second approach has been to get the top three emitters—China (the top emitter), the United States, and India—to come to agreement. In 2013, India agreed to take on legally binding obligations, but not until after 2020, fearful that such obligations would inhibit growth. In late 2014, China agreed for the first time to stop its emissions from growing by 2030, and the United States announced new targets for reducing carbon emissions. These commitments proved to be a critical impetus for commitments by other states in the 2015 UN climate change talks. These events showed the key importance of top-level leadership taking the initiative.

For still others, given the reality of global warming and the likely continued failure of efforts to slow or halt it, a third approach is to shift resources into preparing for and remediating its effects. For example, 80 percent of the world's population lives near a coastline and some states are already vulnerable, so mitigation efforts must, and are, becoming a major priority; neighborhoods have been evacuated and seawalls constructed. The Netherlands has made major strides in adopting unique approaches, not only constructing walls, but also using less concrete to permit water seepage and constructing reservoirs and parking garages for alternative water storage. However, for vulnerable poorer states, the financial costs of these kinds of initiatives are too high.

In December 2015, following two weeks of intensive negotiations, the 195 participants in the Paris climate change talks reached an accord replacing the Kyoto Protocol. By this time, the effects of climate change on humans were being felt, not just on small island states, as noted above, but more generally. Then French president François Hollande expressed the urgency: "Never have the stakes been so high because this is about the future of the planet, the future of life."[16] In a grand bargain, states agreed in the Paris Agreement to keep the increase in global average temperature to "well below" 2 degrees Celsius and to pursue efforts to limit warming to 1.5 degrees Celsius. The targets essential to reach that goal are aspirational: abandoning fossil fuels by 2050 *and* supporting growth in renewable sources of energy. States agreed to both curb the emission of greenhouse gases and promote carbon-absorbing sinks like forests. And perhaps most importantly, states agreed to a process to ensure transparency and accountability by publishing climate plans every five years, beginning in 2020. While the submission of plans is mandatory, meeting the targets is not legally binding. Finally, participants agreed that key developed countries should take the lead. In the end, what made the Paris Agreement possible was the earlier negotiations between the United States and China, whereby China agreed to curb its emissions over the long term. In addition, the developed countries agreed to support the efforts of developing countries to mitigate climate change, with a $100 billion Green Climate Fund. The agreement entered into force in 2016.

Global warming and climate change are not solved by this agreement, but supporters assert that a structure now exists to tackle the problem in an effective way. However, the decision in 2017 by U.S. president Donald Trump to withdraw from the Paris Agreement and to not continue financial support for the climate fund represents a setback. Since the agreement is not a treaty under American law, the president has the authority to make that decision; however, there is a "waiting period," so the soonest withdrawal would be in 2020. The administration's rationale is based on domestic factors: it asserts that American jobs are negatively affected by the agreement; the "imposed" regulations undermine American energy independence; and payments to the climate fund are wasteful.

Critics of the U.S. decision to withdraw both dispute the domestic rationale and point to the troubling international implications. Withdrawal by the United States, the world's second-largest emitter of greenhouse gases, undercuts the collective effort to reduce emissions and make the transition to a renewable energy future. And backsliding by the United States may lead others to reduce their commitment. Clearly, U.S. leadership on the issue is being jeopardized and some fear new leadership will be exercised by China and Europe, displacing the United States.

The Trump administration is confronting strong support for the agreement from those in the business community who are already heavily invested in green technology, from civil society actors including environmental NGOs, and from numerous private transnational regulatory organizations like the Carbon Disclosure Project, the Climate Bonds Initiative, the Sustainable Forestry Initiative, and the Global Reporting Initiative. Operating through markets, these coalitions of business and civil society are writing and implementing key voluntary rules on carbon emissions, green buildings, and environmental disclosure.[17] Key substate advocates are among the strongest supporters of the Paris Agreement. California, itself the world's sixth-largest economy, has already taken aggressive action to reduce emissions, increase the use of renewable energy sources, and push for tougher automobile emission standards, joining with 34 other states, including New York and Massachusetts. And these states are forging memos of understanding with Mexico, Canada, and various provinces of Canada and working with governments of other Paris Agreement members like China. Along with comparable activities in Europe, these institutional forums provide support for the agreement, even without the participation of the current U.S. administration.

Climate change clearly will continue to be a high-priority agenda item across a wide spectrum of state interests, including economic development and national security. Climate change is an issue that brings with it both very real threats and opportunities in the twenty-first century, and any efforts to counter climate change will proceed slowly.

Natural Resource Issues

The belief in the infinite supply of natural resources was not unreasonable throughout much of human history, as people migrated to uninhabited or only sparsely inhabited lands. Trading for natural resources became a mainstay of economic activity once people recognized that natural resources were not uniformly distributed. Radical Marxist thinkers challenged the assumption of an infinite supply of key economic resources. According to Lenin, one of the reasons for imperialism was the inevitable quest for new sources of raw materials. Capitalist states depended on overseas markets *and* resources, precisely because resources are unevenly distributed. From this assertion, Lenin also drew his explanation for why imperialism necessarily resulted in war: capitalist states would be compelled to use armed force to secure the natural resources their factories demanded.

Nowadays, we are keenly aware that natural resources *are* limited and that states do compete for resources. The example of freshwater, linked to pollution, climate change, and population, helps highlight the importance of natural resources as a transnational issue.

Perhaps the most crucial transnational resource issue is freshwater because it is necessary for all forms of life—human, animal, and plant. Only 3 percent of the earth's water is fresh (one-third lower than in 1970). Freshwater is political because it is unevenly distributed; by 2050, the global demand for fresh water is predicted to increase by 40 percent and one quarter of the world's population will live in countries facing moderate or severe water-shortage problems. Others live in states with abundant supplies. Water is also unequally used: agriculture accounts for about two-thirds of the use of water, industry about one-quarter, and human consumption slightly less than one-tenth. But 1.1 billion people have no access to improved drinking water, and one-third of those live in Africa. Climate change is apt to make the situation worse since 70 percent of the world's total supply of freshwater is leaking away from the polar ice caps. And some new technologies may be using freshwater faster than it is replenished, leading to unanticipated consequences. The use of water as an aid to natural gas and petroleum extraction (a process most commonly known as "fracking") threatens shortages in some locales and has caused contamination issues.

Three examples illustrate the international controversies and repercussions of the limited supply of freshwater. First, the Middle East has long been an area where freshwater is a contested resource. Since the 1960s, Israel has adopted methods to preserve scarce water resources, adopting drip irrigation, recycling 86 percent of its wastewater, and piping water long distances from the north to the parched Mediterranean coast. And the country has been a leader in desalination: now one-third of the country's drinking water comes from seawater. But that does little to help the Palestinians on the West Bank as they are not connected to Israel's water grid. With a doubling of the population, Palestinians have access to less than the amount recommended. The situation is dire in the Gaza Strip, where the shortfall is exacerbated by inadequate infrastructure, resulting in polluted water. There is no solution to the water crisis in either the West Bank or Gaza without Israel's participation.

A second conflict over water surrounds Ethiopia's Grand Renaissance Dam, scheduled for completion in 2019. It will be Africa's largest hydropower dam, encompassing 685 square miles. Egypt, the downstream state, relies totally on the waters of the Nile River, and is not pleased by the anticipated lower river flows. With agriculture threatened, Egypt sees access to river water as an issue of national security. Under an agreement reached during the colonial era, Egypt and Sudan got most of the Nile's waters for their own use, while Ethiopia was cut out of that arrangement. The Grand Renaissance Dam would change that historic allocation. No wonder during 2013 talks on the issue, Egyptian authorities reported that Egypt was keeping all options open. While not calling for war, Egypt has made it clear that its water security cannot be violated; the livelihood of its population is at stake.

The third example involves the Mekong River, where the story is much the same. With its origins in Tibet, the river serves as the rice bowl and fishing grounds for the inhabitants along its banks in Myanmar, Laos, Thailand, Cambodia, and Vietnam. But the construction of five hydropower dams in China (with 14 more planned) affects the rate of flow along the river, the balance of its nutrients, and the quality of the water reaching downstream users. And the lower Mekong Delta itself is experiencing rising seawater, which threatens crops and fields, making farming impossible. Demand for freshwater resources increases as the population increases.

Population Dynamics

Recognition of the potential world population problem occurred centuries ago. In 1798, Thomas Malthus posited a key relationship. If population grows unchecked, it will increase at a geometric rate (1, 2, 4, 8, . . .), whereas food resources will increase at an arithmetic rate (1, 2, 3, 4, . . .). Very quickly, he postulated, population increases will outstrip food production. This scenario is called the **Malthusian dilemma.** Although Malthus did not think productivity would keep up with population growth rates, he did acknowledge wars, famine, or moral restraint as ways to check excessive population.[18] Three centuries later, *The Limits to Growth*, an independent report issued by the Club of Rome in 1972, systematically investigated trends in population, agricultural production, natural resource use, and industrial production—as well as pollution and the intricate feedback loops that link these trends. Its conclusion was pessimistic: the earth would reach natural limits to population growth within a relatively short time.[19]

Neither Malthus nor the Club of Rome proved to be correct. Malthus did not foresee the technological changes that would lead to much higher rates of food production, nor did he predict the **demographic transition**—a situation in which population growth rates would not proceed unchecked. Although improvements in economic development led at first to lower death rates and hence to a greater population increase, over time, as the lives of individuals improved, women became more educated, people moved to urban areas, and birthrates dropped dramatically. The advent of safe, reliable birth-control technologies also led to a decline in birthrates. Likewise, the Club of Rome's predictions proved too pessimistic, as technological change stretched resources beyond the limits predicted in its 1972 report. Although Malthus and the Club of Rome missed some key trends, their prediction that the world's population would increase dramatically has proved correct. The population has increased from 800 million in 1776 to 7.5 billion in 2017. The UN estimates that by 2100 the global population will reach 11.2 billion; that prediction suggests that the rate of growth will decline. In fact, the relative rate of growth of the world's population has declined much faster than expected. But several key observations make population and population growth rates cause for concern.

First, the population increase is not uniformly distributed. Women in Africa averaged 4.7 births in 2016; in Asia and Latin America, 2.2 births; in North America, 1.9 births; and in Europe 1.6 births. Clearly, a significant demographic divide exists between the rich with low population growth rates and the poorer states, particularly in Africa, with higher population growth rates. These divides have politically sensitive consequences, as poor states labor under the burden of the population explosion while attempting to meet the economic consumption standards of North America and Europe.

Realists see two threats emerging from these demographic trends that could destabilize the balance of power. First, states with burgeoning populations and insufficient food might seek to expand their territory or acquire food by means of war. Second, surplus males, who might otherwise turn to domestic crime or destabilize the state from within, might be channeled into state militaries and "expended" in aggressive interstate wars. Radicals see these possibilities as confirming that the South needs economic development for more than simply material needs. Liberal feminists would argue that whenever economic life improves (especially when that improvement has resulted from greater educational and workplace opportunities for women), women tend to have fewer and healthier babies, more of whom survive to adulthood. As a state's economic fortunes improve, so does access to health care and family planning. Better education for parents and their children, in turn, opens more economic opportunity, and the cycle reinforces itself. Thus, closing the development gap leads to a self-reinforcing spiral of economic improvement and demographic balance.

In addition, rapid rates of overall population growth and high levels of economic development mean increased demands for natural resources—in particular, arable land and freshwater. For countries that already have large populations, such as China, India, and Bangladesh, the problem is severe. In Bangladesh and Nepal, the growing population is forced onto increasingly marginal land. In Nepal, human settlements at higher elevations have resulted in deforestation, as people cut down trees for fuel, leading to hillside erosion, landslides, and other "natural" disasters. In Bangladesh, population pressures have led to settlements on deltas, which are vulnerable to monsoonal flooding; this settlement strips topsoil, decreases agricultural productivity, and, especially when coupled with rising seawaters, dislocates millions of individuals. That is one of the reasons that Bangladeshis seek refuge in India.

Accelerating demand for natural resources occurs in the developed world as well. As the smaller (even slightly declining) population becomes more economically affluent, it demands more energy and resources to support higher standards of living—more living space, larger houses, and more highways. Wealthier people, especially those in the United States, also produce more garbage per person than in the developing world, and much is not recycled, leading to a high demand for domestic landfill space and a profitable business in exporting garbage to the developing world.

High population growth rates lead to numerous ethical dilemmas for state and international policy makers. How can state economic growth rates be sustained without an increasing population? After all, the number of people matters for economic growth. How can population growth rates be curbed without leading to a reduction in state growth and without infringing on individual rights to procreate? How can developed countries promote lower birthrates in the developing world without sounding racist or ethnocentric and without jeopardizing the economic growth necessary to move people out of poverty? Can policies be developed that both improve the standards of living for those already born and guarantee equally high standards and improvements for our descendants?

Population becomes a classic collective-goods problem. It is eminently rational for a couple in the developing world to have more children: children provide valuable labor and often earn money in the wage economy, contributing to family well-being. Children are the social safety net for families in societies where no governmental programs exist. But what is economically rational for each couple is not environmentally sustainable for the collectivity. The amount of land in the commons shrinks on a per capita basis, and the overall quality of the resource declines. Over time, the finite resources of the commons have a decreasing capacity to support the population: Adam Smith's famous "invisible hand," when considered in the context of a commons, may therefore lead not to collective benefit but to collective disaster.

What actions can be taken with respect to population to alleviate or mitigate these dilemmas? The biologist Garrett Hardin's solution, using coercion to prohibit procreation, is politically untenable and pragmatically difficult, as China discovered with its one-child policy. Relying on group pressure to force individual changes in behavior is also unlikely to work in the populous states.[20] Leaving coercion aside, even if individuals may desire smaller families, family-planning methods may be unavailable to them.

The Dilemmas of Population Decline

As in the global environment, the connections, causes, and consequences of global population growth and decline have proven not only interlinked but also complex. In many Western states, including Europe and Russia, as well as in Japan, Korea, and China, not only has population growth slowed, but it is also in decline, and the population is aging. These regions all share a remarkable trend of increasing women's access to education and career employment outside the home. As a result, one of the world's most powerful demographic trends—women are having fewer babies and having babies later in life—can be explained by the extraordinary demands of education and career. The aggregation of these individually rational decisions is a declining birthrate. In China, this dramatic decline may have been due not to individual choice but to the government policy of one child per couple instituted in 1978. But in 2015, China rescinded the one-child policy, recognizing the deleterious economic consequences of a declining population. Rather ironically, Chinese fertility rates were already declining before the one-child policy, and lifting the restriction on the number of children is not having the desired effect. In 2017, the number of births in China fell. By the end of 2100, the Chinese population may well fall below 1 billion for the first time since 1980. Over one-half of the world is now below the population replacement level.

In China and India as well, the problem is also a surplus of males, since males are still preferred for cultural reasons and sex-selective abortions have become increasingly common. From 2010 to 2015, the sex ratio at birth was 116 boys to 100 girls in China and 111 boys to 100 girls in India, above the 105 to 100 natural ratio. As soon as 2020, China is expected to have 30 million more men than women of the same age, leading to what is called the "marriage squeeze." This imbalance, referred to locally as "bare branches," leads to prostitution and the sale of brides, and, some scholars suggest, actually threatens domestic and international security.[21] In these countries, there is some evidence that sex selection appears to be declining as government policies support prizing girls.

In Russia, characterized by one demographer as a "demographic disaster," there has been a steep decline in population, due to a combination of two decades of dramatic underinvestment in health care and education, widespread alcoholism, and heart disease. This decline has occurred despite significant immigration into Russia from the Central Asian states.[22] This not only slows state economic growth but also weakens state power, as population size is one indicator of that power.

One exception to the pattern of population growth decline is the Nordic countries (in particular Norway and Sweden), where parental leave and strongly enforced anti-discrimination policies make it possible for women to avoid having to choose between becoming mothers and obtaining higher education and lifetime employment.

What is clear about world population growth and decline, and the disparities among regions, is that the problems and opportunities they create are international. Decisions affect not just states with high rates of population growth but also their neighbors, as people on overcrowded land contend for scarce resources, seek a better life in other countries through migration, or may turn to violence to get more desirable space.

States are not the only actors affected by population pressures: this issue affects individuals, couples, and communities, along with their deepest-held religious and humanistic values. Population pressures also involve the nongovernmental community, including groups such as Population Connection and the Population

Council that try to change public attitudes about population and procreation, as well as the Catholic church and fundamentalist Islamic sects that oppose artificial restrictions on family size. And they involve intergovernmental organizations such as the World Bank, charged with promoting sustainable development and yet hamstrung by the wishes of some member states to refrain from directly addressing the population issue. Perhaps most important, the population issue intersects inextricably with other environmental issues. Populations put demands on land use for enhanced agricultural productivity; they need natural resources and energy resources. Thus, ironically, population may well be the pivotal global environmental issue, but it may also be the one that states and other international actors can do the least about resolving.

Environmental NGOs in Action

Nongovernmental organizations (NGOs) have played a vital role in environmental issues since the 1960s. Their numbers have grown, and their interests are diverse. They range from the Nature Conservancy and the Rainforest Action Network to the Earth Island Institute and the Climate Coalition.

Human action has caused significant damage to our environment, but the political response has rarely proved commensurate with the harm. Many well-intentioned efforts, like cleaning landfills, fail to address the larger problems of overconsumption and pollution of natural resources.

NGOs perform a number of key functions in environmental affairs. First, they often act as international critics, using the media to publicize their dissatisfaction and get environmental issues onto international and state agendas. For example, Greenpeace's condemnation of Brazil's unsustainable cutting of mahogany trees led that country to stop all mahogany exports until forestry practices could be improved. Second, NGOs may function through intergovernmental organizations, working to change the organizations from within. For example, NGOs transformed the International Whaling Commission from a body that limited whaling through quotas into one that banned whale hunting altogether. Third, NGOs can aid in monitoring and enforcing environmental regulations, by either pointing out problems or actually carrying out onsite inspections. For example, TRAFFIC, the wildlife-trade-monitoring program of the World Wide Fund for Nature and the International Union for Conservation of Nature (IUCN), is authorized to conduct inspections under the Convention on International Trade in Endangered Species of Wild Fauna and Flora (CITES). Fourth, NGOs may function as part of transnational communities of experts, serving with counterparts in intergovernmental organizations and state agencies to try to change practices and procedures on an issue. One such epistemic community formed around the Mediterranean Action Plan of the UN Environment Programme. Experts gathered to discuss ways to improve the quality of seawater, share data, and, ultimately, establish monitoring programs. These same individuals also became active in domestic-bargaining processes, fostering learning among government elites. Finally, and perhaps most important, NGOs can attempt to influence state environmental policy directly, providing information about policy options, sometimes initiating legal proceedings, and lobbying directly to a state's legislature or bureaucracy. For climate change, several epistemic communities have been active. Yet in the long run, despite the increased roles of NGOs and epistemic communities, it is still states that have primary responsibility for taking action.

Contending Perspectives on the Environment

What has made many environmental issues so politically controversial at the international level is that states have tended to divide along the developed/developing—North/South—economic axis (although some developed states have been more accommodating than others). From the perspective of some in the developed world, many environmental issues appear to stem from the population explosion, which they take to be a problem of the developing world, and furthermore, a problem over which governments in those parts of the world have some control. In this view, the developing world's governments must enact policies that slow population growth rates, leading to a decrease in the pressure on scarce natural resources and diminishing the negative externality of pollution locally, regionally, and internationally.

States of the developing South perceive the environmental issue differently. They correctly point to the fact that many environmental problems—including the overuse of natural resources and the pollution issues of ozone depletion and greenhouse gas emissions—are the result of the industrial world's excesses. By exploiting the environment in an unsustainable way, by misusing the commons, the developed countries were able to achieve high levels of—depending upon one's point of view—either economic development or consumption. Putting restrictions on developing countries by not allowing them to exploit their natural resources or by limiting their use of fossil fuels may impede their development. Thus, because the developed states have been responsible for most of the environmental excesses, it is they who should bear the burden of reduced energy consumption and environmental cleanup.

The challenge in addressing transnational environmental issues is to negotiate a middle ground that reflects the reality that both sides are, in fact, correct. High population growth rates are a problem in the South—one that will not be alleviated until higher levels of economic development are achieved. Overuse of natural resources is primarily a problem of the North. Powerful economic interests in the North are continually reminding us that changes in resource use may lead to a lower standard of living. An offshoot of both problems is pollution, which in the South stems primarily from land- and water-resource overuse due to excessive population, and in the North stems primarily from the by-products and negative externalities of industrialization. Thus, more than the other transnational issues, environmental issues involve trade-offs between economic interests and environmental sustainability.

Realists, liberals, and constructivists do not all have the same degree of concern for environmental issues, although each group has modified its perspectives in response to changing conditions. Realists' principal emphasis has been on state security, although some have identified human security concerns. Both types of security require a healthy and strong population, near self-sufficiency in food, and a dependable supply of natural resources. Making the costs of natural resources or the costs of pollution abatement too high diminishes a state's ability to make independent decisions. So, for example, Iceland's dependency on cod fishing as an industry made it much more vulnerable both to unsustainable harvesting practices by its own fisheries and those of Britain and the United States and to global warming, which has caused cod populations to move to deeper or more northerly waters. The implication is that for countries like Iceland, sovereignty is necessarily abridged, and the security of Iceland's citizens cannot be guaranteed by the state.

The Environment: A View from Indonesia

Agricultural production, forestry, and mining are all key sectors in the economy of Indonesia, an archipelago nation of 5,000 islands and approximately 261 million people. The islands, a center of biodiversity, support the world's third-largest rain forest and peatland. Over 20 million indigenous people live in these fragile lands, depending on the nontimber forest products for their livelihood.

The Indonesian government is committed to the country's economic development, using the capital from domestic and foreign-owned companies to invest in plantations for producing export crops like palm oil, timber products such as wood and paper, and minerals. The deforestation, second only to that of Brazil, and the burning of peatlands have led to serious clashes among groups and have had major environmental consequences in both Indonesia and neighboring countries. The Indonesian government recognizes the problem.

Deforestation has significant consequences for the environment: soil is eroded; crops are incapable of regeneration; and animal species are lost and biodiversity is threatened. And in Indonesia, deforestation is often accompanied by burning of the ancient peatlands, an estimated 12 percent of Indonesia's territory. This led to massive forest fires in 1987, 1994, 1997–98, 2005–2006, 2012, 2015, and 2017. The 2015 fires and the accompanying haze cost Indonesia $16.1 billion in losses. Schools and hospitals were closed; over the long term, an estimated 100,000 people will die prematurely due to smoke inhalation from the 2015 fires. The fires resulted in haze over Indonesia as well as neighboring Malaysia, Thailand, and Singapore, causing a regional crisis—a condition referred to as "the new normal."

In addition, deforestation and burning of peatlands lead to an increase in greenhouse gas emissions and contribute to global warming for three reasons. First, the carbon from burned trees rises into the atmosphere. Second, while alive, the trees are a major carbon sink, meaning they absorb more carbon than they release; this benefit is lost when the trees are cut down. Third, the peatlands are a carbon-rich environment, and the carbon is released through burning. The country is already one of the world's largest emitters of greenhouse gases, releasing the amount of carbon dioxide equivalent to the annual emissions of Great Britain. As the Indonesian government now acknowledges, the future projections are even more troubling. A reputable study published in *Nature* in 2013 predicts that by 2029 Indonesia will be one of the first developing tropical countries to feel the direct effects of climate change. Rice production and fisheries will decline; flooding along the 50,000 miles of coastline will increase; and intense storms and saltwater intrusion will deplete agricultural and forest resources.[a]

Indonesia has an increasingly strong national interest in slowing down deforestation and burning and thus reducing its greenhouse emissions. The central government has made restoration of peatlands a priority and has banned activity on some peatlands. Monitoring of these sites has improved. But that does not appear to be sufficient, as the economic imperatives of development and of the interest of large corporations take precedence. And the government does not have the capacity to closely monitor the activities on this vast archipelago.

Beyond the regional and international dimensions of the deforestation problem, the

Burning of peatlands and clearing forested land for export agriculture has resulted in severe air pollution and contributes to climate change.

Indonesian government must also remain sensitive to the human security needs of its poorest population. Many of the forest-dependent communities clash with national authorities over the forest's use. Decentralization of control, urged in part to respect the wishes of forest-dependent communities and advocated by the World Bank, has created new loci of corruption as local governments fight businesses and each other regarding how to best use forest resources.

Such clashes can also be seen in the mining sector, a significant earner of foreign exchange. Gold, copper, and coal are mined throughout Indonesia and are viewed by government officials as a vital part of the country's economic development. To extract the highest profits, mining companies often disregard environmental protocols, resulting in polluted water, air, and topsoil. In 2006, Newmont Mining Corporation, a U.S.-based gold producer, paid Indonesia $30 million in a settlement to compensate for emitting toxic mercury vapors into the air. Other mining clashes involve the world's largest gold mine, owned by American mining company Freeport-McMoRan; there have been conflicts between the government and the company for years. In 2017, an agreement was reached; the company would transfer to Indonesia a 51 percent stake in the mine and would build more smelters in the country to create more jobs.

Countervailing pressures continue to advocate for greater environmental protection. Many of Indonesia's 3,000 NGOs work on deforestation, conflicts over natural resources, preservation of coastal and marine resources, and climate change issues. Indonesian-based umbrella NGOs like WALHI and Siemenpuu publicize abuses and institute legal proceedings, frequently teaming with international NGOs such as the World Wide Fund for Nature and Greenpeace to establish more sustainable environmental initiatives. In general, these groups contend that the Indonesian government's commitment is too weak and that its laws are not being enforced. The government disagrees and points to its new authority in key economic sectors.

a. Camilo Mora et al., "The Projected Timing of Climate Departure from Recent Variability," *Nature* 502 (October 10, 2013): 183–87.

FOR CRITICAL ANALYSIS

1. What pressures can states in the region affected by the haze put on Indonesia to improve enforcement of burning bans?

2. Many economists argue that economic development should take priority and commitment to the environment will follow. What is the problem with this view?

3. How does global warming provide more incentive for the Indonesian government to act?

Thus, realists fit environmental issues into the theoretical concepts of the state, power, sovereignty, and the balance of power.

Realists and economic nationalists clearly recognize that controversies over natural resources and resource scarcity may lead to violence and even war. Drawing on Malthusian logic, political scientist Thomas Homer-Dixon modeled how the degradation of renewable natural resources may lead to violence: as resources such as freshwater or arable land decline in quality or quantity, individuals and groups will compete for these vital resources, resulting in violent conflict.[23] Many years later, he added that climate change may also lead to insecurity and violence, a view consistent with the popular wisdom. Jared Diamond's book *Collapse: How Societies Choose to Fail or Succeed* documents how the struggle for scarce resources led to the collapse of empires in the past and to state failure in Rwanda and Burundi, resulting in the abrogation of human rights.[24]

The relationship between environmental and resource issues and conflict is a complex one. Recent research is focusing more narrowly on the possible link between climate change and violent conflict. A 2017 study of all the empirical studies so far about this relationship finds that a majority of studies (62.3 percent) find evidence that climate variables are associated with higher levels of violent conflict; there are small increases in violent conflict associated with climate change variables. But divergent methodologies and operationalization of key variables make systematic assessment of the studies problematic.[25] There is anecdotal evidence. Jeffrey Gettleman generalizes from his analysis of the land-conflict relationship in Kenya, "Population swells, climate change, soil degradation, erosion, poaching, global food prices and even the benefits of affluence are exerting incredible pressure on African land. They are fueling conflicts across the continent, from Nigeria in the west to Kenya in the east."[26]

Nonrenewable resources such as oil may lead to particularly violent conflicts, because such resources are vital for industry, economic health and welfare, and national security and there are few viable substitutes. How else can we explain the conflict over remote and uninhabited islands in the South China Sea? Only with the possibility of oil or other natural resources beneath the waters surrounding the islands does the conflict make sense. Changes in the distribution of these resources may lead to a shift in the balance of power, creating an instability that may lead to war, just as realists fear. In contrast, issues such as ozone depletion or global warming are not particularly conducive to violent interstate conflict. In these cases, the commons and responsibility for its management are diffuse.

Liberals provide useful insights into addressing environmental issues. Their broadened view of security, coupled with the credence they give to the notion of an interdependent international system—perhaps even one so interconnected as to be called an international society—makes environmental issues ripe for international action. Because liberal perspectives can accommodate a greater variety of different actors, including domestic and nongovernmental organizations, liberals see environmental and human rights issues as legitimate, if not key, international issues of the twenty-first century. Unlike realists, who fear dependency on other countries because it may diminish state power and therefore limit state action, liberals acknowledge interdependence and have faith in the technological ingenuity of individuals to be able to solve many of the natural resource dilemmas. They, too, are keenly aware of how the environment affects the lives of individuals.

Constructivists, too, remind us of the salient discourses on environmentalism and sustainability. How political and scientific elites define the problems and how these definitions change over time as new ideas become rooted in their belief sets are of major interest to constructivists. In the face of the international nature of environmental problems and their solutions, the core concepts of sovereignty may be challenged. One of the major intellectual tasks for constructivists has been to uncover the roots and practices of sovereignty.[27]

THE IMPACT OF HUMAN SECURITY ISSUES ON INTERNATIONAL RELATIONS PRACTICE AND THEORY

Transnational human security issues have effects on three major areas of international relations practice and theory. First, from a practice standpoint, the interconnectedness of the issues within health, the environment, human rights, and migration affects international bargaining. When states choose to go to the bargaining table, many issues are often at stake, and states may be willing to make trade-offs between issues to achieve a desired result. For example, in the aftermath of the 1973 oil embargo and in the face of supply shortages, the United States negotiated with Mexico, an oil exporter. In return for more assured petroleum supplies, the United States began to clean up the Colorado River, agreed to construct a desalination plant at the U.S.-Mexico border, and helped Mexican residents reclaim land in the Mexicali Valley for agriculture.

Other issues, however, are less accommodating to negotiation, particularly if state security is at stake. The United States was unwilling to compromise by signing the Convention on the Prohibition of the Use, Stockpiling, Production, and Transfer of Anti-Personnel Mines and on Their Destruction because of the security imperative to preserve the heavily mined border between North and South Korea. Supporters of the treaty framed the argument in human security terms: innocent individuals, including vulnerable women and children, are killed or maimed by such weapons, which must be eliminated. Yet in this case, the United States decided not to sign the treaty because of South Korean state security. And in the case of the contemporary migration crisis in Europe, states are confronted by conflicting demands: the demand by many to accept new refugees in the name of human rights versus the demand by many others to protect the state's citizens from outsiders who may cause harm. Faced with that dilemma, some states, like Germany, did accept refugees, while others, like Hungary, refused. Negotiations within the European Union over acceptance of refugees broke down. Bargaining is a much more complicated process in the age of transnational issues in which human security and state security may be in conflict.

Second, human security issues pose direct challenges to state sovereignty, setting off major debates about the nature of sovereignty. In Chapter 2, we traced the roots of sovereignty to the Westphalian revolution: the development of the notion that states enjoy internal autonomy and cannot be subjected to external authority. That principle—noninterference in the domestic affairs of other states—was embedded in the UN Charter.

Yet the rise of nonstate actors—multinational corporations, nongovernmental organizations, and supranational organizations such as the European Union—and the forces of globalization undermine Westphalian ideals of state sovereignty. Communicable diseases, the environment, human rights, and migration were traditionally sovereign state concerns, and interference by outside actors was unacceptable. After World War II, those norms began to change, a process that continues today. This is one of the main reasons that discussion has turned to a power shift: an erosion of state authority and the severe weakening of state power overall. Issues that once were the exclusive hallmark of state sovereignty are increasingly susceptible to scrutiny and intervention by global actors. When fragile or failing states cannot protect their own people from disease, violence, or environmental disasters, others might want to step in either for realist reasons (to protect their own) or for liberal reasons (to protect the "other"). Yet traditions of sovereignty mitigate against such interventions.

How, then, should we think about sovereignty today? How has sovereignty been transformed? Mainstream theories in the realist and liberal traditions tend to talk of an erosion of sovereignty. Constructivists go further, probing how sovereignty is and always has been a contested concept. There have always been some issues wherein state control and authority are secure and others wherein authority is shared or even undermined. After all, sovereignty is a socially constructed institution that varies across time and place. Transnational issues such as health, the environment, and human rights permit us to examine in depth long-standing but varying practices of sovereignty. These issues give rise to new forms of authority and new forms of governance, stimulating us to reorient our views of sovereignty.[28]

Third, transnational issues pose critical problems for international relations scholars and for the theoretical frameworks introduced at the beginning of this book. Adherents of each framework have been forced to rethink key assumptions and values, as well as the discourse of their theoretical perspective, to accommodate transnational human security issues.

The very core propositions of realist theory—the primacy of the state, the clear separation between domestic and international politics, and the emphasis on state security—are made problematic. Issues of health and disease, the environment, human rights, and migration, along with others such as drug and human trafficking and transnational crime, are problems that no single state can effectively address alone. These issues have broken down the divide between the international and the domestic. Although they may threaten state security, they have no traditional military solution, even for a great power or superpower.

Realists have generally adopted a nuanced argument consonant with realist precepts. Although most realists admit that other actors have gained power relative to the state, they contend that state primacy is not in jeopardy. Competitive centers of power at the local, transnational, or international level do not necessarily or automatically lead to the erosion or elimination of state power. Most significant, the fundamentals of state security are no less important in this age of globalization than they were in the past. What has changed is that the decreasing salience of interstate and nuclear war as challenges to state and interstate security has forced a broadening of security discourse to encompass numerous aspects of human security. For humans to be secure, not only must state security be ensured, but economic security, environmental security, human rights security, and health and well-being must be secured as well. One form of security does not replace another; each augments the rest. Thus, although these issues have forced realists to add qualifications to their theory, they have preserved it and enhanced its theoretical usefulness.

Human security issues are consistent with liberals' belief in the importance of individuals and the possibility of both cooperative and conflictual interests. After all, it is liberals who introduced the notion that many other issues may be as important as physical security. They see power as a multidimensional concept. Later versions of liberal thinking, such as neoliberal institutionalism, recognized the need for international institutions to facilitate state interactions, to ensure transparency, and to add new issues to the international agenda. Though not denying the importance of state security, they quickly embraced the notion of other forms of security compatible with health, environmental, and human rights issues.

Constructivists have presented a different approach for analyzing transnational issues. They have alerted us to the nuances of the changing discourse embedded in discussions of health, the environment, and human rights. They have illustrated how both material factors and ideas shape debates over these issues. They have called attention to the importance of norms in influencing and changing individual and state behavior. More directly than other theorists, constructivists have begun to explore the varying impacts of these issues on the traditional concepts of the state, national identity, and sovereignty.

Issues of Human Security: Effects on International Relations

On practice:

▶ **Bargaining:** there is more possibility of trade-offs, along with greater complexity; objectives are harder to achieve if state security and human security conflict.

▶ **State sovereignty:** issues that were once domestic have become international; the rise of nonstate actors undermines sovereignty.

On perspectives:

▶ **Realism:** assumptions about unitary states and separation of domestic and international issues have become problematic.

▶ **Liberalism:** embrace of other forms of security may undermine state security.

▶ **Constructivism:** there is a continual need to rethink notions of state, identity, sovereignty, and emergent norms.

WILL TRANSNATIONAL ISSUES LEAD TO GLOBAL GOVERNANCE?

Recognition of transnational human security issues and their effects has led some scholars and pundits to conclude that we need to conceptualize governance processes differently than we have in the past. The processes of interaction among the various actors in international politics are now more frequent and intense, ranging from conventional ad hoc cooperation and formal organizational collaboration to nongovernmental and network collaboration and even virtual communal interaction on the Internet. These changes imply an increasing role for the regulatory capacity of norms. **Global governance** implies that through various structures and processes, actors can coordinate interests and needs in the absence of a unifying political authority. Global governance implies a multiple-actor, multiple-process, decentralized framework; in its idealized form, it presupposes a global civil society. The political scientist Ronnie Lipschutz describes the essential component of global civil society:

> While global civil society must interact with states, the code of global civil society denies the primacy of states or their sovereign rights. This civil society is "global" not only because of those connections that cross national boundaries and operate

within the "global, nonterritorial region," but also as a result of a growing element of global consciousness in the way the members of global civil society act.[29]

There are many skeptics who do not believe that anything approaching global governance, however defined, is possible or desirable. For realists, there can never be global governance because the more closely it is approached, the more dangerous it is perceived to be, and the more likely a countervailing authority or alliance is to halt or reverse the process of convergence. Outcomes are determined by relative power positions rather than by law or other regulatory devices, however decentralized and diffuse those devices might be. For Kenneth Waltz, the quintessential neorealist, the anarchic structure of the international system is the core dynamic. For other realists, such as Hans Morgenthau, there is space for both international law and international organization, but each is relatively insignificant in the face of power politics and the national interest. Few realists would talk in global governance terms. Liberals might be less skeptical, although they may fear that the presence of multiple, sometimes powerful, actors might turn the focus away from the individual, thus undermining democratic values and cultural diversity.

Still others, like some constructivists, fear domination by hegemons that would structure global governance processes to their own advantage. Skepticism about the possibility of global governance does not necessarily diminish the fact that there may be a need for it in the age of globalization.

IN SUM: CHANGING YOUR WORLD

In these 11 chapters, we have explored the historical development of international relations, from the development of the state system to notions of an international system and community and global governance. We have introduced different ideas—realism, liberalism, and constructivism—that help us organize our ideas about the role of the international system, the state, the individual, and intergovernmental and nongovernmental organizations in international relations. From these perspectives, we have examined the major issues of the day and analyzed how these issues affect interstate bargaining, conflict, sovereignty, and even the study of international politics.

A citizenry able to articulate these arguments is better able to explain the whys and hows of events that affect our lives. A citizen who can understand these events is better able to make and support informed policy choices. In the transnational era of the twenty-first century, as economic, political, social, and environmental forces both above the state and within the state assume greater saliency, the role of individuals becomes all the more demanding—and all the more important.

Discussion Questions

1. Explain why migration is both a human rights issue and a humanitarian issue.

2. Find two news articles that explain how receiving states are addressing the influx of new migrants.

3. International cooperation on health has traditionally been viewed as a functionalist issue, but increasingly the issue has been politicized. What has changed? With what effect? Cite specific examples.

4. Global warming, unlike some other environmental issues, is a problem of the global commons. Why are problems of the global commons particularly difficult to solve?

5. Select two news accounts that address the trade-off between economic development and environmental sustainability. Can these two objectives be harmonized in the twenty-first century? Why or why not?

Key Terms

demographic transition (p. 427)

epistemic community (p. 415)

global governance (p. 440)

internally displaced people (IDPs) (p. 404)

Malthusian dilemma (p. 427)

negative externalities (p. 420)

noncommunicable diseases (NCDs) (p. 415)

non-refoulement (p. 404)

refugees (p. 404)

NOTES

Chapter 1

1. Steven Pinker, *The Better Angels of Our Nature: Why Violence Has Declined* (New York: Viking Books, 2011), p. xxi; and Martin Dempsey, quoted in Micah Zenko, "Most. Dangerous. World. Ever.," *Foreign Policy*, February 26, 2013, http://foreignpolicy.com/2013/02/26/most-dangerous-world-ever/ (accessed 12/21/17). See also Human Security Report Project, *The Decline in Global Violence: Evidence, Explanation, and Contestation*, March 3, 2014, https://reliefweb.int/sites/reliefweb.int/files/resources/HSRP_Report_2013_140226_Web.pdf (accessed 12/21/17); and Carnegie Council for Ethics in International Affairs, "Is the World Becoming More Peaceful?" September 27, 2012, https://www.carnegiecouncil.org/studio/multimedia/20120927-is-the-world-becoming-more-peaceful (accessed 12/21/17).

2. Stephen M. Walt, "International Relations: One World, Many Theories," *Foreign Policy* 110 (Spring 1988): 30.

3. Thucydides, *History of the Peloponnesian War*, trans. Rex Warner, rev. ed. (Harmondsworth, UK: Penguin, 1972).

4. See Jeffrey Record and W. Andrew Terrill, "Iraq and Vietnam: Differences, Similarities, and Insights" (Carlisle, PA: Strategic Studies Institute, U.S. Army War College, 2004), http://ssi.armywarcollege.edu/pdffiles/00367.pdf (accessed 11/15/17).

5. Stephen Krasner, "Israel: Munich or Helsinki," *Omphalos: Middle East Conflict in Perspective*, August 28, 2015, www.lawfareblog.com/israel-munich-or-helsinki (accessed 1/23/18). For more on the use of historical analogies, see Yuen Foong Khong, *Analogies at War: Korea, Munich, Dien Bien Phu, and the Vietnam Decision of 1965* (Princeton, NJ: Princeton University Press, 1992).

6. Plato, *The Republic*, trans. Desmond Lee (Harmondsworth, UK: Penguin, 1955).

7. Aristotle, *The Politics*, ed. Trevor J. Saunders, trans. T. A. Sinclair (Harmondsworth, UK: Penguin, 1981).

8. Thomas Hobbes, *Leviathan*, ed. C. B. Macpherson (Harmondsworth, UK: Penguin, 1968).

9. Jean-Jacques Rousseau, *Discourse on the Origin and Foundations of Inequality among Men*, in *Basic Political Writings of Jean-Jacques Rousseau*, ed. and trans. Donald A. Cress (Indianapolis, IN: Hackett Publishing, 1987).

10. Jean-Jacques Rousseau, "On the Social Contract," bk. 2, chap. 1, in *Basic Political Writings of Jean-Jacques Rousseau*, p. 153.

11. Rousseau, "Social Contract," bk. 1, chap. 6, p. 148.

12. See Immanuel Kant, *Idea for a Universal History from a Cosmopolitan Point of View* (1784) and *Perpetual Peace: A Philosophical Sketch* (1795), both reprinted in *Kant Selections*, ed. Lewis White Beck (New York: Macmillan Co., 1988).

13. See, for example, Michael Walzer, *Just and Unjust Wars. A Moral Argument with Historical Illustrations* (New York: Basic Books, 1977); and Jack Donnelly, *Universal Human Rights in Theory and Practice*, 2nd ed. (Ithaca, NY: Cornell University Press, 2003).

14. J. David Singer and Melvin Small, *The Wages of War, 1816–1965: A Statistical Handbook* (New York: Wiley, 1972).

15. Wade M. Cole, "Mind the Gap: State Capacity and the Implementation of Human Rights Treaties," *International Organization* 69 (Spring 2015): 410.

16. Meredith Reid Sarkees, "Defining and Categorizing Wars," in *Resort to War: A Data Guide to Inter-State, Extra-State, Intra-State, and Non-State Wars, 1816–2007*, ed. Meredith Reid Sarkees and Frank Whelon Wayman (Washington, DC: CQ Press, 2010).

17. Emilie M. Hafner-Burton and James Ron, "Seeing Double: Human Rights Impact through Qualitative and Quantitative Eyes," *World Politics* 61:2 (April 2009): 360–401.

18. Peter J. Katzenstein, ed., *The Culture of National Security: Norms and Identity in World Politics* (New York: Columbia University Press, 1996).

19. Cynthia Weber, *Simulating Sovereignty: Intervention, the State, and Symbolic Exchange* (Cambridge, UK: Cambridge University Press, 1995).

20. Karen T. Litfin, ed., *The Greening of Sovereignty in World Politics* (Cambridge, MA: The MIT Press, 1998).

21. Christine Sylvester, "Empathetic Cooperation: A Feminist Method for IR," *Millennium: Journal of International Studies* 23:2 (1994): 315–34.

22. See articles in Clifford Bob, ed., *The International Struggle for New Human Rights* (Philadelphia: University of Pennsylvania Press, 2009).

Chapter 2

1. Jean Bodin, *Six Books on the Commonwealth*, trans. M. J. Tooley (Oxford: Basil Blackwell, 1967), p. 25.

2. Bodin, *Commonwealth*, p. 28.

3. Bodin, *Commonwealth*, p. 28.

4. Adam Smith, *An Inquiry into the Nature and Causes of the Wealth of Nations* (New York: Modern Library, 1937).

5. John Locke, *Two Treatises on Government* (Cambridge, UK: Cambridge University Press, 1960).

6. Hilaire Belloc, as quoted in John Ellis, *A Social History of the Machine Gun* (New York: Random House, 1975), p. 18.

7. Quoted in A. C. Walworth, *Woodrow Wilson* (Baltimore, MD: Penguin, 1969), p. 148.

8. E. H. Carr, *The Twenty Years' Crisis, 1919–1939: An Introduction to the Study of International Relations* (New York: Harper Torchbooks, 1939, rep. 1964), p. 224.

9. P. M. H. Bell, *The Origins of the Second World War in Europe* (New York: Longman, 1986), pp. 151–52.

10. John W. Dower, *War without Mercy: Race and Power in the Pacific War* (New York: Pantheon Books, 1986).

11. George F. Kennan ["X"], "The Sources of Soviet Conduct," *Foreign Affairs* 25 (July 1947): 566–82.

12. Quoted in Charles W. Kegley Jr. and Eugene R. Wittkopf, *World Politics: Trend and Transformation*, 5th ed. (New York: St. Martin's, 1995), p. 94.

13. Joseph Stalin, "Reply to Comrades," *Pravda*, August 2, 1950.

14. Mikhail Gorbachev, "Reality and Guarantees for a Secure World," as reported in Foreign Broadcast Information Service, Daily Report, Soviet Union, September 17, 1987, p. 25.

15. For an extensive discussion of populism, see the articles in *Foreign Affairs* 95:6 (November/December 2016), "The Power of Populism." See especially Pankaj Mishra, "The Globalization of Rage: Why Today's Extremism Looks Familiar," pp. 46–54. That article is based on a book by the same author, *Age of Anger: A History of the Present* (New York: Farrar, Straus, and Giroux, 2017).

16. Condoleezza Rice, *Democracy: Stories from the Long Road to Freedom* (New York: Twelve, 2017), p. 441.

Chapter 3

1. Lisa L. Martin and Beth A. Simmons, "International Organizations and Institutions," in *Handbook of International Relations*, 2nd ed., ed. Walter Carlsnaes, Thomas Risse, and Beth A. Simmons (London: Sage, 2013), p. 328.

2. Thucydides, *History of the Peloponnesian War*, trans. Rex Warner, rev. ed. (Harmondsworth, UK: Penguin, 1972).

3. Augustine, *Confessions* and *City of God*, in *Great Books of the Western World*, ed. Robert Maynard Hutchins, vol. 18 (Chicago: Encyclopedia Britannica, 1952, 1986).

4. Thomas Hobbes, *Leviathan*, ed. C. B. Macpherson (Harmondsworth, UK: Penguin, 1968), p. 13.

5. Hans J. Morgenthau, *Politics among Nations: The Struggle for Power and Peace*, 5th ed., rev. (New York: Knopf, 1978).

6. John J. Mearsheimer, "The False Promise of International Institutions," *International Security* 19:3 (Winter 1994–95): 5–49.

7. John Herz, "Idealist Internationalism and the Security Dilemma," *World Politics* 2:2 (January 1950): 157–80.

8. Kenneth N. Waltz, *Theory of International Politics* (Reading, MA: Addison-Wesley, 1979).

9. Kenneth N. Waltz, "Realist Thought and Neorealist Theory," in *Controversies in International Relations Theory: Realism and the Neoliberal Challenge*, ed. Charles W. Kegley Jr. (New York: St. Martin's, 1995), pp. 67–82.

10. Robert Gilpin, *War and Change in World Politics* (Cambridge, UK: Cambridge University Press, 1981), p. 210.

11. Montesquieu, *The Spirit of the Laws*, vol. 36, ed. David Wallace Carrithers (Berkeley: University of California Press, 1971), p. 23.

12. Immanuel Kant, *Perpetual Peace*, ed. Lewis White Beck (New York: Macmillan, 1957).

NOTES \\ N-3

13. Robert O. Keohane and Joseph S. Nye Jr., *Power and Interdependence* (Boston: Little Brown, 1977).

14. Robert Axelrod and Robert O. Keohane, "Achieving Cooperation under Anarchy: Strategies and Institutions," in *Cooperation under Anarchy*, ed. Kenneth Oye (Princeton, NJ: Princeton University Press, 1986), pp. 226–54.

15. Andrew Moravcsik, "Taking Preferences Seriously: A Liberal Theory of International Politics," *International Organization* 51:4 (Autumn 1997): 513–53.

16. Ted Hopf, "The Promise of Constructivism in International Relations Theory," *International Security* 23:1 (Summer 1989): 172.

17. Thomas U. Berger, "Norms, Identity, and National Security in Germany and Japan," in *The Culture of National Security: Norms and Identity in World Politics*, ed. Peter J. Katzenstein (New York: Columbia University Press, 1996), p. 318.

18. Alexander Wendt, "Anarchy Is What States Make of It: The Social Construction of Power Politics," *International Organization* 46:2 (Spring 1992): 396. For a more complete analysis, see Alexander Wendt, *Social Theory of International Politics* (Cambridge, UK: Cambridge University Press, 1999).

19. Joseph S. Nye Jr., *Soft Power: The Means to Success in World Politics* (New York: Public Affairs, 2004).

20. Karl Marx, *Capital: A Critique of Political Economy*, trans. Ben Fowkes (New York: Random House, 1977).

21. John A. Hobson, *Imperialism: A Study*, ed. Philip Siegelman (Ann Arbor: University of Michigan Press, 1965).

22. Vincent Ferraro, "Dependency Theory: An Introduction," in *The Development Economics Reader*, ed. Giorgio Secondi (London: Routledge, 2008), pp. 58–64.

23. J. Ann Tickner, "Hans Morgenthau's Principles of Political Realism: A Feminist Reformulation," *Millennium: Journal of International Studies* 17:3 (1988): 429–40.

24. Cynthia Enloe, *Bananas, Beaches, and Bases: Making Feminist Sense of International Politics*, 2nd ed. (Berkeley: University of California Press, 2014).

25. John J. Mearsheimer, "Why the Ukraine Crisis Is the West's Fault: The Liberal Delusions That Provoked Putin," *Foreign Affairs* 93:5 (September/October 2014): 77–93.

26. Sophie Pinkham, "How Annexing Crimea Allowed Putin to Claim He Had Made Russia Great Again," *Guardian*, March 22, 2017.

27. Carl Gershman, quoted in Mearsheimer, "Why the Ukraine Crisis Is the West's Fault."
Chapter 4

1. Kenneth N. Waltz, *Man, the State, and War* (New York: Columbia University Press, 1954); and J. David Singer, "The Levels of Analysis Problem," in *International Politics and Foreign Policy*, ed. James N. Rosenau, rev. ed. (New York: Free Press, 1961), pp. 20–29.

2. Kenneth N. Waltz, "International Structure, National Force, and the Balance of World Power," *Journal of International Affairs* 21:2 (1967): 229.

3. Kenneth N. Waltz, "Why Iran Should Get the Bomb," *Foreign Affairs* 91:4 (July/August 2012): 5.
N-4 \\ NOTES

4. Paul M. Kennedy, *The Rise and Fall of the Great Powers: Economic Change and Military Conflict from 1500 to 2000* (New York: Random House, 1987).

5. Robert O. Keohane, *After Hegemony: Cooperation and Discord in the World Political Economy* (Princeton, NJ: Princeton University Press, 1984).

6. Robert O. Keohane and Joseph S. Nye, *Power and Interdependence*, 3rd ed. (New York: Longman, 2001).

7. G. John Ikenberry, *After Victory. Institutions, Strategic Restraint, and the Rebuilding of Order After Major Wars* (Princeton, NJ: Princeton University Press, 2001), p. 50.

8. Martha Finnemore, *The Purpose of Intervention: Changing Beliefs about the Use of Force* (Ithaca, NY: Cornell University Press, 2003), p. 94.

9. See Alexander Wendt, *Social Theory of International Politics* (Cambridge, UK: Cambridge University Press, 1999).

10. Robert Gilpin, *War and Change in World Politics* (Cambridge, UK: Cambridge University Press, 1981).

11. Finnemore, *Intervention*, p. 95.

12. See Martha Finnemore, *National Interests in International Society* (Ithaca, NY: Cornell University Press, 1996), chap. 1.

13. Alfred T. Mahan, *The Influence of Seapower upon History, 1660–1783* (Boston: Little, Brown, 1897).

14. Halford Mackinder, "The Geographical Pivot of History," *Geographical Journal* 23 (April 1904): 434.

15. Joseph S. Nye Jr., *Soft Power: The Means to Success in World Politics* (New York: Public Affairs, 2004).

16. Andrew Mack, "Why Big Nations Lose Small Wars: The Politics of Asymmetric Conflict," *World Politics* 27:2 (January 1975): 175–200.

17. Joseph S. Nye Jr., *The Future of Power* (New York: Public Affairs, 2011).

18. Hans J. Morgenthau, *Politics among Nations: The Struggle for Power and Peace*, brief ed., ed. Kenneth W. Thompson (New York: McGraw-Hill, 1993), p. 5.

19. Robert G. Herman, "Identity, Norms, and National Security: The Soviet Foreign Policy Revolution and the End of the Cold War," in *The Culture of National Security: Norms and Identity in World Politics*, ed. P. J. Katzenstein (New York: Columbia University Press, 1996), pp. 271–316.

20. Margaret G. Hermann, "Explaining Foreign Policy Behavior Using the Personal Characteristics of Political Leaders," *International Studies Quarterly* 24:1 (March 1980): 7–46.

21. Stephen Benedict Dyson, "Personality and Foreign Policy: Tony Blair's Iraq Decisions," *Foreign Policy Analysis* 2:3 (July 2006): 289.

22. Betty Glad, "Why Tyrants Go Too Far: Malignant Narcissism and Absolute Power," *Political Psychology* 23:1 (2002): 6.

23. Michael C. Horowitz, Allan C. Stam, and Cali M. Ellis, *Why Leaders Fight* (New York: Cambridge University Press, 2015).

NOTES \\ N-5

24. Ole Holsti, "The Belief System and National Images: A Case Study," *Journal of Conflict Resolution* 6 (1962): 244–52.

25. Irving L. Janis, *Victims of Groupthink: A Psychological Study of Foreign-Policy Decisions and Fiascoes* (Boston: Houghton Mifflin, 1972), p. 9.

26. Robert Jervis, "Hypotheses on Misperception," *World Politics* 20:3 (April 1968): 454–79.

27. Quoted in Mijib Marshall, "After Karzai," *The Atlantic*, July/August 2014, 56.

28. Pamela Johnston Conover, Karen A. Mingst, and Lee Sigelman, "Mirror Images in Americans' Perceptions of Nations and Leaders during the Iranian Hostage Crisis," *Journal of Peace Research* 17:4 (1980): 325–37.

29. Johanna McGeary, "The End of Milošević," *Time*, October 16, 2000, 60.

30. "Top Global Thinkers: Mohamed ElBaradei, Wael Ghonim," *Foreign Policy* (December 2011): 36.

31. Malala Yousafzai, *I Am Malala: The Girl Who Stood Up for Education and Was Shot by the Taliban* (London: Weidenfeld & Nicolson, 2013); and *He Named Me Malala*, directed by Davis Guggenheim (Fox Searchlight Pictures and National Geographic Channel, 2015).
Chapter 5

1. Reuters, "U.S. to Search Russian Consulate in San Francisco, Says Moscow," September 1, 2017, www.reuters.com/article/us-russia-usa-searches/u-s-to-search-russian-consulate-in-san-francisco-says-moscow-idUSKCN1BC5YX (accessed 12/4/17).

2. James N. Rosenau, *Turbulence in World Politics: A Theory of Change and Continuity* (Princeton, NJ: Princeton University Press, 1990), pp. 117–18.

3. Graeme Wood, "Limbo World," *Foreign Policy* (January/February 2010): 49.

4. Quoted in Yaroslav Trofimov, "The Stateless Nation," *Wall Street Journal*, June 20–21, 2015, C2.

5. Minxin Pei, "The Paradoxes of American Nationalism," *Foreign Policy* 134 (May/June 2003): 31–37.

6. Robert D. Putnam, "Diplomacy and Domestic Politics: The Logic of Two-Level Games," *International Organization* 42:3 (Summer 1988): 427–69.

7. Putnam, "Two-Level Games," 434.

8. Raymond Cohen, *Negotiating across Cultures: Communication Obstacles in International Diplomacy*, 2nd ed. (Washington, DC: U.S. Institute of Peace, 1997).

9. David A. Baldwin, *Economic Statecraft* (Princeton, NJ: Princeton University Press, 1985).

10. Thomas Biersteker, Sue E. Eckert, Marcos Tourinho, and Zuzana Hudakova, *The Effectiveness of United Nations Targeted Sanctions: Findings from the Targeted Sanctions Consortium*, http://repository.graduateinstitute.ch/record/287976/files/effectiveness_TCS_nov_2013.pdf (accessed1/4/18).

11. Thomas C. Schelling, *Arms and Influence* (New Haven, CT: Yale University Press, 1966).

12. Norman M. Naimark, *The Russians in Germany: A History of the Soviet Zone of Occupation, 1945–1949* (Cambridge, MA: Harvard University Press, 1995).
N-6 \\ NOTES

13. Brendon O'Connor and Srdjan Vucetic, "Another Mars-Venue Divide? Why Australia Said 'Yes' and Canada Said 'Non' to Involvement in the 2003 Iraq War," *Australian Journal of International Affairs* 64:5 (November 2010): 526–48.

14. Immanuel Kant, *Perpetual Peace: A Philosophical Sketch* (1795), reprinted in *Kant Selections*, ed. Lewis White Beck (New York: Macmillan, 1988).

15. See, for example, William J. Dixon, "Democracy and the Peaceful Settlement of International Conflict," *American Political Science Review* 88 (1994): 14–32; Joe D. Hagan, "Domestic Political Systems and War Proneness," *Mershon International Studies Review* 38:2 (October 1994): 183–207; Erik Gartzke, "The Capitalist Peace," *American Journal of Political Science* 51:1 (2007): 166–91; Seung-Whan Choi, "Beyond Kantian Liberalism: Peace through Globalization?" *Conflict Management and Peace Science* 27:3 (2010): 272–95.

16. See Monica Duffy Toft, Daniel Philpott, and Timothy Samuel Shah, *God's Century: Resurgent Religion and Global Politics* (New York: W. W. Norton, 2011).

17. Samuel P. Huntington, *The Clash of Civilizations and the Remaking of World Order* (New York: Simon & Schuster, 1996).

18. Audrey Kurth Cronin, "ISIS Is Not a Terrorist Group: Why Counterterrorism Won't Stop the Latest Jihadist Threat," *Foreign Affairs* 94:2 (March/April 2015): 87–98.

19. Rebecca Wright and Ben Westcott, "At Least 30,000 Rohingya Trapped in Myanmar Mountains without Food," CNN, September 4, 2017, www.cnn.com/2017/09/04/asia/rohingya-refugees-myanmar-military/index.html (accessed 12/4/17).

20. Jack Snyder, *From Voting to Violence: Democratization and Nationalist Conflict* (New York: W. W. Norton, 2000).

21. See Moisés Naím, *Illicit: How Smugglers, Traffickers, and Copycats Are Hijacking the Global Economy* (New York: Doubleday, 2005).

22. Fund for Peace, *Fragile State Index 2017—Annual Report*, May 14, 2017, http://fundforpeace.org/fsi/2017/05/14/fragile-states-index-2017-annual-report/ (accessed 8/21/17).

Chapter 6

1. Chris Hedges, *What Every Person Should Know about War* (New York: Free Press, 2003), p. 1.

2. Data come from the Institute for Economics and Peace, "Global Peace Index 2017," http://visionofhumanity.org/indexes/global-peace-index/ (accessed 12/12/17).

3. Charles Tilly, "Reflections on the History of European State-Making," in *The Making of National States in Western Europe* (Princeton, NJ: Princeton University Press, 1975), p. 42.

4. Andrew Mack, "Why Big Nations Lose Small Wars: The Politics of Asymmetric Conflict," *World Politics* 27:2 (January 1975): 175–200.

5. Ivan Arreguín-Toft, "How the Weak Win Wars: A Theory of Asymmetric Conflict," *International Security* 26:1 (Summer 2001): 105.

6. Audrey Kurth Cronin, "Behind the Curve: Globalization and International Terrorism," *International Security* 27:3 (Winter 2002/3): 33.

7. Audrey Kurth Cronin, "ISIS Is Not a Terrorist Group: Why Counterterrorism Won't Stop the Latest Jihadist Threat," *Foreign Affairs* 94:2 (March/April 2015): 90.

8. See, for example, Dan Caldwell and Robert E. Williams Jr., *Seeking Security in an Insecure World* (Lanham, MD: Rowman & Littlefield, 2006); and Walter Enders and Todd Sandler, "Distribution of Transnational Terrorism among Countries by Income Classes and Geography after 9/11," *International Studies Quarterly* 50:2 (June 2006): 367–68.

9. Ronald Deibert, "Cyber-Security," in *Routledge Handbook of Security Studies*, 2nd ed., ed. Myriam Dunn Cavelty and Thierry Balzacq (New York: Routledge, 2016), p. 172.

10. John J. Mearsheimer, *The Tragedy of Great Power Politics* (New York: W. W. Norton, 2001), p. 32.

11. A. F. K. Organski, *World Politics* (New York: Knopf, 1958), chap. 12; and A. F. K. Organski and Jacek Kugler, *The War Ledger* (Chicago: University of Chicago Press, 1980).

12. San Pil Chun, 선군정치대한이해 [Understanding Sŏn'gun policy] (Pyongyang Press: Pyongyang, 2004), p. 15.

13. Jacques E. C. Hymans, "Assessing North Korean Nuclear Intentions and Capacities: A New Approach," *Journal of East Asian Studies* 8:2 (2008): 259–82.

14. Quoted in Michael Dobbs, "Serbian Nationalism Lifts Milosevic," *Washington Post*, March 30, 1999.

15. George W. Bush, "The National Security Strategy of the United States of America," September 17, 2002, http://georgewbush-whitehouse.archives.gov/nsc/nss/2002/index .html (accessed 2/1/10).

16. See Glenn Snyder, *Deterrence and Defense* (Princeton, NJ: Princeton University Press, 1961); and Alexander L. George and Richard Smoke, *Deterrence in American Foreign Policy: Theory and Practice* (New York: Columbia University Press, 1974).

17. For a complete treatment, see Inis Claude, *Power and International Relations* (New York: Random House, 1962), pp. 94–204.

18. Alexander Wendt, "Anarchy Is What States Make of It: The Social Construction of Power Politics," *International Organization* 46:2 (Spring 1992): 391–425; Jeffrey T. Checkel, "International Institutions and Socialization in Europe: Introduction and Framework," *International Organization* 59:4 (Autumn 2005): 801–26.

19. For contemporary views, see Michael Walzer, *Just and Unjust Wars*, 4th ed. (New York: Basic Books, 2006).

20. These statistics were reported in Charlie Savage and Scott Shane, "U.S. Reveals Death Toll from Airstrikes Outside War Zones," *New York Times*, July 1, 2016.

21. Matthew C. Waxman, "Cyber Strategy & Policy: International Law Dimensions," testimony before the Senate Armed Services Committee," March 2, 2017, www.armed-services.senate .gov/imo/media/doc/Waxman_03-02-17.pdf (accessed 3/27/2017).

22. Oona A. Hathaway et al., "The Law of Cyber-Attack," *California Law Review* 100:4 (2012): 817–85.

23. John Arquilla, "Foreword: Ethics for the Coming Epoch of Conflict," in *Binary Bullets: The Ethics of Cyberwarfare*, ed. Fritz Allhoff, Adam Henschke, and Bradley Jay Strawser (Oxford: Oxford University Press, 2016), p. viii.

Chapter 7

1. Robert O. Keohane, *After Hegemony: Cooperation and Discord in the World Political Economy* (Princeton, NJ: Princeton University Press, 1984); Robert Axelrod and Robert O. Keohane, "Achieving Cooperation under Anarchy: Strategies and Institutions," *World Politics* 38:1 (1985): 226–54.

2. These data come from two sources. C. N. Trueman, "The Nuclear Arms Race," The History Learning Site, March 9, 2015, August 16, 2016, http://historylearningsite.co.uk (accessed 12/15/17); John Swift, "The Soviet-American Arms Race," *History Review*, March 2009.

3. Robert Axelrod, *The Evolution of Cooperation* (New York: Basic Books, 1984).

4. James D. Morrow, "When Do States Follow the Laws of War?" *American Political Science Review* 101:3 (August 2007): 559–72.

5. Bruce Russett and John Oneal, *Triangulating Peace: Democracy, Interdependence, and International Organizations* (New York: W. W. Norton, 2000).

6. Norman Angell, *The Great Illusion* (New York: Cosimo, 2010; originally published in 1909 under the title *Europe's Optical Illusion*).

7. Keohane, *After Hegemony*, p. 97.

8. Alexander Wendt, "Anarchy Is What States Make of It: The Social Construction of Power Politics," *International Organization* 46:2 (1992): 391–425.

9. Thomas Risse-Kappen, "Collective Identity in a Democratic Community: The Case of NATO," in *The Culture of National Security: Norms and Identity in World Politics*, ed. Peter J. Katzenstein (New York: Columbia University Press, 1996), pp. 357–99.

10. Wendt, "Anarchy," 391–425.

11. Karen J. Alter, *The New Terrain of International Law: Courts, Politics, Rights* (Princeton, NJ: Princeton University Press, 2014).

12. Abram Chayes and Antonia Handler Chayes, "On Compliance," *International Organization* 47:2 (1993): 175–205.

13. Thomas M. Franck, *The Power of Legitimacy among Nations* (Oxford: Oxford University Press, 1990).

14. Andrew Moravcsik, "Taking Preferences Seriously: A Liberal Theory of International Politics," *International Organization* 51:4 (1997): 513–53; Anne-Marie Slaughter, "A Liberal Theory of International Law," *Proceedings of the ASIL (American Society of International Law) Annual Meeting* 94 (April 5–8, 2000): 240–49.

15. Moisés Naím, *Illicit: How Smugglers, Traffickers, and Copycats Are Hijacking the Global Economy* (New York: Anchor Books, 2006), p. 5.

16. Barnett Lotstein, quoted in Associated Press, "Escape to Mexico Blocks Death Penalty," *USA Today*, January 17, 2008.

17. Bob Baker, "Force Mexico to Extradite," *Denver Post*, May 18, 2005.

Chapter 8

1. Thomas L. Friedman, *The Lexus and the Olive Tree: Understanding Globalization* (New York: Farrar, Straus, and Giroux, 1999), p. 257.

2. Some of the material in this chapter is drawn from Margaret P. Karns, Karen A. Mingst, and Kendall W. Stiles, *International Organizations: The Politics and Processes of Global Governance*, 3rd ed. (Boulder, CO: Lynne Rienner, 2015); and Karen A. Mingst, Margaret P. Karns, and Alynna J. Lyon, *The United Nations in the 21st Century*, 5th ed. (Boulder, CO: Westview Press, 2017).

3. See "The Retreat of the Global Company," *The Economist*, January 28, 2017, 18–22; and "The Rise of the Superstars," *The Economist*, September 17, 2016, 3–16.

4. Robert Gilpin, "Three Models of the Future," *International Organization* 29:1 (Winter 1975): 39.

5. Sir Norman Angell, *The Great Illusion* (New York: Putnam, 1933).

6. "The Sticky Superpower," *The Economist*, October 3, 2015, 8.

7. See Eswar Prasad, "A Middle Ground," *Finance and Development* 54:1 (March 2017): 1–5; and Barry Eichengreen, "The Renminbi Goes Global," *Foreign Affairs* (March/April 2017): 157–63.

8. "The Sticky Superpower," 12.

9. Antoni Estevadeordal and Alan M. Taylor, *Is the Washington Consensus Dead? Growth, Openness, and the Great Liberalization, 1970s–2000s*, Working Paper 14264 (Cambridge, MA: National Bureau of Economic Research, August 2008).

10. Data on tariffs reported in Keith Bradsher and Karl Russell, "Building Trade Walls," *New York Times*, March 7, 2017, B6.

11. "The Sticky Superpower," 8.

12. See John McCormick and Jonathan Olsen, *The European Union: Politics and Policies* (Boulder, CO: Westview, 2014).

13. Jorge G. Castañeda, "NAFTA's Mixed Record: The View from Mexico," *Foreign Affairs* 93:1 (January/February 2014): 134.

14. James McBride, "NAFTA's Economic Impact," Council on Foreign Relations Backgrounder, January 24, 2017.

15. Danielle Renwick, "Mercosur: South America's Fractious Trade Bloc," Council on Foreign Relations Backgrounder, October 5, 2016.

16. Jagdish Bhagwati, *Termites in the Trading System: How Preferential Agreements Undermine Free Trade* (New York: Oxford University Press, 2008).

17. David S. Christy Jr., "Round and Round We Go," *World Policy Journal* 25:2 (Summer 2008): 24.

18. Paul Collier, *The Bottom Billion: Why the Poorest Countries Are Failing and What Can Be Done about It* (New York: Oxford University Press, 2007).

19. Nancy Birdsall and Francis Fukuyama, "The Post-Washington Consensus: Development after the Crisis," *Foreign Affairs* 90:2 (March/April 2011): 45–53.

20. Daron Acemoglu and James A. Robinson, *Why Nations Fail: The Origins of Power, Prosperity, and Poverty* (New York: Crown Business, 2012).

21. David Roodman, *Due Diligence: An Impertinent Inquiry into Microfinance* (Washington, DC: Center for Global Development, 2012).

22. Abhuijit Banerjee, Dean Karlan, and Jonathan Zinman, "Six Randomized Evaluations of Microcredit: Introduction and Further Steps," *American Economic Journal: Applied Economics* 7:1 (2015): 1–21.

23. "Cash Transfers: Changing the Debate on Giving Cash to the Poor," Innovations for Poverty Action, www.poverty-action.org/impact/cash-transfers-changing-debate-giving -cash-poor_ (accessed 1/5/18).

24. United Nations, *The Millennium Development Goals Report 2015*, www.un.org /millenniumgoals/2015_MDG_Report/pdf/MDG%202015%20rev%20(July%201).pdf (accessed 1/5/18).

25. John McArthur, "Seven Million Lives Saved: Under-5 Mortality since the Launch of the Millennium Development Goals," Brookings Institution, September 25, 2014, www.brookings .edu/research/papers/2014/09/under-five-child-mortality-mcarthur (accessed 1/5/18).

26. Scott Wisor, "The Impending Failure of the Sustainable Development Goals," *Ethics and International Affairs*, September 30, 2014, www.ethicsandinternationalaffairs.org/2014 /the-impending-failure-of-the-sustainable-development-goals (accessed 10/19/15).

27. Quoted in "Special Report, State Capitalism: The Visible Hand," *The Economist*, January 21, 2012, 5.

28. C. Fred Bergsten, "Why the Euro Will Survive: Completing the Continent's Half-Built House," *Foreign Affairs* 91:5 (September/October 2012): 16–17; and Timothy Garton Ash, "The Crisis of Europe: How the Union Came Together and Why It's Falling Apart," *Foreign Affairs* 91:5 (September/October 2012): 7–8.

29. Bergsten, "Why the Euro Will Survive," 22. For a more general assessment of the viability of the EU, see Wallace J. Thies, "Is the EU Collapsing?" *International Studies Review* 14 (2012): 225–39.

30. "Africa's Hopeful Economies. The Sun Shines Bright," *The Economist*, December 3, 2011, 82–84.

31. Jeffrey Gettleman, "'Africa Rising'? 'Africa Reeling' May Be More Fitting Now," *New York Times*, October 17, 2016.

32. Roger Altman, "The Great Crash, 2008: A Geopolitical Setback for the West," *Foreign Affairs* 88:1 (January/February 2009): 13.

33. William Easterly, *The White Man's Burden: Why the West's Efforts to Aid the Rest Have Done So Much Ill and So Little Good* (New York: Penguin, 2006); and Joseph E. Stiglitz, *Globalization and Its Discontents* (New York: W. W. Norton, 2002).

34. Jane Perlez and Yufan Huang, "Behind China's $1 Trillion Plan to Shake Up the Economic Order," *New York Times*, May 13, 2017. See also Yinan Zhang, "One Belt, One Road, and the Chinese Tributary System in the 21st Century," *Berkeley APEC Study Center Newsletter*, Winter 2016/17, 9–11.

Chapter 9

1. Joseph M. Grieco, "Anarchy and the Limits of Cooperation: A Realist Critique of the Newest Liberal Institutionalism," in *Neorealism and Neoliberalism: The Contemporary Debate*, ed. David A. Baldwin (New York: Columbia University Press, 1993), p. 117.

2. David Mitrany, *A Working Peace System* (London: Royal Institute of International Affairs, 1946), p. 40.

3. Garrett Hardin, "The Tragedy of the Commons," *Science* 162 (December 13, 1968): 1243–48. See also Mancur Olson Jr., *The Logic of Collective Action: Public Goods and the Theory of Groups* (New York: Schocken, 1968).

4. Margaret P. Karns and Karen A. Mingst, "The United States and Multilateral Institutions: A Framework," in *The United States and Multilateral Institutions: Patterns of Changing Instrumentality and Influence*, ed. Margaret P. Karns and Karen A. Mingst (Boston: Unwin Hyman, 1990), pp. 1–24.

5. See Karen A. Mingst. Margaret P. Karns, and Alynna J. Lyon, *The United Nations in the 21st Century*, 5th ed. (Boulder, CO: Westview, 2017).

6. See Bruce Cronin and Ian Hurd, "Conclusion: Assessing the Council's Authority," in *The UN Security Council and the Politics of International Authority*, ed. Bruce Cronin and Ian Hurd (New York: Routledge, 2008), pp. 199–214; and Jeremy Greenstock, "The Security Council in a Fragmenting World," in *The UN Security Council in the 21st Century*, ed. Sebastian von Einsiedel, David M. Malone, and Bruce Stagno Ugarte (Boulder, CO: Lynne Rienner, 2016), pp. 815–26.

7. Jonathan Tepperman, "Where Are You, Ban Ki-Moon?" *New York Times*, September 24, 2013, www.nytimes.com/2013/09/25/opinion/tepperman-where-are-you-ban-ki-moon .html (accessed 1/8/18).

8. Charles T. Hunt, "All Necessary Means to What Ends? The Unintended Consequences of the 'Robust Turn' in UN Peace Operations," *International Peacekeeping* 24:1 (2017): 108–31.

9. Paul F. Diehl and Alexandru Balas, *Peace Operations*, 2nd ed. (Malden, MA: Polity Press, 2014), chap. 4. See also Séverine Autesserre, *Peaceland: Conflict Resolution and the Everyday Politics of International Intervention* (New York: Cambridge University Press, 2014), chap. 1.

10. See, for example, Virginia Page Fortna, "Does Peacekeeping Keep Peace? International Intervention and the Duration of Peace after Civil War," *International Studies Quarterly* 28:2 (June 2004): 269–92; and Virginia Page Fortna, *Does Peacekeeping Work? Shaping Belligerents' Choices after Civil War* (Princeton: Princeton University Press, 2008).

11. John Karlsrud, "The UN at War: Examining the Consequences of Peace-Enforcement Mandates for the UN Peace-Keeping Operations in the CAR, the DRC, and Mali," *Third World Quarterly* 36:1 (2015): 41.

12. Thomas Biersteker, Sue E. Eckert, Marcos Tourinho, and Zuzana Hudáková, *The Effectiveness of United Nations Targeted Sanctions: Findings from the Targeted Sanctions Consortium (TSC)*, Graduate Institute Geneva, November 2013, p. 15, http://repository.graduateinstitute.ch /record/287976/files/effectiveness_TCS_nov_2013.pdf (accessed 1/18/18).

13. Gary Clyde Hufbauer, Jeffrey J. Schott, Kimberly Ann Elliott, and Barbara Oegg, *Economic Sanctions Reconsidered*, 3rd ed. (Washington, DC: Peterson Institute for International Economics, 2007), p. 141.

14. See Franz Baumann, "United Nations Management—An Oxymoron?" *Global Governance* 22:4 (October–December 2016): 461–72. For a comprehensive assessment of problems and prospects for the future, see Independent Commission on Multilateralism Chair Kevin Rudd, *UN 2030: Rebuilding Order in a Fragmenting World*, International Peace Institute, August 2016, www.ipinst.org/wp-content/uploads/2016/08/IPI-ICM-UN-2030-Chairs -Report2FINAL.pdf (accessed 1/8/18).

15. Immanuel Kant, "Idea for a Universal History from a Cosmopolitan Point of View" (1784), reprinted in *Kant Selections*, ed. Lewis White Beck (New York: Macmillan, 1988); and Jean-Jacques Rousseau, "State of War," "Summary," and "Critique of Abbé Saint-Pierre's Project for Perpetual Peace," in *Reading Rousseau in the Nuclear Age*, trans. and ed. Grace G. Roosevelt (Philadelphia: Temple University Press, 1990), pp. 185–229.

16. This section draws on Margaret P. Karns, Karen A. Mingst, and Kendall W. Stiles, *International Organizations: The Politics and Processes of Global Governance*, 3rd ed. (Boulder, CO: Lynne Rienner, 2015), chap. 5.

17. This section on NGOs draws on Karns, Mingst, and Stiles, *International Organizations*, 3rd ed., chap. 6.

18. Maria Ivanova, "The Contested Legacy of Rio+20," *Global Environmental Politics* 13:4 (November 2013): 4.

19. Thomas Carothers, "The Closing Space Challenge: How Are Funders Responding?" Carnegie Endowment for International Peace, November 2, 2015, http://carnegie endowment.org/2015/11/02/closing-space-challenge-how-are-funders-responding -pub-61808 (accessed 1/8/18).

20. See Alexander Cooley and James Ron, "The NGO Scramble: Organizational Insecurity and the Political Economy of Transnational Action," *International Security* 27:1 (Summer 2002): 5–39.

21. See, for example, William DeMars, *NGOs and Transnational Networks: Wild Cards in World Politics* (London: Pluto, 2005); and Volker Heins, *Nongovernmental Organizations in International Society: Struggles over Recognition* (New York: Palgrave Macmillan, 2008).

22. Fiona Terry, *Condemned to Repeat? The Paradox of Humanitarian Action* (Ithaca, NY: Cornell University Press, 2002); and Sarah Kenyon Lischer, "Military Intervention and the Humanitarian 'Force Multiplier,'" *Global Governance* 13:1 (January–March 2007): 99–118.

23. For pathbreaking theoretical and empirical work, see Martha Finnemore, *National Interests in International Society* (Ithaca, NY: Cornell University Press, 1996); Martha Finnemore, *The Purpose of Intervention: Changing Beliefs about the Use of Force* (Ithaca, NY: Cornell University Press, 2003); and Margaret E. Keck and Kathryn Sikkink, *Activists beyond Borders: Advocacy Networks in International Politics* (Ithaca, NY: Cornell University Press, 1998).

24. Michael Barnett and Martha Finnemore, *Rules for the World: International Organizations in Global Politics* (Ithaca, NY: Cornell University Press, 2004). See also Michael Barnett and Martha Finnemore, "The Politics, Power, and Pathologies of International Organizations," *International Organization* 53:4 (Autumn): 699–732; and Grieco, "Anarchy and the Limits of Cooperation," p. 117.

GLOSSARY

anarchy the absence of a hierarchically superior, coercive authority that can create laws, resolve disputes, or enforce law and order in a system (Ch. 3)

arms control regulation of arms proliferation, including restrictions on research, manufacture, or deployment of weapons systems (Ch. 6)

asymmetric conflict conflict between a more powerful party and a significantly weaker party (Ch. 6)

balance of payments a country's current and capital account balances; may be positive (surplus) or negative (deficit) (Ch. 8)

balance of power any system in which actors (e.g., states) enjoy relatively equal power, such that no single state or coalition of states is able to dominate other actors in the system (Ch. 2)

balancing taking actions to offset the power of more powerful states (Ch. 3)

bandwagoning a process in which states that might have opposed a threatening state choose to ally with it instead (Ch. 3)

behavioralism an approach to the study of social science and international relations that posits that individuals and units like states act in regularized ways; leads to a belief that behaviors can be described, explained, and predicted (Ch. 1)

Beijing Consensus an alternative to economic liberalism; a development model that advocates experimenting with policies in state capitalism, with the government playing an active role in picking economic winners and losers (Ch. 8)

belief system the organized and integrated perceptions of individuals that form a relatively integrated set of images (Ch. 4)

bipolar describes a system in which the distribution of the power to conquer is concentrated in two states or coalitions of states (Ch. 4)

BRICS an informal group of emerging economic powers, including Brazil, Russia, India, China, and South Africa (Ch. 8)

bureaucratic politics a model of foreign policy making that posits that national decisions are the outcomes of bargaining among bureaucratic groups having competing interests (Ch. 5)

caliphate a religious territory headed by a caliph, a spiritual leader of Islam (Ch. 2)

capital accounts measure of the flows of capital between countries, including foreign direct investment and portfolio investment in and out (Ch. 8)

capitalism the economic system in which the ownership of the means of production is in private hands; the system operates according to market forces whereby capital and labor move freely (Ch. 2)

cognitive consistency the tendency to accept information that is compatible with what has previously been accepted, often ignoring inconsistent information (Ch. 4)

Cold War the era in international relations between the end of World War II and 1990, distinguished by ideological, economic, political, and military rivalry between the Soviet Union and the United States (Ch. 2)

collective good a public good that is available to all regardless of individual contribution—for example, the air, the oceans, or Antarctica—and that no one owns or is individually responsible for (Ch. 9)

collective security the idea that aggression by a state should be defeated collectively because aggression against one state is aggression against all (Ch. 3)

colonialism the practice of settling people from a home country among indigenous peoples of a distant territory (Ch. 2)

comparative advantage the ability of a country to make and export a good more efficiently than other countries can; the basis for the liberal economic principle that countries benefit from free trade among nations (Ch. 8)

compellence a strategy in which a state threatens to use force to try to get another state to do something or to undo an act it has undertaken (Ch. 5)

complex interdependence the idea that states are connected through multiple channels (both formal and informal), there is no hierarchy of issues, and the result is a decline in the use of military force (Ch. 3)

complex peacekeeping multidimensional operations using military and civilian personnel, often including traditional peacekeeping and nation-building activities; more dangerous because not all parties have consented and because force is usually used (Ch. 9)

containment a foreign policy designed to prevent the expansion of an adversary by blocking its opportunities to expand through foreign aid programs or through use of coercive force; the major U.S. policy toward the Soviet Union during the Cold War era (Ch. 2)

credibility the quality of having both the ability and incentive to act using a certain policy such that other states believe it will be carried out (Ch. 5)

crimes against humanity international crimes, including murder, enslavement, ethnic cleansing, and torture, committed against civilians, as codified in the Rome Statute (Ch. 10)

cultural relativism the belief that human rights, ethics, and morality are determined by cultures and history and therefore are not universally the same (Ch. 10)

current accounts measure of net border flows between countries of goods, services, governmental transfers, and income on capital investments (Ch. 8)

cyberspace the environment in which communication over computer networks flows (Ch. 6)

cyberwarfare state actions taken to penetrate another state's computers or networks for the purpose of causing damage or disruption (Ch. 6)

demographic transition the situation in which increasing levels of economic development lead to falling death rates, followed by falling birthrates (Ch. 11)

dependency theory a strand of the radical school of thought that seeks to explain the underdevelopment of dominated states (Ch. 3)

derivatives financial instruments often derived from an asset (mortgages, loans, foreign exchange, interest rates) that parties agree to exchange over time; a way of buying and selling risk in international financial markets (Ch. 8)

détente the easing of tense relations; in the context of this volume, détente refers to the relaxation and reappraisal of threat assessments by political rivals, for example, the United States and Soviet Union during the later years of the Cold War (Ch. 2)

deterrence a strategy in which a state commits to punishing a target state if that state takes an undesired action; threats of actual war are used as an instrument of policy to dissuade a state from pursuing certain courses of action (Ch. 5)

diplomacy the process in which states try to influence the behavior of other actors by bargaining, negotiating, taking a specific action or refraining from such an action, or appealing to the foreign public for support of a position (Ch. 5)

disarmament reduction of the number of arms and limitations on the types of weapons employed by a state (Ch. 6)

discourse the way we choose to talk about ourselves and others (Ch. 3)

domino effect a metaphor that posits that the loss of influence over one state to an adversary will necessarily lead to a subsequent loss of control over neighboring states, just as dominos fall one after another (Ch. 2)

economic interdependence a relationship in which states rely on one other for goods and/or economic gain (Ch. 7)

economic radicalism beliefs, drawn from Marxist and neo-Marxist writing, that poor labor conditions, colonial expansion, and divisions between the rich and poor can be blamed on international capitalism (Ch. 8)

engagement a type of statecraft in which a state entices a target state to act in a desired way by rewarding moves it makes in a desired direction (also called positive sanctions) (Ch. 5)

epistemic community community of experts and technical specialists who share a set of beliefs and a way to approach problems (Ch. 11)

ethnonational movements self-conscious communities that share an ethnic affiliation and participate in organized political activity (Ch. 5)

European Union (EU) a union of 28 European states, formerly the European Economic Community; designed originally during the 1950s for economic integration, but since expanded into a closer political and economic union (Ch. 9)

evoked set details from a present situation that are similar to information gleaned from past situations (Ch. 4)

exchange rates the price of one currency in relation to another; rates may float with the market or be fixed by governments (Ch. 8)

external balancing allying with other states to offset the power of more powerful states (Ch. 3)

extradition the process of delivering an individual from the territory of one state to another state for prosecution or to serve a sentence (Ch. 7)

fiscal policies policies affecting a government's budget, including the level of government spending and the tax rates (Ch. 8)

foreign direct investment (FDI) investment in a state, usually by multinational corporations, through establishing a manufacturing facility or financing investments in extractive industries or transportation (Ch. 8)

fragile states states with an inability to exercise a monopoly on the legitimate use of force within their territory, make collective decisions because of the erosion of legitimate authority, interact with other states in the international system, and/or provide public services (Ch. 5)

General Agreement on Tariffs and Trade (GATT) founded by treaty in 1947 as the Bretton Woods institution responsible for negotiating a liberal international trade regime that included the principles of nondiscrimination in trade and most-favored-nation status; re-formed as the World Trade Organization in 1995 (Ch. 8)

General Assembly one of the major organs of the United Nations; generally addresses issues other than peace and security; each member state has one vote; operates with six functional committees composed of all member states (Ch. 9)

genocide the systematic killing or harming of a group of people based on national, religious, ethnic, or racial characteristics, with the intention of destroying the group (Ch. 10)

global governance structures and processes that enable actors to coordinate interdependent needs and interests in the absence of a unifying political authority (Ch. 11)

globalization the growing integration of the world in terms of politics, economics, and culture (Ch. 5)

Group of 7 (G7) a group of the traditional economic powers (United States, Japan, Germany, Great Britain, France, Italy, Canada) that meets annually to address monetary cooperation; when Russia joins, the G8 discussions turn to political issues (Ch. 8)

Group of 77 a coalition of about 125 developing countries that presses for reforms in economic relations between developing and developed countries; also referred to as the South (Ch. 9)

Group of 20 a group of finance ministers and heads of central banks (and, recently, heads of state) of major economic powers, including China, Russia, Australia, Argentina, Brazil, Indonesia, Mexico, South Africa, South Korea, and Turkey, as well as representatives from the G7; meets periodically to discuss economic issues (Ch. 9)

groupthink the tendency of individuals to strive for cohesion and sometimes unanimity to achieve cohesion, at the risk of not examining alternative policies (Ch. 4)

Heckscher-Ohlin theory theory that a country will export goods that make intensive use of the factors of production in which it is well-endowed (Ch. 8)

hegemon a dominant state that has a preponderance of power; often establishes and enforces the rules and norms in the international system (Ch. 2)

horizontal enforcement a process whereby states work to elicit compliance with international law by other states (Ch. 7)

humanitarian intervention actions by states, international organizations, or the international community in general to intervene, usually with coercive force, to alleviate human suffering without necessarily obtaining consent of the state (Ch. 10)

human security a broadened concept of security that includes the protection of individuals from systematic violence, environmental degradation, and health disasters (Ch. 9)

hypotheses specific *falsifiable* statements that question the proposed relationship among two or more concepts (Ch. 3)

imperialism the policy and practice of extending the domination of one state over another through territorial conquest or economic domination (Ch. 2)

intergovernmental organizations (IGOs) international agencies or bodies established by states and controlled by member states that deal with areas of common interest (Ch. 9)

internal balancing a state's building up its own military resources and capabilities in order to be able to stand against more powerful states (Ch. 3)

internally displaced people (IDPs) individuals who have been uprooted from their homes, often due to civil strife, but remain in their home country (Ch. 11)

International Bill of Rights the collective name for the Universal Declaration of Human Rights, the International Covenant on Civil and Political Rights, and the International Covenant on Economic, Social, and Cultural Rights (Ch. 10)

international cooperation adoption of behavior by states that is consistent with the preferences of other states in order to achieve common objectives (Ch. 7)

international humanitarian law a body of law composed of the four Geneva Conventions and protocols protecting individuals during war, including wounded military, prisoners of war, and civilians (Ch. 10)

international institutions organizations and sets of rules such as international treaties meant to govern international behavior (Ch. 3)

international law a body of rules and norms regulating interactions among states, between states and IGOs, and among IGOs, states, and individuals (Ch. 7)

International Monetary Fund (IMF) the Bretton Woods institution originally charged with helping states deal with temporary balance-of-payments problems; now plays a broader role in assisting debtor developing states by offering loans to those who institute specific policies or structural adjustment programs (Ch. 8)

international relations the study of the interactions among various actors (states, international organizations, nongovernmental organizations, and subnational entities like bureaucracies, local governments, and individuals) that participate in international politics (Ch. 1)

interstate wars wars between states (Ch. 6)

intrastate wars wars that take place within a state (also known as civil wars) (Ch. 6)

jus ad bellum laws that deal with when it is just/legal to go to war (Ch. 6)

jus in bello laws that define what acts are considered legal and illegal when fighting a war (Ch. 6)

League of Nations the international organization formed at the conclusion of World War I for the purpose of preventing another war; based on collective security (Ch. 2)

legitimacy the moral and legal right to rule, which is based on law, custom, heredity, or the consent of the governed (Ch. 2)

legitimate describes laws that are supported logically and justifiably (Ch. 7)

macroeconomic policies government policies designed to address macroeconomic conditions, including fiscal and monetary policies (Ch. 8)

Malthusian dilemma the scenario in which population growth rates will increase faster than agricultural productivity, leading to food shortages; named after Thomas Malthus (Ch. 11)

mercantilism economic theory that international commerce should increase a state's wealth, especially gold; state power is enhanced by a favorable balance of trade (Ch. 8)

microeconomic policies government policies adopted to affect regulations, subsidies, competition, and antitrust actions (Ch. 8)

mirror image a psychological mechanism in which one sees in one's opponent the opposite of characteristics seen in oneself; one views the opponent as hostile and uncompromising, whereas one views oneself as friendly and compromising (Ch. 4)

monetary policies policies affecting national interest rates or exchange rates, designed to affect employment and inflation rates (Ch. 8)

moral hazard problem that occurs when states or individuals are not made to pay for the consequences of their reckless behavior; they have little incentive to change that behavior (Ch. 8)

most-favored-nation (MFN) principle principle in international trade agreements whereby one state promises to give another state the same treatment in trade as the first state gives to its most-favored trading partner (Ch. 8)

multilateralism the conduct of international activity by three or more states in accord with shared general principles, often, but not always, through international institutions (Ch. 4)

multipolar describes a system in which the distribution of the power to conquer is concentrated in more than two states (Ch. 4)

nation a group of people sharing a common language, history, or culture (Ch. 5)

nationalism a sense of national consciousness in which people identify with a common history, language, or customs, often placing primary emphasis on one's own nation's culture and interests over those of other nations (Ch. 2)

national security the ability of a state to protect its interests, secrets, and citizens from threats—both external and internal—that endanger it (Ch. 6)

nation-state the coincidence between state and nation; the entity formed when people sharing the same historical, cultural, or linguistic roots form their own state with borders, a government, and international recognition (Ch. 5)

negative externalities costly (harmful) unintended consequences of economic exchange (Ch. 11)

noncommunicable diseases (NCDs) diseases that are not directly transferred between individuals or groups, including heart disease, respiratory illnesses, diabetes, and obesity (Ch. 11)

non-refoulement principle that refugees cannot be forced to return to their country of origin, because of fear of persecution on the grounds of race, ethnicity, or membership in a social group (Ch. 11)

nontariff barriers restrictions on international trade other than tariffs, including quantitative restrictions and quotas; designed to protect health, safety, national security, or competitiveness (Ch. 8)

normative relating to ethical rules; in foreign policy and international affairs, standards suggesting what a policy should be (Ch. 1)

norms collective expectations for the proper behavior of actors with a given identity (Ch. 3)

North Atlantic Treaty Organization (NATO) military and political alliance between Western European states and the United States established in 1949 for the purpose of defending Europe from aggression by the Soviet Union and its allies; in the post–Cold War era, the alliance expanded to include Eastern European states (Ch. 2)

offshore financial centers states or jurisdictions with few regulations on banking and financial transactions, often with low taxation; used by individuals and international banks to transfer funds (Ch. 8)

organizational politics a model of foreign policy making that highlights the role that subnational governmental organizations play in the construction of foreign policy, emphasizing their standard operating procedures and processes (Ch. 5)

peacebuilding post-conflict political and economic activities designed to preserve and strengthen peace settlements; includes civil administration, elections, and economic development activities (Ch. 9)

pluralist model a model of foreign policy making that focuses on the role that societal groups play in influencing national decisions (Ch. 5)

populism belief that champions the common person, contrasting people's concerns with those of the elite; adherents often oppose big business and financial interests (Ch. 2)

portfolio investment investment in another state by purchasing stocks or bonds, without taking direct control of the investments (Ch. 8)

power the ability not only to influence others but also to control outcomes so as to produce results that would not have occurred naturally (Ch. 4)

power potential a measure of the power an entity like a state could have, derived from a consideration of both its tangible and intangible resources; states may not always be able to transfer their power potential into actual power (Ch. 4)

prisoner's dilemma a theoretical game in which rational players (states or individuals) choose options that lead to outcomes (payoffs) such that all players are worse off than under a different set of choices (Ch. 7)

protectionism state policies imposing barriers to restrict imports for a variety of reasons (Ch. 8)

public diplomacy the process of targeting both foreign publics and elites, attempting to create an overall image that enhances a country's ability to achieve its objectives (Ch. 5)

rational actors actors that make decisions by weighing the costs and benefits of various options against the goal to be achieved (Ch. 3)

refugees individuals who flee from their country of nationality because of fear of persecution on the grounds of race, ethnicity, or membership in a social group (Ch. 11)

relative gains how much more one state gains over another (Ch. 3)

responsibility to protect (R2P) emerging norm that the international community should help individuals suffering at the hands of their own state or others when the home state fails to provide security (Ch. 10)

rollback a strategy of using, or threatening the use of, armed force to aggressively coerce an adversary into abandoning occupied territory (Ch. 2)

sanctions a type of statecraft in which a state threatens to act, or takes actual actions, to punish a target state for moves it makes in a direction not desired (also called negative sanctions) (Ch. 5)

satisficing settling for a decision that is a minimally acceptable solution, even if that decision is not the best possible outcome (Ch. 5)

Security Council one of the major organs of the United Nations; charged with the responsibility for peace and security issues; includes five permanent members with veto power and ten nonpermanent members chosen from the General Assembly (Ch. 9)

security dilemma the situation in which each state tries to increase its own power to protect itself, but this increased power is seen as a threat by other states, leading them to be more insecure and thus to seek to increase their own power, which, in turn, makes others more insecure (Ch. 3)

shadow of the future states' expectations that they will continue to interact in the future (Ch. 7)

smart power a combination of the hard power of coercion and the soft power of persuasion and attraction (Ch. 4)

smart sanctions limited sanctions targeted to hurt or support specific groups or people; used to avoid the high humanitarian costs of general sanctions (Ch. 5)

socialism an economic and social system that relies on intensive government intervention or public ownership of the means of production in order to distribute wealth among the population more equitably; in radical Marxist theory, the stage between capitalism and communism (Ch. 2)

socialization the process through which one adopts the identities of other groups (Ch. 3)

soft power the power of a state to attract others and influence their behavior because of the legitimacy of its values or policies (Ch. 4)

sovereignty the authority of the state, based on recognition by other states and by nonstate actors, to govern matters within its own borders that affect its people, economy, security, and form of government (Ch. 2)

sovereign wealth funds state-controlled investment companies that manage large foreign-exchange reserves in capital-surplus countries like China or in petroleum-exporting countries like Norway, the Gulf states, and Saudi Arabia (Ch. 8)

state an organized political unit that has a geographic territory, a stable population, and a government to which the population owes allegiance and that is legally recognized by other states (Ch. 5)

statecraft strategies for action vis-à-vis other states (Ch. 5)

structural adjustment programs IMF policies and recommendations aimed at guiding states out of balance-of-payments difficulties and economic crises, in ways consistent with the Washington Consensus (Ch. 8)

summits talks and meetings among the highest-level government officials from different countries (Ch. 2)

superpowers highest-power states as distinguished from other great powers; term coined during the Cold War to refer to the United States and the Soviet Union (Ch. 2)

sustainable development an approach to economic development that tries to reconcile current economic growth and environmental protection with the needs of future generations (Ch. 8)

system an assemblage of units, objects, or parts united by some form of regular interaction, in which a change in one unit causes changes in the others (Ch. 4)

tariffs taxes imposed on imports that raise the price of the goods; designed to protect domestic producers from competition by foreign producers (Ch. 8)

terrorism a violent act that is political in nature or intent, is committed by nonstate actors, and targets noncombatants (a form of asymmetric conflict) (Ch. 6)

theoretical perspectives sets of theories united by some common themes such as actors, concepts, and issues (Ch. 3)

theory a collection of propositions that combine to explain phenomena by specifying the relationships among a set of concepts (Ch. 3)

Third Reich the German state from 1933 to 1945, a time that coincides with the rule of Adolf Hitler and his National Socialist Worker's Party, or Nazis (Ch. 2)

track-two diplomacy the process of using individuals outside the government to carry out negotiations with other states (Ch. 5)

traditional peacekeeping the use of multilateral third-party military forces to achieve several different objectives: containing interstate conflict, enforcing cease-fires, and separating military forces; used during the Cold War to prevent conflict among the great powers from escalating (Ch. 9)

transaction costs the costs of making an exchange (Ch. 7)

transnational movements groups of people from different states who share religious, ideological, or policy beliefs and work together to change the status quo (Ch. 5)

treaties explicitly written agreements among states that lay out rights and obligations (sometimes called conventions, covenants, or protocols) (Ch. 7)

Treaties of Westphalia treaties ending the Thirty Years' War in Europe in 1648; in international relations, represent the beginning of state sovereignty within a territorial space (Ch. 2)

unconventional warfare warfare distinguished by willingness to flout restrictions on legitimate targets of violence or refuse to accept the traditional outcomes of battles as an indicator of victory or defeat (Ch. 6)

unipolar describes a system in which the power to conquer all other states in the system combined resides within a single state (Ch. 4)

universal jurisdiction a legal concept in which states may claim jurisdiction over an individual in another state if that individual's conduct is sufficiently heinous to violate the laws of all states (Ch. 7)

vertical enforcement a legal process whereby one actor works to constrain the actions of another actor over which it has authority in order to secure its compliance with the law (Ch. 7)

war an organized and deliberate political act by an established political authority that causes 1,000 or more deaths in a 12-month period and involves at least two actors capable of harming each other (Ch. 6)

war on terrorism a declaration by a society of its intent to use its material and nonmaterial resources to defeat those using terror, often nonstate actors targeting noncombatants to instill fear in the population (Ch. 2)

Warsaw Pact the military alliance formed by the states of the Soviet bloc in 1955 in response to the rearmament of West Germany and its inclusion in NATO; permitted the stationing of Soviet troops in Eastern Europe (Ch. 2)

Washington Consensus a version of economic liberalism that holds that only through specific liberal economic policies—including privatization, trade liberalization, government deregulation, and broad tax reform—can economic development occur (Ch. 8)

weapons of mass destruction (WMD) nuclear, chemical, biological, and radiological weapons that can kill or bring major harm to large numbers of people or structures (Ch. 2)

World Bank a global lending agency focused on financing projects in developing countries; formally known as the International Bank for Reconstruction and Development, it was established as one of the key Bretton Woods institutions to deal with reconstruction and development after World War II (Ch. 8)

World Trade Organization (WTO) intergovernmental organization designed to support the principles of liberal free trade; includes enforcement measures and dispute settlement mechanisms; established in 1995 to replace the General Agreement on Tariffs and Trade (Ch. 8)

CREDITS

Frontmatter: Pg. iii (left): Philippe Huguen/AFP/Getty Images; (right): Anthony Wallace/AFP/Getty Images.

Chapter 01: Pg. 2: Paula Bronstein/Getty Images; Pg. 5: Maya Hautefeuille/AFP/Getty Images; Pg. 8: Steve Liss/The LIFE Images Collection/Getty Images.

Chapter 02: Pg. 18: Yichuan Cao/NurPhoto via Getty Images; Pg. 25: Private Collection/Photo © Bonhams, London, UK/Bridgeman Images; Pg. 29: Art Media/Print Collector/Getty Images; Pg. 30: 'Countries that have been under European control' from "Map: European colonialism conquered every country in the world but these five," by Max Fisher. Vox.com, February 24, 2015. http://www.vox.com/2014/6/24/5835320/map-in-the-whole-world-only-these-five-countries-escaped-european. Reprinted by permission of Vox Media, Inc.; Pg. 51: Bettmann/Getty Images; Pg. 57: David Turnley/Corbis/VCG via Getty Images.

Chapter 03: Pg. 66: Chip Somodevilla/Getty Images; Pg. 70: ©RIA Novosti/The Image Works; Pg. 84: dpa picture alliance/Alamy Stock Photo; Pg. 91: Tharaka Basnayaka/NurPhoto/Sipa/Newscom; Pg. 95: Dado Galdieri/Bloomberg via Getty Images; Pg. 100: Sasha Mordovets/Getty Images.

Chapter 04: Pg. 106: Fayez Nureldine/AFP/Getty Images; Pg. 115: DigitalGlobe via Getty Images; Pg. 121: Rick Wilking/AFP/Getty Images; Pg. 127: Jochen Eckel/Bloomberg via Getty Images; Pg. 130: Xinhua/Zhang Shuo via Getty Images; Pg. 143: Giuseppe Ciccia/NurPhoto via Getty Images.

Chapter 05: Pg. 148: Beck Diefenbach/Reuters/Newscom; Pg. 153: Ahmad Al-Rubaye/AFP/Getty Images; Pg. 155: Gali Tibbon/AFP/Getty Images; Pg. 165: Emmanuel Dunand/AFP/Getty Images; Pg. 177: Louisa Gouliamaki/AFP/Getty Images.

Chapter 06: Pg. 186: Ian Hanning/REA/Redux; Pg. 190: Charles Caratini/Sygma via Getty Images; Pg. 201: Nawras Aamer/Epa/REX/Shutterstock; Pg. 208: Chuck Kennedy/MCT/MCT via Getty Images; Pg. 215: KCNA/EPA-EFE/REX/Shutterstock; Pg. 227: Pacific Press/Alamy Stock Photo.

Chapter 07: Pg. 232: AP Photo/Efrem Lukatsky, File; Pg. 240: Jesco Denzel/AP/Shutterstock; Pg. 249: UN Photo; Pg. 259: Nicolas Economou/NurPhoto via Getty Images; Pg. 265: Raul Arboleda/AFP/Getty Images.

Chapter 08: Pg. 268: CrowdSpark/Alamy Stock Photo; Pg. 284: Jenny Vaughan/AFP/GettyImages; Pg. 293: Bullit Marquez/AFP/Getty Images; Pg. 305: Sven Torfinn/Panos Pictures; Pg. 312: Ted Aljibe/AFP/Getty Images.

Chapter 09: Pg. 318: Jason Szenes/UPI/Newscom; Pg. 324: Amos Gumulira/AFP/Getty Images; Pg. 334: Albert Gonzalez Farran/AFP/Getty Images; Pg. 351: Neil Hall/EPA-EFE/REX/Shutterstock; Pg. 356: Marta Nascimento/REA/Redux.

Chapter 10: Pg. 364: Afolabi Sotunde/Reuters/Newscom; Pg. 368: Jonas Bendiksen/Magnum Photos; Pg. 377: Arindam Shivaani/NurPhoto/Getty Images; Pg. 382: AP Photo/Seattlepi.com, Joshua Trujillo; Pg. 384: Grigoris Siamidis/NurPhoto/Sipa/Newscom; Pg. 392: Waseem Nikzad/AFP/Getty Images.

Chapter 11: Pg. 400: Fabrizio Villa/Polaris/Newscom; Pg. 405: UNHCR, Figure 1: "Trend of global displacement & proportion displaced, 1997-2016," from Global Trends: Forced Displacement in 2016. Reprinted by permission of UNHCR, the UN Refugee Agency.; Pg. 410: Mohammed Mohammed/Xinhua News Agency/Newscom; Pg. 414: UNAIDS, Figure: "Antiretroviral therapy coverage and number of AIDS-related deaths, global, 2000–2015," from Global AIDS Update, 2016. Reprinted by permission of UNAIDS.; Pg. 431: Courtesy Paul McCormick/NOAA Marine Debris Program; Pg. 435: Maulana / Barcroft Media via Getty Images.

INDEX

Page numbers in *italics* refer to boxes, figures, maps, and tables.

atomic bombing of Japan, 42, 196, 226
AU (African Union), 195, 333–34, 351, 352,
    397
Augustine, Saint, 74, 75, 224
Aung San Suu Kyi, 319, 406
Australia
    bipolarity and, 111, *112*
    cyberattack in, 187
    foreign policy decision making and, 170,
        171
    in Group 20, 295
    mutual legal assistance treaties and, 258
    natural sources of power, 125
    TPP and, 294
    World War II and, 41
Austria
    alliances in the nineteenth century, 33
    annexation of, 42
    collective actions in, 142
    Concert of Europe and, 26, 28
    Napoleonic Wars and, 24
    natural sources of power, 127
    post-World War I, 36
    Westphalian system and, 22
Austria-Hungary, 33, 34–36, 37, 111, *112*,
    192
avian flu, 411
"axis of evil," 88, 164
Axis powers (World War II), 40–41
Axworthy, Lloyd, 376
Azavedo, Roberto, 312

Bahama, 422
Bahrain, 61, 353
Baker, Bob, 261
balance of payments, 273–74
balance of power
    Cold War and, 53
    collapse of, 33–36
    definition of, 32
    deterrence and, 217
    Kuwait and, 78
    in managing insecurity, 213, 216
    in the nineteenth century, 29, 32–33
    polarity systems and, 111, *112*, 113, 116
    realist view of, 73, 77

Balfour Doctrine, 36
bandwagoning, 78
Bangladesh
    genocide in, 386
    international trade and, 285
    malaria in, 410
    microfinance and, 299
    population issues in, 428
Ban Ki-moon, 329
Bank of England, 307
bargaining, 157–58, 440
Barnett, Michael, 362
Basque people, 153, 200
Bayer, 274
behavioralism, 11–14, *16*
Beijing Consensus, 302
Belarus, 223
Belgium
    Cold War and, 53
    European Union and, 341
    formation of, 27
    independence of, 32
    terrorism and, 204
    World War I and, 35
belief system, 136
Bellamy, Alex, 409
Ben Ali, Zine al-Abidine, 61, 144
Berger, Thomas, 88
Bergsten, C. Fred, 309
Berlin, Congress of, 29
Berlin blockade, 46, 47, *47*
Berlin Wall, 47, *47*, 54, 142
Bermuda, 281
Better Angels of Our Nature, The (Pinker), 3
Bhagwati, Jagdish, 294
Bill of Rights, 367
BINGOs (business and industry NGOs),
    353
bin Laden, Osama, 176, 199, *202*
    death of, 358
    locating, 411, 416
    in September 11, 2001, attacks, 59
biological weapons, 78
bipolar systems, 80, 111, *112*
Bismarck, Otto von, 129
Blair, Tony, 134
Bodin, Jean, 21

Boko Haram, 193, *202*, 364–66, 392
Bonaparte, Napoleon, 24–26, 196
Bosnia
    human rights and, 386–87
    truth commissions and, 390
    UN operations in, 55, 331, *332*
    violence against women in, 392
    war crimes in, 254, 388
Botswana, 252, 413, 414
Bouazizi, Mohamed, 144
Brazil
    as BRICS country, 295, 313
    deforestation and, 432, 434
    financial crisis and, 281
    HIV/AIDS and, 413–14
    international development and, 303
    international finance and, 280
    international trade and, 286
    natural resource issues in, 432
    natural sources of power, 125, 127
    nuclear weapons and, 223, 233
    polarity and, 113
    refugees and, 407
    slavery in, 369
    UN Security Council and, 396
Bretton Woods institutions, 275, *276,* 277–79
Brexit, 60, 61, 63, 142, 288, 290, 309, 314, *344,* 348–51
BRICS countries, 295, 313
#BringBackOurGirls campaign, 364–65
Britain, *see* Great Britain
Britain, Battle of, 39–40
British East India Company, 270, 274
British Virgin Islands, 281
Brooks, Rosa, 397
Brzezinski, Zbigniew, 399
bubonic plague, 409–10
Buddhism, 367
Bulgaria
    bipolarity and, *112*
    Greece and, 325
    post-World War I, 39
    post-World War II, 43
Burkina Faso, 352, 380, 407
Burma, *see* Myanmar

Burundi
    civil war in, 193
    genocide in, 58
    violence against women in, 392
Bush, George W.
    on Iran, 88
    Iraq War and, 164, 208, 220
    Kyoto Protocol and, 422–23
    public opinion and, 141
business and industry NGOs (BINGOs), 353

Cambodia
    communism and, 49
    human rights and, 386
    truth commissions and, 390
    UN operations in, 331
Cameron, David, 347
Cameroon, 29, 178, 253, 350
Canada
    bipolarity and, *112*
    Cold War and, 52
    environmental issues and, 425
    foreign policy decision making and, 170, 171
    in Group of 7, 278
    human rights and, 260, 376–77
    international finance and, 281
    international trade and, 284
    mutual legal assistance treaties and, 258
    NAFTA and, 290–92
    Native American nations and, 152–53
    SARS outbreak and, 411
    sources of power, 125, 129
    TPP and, 294
Canada, Judge v., 260
CAP (Common Agricultural Policy), 285, 289
capital accounts, 273
capitalism, 43–44
    Marxist view of, 272
    natural resources and, 425
    post-Cold War era, 57
    radical view of, 92–96
    Westphalian system and, 23

carbon dioxide emissions, 421, *421*, 422–23, 424–25

Carbon Disclosure Project, 425

Caribbean, 265

Caribbean Community, 351

Carr, E. H., 38

Carrefour, 274

Carson, Rachel, 419

Carter, Jimmy, 159

Castaneda, Jorge, 291

Castro, Fidel, 162

Catalonia, 153

Catholic Church
    international law and, 246
    population issues and, 431

Catholic Relief Services, 299, 355

Cayman Islands, 281

CEC (Council of Europe's Convention on Cybercrime), 205

CEDAW (Convention on the Elimination of All Forms of Discrimination Against Women), 249, *372*, 376, 391, 393

Centers for Disease Control and Prevention, 415

Central African Republic, 183, 334–35, 336, 337, 338, 407

Central America
    colonialism and, 126
    drug trafficking in, national model against, 265
    refugees from, 407
    UN operations in, 331

Central Intelligence Agency (CIA), *202,* 411

CERTs (computer emergency response teams), 206

CFCs (chlorofluorocarbons), 322, 420

Chad, 178, 193, 252

Chamberlain, Neville, 137

Chechnya, 207, 211

chemical weapons, 78, 250

Chemical Weapons Convention, 222

Cheney, Dick, 379

Chiang Kai-shek, 197

Chile, 269, 280, 287, 294

China
    Africa and, 114–15
    balance of power and, 77, 216

as BRICS country, 295, 313

bubonic plague in, 409

carbon dioxide emissions of, 421, *421,* 422–23, 424

civil wars and, 197

Cold War and, 49, 50

communism and, 47, 49, 50, 153

cyberwarfare and, 204, 205

environmental issues and, 420, 422–23, 424, 425

ethnonational movements and, 179–81

foreign policy elites and, 140

freshwater issue and, 427

global financial crisis and, 306, 307, 309–10

HIV/AIDS and, 413

human rights and, 355, 378, 380, 396, 398

imperialism and, 30

international development and, 302–3

international finance and, 280

international law and, 254

international system and, 114–15

international trade and, 284, 286, 287, 293

Japan and, 30, 38, 41, 64, 197, 220

Kyoto Protocol and, 422–23

map of, *180*

military forces of, 60, 63, 115

nationalism and, 153, 156

nuclear weapons and, 115

oil and, 151, 397

One-China policy, 115, 156

Paris Agreement and, 424, 425

polarity and, 111, *112*

population policy of, 429–30

post-World War I, 38

public diplomacy and, 158

Rape of Nanking in, 38, 64

SARS outbreak and, 411

sources of power, 126–27, 129–30

South Korea and, 221–22

Spratly Islands and, 63, 151

Taiwan and, 153, 156, 166

technology and, 173–74

China (*continued*)
   transnational crime and, 182
   United States and, 114, 239, 263, 266
   UN Security Council and, 326, 336, 338, 396, 406
   World War II and, 41
   WTO and, 114, 286
chlorofluorocarbons (CFCs), 322, 420
cholera, 183, 410, 411
Christianity
   on dignity of individuals, 367
   imperialism and, 28, 29, 31
   Westphalian world and, 21
Churchill, Winston, 42, 129
CIA (Central Intelligence Agency), *202*, 411
Cingranelli-Richards (CIRI) Human Rights Dataset, 13
CITES (Convention on International Trade in Endangered Species of Wild Fauna and Flora), 432
City of Thorns (Rawlence), 406–7
civil rights movement, 198
civil wars, *see* intrastate wars (civil wars)
CJEU (Court of Justice of the European Union), 346
class
   industrialization and, 26
   Marxist view of, 9, 93
class analysis, 9
Clausewitz, Carl von, 189
Climate Bonds Initiative, 425
climate change, 420–25
   deforestation and, 434–35
   human cost of, 420, 422
   natural resource issues and, 426
   ozone depletion and global warming in, 420–25, *421*, 433
Climate Coalition, 431
Clinton, Hillary Rodham, 158
Clooney, Amal, 388
Club of Rome, 427
coal-burning power plants, 420
cognitive consistency, 137, *138*
Cohen, Dara Kay, 393
Colbert, Jean-Baptiste, 271
Cold War, 42, 216

arms control agreements during, 221
in Asia and Latin America, 49–52
bipolarity and, 111, *112*
containment strategy and, 43, 50, 77
end of, 56–57
foreign policy decision making and, 166
important events of, *47–48*
nuclear weapons and, 46, 236
origins of, 42–46
proxies in, 46, *47*, 52–52, 120
as series of confrontations, 46–47, *47–48*
Cole, Wade M., 12
Collapse (Diamond), 436
collective goods, 321–22, 418, 429
collective rights, 367
collective security, 82–83, 118, 219–20
Colombia, 144, 259, 264–65, 288
colonialism, 28–32, 45, 271
commercial peace theory, 210
Common Agricultural Policy (CAP), 285, 289
communism
   Cambodia and, 49
   China and, 47, 49, 50, 153
   Cold War and, 47
   Cuba and, 47, 54
   Greece and, 43
   Laos and, 49
   North Korea and, 47, 49–50
   post–World War I, 38
   rise of, 36
   Soviet Union and, 43, 44, *47*, 56
   Vietnam and, 47, 49, 50–52
Comoros Islands, 352
comparative advantage, 283–85
compellence, 164
complex interdependence, 83–84
complex (or multidimensional) peacekeeping, 331–35, *332*
Comprehensive Anti-Apartheid Act, 162
computer emergency response teams (CERTs), 206
Concert of Europe, 26–28, 33, 324
Confucianism, 367
Congo, *see* Democratic Republic of Congo
Congress of Berlin, 29

Congress of Versailles, 371
Congress of Vienna, 26, 27, 369
constructive engagement policy, 162
constructivism, 69, 86–89, 92
  discourse analysis and, 14–15
  on environmental issues, 433, 437
  feminist critiques and, 97
  on foreign policy decision making,
    170–72
  on foreign policy elites, 145
  on global governance, 441
  on health and communicable disease, 417
  on human rights, 89, 398
  on human security, 439, 440
  on identity, 87–88, 123, 211, 409
  on IGOs, 361–62
  on individuals, 92, 133, 145, 146, 439
  on international cooperation, 244–46
  on international law, 256–57
  on international system, 92, 123
  international system and, 117, 118–19, 123
  on migration, 409
  on national interest, 124–25, 145
  on NGOs, 361–62
  on norms, 86–87, 92, 244, 245–46
  on power, 89
  on Russia-Ukraine conflict, 98, 103–4,
    123
  on security, 222–24
  on soft power, 131
  on sovereignty, 89, 398, 438, 439
  on state, 5, 87, 92, 123, 124–25, 131, 439
  on transnational issues, 439
  on war, 211–12, 222–24
containment strategy, 43, 50, 77
Convention Against Torture, 257
Convention against Torture and Other
  Cruel, Inhuman, or Degrading Treatment
  or Punishment, *373*, 378, 379
conventional war, 195–96
Convention Concerning Indigenous and
  Tribal Peoples in Independent Countries,
  373
Convention for the Protection of All Persons
  from Enforced Disappearance, *373*
Convention on Cluster Munitions, 227

Convention on International Trade in
  Endangered Species of Wild Fauna and
  Flora (CITES), 432
Convention on the Elimination of All
  Forms of Discrimination against Women
  (CEDAW), 249, *372*, 376, 391, 393
Convention on the Prevention and
  Punishment of the Crime of Genocide,
  373, *385*, 385–86
Convention on the Prohibition of the Use,
  Stockpiling, Production, and Transfer
  of Anti- Personnel Mines and on Their
  Destruction, 437
Convention on the Rights of Persons with
  Disabilities, *374*, 381
Convention on the Rights of the Child, *373*
Convention Relating to the Status of
  Refugees, 371, *373*, 404, 405
Convention to Ban Landmines, 359
cooperation, international, *see* international
  cooperation
Correlates of War project, 12–13, 16
Costa Rica, 252
Côte d'Ivoire, *161*, 380, 407
Council of Europe's Convention on
  Cybercrime (CEC), 205
Council of Ministers (EU), 343–44, 345
Council of the European, 252
Counter-Terrorism Committee, UN, 337
Court of Justice of the European Union
  (CJEU), 346
Cousteau, Jacques, 419
credibility, 157
Crimea, annexation of, 8, 57, 60, 62–63, 99,
  101, 136, 207, 346, 395–96
Crimean War (1854-56), 26, 32
crimes against humanity, 386, *387*
criminal law, international, 258–61
critical theory, 96–97
Croatia
  EU membership and, 347
  human rights and, 386–87
  NATO and, 386
  rape and, 392
  UN operations in, *332*
  war crimes in, 254

elites, *see* foreign policy elites

Emory University, 159

endangered species, protection of, 419, 432

enforcement

mechanisms of international law, 250, *251, 252*–55

United Nations and, 330–37, *332*

engagement, positive, 160, *161,* 162

England, *see* Great Britain

Enlightenment, 9, 81–82, 209

Enloe, Cynthia, 97

Entente Cordiale, 34

environmental issues, 417–37, 438

collective goods and, 418

constructivist view of, 433, 437

deforestation, 434–35

global conferences on, 354

liberal view of, 122, 433, 436–37

natural resource issues, 425–27, 433

NGOs and, 355–56, 425, 431–32, 435

pollution and climate change, 419–25, *421,* 433

population issues, 427–31, 436

realist view of, 433, 436

sustainability and, 418–19, 422, 431

system change and, 122

epistemic communities, 415, 417

Erdoğan, Recep Tayyip, 348

Eritrea, 159, 193, *331,* 400

Estonia, 42, 63, 204

ethics in international law, *251,* 256–57

Ethiopia

civil war and, 193, 195

Cold War and, 46, *47*

colonialism and, 29

Eritrea and, 159

migrants and, 407

natural resource issues and, 426

natural sources of power, 128

post–World War I, 38

UN operations in, *331*

Ethiopia-Eritrea War (1999-2000), 193

ethnic cleansing, 183, 386–87, 406

ethnonational movements, 152–53, *174,* 179–81

EU, *see* European Union (EU)

EU Emissions Trading System, 423

Eurasia, 126, *421*

euro (currency), *344*

Euromaidan Revolution, 143

Europe

balance of power and, 29, 32–33

bubonic plague in, 409–10

carbon dioxide emissions of, *421*

colonialism and, 28–32

Concert of Europe, 26–28, 33, 324

economic integration in, 288–90

global financial crisis of 2008 and, 60–61, 306–7, 314

HDI and, *297*

imperialism and, 28–32

industrialization in, 26, 29, 32, 34

maps of, *22, 27, 30, 35, 40, 45*

during Napoleonic Wars, 24–26

in the nineteenth century, 23–36

peace at the core of, 26–28

population issues and, 428

solidification of alliances, 33–34

Thirty Years War in, 20, 21

Westphalian system and, 20–23

See also specific countries

European Atomic Energy Community, 341

European Central Bank, 307, 308

European Coal and Steel Community, 341, *344*

European Commission, 343, 345, 346

European Constitution, *344*

European Council, 343

European Court of Human Rights, 381

European Court of Justice (ECJ), 145, *251,* 252, 348, 350

European Defense Community, 341

European Economic Community (EEC), 341, *344*

"European" identity, 31

European Monetary Union, 289, *344*

European Parliament, 252, 343

European Stability Mechanism, 311

European Union (EU), 239, 340–51

Brexit and, 60, 61, 63, 142, 288, 290, 309, 314, *344,* 348–51

Colombia and, 264

Common Agricultural Policy, 285

economic integration and, 288–90

Eurozone sustainability and, 61, 308
historical evolution of, 341–43
human rights and, 378
international law and, 252, 254, 260
international political economy and,
288–90
international trade and, 286–87, 348–49
Kosovo and, 151
map of, *342*
Myanmar and, 406
neoliberal institutionalist view of, 85
polarity and, *112*
policies and problems, 346–47, 350
principal institutions of, *345*
public opinion polling in, 141
refugees and, 405–6, 438
Russia and, 98, 99
sanctions imposed by, 99, 163, 335
significant events in the development of,
344
structure of, 288–90
Ukraine and, 102–3, 123
Eurozone financial crisis (2009), 307–9, 314,
344
evoked set, 137, *138*
exchange rates, 273
Exogenous Shocks Facility, 307
external balancing, 76
extradition, 258, 259, 260
extreme poverty, 304
extremist Islamic fundamentalism, 175–78,
199
Exxon Mobil, 274

Facebook, 143, 144, 151, 354
fascism, 37, 38, 39, 40
FDI (foreign direct investment), 279–80
Federal Aviation Administration, *251*
federalism, 340
feminists
critiques of IR theories, 96–98
on health and communicable disease, 417
on population, 428
women's rights and, 394
Ferdinand, Franz, 34
Field Support, UN Department of, 337

financial crises, 303, 306
Asian crisis of 1990s, 281–82, 303
Eurozone crisis of 2009, 307–9
global crisis of 2008-2009, 60–61,
306–7, 314
Mexican crisis of 1982, 303
responses to, 309–12
Finland, 42, 101, 325
Finnemore, Martha, 119, 362
fire-in-a-theater, 87
FIRST (Forum of Incident Response and
Security Teams), 206
first-strike capability, 164
First UN Emergency Force (UNEF I),
331
fiscal policies, 272–73
force, exercising power via, 163–65
Ford, 274
Ford, Gerald, 77
Foreign Affairs (Kennan), 43
foreign direct investment (FDI), 279–80
foreign policy
Cold War view on, 43
IGOs and, 323
masculinization of, 97
post-Cold War era, 57
Foreign Policy, 183
foreign policy decision making
constructivist view of, 170–72
liberal view of, 167–70, *168*
models of, 165–72, *167*
foreign policy elites, 133
individual decision making by, 136–39,
138
influence of situational factors on,
139–40, *140*
information-processing mechanisms of,
136–39, *138*
personality and personal interests of,
133–34, *135,* 136
Forum of Incident Response and Security
Teams (FIRST), 206
"Four Freedoms" (Roosevelt), 371
Fourteen Points, 36, 37–38
fracking process, 426
Fragile State Index, 183
fragile states, *174,* 182–83, 438

France
 Algeria and, 130
 alliances in the nineteenth century, 33
 attack in Nice, 187, 188, 201
 balance of power and, 32, 33
 bipolarity and, 111, *112*
 Cold War and, 47, 49
 colonialism and, 29, 45, 197
 Concert of Europe and, 26, 28
 cyberattack in, 187
 ethnonationalists and, 153
 European Union and, 341
 Germany and, 32
 in Group of 7, 278
 Libya and, 61
 multipolarity and, 111, *112*
 Napoleonic Wars and, 23, 24–26
 post–World War I, 37, 39
 post–World War II, 119
 sources of power, 130
 terrorism and, 204
 UN Security Council and, 326, 336
 Westphalian system and, 22
 World War I and, 34, 36, 192
 World War II and, 39, 40, 192
Franco-Prussian War (1870), 33, 34
Frederick II, 22
Freedom House, 375
Freeport-McMoRan, 435
free trade, 82, 85, 290, 348–49
French Revolution (1789), 23, 24, 152, 196
freshwater issues, 426
Friedman, Thomas, 269
Friends of the Earth International, 355
functionalism, 321, 346
Fund for Peace, 183

Gambia, 389
Gandhi, Mohandas, 129, 139, 198, 199
Garrett, Laurie, 412
GATT, *see* General Agreement on Tariffs
 and Trade (GATT)
Gazprom, 274
GDP (gross domestic product), 281, 414,
 415–16

gender roles, 97
General Agreement on Tariffs and Trade
 (GATT), 275, *276, 278, 285–86*
  see also World Trade Organization
  (WTO)
General Assembly, UN, *see* UN General
 Assembly
General Motors, 274
generic drugs, intellectual-property
 protection rules on, 413–14
Geneva Conventions, 41, 195, 226, 240–41,
 255, 257, 370, 396
genocide, 384–90, *385, 387*
 in Burundi, 58
 Convention on the Prevention and
  Punishment of Genocide, *373, 385,*
  385–86
 definition of, *385*
 human rights and, 396
 in Myanmar, 406
 punishing guilty individuals for, 388–89
 rape as, 392
 rebuilding truth commissions on, 390
 in Rwanda, 58, 59, 190, 191, 304
 during World War II, 41, 254, 371, 385
geographic size and position, as sources of
 power, 125–26
Georgia, 98, 143, 204
Germany
 alliances in the nineteenth century,
  33–34
 balance of power and, 32, 33, 213
 colonialism and, 31
 conventional war and, 195
 division of, 42, 47
 European Union and, 341
 Eurozone sustainability and, 61, 308
 France and, 32
 in Group of 7, 278
 imperialism and, 29
 industrialization and, 29, 32, 33
 international finance and, 280
 multipolarity and, *112*
 national identity of, 88–89
 nuclear weapons and, 89
 Poland and, 325

post-World War I, 36–37, 38
post-World War II, 43, 88
public diplomacy and, 158
refugees and, 406, 438
sources of power, 126, 129
unification of, 27, 28, 32, *47*, 152
World War I and, 34–36, 68
World War II and, 8, 38, 39–41, 192, 209, 213
Gettleman, Jeffrey, 436
GGE (Group of Governmental Experts), 206
Ghana
global financial crisis and, 309, 310
migrants from, 407
Ghonim, Wael, 143–44
Gilpin, Robert, 80, 120, 274
Glad, Betty, 134
glasnost, 54, 55, 57
global financial crisis of 2008, 60–61, 306–7, 314
Global Fund to Fight AIDS, Tuberculosis, and Malaria, 413
global governance, 440–41
globalization
as challenge to state power, *174,* 174–75, 438
of conflict, 45–46
definition of, 269–70
of women's rights, 390–94
see also economic globalization
Global Network of People Living with HIV/ AIDS, 414
Global Outbreak Alert and Response Network, 411
global peace index, 190
Global Reporting Initiative, 425
Global Slavery Index, 370
global warming, 420–25, *421,* 433
GONGOs (government-organized NGOs), 353
good neighbor principle of cooperation, 418
Gorbachev, Mikhail, *47,* 54, 55, 57, 72, 132, 134, 140
government-organized NGOs (GONGOs), 353

Grameen Bank, 299
Great Britain
abolitionists and, 369
alliances in the nineteenth century, 33–34
balance of power and, 32–34, 213
carbon dioxide emissions of, 434
civil wars and, 74
Cold War and, 47
colonialism and, 30, 31, 45, 126, 197
Concert of Europe and, 26, 28
cyberattack in, 187
foreign policy elites and, 134, 137
in Group of 7, 278
hegemony of, 116
imperialism and, 29, 31
industrialization and, 26, 33, 271–72
Iraq and, 59, 134, 346
Law of the Sea Treaty and, 250
Malayan Emergency and, 197
multipolarity and, 111, *112*
Napoleonic Wars and, 24, 25, 26
nuclear weapons and, 15, 133
post-World War I, 36, 37, 39
post-World War II, 42, 119
public diplomacy and, 158
public input in, 142
sources of power, 126, 129
Torrey Canyon oil spill in, 419
UN Security Council and, 326, 336
vote to leave the EU, 60, 61, 63, 142, 288, 290, 309, 314, *344, 348–51*
Westphalian system and, 22
World War I and, 35–36, 192
World War II and, 39–41, 192, 213
Great Illusion, The (Angell), 242
"Great War," *see* World War I (1914-18)
Greece
Bulgaria and, 325
communism and, 43
Eurozone sustainability and, 61, 307–8
independence of, 27, 32
Turkey and, 259, 336
Green Movement, 144
Green Climate Fund, 424
Greenham Common Peace Camp, 15

World War II and, 38, 39–40, 212

HIV/AIDS, 329, 354, 355, 403, 412–14, 415

Hobbes, Thomas
    on anarchy, 9, 74
    on individuals, 9, 74
    Leviathan, 9, *10,* 74
    on state, 9, 74–75
    on state of nature, 9, 213

Hobson, John A., 93

Ho Chi Minh, 49, 50

Holland, 32
    see also Netherlands

Hollande, François, 424

Holocaust, 371, 385, 386

Holsti, Ole, 136

Holy Alliance of 1815, 33

Homer-Dixon, Thomas, 436

Honduras, 265, 349

H1N1 virus, 411

Hong Kong, 120

Hopf, Ted, 86–87

horizontal enforcement, *251,* 254–55

HSBC Holdings, 274

Hudson's Bay Company, 270, 274

Human Development Index (HDI), 295, *297,* 304

Human Development Report, 403

humanitarian intervention, 394–97

human nature
    economic liberalism on, 277
    liberal view of, 5, 81–82, 122
    realist view of, 79, 97, 122

human rights, 365–99
    behavioralist view of, 12–13
    constructivist view of, 89, 398
    as emerging international responsibility, 370–71, *372–74*
    foundations of, 367–70
    genocide and, *see* genocide
    Helsinki Accord and, 8
    High Commissioner for, 337, 380
    HIV/AIDS and, 414
    humanitarian interventions and, 394–97
    IGOs and, 379–81, 383
    international community's role in, 379–84

international law and, 260–61

liberal view of, 122, 398

mass atrocities and, 384–90, *385, 387*

NGOs and, 355, 381–83, 386

public actions and, 143

realist view of, 398

responsibility to protect (R2P), 394–97, 398

states as protectors of, 374–79, 438

system change and, 122

women's rights as, 390–94

Human Rights Watch, 355, 381, 393

human security, 376–77
    constructivist view of, 439, 440
    environment and, 417
    in globalized and transnational world, 403
    impact on international relations practice, 437–38, 440
    impact on international relations theory, 437, 438–40
    liberal view of, 439, 440
    in national security, 189
    realist view of, 439, 440
    United Nations and, 326

human trafficking, 183, 370, *372–73,* 393–94, 408

Humphrey, John, 376

Hungary
    bipolarity and, *112*
    Cold War and, 43, 52
    collective actions in, 142
    global financial crisis and, 307
    post-World War I, 36, 39
    post-World War II, 43
    refusal of refugees, 438

Huntington, Samuel, 175

Hussein, Saddam, 215, 217, 220
    Iraqization policy and, 7
    Kuwait and, 77, 395
    malignant narcissism syndrome and, 134
    removal from power, 59, 73, 100, 149
    sanctions against, 162–63

hydrofluorocarbons (HFCs), 420

hyperinflation, 37

hypotheses, 68–69

Hyundai, 71

IAEA (International Atomic Energy Agency), 144, 323, 335

I Am Malala (Yousafzai), 144

IBM, 71

ICBL (International Campaign to Ban Landmines), 227, 359

ICBMs (intercontinental ballistic missiles), 54, 63

ICC (International Criminal Court), 154, 155, 381, *387*, 388–89, 392, 398

Iceland, 306, 307, 433

ICJ (International Court of Justice), *251*, 252–53, 254, *327*, 387

ICT (information and communications technology), 206, 304

IDA (International Development Association), *276*, 280

Idea for a Universal History (Kant), 10, *10*

identity
    constructivist view of, 87–88, 123, 211, 409
    "European," 31
    in international relations theories, 72

IDPs (internally displaced people), 404–5, *405*, 407, 408

IFC (International Finance Corporation), *276*, 280, 295

IGOs, *see* intergovernmental organizations (IGOs)

IHL (international humanitarian law), 41, 370

Ikenberry, G. John, 118

IMF, *see* International Monetary Fund (IMF)

immigration and asylum, EU on, 349

imperialism
    definition of, 28
    Hobson on, 93
    Lenin on, 425
    in the nineteenth century, 28–32
    radical view of, 93

India
    balance of power and, 77, 216
    as BRICS country, 295, 313
    carbon dioxide emissions of, *421*
    colonialism and, 45, 126
    environmental issues and, 421, 422–23

    ethnonational movements and, 179
    foreign policy elites and, 139
    HIV/AIDS and, 413–14
    human rights and, 368, 386, 396
    independence of, 45, 197
    international trade and, 285, 286, 293
    Kyoto Protocol and, 422–23
    malaria in, 410
    map of, *180*
    multiple nations within, 152
    mutual legal assistance treaties and, 258
    nuclear weapons and, 76, 90, 223, 233
    population issue in, 428, 430
    sources of power, 125, 129
    UN operations in, 330
    WTO agreement and, 91

individuals
    constructivist view of, 92, 133, 145, 146, 439
    decision making and, 74
    economic liberalism on, 277
    foreign policy elites, *see* foreign policy elites
    Hobbes on, 9, 74
    human rights and, 369
    in international relations theories, 72, 132–33
    Kant on, 10–11
    levels of analysis for, 109, *109*, 132, 145–46
    liberal view of, 5, 133, 145–46, 439
    mass publics and, 141–44
    neoliberal institutionalist view of, 83
    private, 144–45
    realist view of, 74, 132–33, 145
    Rousseau on, 10, 11
    Smith on, 23
    track-two diplomacy use of, 159–60

Indochina, 45, 49, 197

Indonesia
    environmental issues and, 434–35
    extremist Islamic fundamentalism and, 178
    financial crisis and, 281
    in Group 20, 295
    independence of, 211
    mutual legal assistance treaties and, 258

natural sources of power, 127
    refugees and, 406
    terrorism and, *202*
    UN operations in, 330
industrialization
    class and, 26
    interstate war and, 192
    in nineteenth-century Europe, 26, 29,
        32, 34
    as tangible source of power, 128
Industrial Revolution, 29–30, 192,
    271–72
information and communications technology
    (ICT), 206, 304
information processing, foreign policy elites
    and, 136–39, *138*
Inquiry into the Nature and Causes of the
    Wealth of Nations, An (Smith), 23, 418
institutions, 82, 83
intellectual-property protection, 413–14
Inter-American Commission on Human
    Rights, 182
intercontinental ballistic missiles (ICBMs),
    54, 63
intergovernmental organizations (IGOs),
    320–53, 362
    affiliated with the UN, 339, *340* (*see also*
        United Nations)
    constructivist view of, 361–62
    creation of, 320–23
    HIV/AIDS epidemic and, 413
    human rights and, 379–81, 383
    liberal view of, 116, 361
    NGOs working with, 432
    other regional organizations, 351–53
    population issue and, 431
    realist view of, 361
    roles of, 323
Intergovernmental Panel on Climate
    Change, 422
Intermediate Range Nuclear Force Treaty
    (1988), 15, 221
internal balancing, 76
internally displaced people (IDPs), 404–5,
    405, 407, 408
International Atomic Energy Agency
    (IAEA), 144, 323, 335

International Bank for Reconstruction and
    Development, *see* World Bank
International Bill of Rights, 371
International Campaign to Ban Landmines
    (ICBL), 227, 359
International Civil Aviation Organization,
    251, 323, 339
International Commission on Intervention
    and State Sovereignty, 395
International Convention on the Abolition
    of Slavery, 369, *372*
International Convention on the
    Elimination of All Forms of Racial
    Discrimination, *372*
International Convention on the Protection
    of the Rights of All Migrant Workers and
    Members of Their Families, *374*
International Convention on the Suppression
    and Punishment of the Crime of
    Apartheid, *372*
international cooperation, 235–46, 266
    constructivist view of, 244–46
    definition of, 234
    international institutions and, 239–41
    liberal view of, 241–43
    neoliberal institutionalist view of,
        238–41
    realist view of, 235–38
    triangular, model of, 264–65
International Court of Justice (ICJ), *251*,
    252–53, 254, *327*, 387
International Covenant on Civil and
    Political Rights, 13, 371, *372*, 378
International Covenant on Economic,
    Social, and Cultural Rights, 371, *372*
International Criminal Court (ICC), 154,
    155, 381, *387*, 388–89, 392, 398
international criminal law, 258–61
International Crisis Group, 413
international development, 295
    goals for, 301–3
    strategies to achieve, 296, *297*,
        298–300
International Development Association
    (IDA), *276*, 280
International Disability Alliance, 381
international finance, 279–82

International Finance Corporation (IFC), *276*, 280, 295

international humanitarian law (IHL), 41, 370

international institutions
  definitions of, 71, 239
  international cooperation and, 239–41
  liberal view of, 86, 210

International Labour Organization, 339, 354

international law, 246–63, 266
  bodies of, 258–63, 266
    international criminal law, 258–61
    UNCLOS, 261–63, *262*, 266
  compliance with, 255–57
  constructivist view of, 256–57
  definition of, 246
  enforcement mechanisms of, 250, *251*, 252–55
  Geneva Conventions, 41
  human rights and, 260–61
  liberal view of, 255, 256–57
  neoliberal institutionalist view of, 255, 256
  realist view of, 254–55, 256, 441
  sources of, 247–50
  on war, 224–30
    cyberattacks, 228–30
    jus ad bellum, 224–26
    jus in bello, 224, 226–28

International Law Commission, 248

International Maritime Organization, 339

International Monetary Fund (IMF), *276*, 278, 310
  Asian financial crisis and, 281–82
  China's rival to, 114
  development strategy and, 296, 298
  economic liberalism and, 275
  global financial crisis of 2008 and, 307
  Greece and, 308
  international monetary policy and, 282–83
  United Nations and, 338

international monetary system, 282–83

International Negotiation Network (Emory University), 159

international order, 118

International Organization for Migration, 370, 408

international political economy, 269–316
  economic globalization and, *see* economic globalization
  economic institutions in, role of, 272–79
    Bretton Woods institutions, 275, *276*, 277–79
    multinational corporations, 274–75
    states, 272–74
  economic liberalism and, *see* economic liberalism
  historical evolution of, 270–72

international relations, 189
  cooperation in, *see* international cooperation
  in daily life, 3–5
  foundational questions of, 6
  impact of human security on, 437–38, 440
  individuals in, *see* individuals
  law and, *see* international law
  theories of, *see* international relations theories
  tools for answering foundational questions in, 6–16, *16*
    alternative approaches, 14–16, *16*
    history, *see* historical context of international relations
    philosophy, 6, 8–11, *10*, *16*
    scientific method, 6, 11–14, *16*
  war and, *see* war

international relations theories, 5–6, 67–104
  behavioralism, 11–14, *16*
  components of, 70–73
  constructivism (*see* constructivism)
  definition of, 68
  feminist critiques of, 96–98
  impact of human security on, 437, 438–40
  liberalism, *see* liberalism
  neoliberal institutionalism, 83–85
  neorealism, *see* neorealism
  postmodernism, 15
  radicalism, *see* radicalism
  realism, *see* realism

International Sanitary Conferences, 410

Iraqization policy, 7
Iraq War (2003), 215
  compellence and, 164
  EU view of, 346–47
  Great Britain and, 134
  lessons of, 7–8, 129
  nuclear weapons and, 208, 209, 220,
    225, 395
  public diplomacy and, 159
  UN Security Council and, 223–24, 250,
    335–36, 346
Ireland, 61, 159, 307
Irish Republican Army, 199, 200
ISIL, *see* Islamic State
ISIS, *see* Islamic State
Islamic State, 62, 176–77, 200, 201, *202*
  ethnonational movements and, 181
  genocide and, 387–88
  human rights and, 369–70
  Iran and, 62
  Iraq and, 60, 62, 129
  Russia and, 62, 66, 67
  Syria and, 3, 60, 62, 194, 225
  United States and, 62
  violence against women, 392
Islam on dignity of individuals, 367
Israel, 158
  bipolarity and, *112*
  Cold War and, *47, 53*
  cyberattacks and, 205
  establishment of, 6, 53
  extremist groups in, 178
  ICJ ruling on, 253
  intangible sources of power, 129
  limited wars and, 192
  natural resource issues and, 426
  nuclear weapons and, 116, 223
  state disputes and, 156, 326
  terrorism and, *202*
  track-two diplomacy and, 159
  Waltz on, 116
  see also Arab-Israeli conflict
Italy
  alliances in the nineteenth century, 33
  European Union and, 341
  Eurozone sustainability and, 308

  in Group of 7, 278
  imperialism and, 29
  industrialization and, 29
  international law and, 260
  League of Nations and, 325
  post-World War I, 38
  protests in, 143
  refugees in, 400, 401
  unification of, 27, 28, 32, 152
  World War II and, 38, 40
IUCN (International Union for the
  Conservation of Nature), 432

Janis, Irving, 138
Japan
  alliances in the nineteenth century,
    33–34
  atomic bombing of, 42, 196, 226
  balance of power and, 34, 216
  China and, 30, 38, 41, 64, 197, 220
  Colombia and, 264
  colonialism and, 45
  conventional war and, 196
  environmental issues and, 420
  foreign policy decision making and, 170
  global financial crisis and, 306, 307
  in Group of 7, 278
  human rights and, 378
  imperialism and, 30
  industrialization and, 34
  international finance and, 280
  international trade and, 287, 293
  invasion of Nanking, 38, 64
  Korea and, 38, 41
  Kyoto Protocol and, 423
  League of Nations and, 325
  national identity of, 88, 89
  in the nineteenth century, 30
  polarity and, 111, *112*
  population issue and, 429
  post-World War I, 38
  post-World War II, 42, 49, 88
  sources of power, 127, 128
  tariffs and, 273
  TPP and, 294

Multilateral Fund for the Implementation of the Montreal Protocol, 256

Multilateral Investment Guarantee Agency (MIGA), *276*, 280

multilateralism, 59, 117–18

multinational corporations (MNCs), 438
  critics of, 310–12, 315
  in dependency theory, 95
  economic globalization and, 272, 287
  international finance and, 279–80
  in international relations theories, 71
  NAFTA and, 290
  role of, 274–75
  system change and, 122

multiple independently targetable reentry vehicles (MIRVs), 54

multipolar systems, 80, 111, *112,* 113, 116

mutual assured destruction (MAD), 46

mutual legal assistance treaties, 258

Myanmar
  civil war in, 193
  human rights and, 386
  malaria in, 410
  Rohingya in, 386, 392, 406
  sanctions against, *161*
  violence against women in, 392

NAFTA (North American Free Trade Agreement), 243, 290–92, 293, 314

Nagasaki, atomic bombing of, 42, 196, 226

Nagorno-Karabakh, 151

Naím, Moisés, 258–59

Namibia, 252, 331, 333, 389

Nanking Massacre, 38, 64

Napoleonic Wars (1799-1815), 23, 24–26

Nasser, Gamal Abdel, 137

nation, definition of, 24, 152

National Institutes of Health, 415

national interest
  constructivist view of, 124–25, 145
  liberal view of, 124, 145
  realist view of, 73, 74, 124, 145

nationalism
  China and, 153–54
  Cold War and, 45
  definition of, 24, 196

  French Revolution and, 196
  globalization and, 60
  Monnet on, 341
  post-World War I and, 37
  Soviet Union and, 56
  war and, 212

national security
  cyberattacks and, 187
  definition of, 188–89
  human security in, 189
  managing, 212–13, 216–24
  vehicle attacks and, 186, 187

National Socialist Worker's (Nazi) Party, 37, 41

nation-states, 152

Native American nations, 152–53

NATO (North Atlantic Treaty Organization)
  Article V of Charter of, 59
  bipolarity and, 111
  expansion of, 98, 134
  expectations of, 239
  formation of, 44, *47*
  human rights and, 386
  Kosovo and, 380–81
  limited military intervention by, 194, 214–15
  natural sources of power, 130
  neoliberal institutionalist view of, 85
  Russia and, 98, 134, 396
  Ukraine and, 102, 210

natural resources
  conflicts over, 425–27, 433
  population issues and, 428–29
  as sources of power, 125–28

Natural Resources Defense Council, 255

natural selection, theory of, 69

Nature, 434

Nature Conservancy, 431

Nazi (National Socialist Worker's) Party, 37, 41

NCDs (noncommunicable diseases), 415

NDB (New Development Bank), 312

negative externalities, 420

negative sanctions, 160, *161,* 162–63

negotiation
  diplomacy and, 157–60
  international trade and, 285–87

neoliberal institutionalism, 83–85, 439
  on anarchy, 118, 238
  on individuals, 83
  on international cooperation, 238–41
  on international law, 255, 256
  on international system, 118
  on prisoner's dilemma, 238–39, 255
  on state, 118
neorealism, 79–80
  on anarchy, 79
  definition of, 78
  on international system, 79, 441
  on power, 79
  Waltz on, 78–79
Nestlé, 274
Netanyahu, Benjamin, 319
Netherlands
  environmental efforts of, 423–24
  European Union and, 341
  formation of, 27
  imperialism and, 29, 211
  international law and, 260
  in the nineteenth century, 32
  oil sanctions and, 162
  Westphalian system and, 22
  World War II and, 39
New Development Bank (NDB), 312
Newmont Mining Corporation, 435
New Zealand, 293, 294
Ngo Dinh Diem, 50
NGOs, *see* nongovernmental organizations
  (NGOs)
Nguyen Van Thieu, 50
Nicaragua, 54, 201, 252, 253
Nicaragua v. United States, 254
Nicolas II, 134
Nicolson, Harold, 157
Nieto, Enrique Peña, 240
Niger, migrants from, 407
Nigeria
  Boko Haram's kidnapping of girls in,
    364–65, 392
  Cameroon and, 253
  civil war and, 193
  extremist Islamic fundamentalism and,
    178

population issue in, 436
  terrorism and, *202*
  transnational crime and, 182
Nixon, Richard, *47,* 77, 140
noncommunicable diseases (NCDs), 415
nongovernmental organizations (NGOs), 4,
  353–60, 362, 438
  business and industry (BINGOs), 353
  constructivist view of, 361–62
  donor-organized (DONGOs), 353
  Ebola outbreak and, 412
  economic development strategies and,
    299
  environmental issues and, 355–56, 425,
    431–32, 435
  functions and roles of, 355–58
  government-organized (GONGOs), 353
  HIV/AIDS epidemic and, 413
  human rights and, 355, 381–83, 386
  influence of, 354–55
  Kenya and, 357
  liberal view of, 85, 116–17, 361
  limits of, 359–60
  organizational politics and, 167–69, 168,
    170
  population issues and, 430–31
  power of, 354–55, 358–59
  realist view of, 360–61
  system change and, 122
  transnational movements and, 178
  WTO and, 311–12
noninterference, principle of, 21, 438
non-refoulement, 404
nontariff barriers, 273
nonviolent resistance, 198
normative element in political life, 10
norms
  constructivist view of, 86–87, 92, 244,
    245–46
  definition of, 72
  in international cooperation, 244–46
  in international law, *251,* 256–57
  in international relations theories, 72–73
  polarity systems and, 116
North America, 126, *421*
  See also specific countries

North American Free Trade Agreement (NAFTA), 243, 290–92, 293, 314

North Atlantic Treaty Organization (NATO), *see* NATO (North Atlantic Treaty Organization)

Northern Ireland, 159, 348
    see also Great Britain

North Korea
    bipolarity and, 111, *112*
    Cold War and, 46, 49–50
    communism and, 47, 49–50
    economic sanctions on, 214
    nuclear weapons and, 3, 18, 50, 63, 120, 205, 211, 214–15, 221–22, 223, 233–34, 239, 318
    South Korea and, 18
    terrorism and, 201
    transnational crime and, 182
    Trump and, 215, 318, 320
    United States and, 49–50, 215

North Vietnam, 46, *47*, 49, 50, 111, 130, 139

Norway
    bipolarity and, *112*
    global financial crisis and, 306
    international finance and, 281
    natural sources of power, 127
    population issue in, 430
    World War II and, 39

no significant harm principle, 418

NPT (Nuclear Nonproliferation Treaty), *47*, 223, 233–34

Ntaganda, Bosco, 389

nuclear deterrence, 163–65, 217–18

Nuclear Nonproliferation Treaty (NPT), *47*, 223, 233–34

nuclear weapons
    China and, 115
    Cold War and, 46, 236
    in Cuban missile crisis, 50
    Germany and, 89
    Great Britain and, 15, 133
    India and, 76, 90, 223, 233
    Iran and, 8, 116, 121, 133, 158
    Iraq and, 208, 209, 220, 225
    Israel and, 116, 223
    Libya and, 78

North Korea and, 3, 18, 50, 63, 120, 205, 211, 214–15, 221–22, 223, 233–34, 239, 318
    Pakistan and, 76, 223, 233
    South Africa and, 223, 233
    South Korea and, 221–22
    Soviet Union and, 43, 46, *47*, 236
    system change and, 120–21
    Ukraine and, 223, 232, 233
    United States and, 42, 46, 196, 236
    World War II and, 42

Nye, Joseph, 81, 117, 129

OAS (Organization of American States), 264, 323, 351–52

Obama, Barack, 72
    Cuba and, 140, 375
    on TPP, 293

OECD (Organization for Economic Cooperation and Development), 264

offensive realism, 78

offshore financial centers, 281

oil
    Angola and, 54
    China and, 151
    economic statecraft and, 162
    embargo in 1973 on, 437
    Kuwait and, 77, 126, 127
    Qatar and, 126
    Torrey Canyon oil spill, 419
    United Arab Emirates and, 126
    violent conflicts over, 436

Oil-for-Food Programme, 338

Oklahoma City Federal Building bombing (1995), 178

Olympic Games, 199

One-China policy, 115, 156

ONGOs (operational NGOs), 353

On War (Clausewitz), 189

OPEC (Organization of the Petroleum Exporting Countries), 162, 306

Open Society Institute, 381

operational NGOs (ONGOs), 353

Operation Barbarossa, 40

Opium War (1842), 30

optimism, 81
Orange Resolution (2004), 143
organizational politics, 167–69, *168*, 170
Organization for Economic Cooperation and Development (OECD), 264
Organization of American States (OAS), 264, 323, 351–52
Organization of Petroleum Exporting Countries (OPEC), 162, 303
Organski, Kenneth, 208
"others, the," 15, *16*
Ottawa Process, 359, 376
Ottoman Empire, 27, 35–36, 37
Outer Space Treaty, 249
Oxfam, 299, 355
ozone depletion, 420–25, *421*, 433

Pakistan
  balance of power and, 216
  drone strikes and, 3, 227
  ethnonational movements and, 179
  global financial crisis and, 307
  malaria in, 410
  nuclear weapons and, 76, 223, 233
  polio vaccinations in, 411, 416
  terrorism and, *202*
  violence against women in, 393
Palestine, 151
  extremist groups and, 178
  ICJ ruling on, 253
  natural resource issues and, 426
  post-World War I, 36
  self-determination and, 199
  state disputes and, 154–55, *156*, 326, 328
  see also Arab-Israeli conflict
Palestine Islamic Jihad, 199
Palestinian Liberation Organization (PLO), 199
Palestinian National Authority, 151, 154
Panama, 52, 258
Paraguay, 238
Paris Agreement, 424, 425
Paris climate change agreement, 237, 424
Pasteur Institute, 415
patriarchal system, 96

peace
  collective security and, 82–83
  Concert of Europe and, 26–28
  decline in violence and, 13
  democratic-peace hypothesis, 172–73
  Fourteen Points on, 38
  Kant on, 10–11
  liberal view of, 86, 121–22, 172, 210
  in nineteenth-century Europe, 26–28
  realist view of, 111, 116, 172
  United Nations and, 325–26
peacebuilding, 331
Peacebuilding Commission, UN, 337–38
peacekeeping
  complex, 331–35, *332*
  multidimensional, 331–35, *332*
  NATO and, 386
  traditional, 330
  United Nations and, 194, 330–35, *331, 332*, 336–337386
Peacekeeping Operations, UN Department of, 337
Pearl Harbor, attack on, 38
Peloponnesian War, 7, 16
People's Republic of China, *see* China
perestroika, 54, 55, 57
Permanent Court of Arbitration, 254, 266
Perpetual Peace (Kant), 10, *10*, 172, 209
personality, foreign policy elites and, 133–34, *135*, 136
Peru, 207
  mining in, 95
  Organization of American States and, 352
  protests against Trans-Pacific Partnership in, 269
  regional trade and, 288
pesticides, 419
Peter the Great, 22
Philippines
  bipolarity and, 111, *112*
  China and, 63, 266
  Cold War and, 49, 50
  extremist Islamic fundamentalism and, 178
  financial crisis and, 281

guerrilla warfare and, 197
imperialism and, 30
Spratly Islands and, 63
terrorism and, 200
"philosopher-kings," 9
philosophical viewpoints on international
relations, 6, 8–11, *10*, *16*
Pinker, Steven, 3, 13
Pinto, Aníbal, 94
Plato, 8–9, *10*, 209
Pledge of Allegiance, 153
PLO (Palestine Liberation Organization),
199
pluralist model of foreign policy decision
making, *168*, 169–70
Poland
annexation of, 42
bipolarity and, *112*
Cold War and, 43
Iraq War and, 346
Lithuania and, 325
in the nineteenth century, 28, 33
post–World War II, 43
Russia and, 101
World War II and, 39, 41
polarity, system
liberal view of, 118
realist view of, 111–16, *112*
polio, 411, 416
political economy, international, *see*
international political economy
polluter pays principle, 419
pollution and climate change, 420–25, *421*,
433
population
as an environmental issue, 427–31, 433,
436
Concert of Europe and, 26–27
radical view of, 428
realist view of, 428
as sources of power, 127–28
Population Connection, 430
Population Council, 430–31
populism, 63
portfolio investment, 280
Portugal, 29, 61, 197, 250, 308

positive engagement, 160, *161*, 162
postmodernism, 15, 96
Potsdam Conference (1945), 42
poverty, extreme, 304
power
constructivist view of, 89
feminist critiques and, 97
industrialization and, 26
neorealist view of, 79
NGOs and, 354–55
post–World War II and, 42
realist view of, 5, 73, 77–78, 97, 111, 113,
254–55
smart, 130
soft, 129–31
state, *see* state power
system change and, 119
see also balance of power
Power and Independence (Keohane and Nye),
117
power potential of states, 125
economic statecraft and, 162
intangible sources of power, 128–31
natural sources of power, 125–28
tangible sources of power, 128
power transition theory, 208–9, 217
Prebisch, Raul, 94
precautionary principle, 419
preventive action principle, 419
principal actors, 73–74
prisoner's dilemma
neoliberal institutionalist view of,
238–39, 255
realist view of, 236–37
prisoners of war, 226, 240–41, 255, 370
private individuals, 144–45
proletariat, 93
protection gap, 407
protectionism, 271
Prussia
alliances in the nineteenth century, 33
Concert of Europe and, 26, 28
multipolarity and, 111, *112*
Napoleonic Wars and, 24, 25, 26
Westphalian system and, 22
public diplomacy, 158–59

public health, *see* health and communicable disease

Public Health Emergency of International Concern, 412

public opinion, impact of, 141–42

Puerto Rico, 30

Purpose of Intervention, The (Finnemore), 119

Putin, Vladimir, 72, 100
   as a foreign policy elite, 134, 136, 137
   Syria and, 67
   Ukraine conflict and, 99, 103, 145–46, 395–96
   UN General Assembly and, 319

Putnam, Robert, 158

Qaddafi, Muammar, 61, 129, 215, 395

Qatar, 126, 159, *161*, 353

Qing dynasty, 30

racial discrimination
   apartheid, *161*, 162, 380
   UN Human Rights Conventions on, *372*

racism, World War II and, 41

radicalism, 69–70, 92–96
   on capitalism, 92–96
   on demographic trends, 428
   dependency theory, 94–96
   economic, 272, 277, 315
   feminist critiques and, 96
   on imperialism, 93
   on international system, 93
   Marxism, 93–94
   on population, 428
   on state, 93, 94
   on women's rights, 394

Radio Sawa, 159

Rainforest Action Network, 431

Rajoy, Mariano, 165

rape, 392–93, 406

Rape during Civil War (Cohen), 393

Rape of Nanking, 38, 64

rational actors, 74

rational model of foreign policy decision making, 165–67, *167*

Rawlence, Ben, 406–7

Reagan, Ronald, 54, 162

Reagan Doctrine, *47*

realism, 69, 73–80
   on anarchy, 73, 110, 113, 238
   on balance of power, 73, 77
   defensive, 77–78
   definition of, 5
   on deterrence, 218
   on diplomacy, 160
   on environmental issues, 433, 436
   feminist critiques and, 97
   on foreign policy decision making, 165–67
   on foreign policy elites, 145
   on global governance, 441
   on health and communicable disease, 416
   on human nature, 79, 97, 122
   on human rights, 398
   on human security, 439, 440
   on IGOs, 361
   on individuals, 74, 132–33, 145
   on international cooperation, 235–38
   on international law, 254–55, 256, 441
   on international system, 5, 110–16, *112*, 117, 119
   on Iraq War (2003), 7–8
   on migration, 408
   on national interest, 73, 74, 124, 145
   neorealism, 78–80
   on NGOs, 360–61
   offensive, 78
   on peace, 111, 116, 172
   on polarity system, 111–16, *112*
   on population, 428
   post–World War I, 38
   on power, 73, 77–78, 97, 111, 113, 254–55
   on prisoner's dilemma, 236–37
   roots of, 73–75
   on Russia-Ukraine conflict, 98, 100–101
   on sanctions, 160
   on security, 74, 76, 100–101, 212–13, 216–18, 439
   on soft power, 130
   on sovereignty, 110, 438
   on state, 5, 73–74, 79, 110–11, 113, 124, 125, 150, 235–36, 439

September 11, 2001, attacks, 59, 88, 141, 200, 204

Serbia
  Bulldozer Revolution, 143
  EU membership and, 350
  human rights and, 386–87
  Kosovo and, 58, 151, 380–81, 386–87
  Milosevic and, 143, 212
  NATO and, 386
  rape and, 392
  World War I and, 34

sex slavery, 369–70, 393

shadow of the future, 239

Shanghai Cooperation Organization (SCO), 205

Shia, 87

Shiites, 176, 200

Short-Term Liquidity Facility, 307

Siemenpuu, 435

Siemens, 274

Sierra Leone
  civil war and, 193
  Ebola outbreak in, 411
  truth commissions and, 390
  war crimes in, 254

Silent Spring (Carson), 419

Singapore
  international development and, 302
  international finance and, 280
  international trade and, 287
  natural sources of power, 127
  SARS outbreak and, 411

Singer, J. David, 12, 14, 109

Singh, Hari, 179

Single European Act (SEA), 288, 342, *344*

Sinopec, 274

Sirisena, Maithripala, 91

Six-Day War (1967), *47, 53*

slavery
  abolition of, 369, 372
  in Libya, 370
  sex, 369–70, 393
  UN Human Rights Conventions on, *372–73*

Slovakia, 63, 347

Small, Melvin, 12, 14

smallpox, 410–11

smart power, 130

smart sanctions, 160

Smith, Adam, 23, 271, 283, 418, 429

Snyder, Jack, 181

socialism, 44, 57

social media
  human rights and, 364–65, 381–82
  private individuals and, 144
  public action and, 143–44
  terrorist groups and, 201

society
  economic liberalism on, 277
  international, 11
  liberal view of, 81
  philosophers' visions of, 9–11

socioeconomic rights, 368, 390–91

Soering v. United Kingdom, 260

soft power, 129–31

Solferino, Battle of, 370

Somalia
  civil war and, 193, 195
  Cold War and, 46, *47*
  disaster relief to, 355
  as fragile state, 183
  humanitarian intervention in, 395
  UN operations in, 331, 352, 396

South (in global economy)
  developing countries in, 330
  Group of 77 and, 330
  responding to climate change, 422

South Africa
  apartheid and, *161,* 162, 380
  as BRICS country, 295, 313
  colonialism and, 31
  foreign policy elites and, 139
  HIV/AIDS and, 413, 414
  international law and, 258, 260, 389
  multiple nations within, 152
  natural sources of power, 126
  nuclear weapons and, 223, 233
  truth commissions and, 390

South African War (1899-1902), 31

South America, 258

South China Sea, 90, 115, 151, 239, 263, 266, 436

South Korea
  bipolarity and, 111, *112*
  Cold War and, 46, 49–50
  foreign policy decision making and, 170
  global financial crisis and, 281, 306
  in Group 20, 295
  international development and, 302
  international finance and, 280
  international trade and, 273, 287
  natural sources of power, 128
  North Korean and, 18
  nuclear weapons and, 221–22
  security of, 437–38
  system change and, 120
South Ossetia, 151
South Sudan
  Darfur and, 6
  election monitoring and, 380
  as fragile state, 183
  independence of, 211
  migrants and, 406, 407
  UN operations and, 331, *332*, 336–37, 338
South Vietnam, 46, *47*, 49, 50–52, 111, 139
Southwest Africa, 29
sovereignty
  Cold War and, 44
  constructivist view of, 89, 398, 438, 439
  definition of, 15
  human security and, 326, 438, 440
  Kant on, 11
  liberal view of, 438
  realist view of, 110, 438
  Rousseau on, 340
  Treaties of Westphalia and, 20–22
sovereign wealth funds, 280–81
Soviet Union
  Afghanistan and, *47*, 52, 55, 57, 132, 137, 197, 331
  arms control agreements of, 221
  balance of power and, 77, 213
  communism and, 43, 44, *47*, 56
  Cuban missile crisis and, 50
  dissolution of, *47*, 55, 216
  emergence of, 34

  foreign policy decision making and, 166–67
  foreign policy elites and, 136
  human rights and, 369
  Marxism and, 44
  nationalism and, 56
  nuclear weapons and, 43, 46, *47*, 236
  polarity and, 111, *112*, 113
  post–World War II, 42, 120
  as superpower, 42, 46
  technology and, 54–55
  World War II and, 39, 40–42, 192, 213
  see also Cold War; Russia and Russian Federation
Spain
  attack in Barcelona, 187
  ethnonationalists and, 153
  Eurozone sustainability and, 61, 307
  Iraq War and, 346
  Napoleonic Wars and, 25
  in the nineteenth century, 30
  slavery in, 369
  terrorism and, 200
Spanish-American War (1898), 30
Spanish Constitutional Court, *251*
Spratly Islands, 63, 151
Sputnik, 47
Stalin, Joseph
  Atlantic Charter and, 42
  horrific crimes of, 56
  Kim Il-Sung and, 49
  malignant narcissism syndrome and, 134
state, 149–84
  Aristotle on, 9
  behavioralist view of, 12–13
  challenges to the, 173–83, *174*
    ethnonational movements, 179–81
    fragile states, 182–83, 438
    globalization, 174–75
    transnational crime, 181–82
    transnational movements, 175–78
  conditions for qualifying as, 151–52
  constructivist view of, 5, 87, 92, 123, 124–25, 131, 439

cooperation between, *see* international
cooperation
definition of, 71
dependency theory on, 94–96
foreign policy decision making and,
165–72, *167, 168*
fragile, 182–83
Hobbes on, 9, 74–75
human rights abuse and, 378–79
IGOs and, 323
international political economy and,
272–74
in international relations theories, 71,
124–25
Kant on, 10
levels of analysis for, 109, *109,* 124, 131
liberal view of, 5, 85, 121–22, 124, 131,
150
Locke on, 24
multiple nations within a, 152–53
in national security, 188–89
nation vs., 152
neoliberal institutionalist view of, 118
Plato on, 8–9
power potential of, 125–31
as protector of human rights, 374–79
radical view of, 93, 94
realist view of, 5, 73–74, 79, 110–11, 113,
124, 125, 150, 235–36, 439
Rousseau on, 9–10
Smith on, 23
Westphalian system and, 21–22
see also sovereignty; state power
State Department, U.S., 159
state of nature, 9, 74
state power, 5, 125
challenges to, 173–83, *174,* 438
Concert of Europe and, 26
diplomacy and, 157–60
economic statecraft and, 160, *161,*
162–63
exercise of, 157–60, *161,* 162–65
intangible sources of, 128–31
natural sources of, 125–28
nature of, 125–31
tangible sources of, 128

Treaties of Westphalia and, 21–22
use of force, 163–65
Strategic Arms Limitations Treaty (SALT
I), *47,* 54
structural adjustment program, 296
structural realism, *see* neorealism
Stuxnet worm, 205, 229
Sudan
civil war in, 6, 193, 211, 407
disaster relief to, 355
as fragile state, 183
human rights and, 386, 389, 395, 397
migrants and, 407
natural resource issues and, 426
refugees and, 407
terrorism and, 201, 204
UN operations and, 331, *332,* 333–34
Suez Canal crisis, 52
Suez crisis (1956), 137
sulfur dioxide emissions, 420
summits, 54
Sunnis, 87, 152, 176, 200, 392
superpowers, 42, 120
see also Cold War
sustainable development, 296, 298, 418–19,
422, 431
Sustainable Development Goals (SDGs),
302, 416
Sustainable Forestry Initiative, 425
Sweden, 406, 430
Switzerland, 127, 142, 211, 260
Sylvester, Christine, 15, 97
symmetrical balance of power, 32
Syria
Arab Spring and, 60, 61, 62, 152
bipolarity and, *112*
chemical weapons and, 250
civil war and, 61, 62, 66, 189, 194–95,
395, 397, 405
Cold War and, *47,* 53
extremist Islamic fundamentalism and,
176, 177–78
human rights and, 397
intangible sources of power, 129
Islamic State and, 3, 60, 62, 194, 225
Israel and, 192, 220

South Africa and, 162
structure of, 326–29, *327*
Switzerland and, 142, 211
weapons of mass destruction and, 59
United States
abolitionists and, 369
AIPAC and, 158
arms control agreements of, 221
balance of power and, 213, 216
Bill of Rights, 367
China and, 114, 239, 263, 266
civil war and, 194, 369
Colombia and, 264
conventional war and, 196
Cuban missile crisis and, 50
cyberattacks and, 187, 205
death penalty in, 260–61
environmental issues and, 420, 422–23, 424–25
European sphere of influence and, 30
foreign policy elites and, 137, 139–40
global financial crisis of 2008 and, 306, 307
in Group of 7, 278
human rights and, 257, 260–61, 398
ICJ jurisdiction and, 254, 389
imperialism and, 30
international finance and, 280
international law and, 254, 260–61
international trade and, 284, 286–87, 293
Iran and, 88
Iraq War and, *see* Iraq War (2003)
Islamic State and, 62
Kyoto Protocol and, 249–50, 422–23
League of Nations and, 37–38
liberalism and, 43
Libya and, 215
Mexico and, 437
mutual legal assistance treaties of, 258
NAFTA and, 290–92
Native American nations and, 152–53
NATO and, 245
North Korea and, 49–50, 215, 438
nuclear weapons and, 42, 196, 236
oil and, 162, 437
Paris Agreement and, 424, 425

polarity and, 111, *112*
post–World War I, 38
post–World War II, 42, 120
public diplomacy and, 158
rape of female soldiers in military of, 393
Russia's role in 2016 presidential election of, 149
sanctions imposed by, 99, 149, *161*, 163, 335
sources of power, 125, 127, 129–30
South Africa and, *161*, 162
as superpower, 42, 46
Syria and, 62
terrorism and, 201, 204
TPP and, 293–94
UN Security Council and, 223–24, 250, 326, 335–36, 346
World War I and, 36, 192
World War II and, 40–42, 192, 196, 213
see also Cold War; war on terrorism
United States, Nicaragua v., 254
Universal Declaration of Human Rights, 371, 376, 391
universal jurisdiction, 254
Universal Periodic Review, 380, 383
Universal Postal Union, 339
UNMEE (UN Mission in Ethiopia and Eritrea), *331*
UNMISS (UN Mission in Republic of South Sudan), *332*
UN Mission in Ethiopia and Eritrea (UNMEE), *331*
UN Organization Stabilization Mission in the Democratic Republic of Congo (Monusco), *332*
UN Peacekeeping Force in Cyprus (UNFICYP), *331*
UNPROFOR (UN Protection Force), *332*
UN Protection Force (UNPROFOR), *332*
UN Relief and Works Agency, 338–39
UN Secretariat, *327,* 328–29
UN Security Council, 326–28, *327*
criminal tribunals and, 388
on Ebola outbreak in 2014, 412
enforcement and, 255, 338
Gorbachev and, 55, 58
on HIV/AIDS, 403, 413